WITHDRAWN

Delicious IN DUNGEON

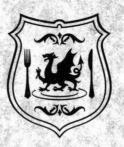

RYOKO KUI

3

Delicious IN DUNGEON

3

Contents

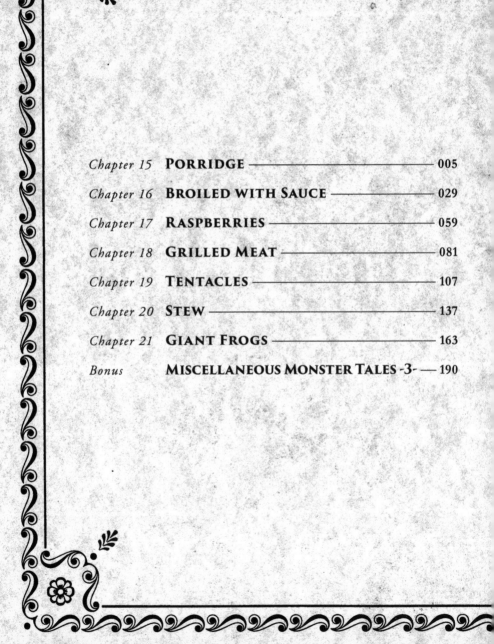

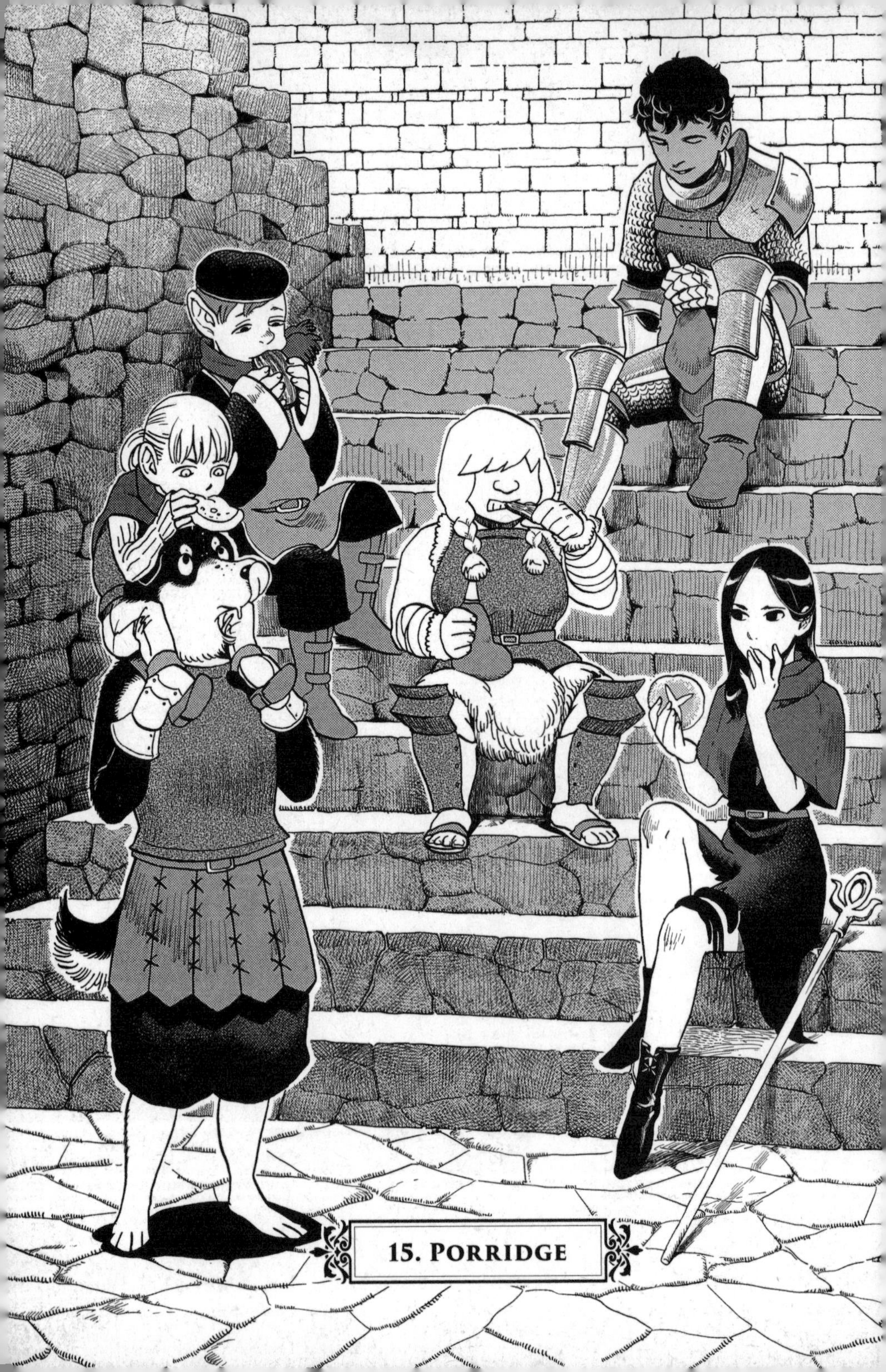

15. Porridge

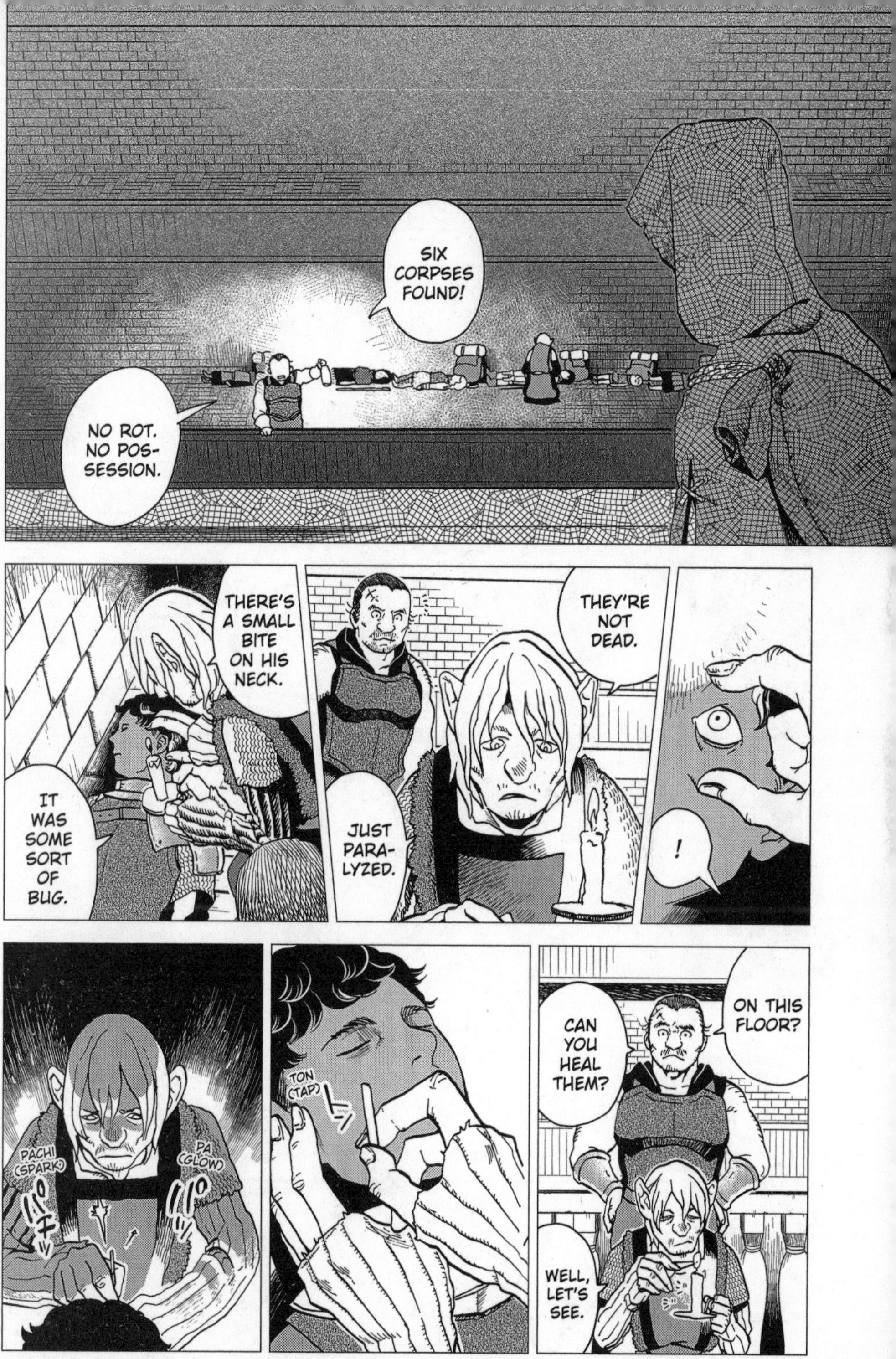
SIX CORPSES FOUND!
NO ROT. NO POSSESSION.
!
THEY'RE NOT DEAD.
JUST PARALYZED.
THERE'S A SMALL BITE ON HIS NECK.
IT WAS SOME SORT OF BUG.
ON THIS FLOOR?
CAN YOU HEAL THEM?
WELL, LET'S SEE.
TON (TAP)
PA (GLOW)
PACHI (SPARK)

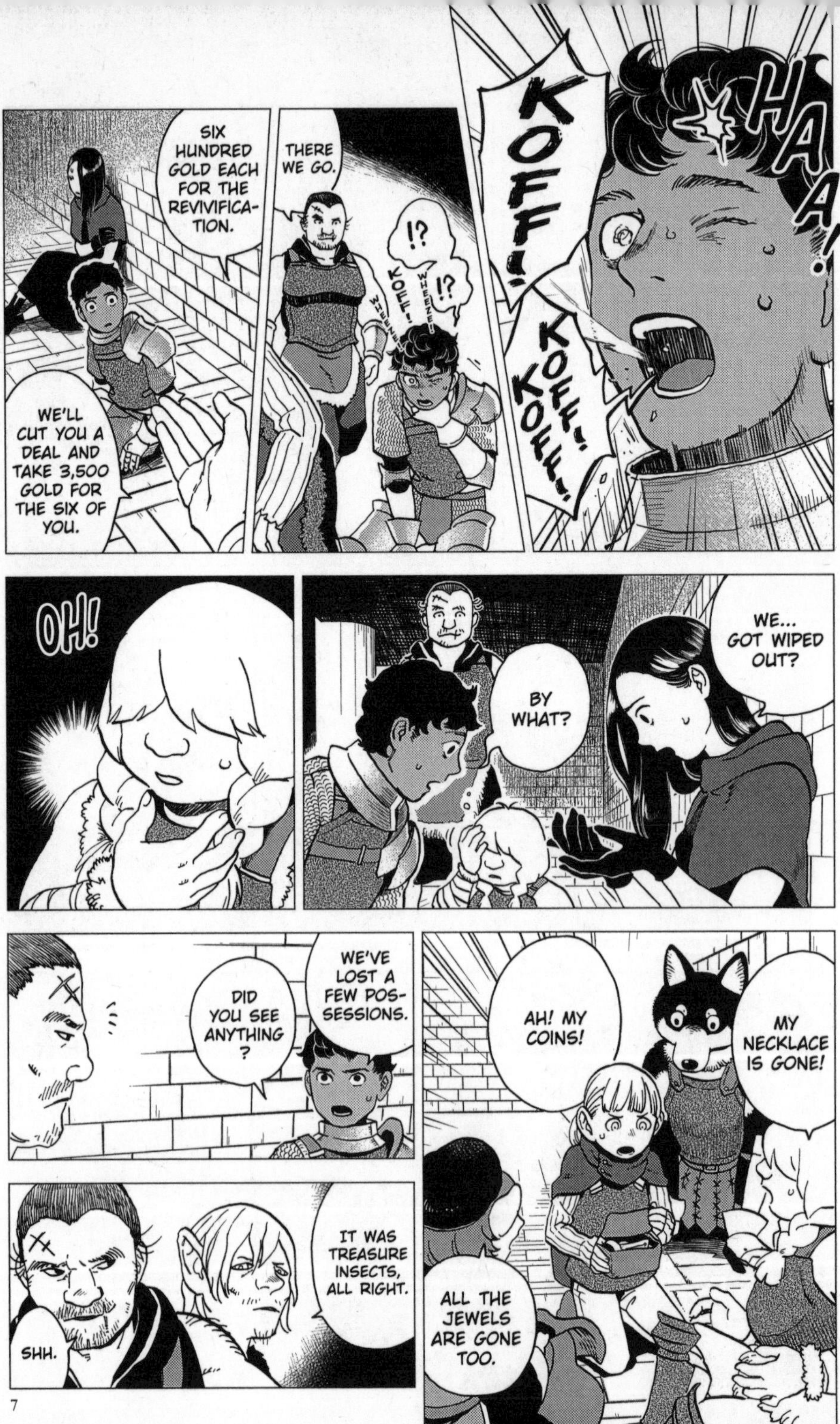
KOFF! KOFF!
KOFF! KOFF!
HAA!
THERE WE GO.
!?
WHEEZE! KOFF!
!?
KOFF! WHEEZE!
SIX HUNDRED GOLD EACH FOR THE REVIVIFICA-TION.
WE'LL CUT YOU A DEAL AND TAKE 3,500 GOLD FOR THE SIX OF YOU.
WE... GOT WIPED OUT?
BY WHAT?
OH!
MY NECKLACE IS GONE!
AH! MY COINS!
ALL THE JEWELS ARE GONE TOO.
WE'VE LOST A FEW POS-SESSIONS.
DID YOU SEE ANYTHING?
IT WAS TREASURE INSECTS, ALL RIGHT.
SHH.

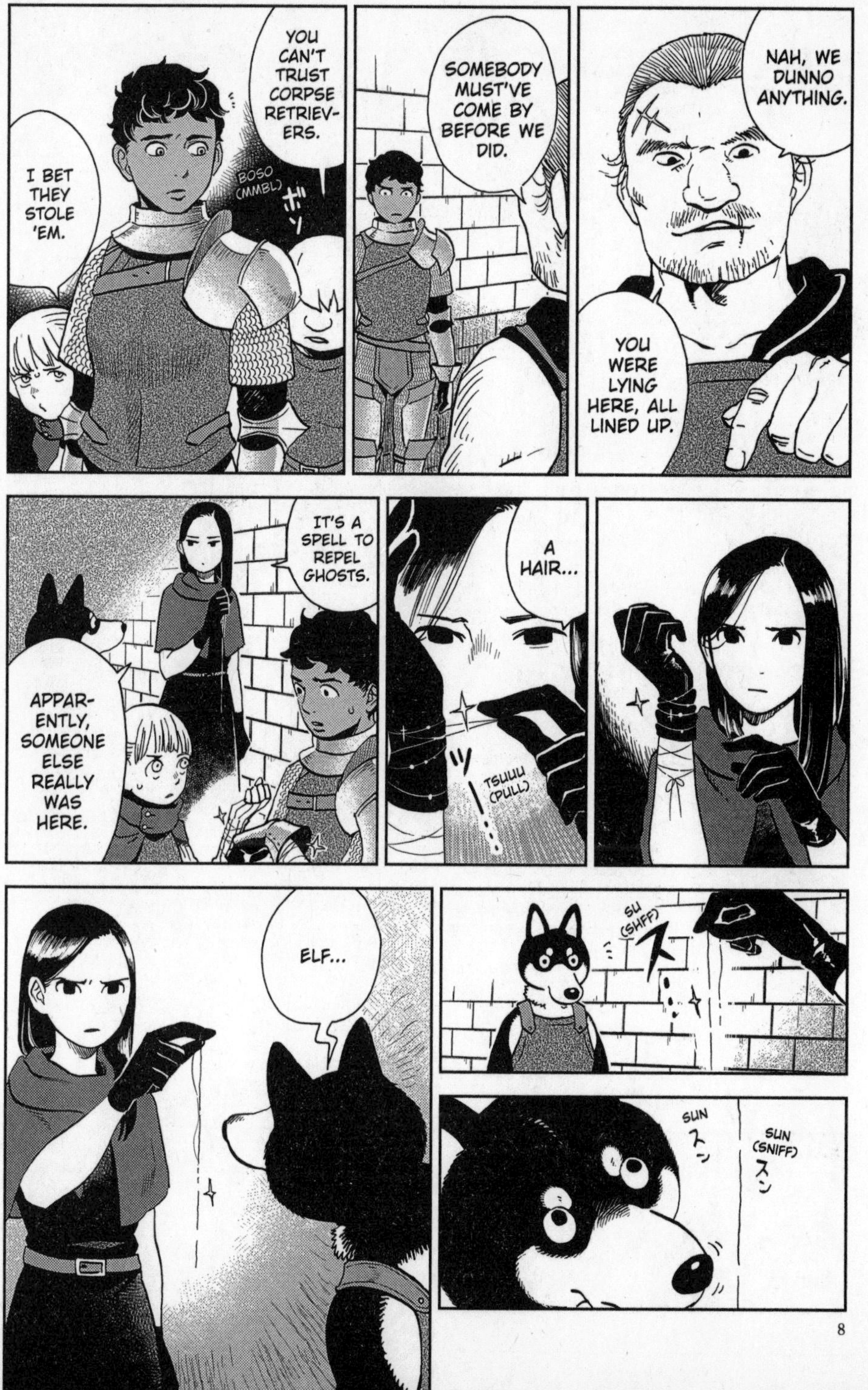

NAH, WE DUNNO ANYTHING.
YOU WERE LYING HERE, ALL LINED UP.
SOMEBODY MUST'VE COME BY BEFORE WE DID.
YOU CAN'T TRUST CORPSE RETRIEVERS.
BOSO (MMBL) ボソ
I BET THEY STOLE 'EM.
A HAIR...
TSUUU (PULL) ツー
IT'S A SPELL TO REPEL GHOSTS.
APPARENTLY, SOMEONE ELSE REALLY WAS HERE.
SU (SHFF) ス
SUN (SNIFF) スン
SUN スン
ELF...

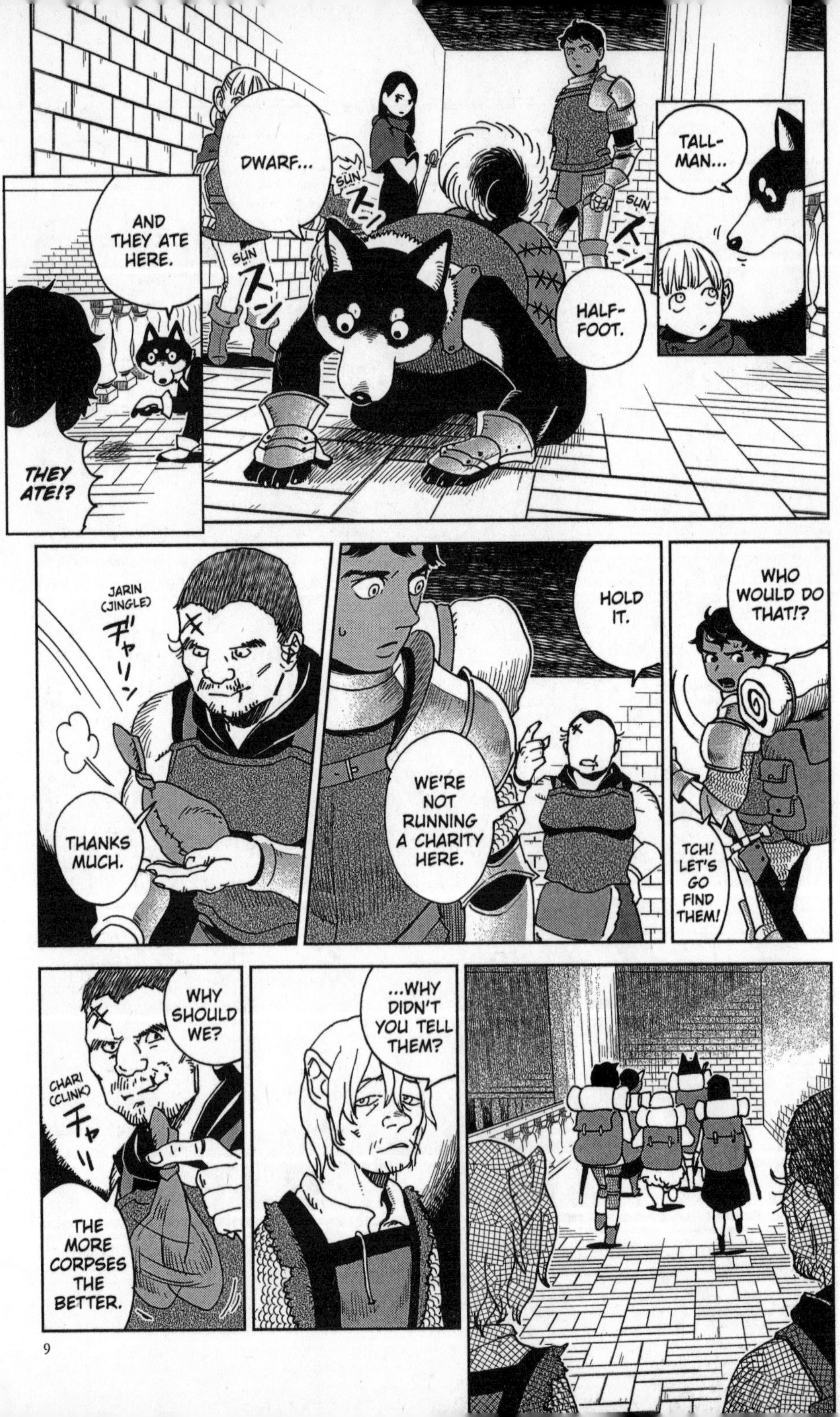
TALL-MAN...
SUN
スン
HALF-FOOT.
SUN
スン
DWARF...
SUN
スン
AND THEY ATE HERE.
THEY ATE!?
WHO WOULD DO THAT!?
TCH! LET'S GO FIND THEM!
HOLD IT.
WE'RE NOT RUNNING A CHARITY HERE.
JARIN (JINGLE)
ジャリン
THANKS MUCH.
...WHY DIDN'T YOU TELL THEM?
WHY SHOULD WE?
CHARI (CLINK)
チャリ
THE MORE CORPSES THE BETTER.

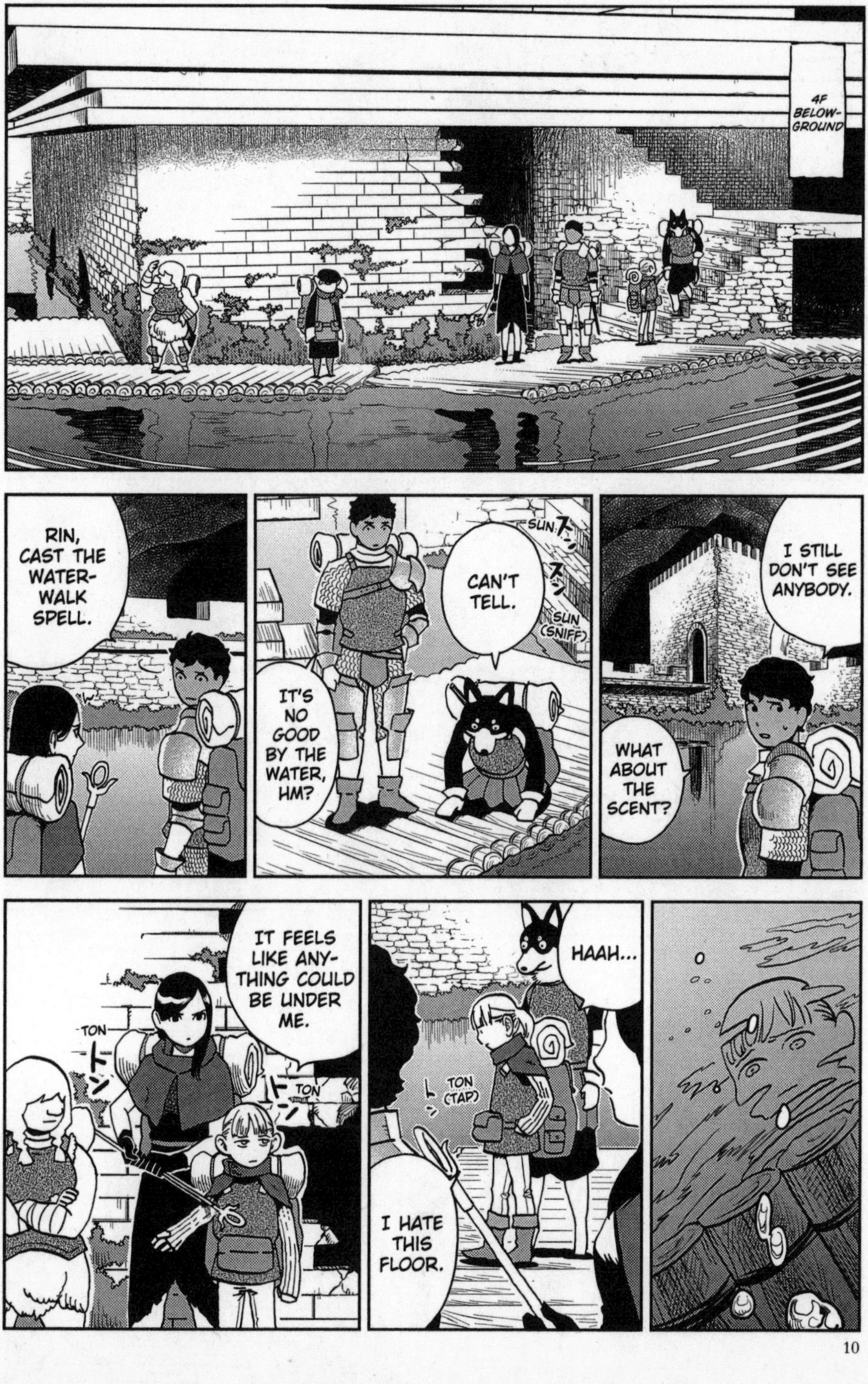
4F BELOW-GROUND
I STILL DON'T SEE ANYBODY.
WHAT ABOUT THE SCENT?
SUN
CAN'T TELL.
SUN (SNIFF)
IT'S NO GOOD BY THE WATER, HM?
RIN, CAST THE WATER-WALK SPELL.
HAAH...
TON (TAP)
I HATE THIS FLOOR.
IT FEELS LIKE ANYTHING COULD BE UNDER ME.
TON
TON

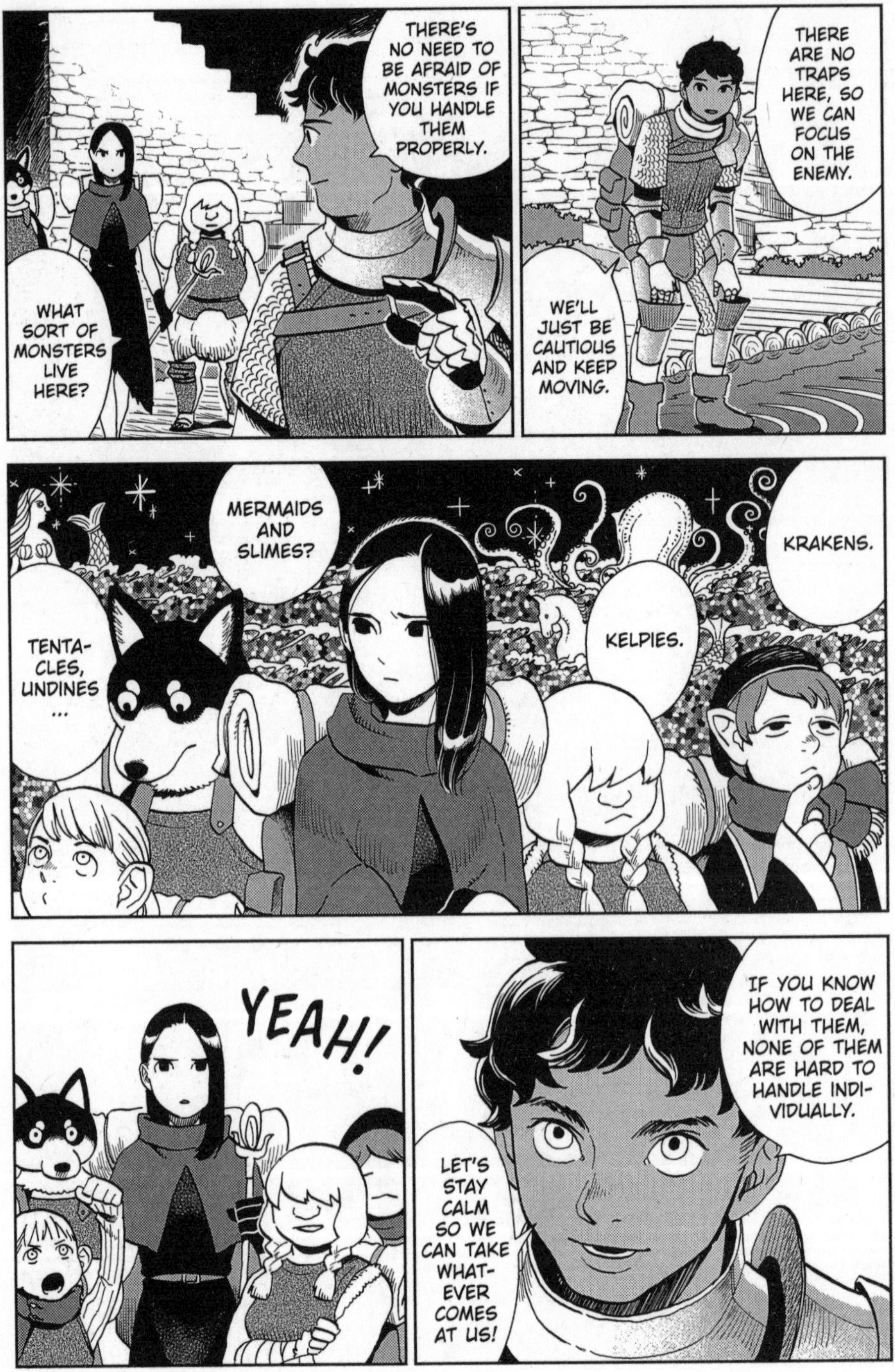
THERE ARE NO TRAPS HERE, SO WE CAN FOCUS ON THE ENEMY.
WE'LL JUST BE CAUTIOUS AND KEEP MOVING.
THERE'S NO NEED TO BE AFRAID OF MONSTERS IF YOU HANDLE THEM PROPERLY.
WHAT SORT OF MONSTERS LIVE HERE?
KRAKENS.
KELPIES.
MERMAIDS AND SLIMES?
TENTA-CLES, UNDINES ...
IF YOU KNOW HOW TO DEAL WITH THEM, NONE OF THEM ARE HARD TO HANDLE INDI-VIDUALLY.
LET'S STAY CALM SO WE CAN TAKE WHAT-EVER COMES AT US!
YEAH!

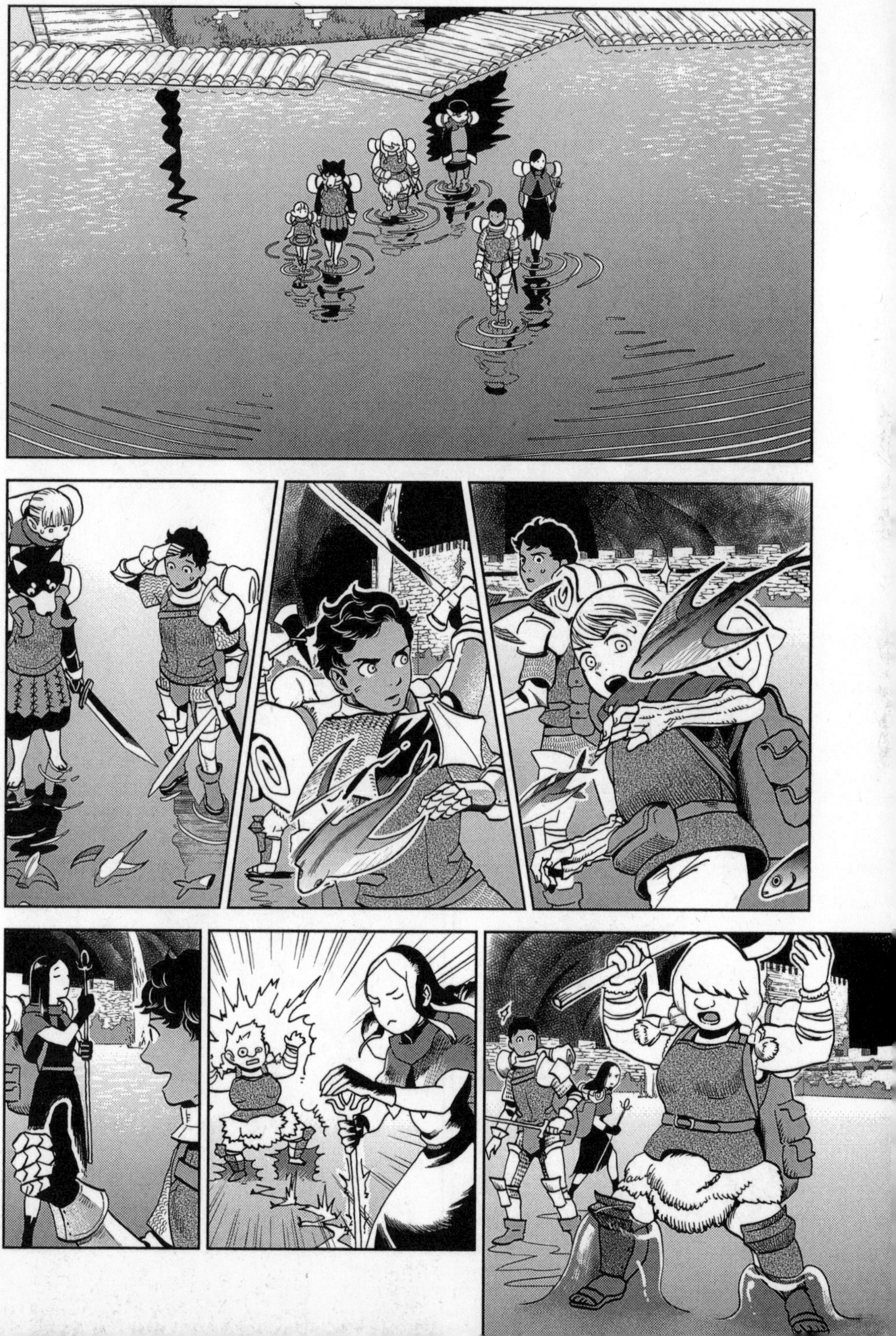

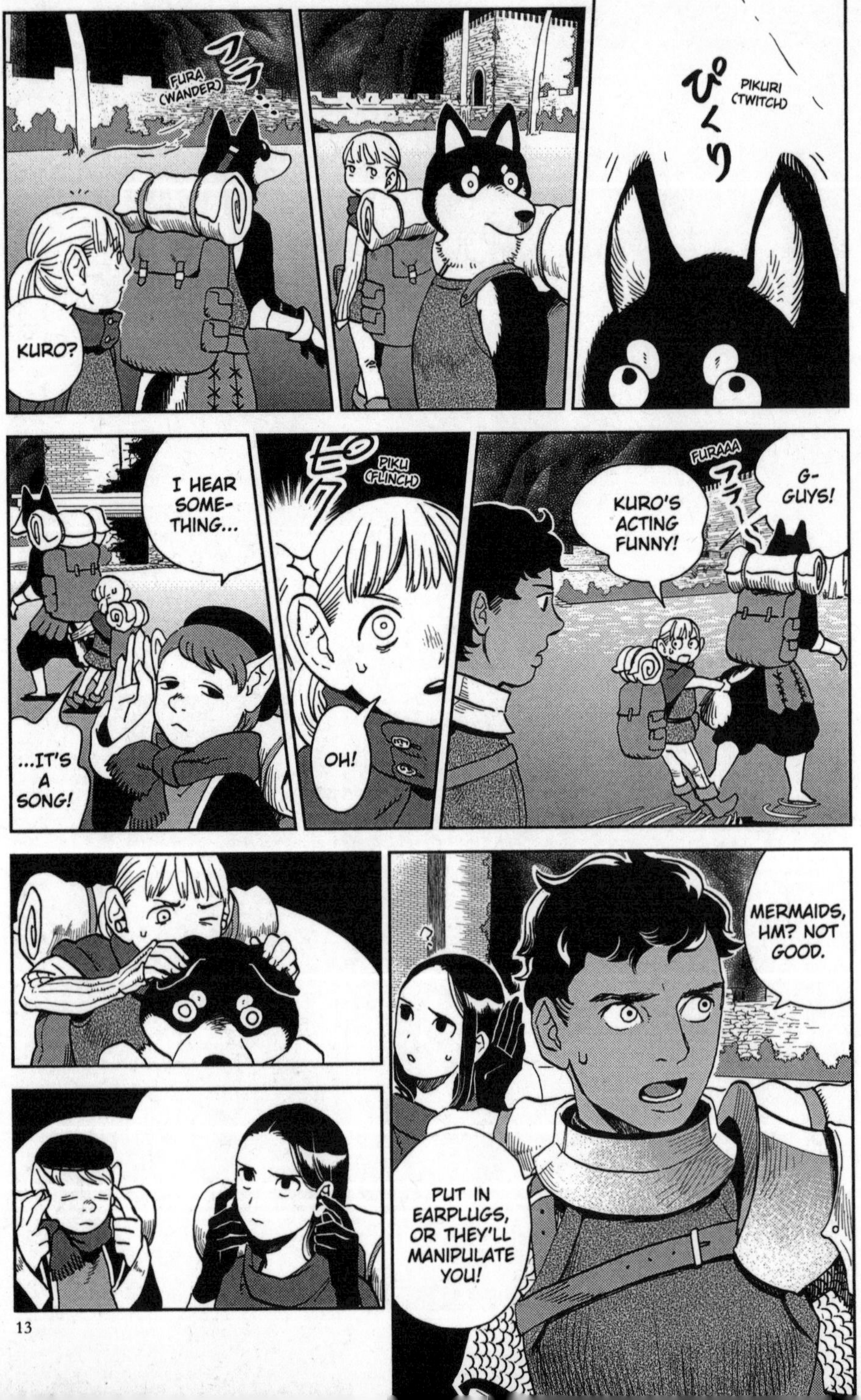
ぴくり
PIKURI (TWITCH)
FURA (WANDER)
KURO?
FURAAA
G-GUYS!
KURO'S ACTING FUNNY!
PIKU (FLINCH)
OH!
I HEAR SOMETHING...
...IT'S A SONG!
MERMAIDS, HM? NOT GOOD.
PUT IN EARPLUGS, OR THEY'LL MANIPULATE YOU!

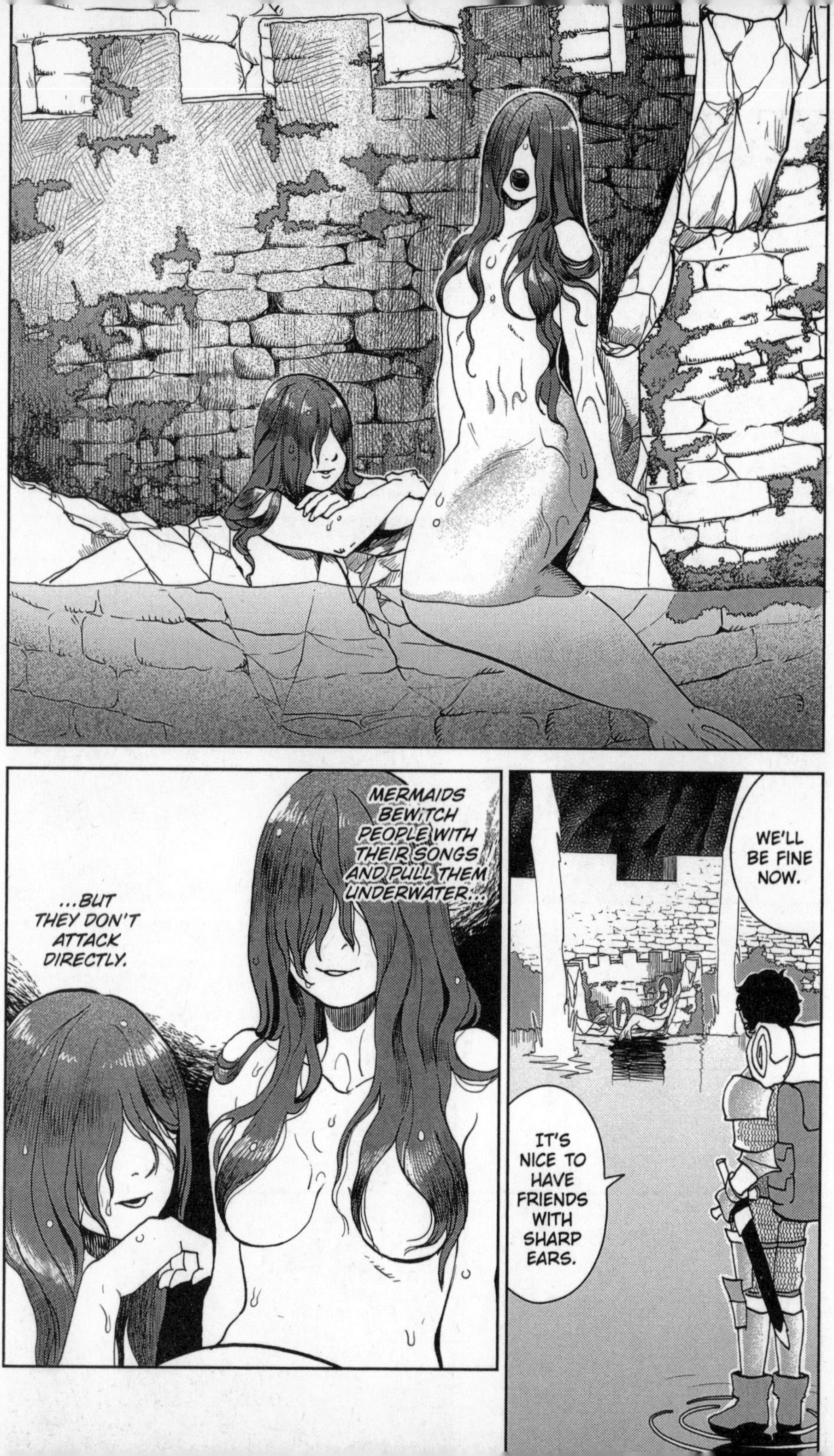
WE'LL BE FINE NOW.
IT'S NICE TO HAVE FRIENDS WITH SHARP EARS.
MERMAIDS BEWITCH PEOPLE WITH THEIR SONGS AND PULL THEM UNDERWATER...
...BUT THEY DON'T ATTACK DIRECTLY.

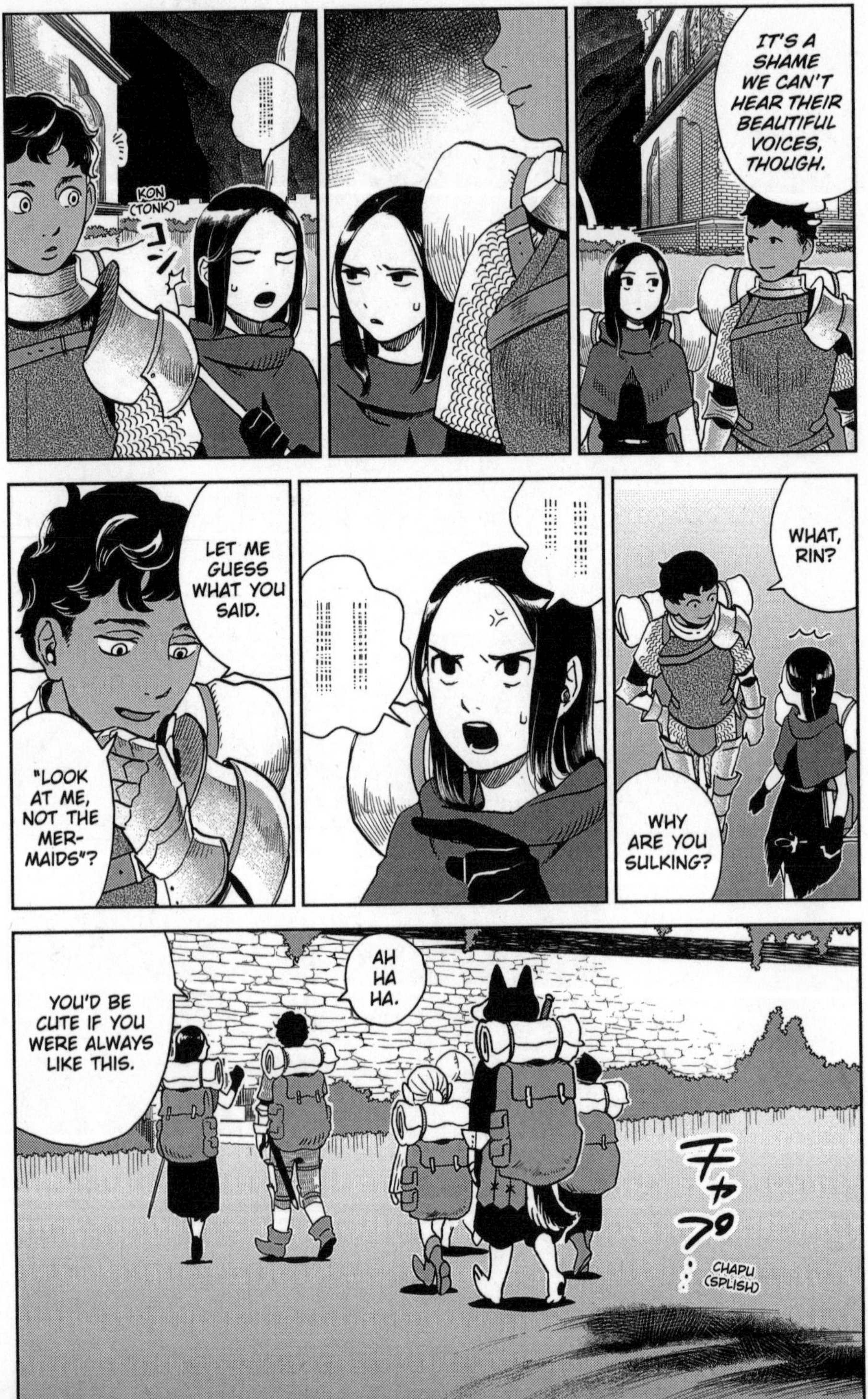
IT'S A SHAME WE CAN'T HEAR THEIR BEAUTIFUL VOICES, THOUGH.
KON (TONK)
WHAT, RIN?
WHY ARE YOU SULKING?
LET ME GUESS WHAT YOU SAID.
"LOOK AT ME, NOT THE MER-MAIDS"?
AH HA HA.
YOU'D BE CUTE IF YOU WERE ALWAYS LIKE THIS.
CHAPU (SPLISH)

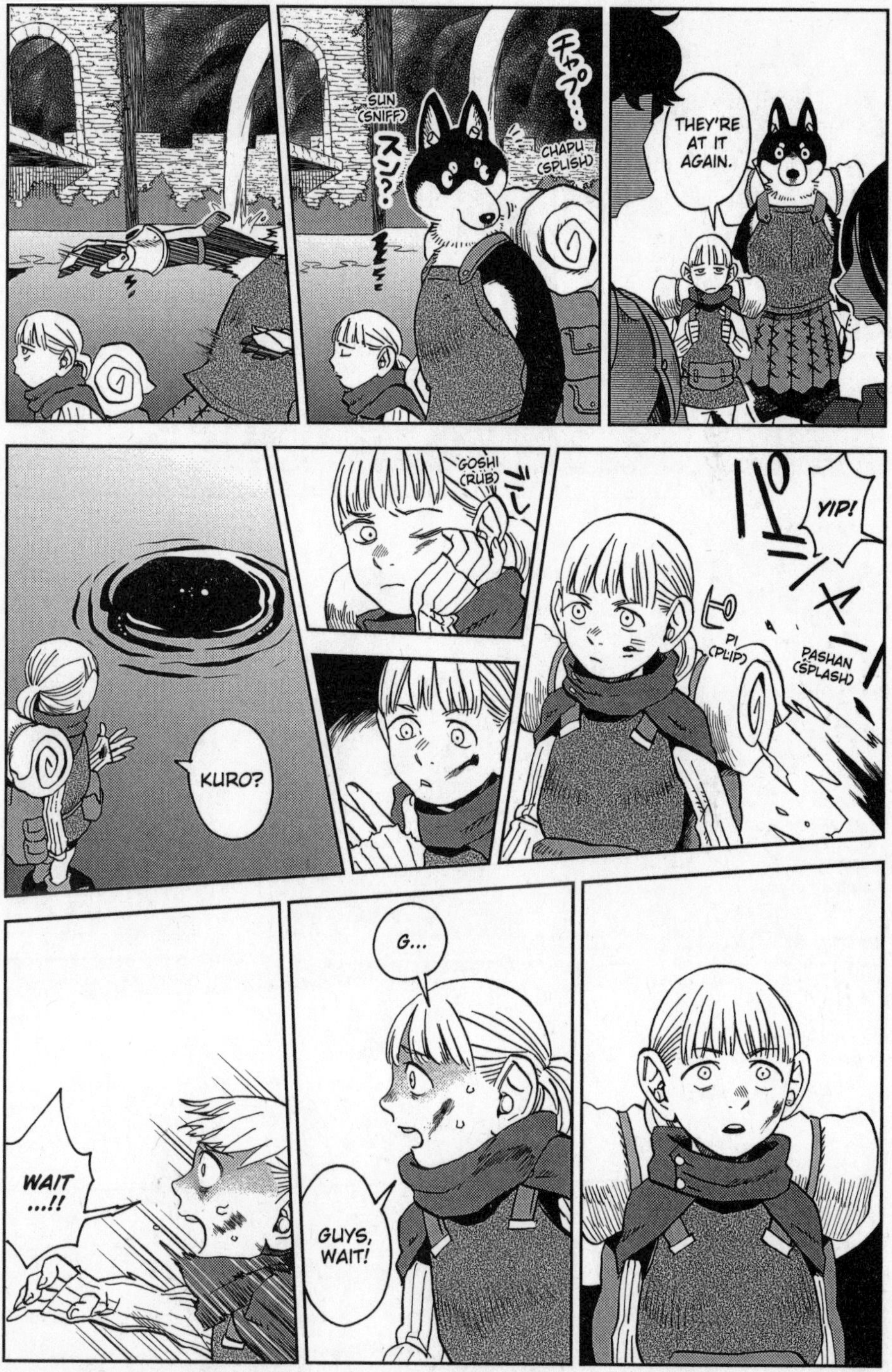
THEY'RE AT IT AGAIN.
チャプ…
CHAPU (SPLASH)
スン?
SUN (SNIFF)
YIP!
パシャーン
PASHAN (SPLASH)
ピ
PI (PLIP)
ゴシ
GOSHI (RUB)
KURO?
G...
GUYS, WAIT!
WAIT ...!!

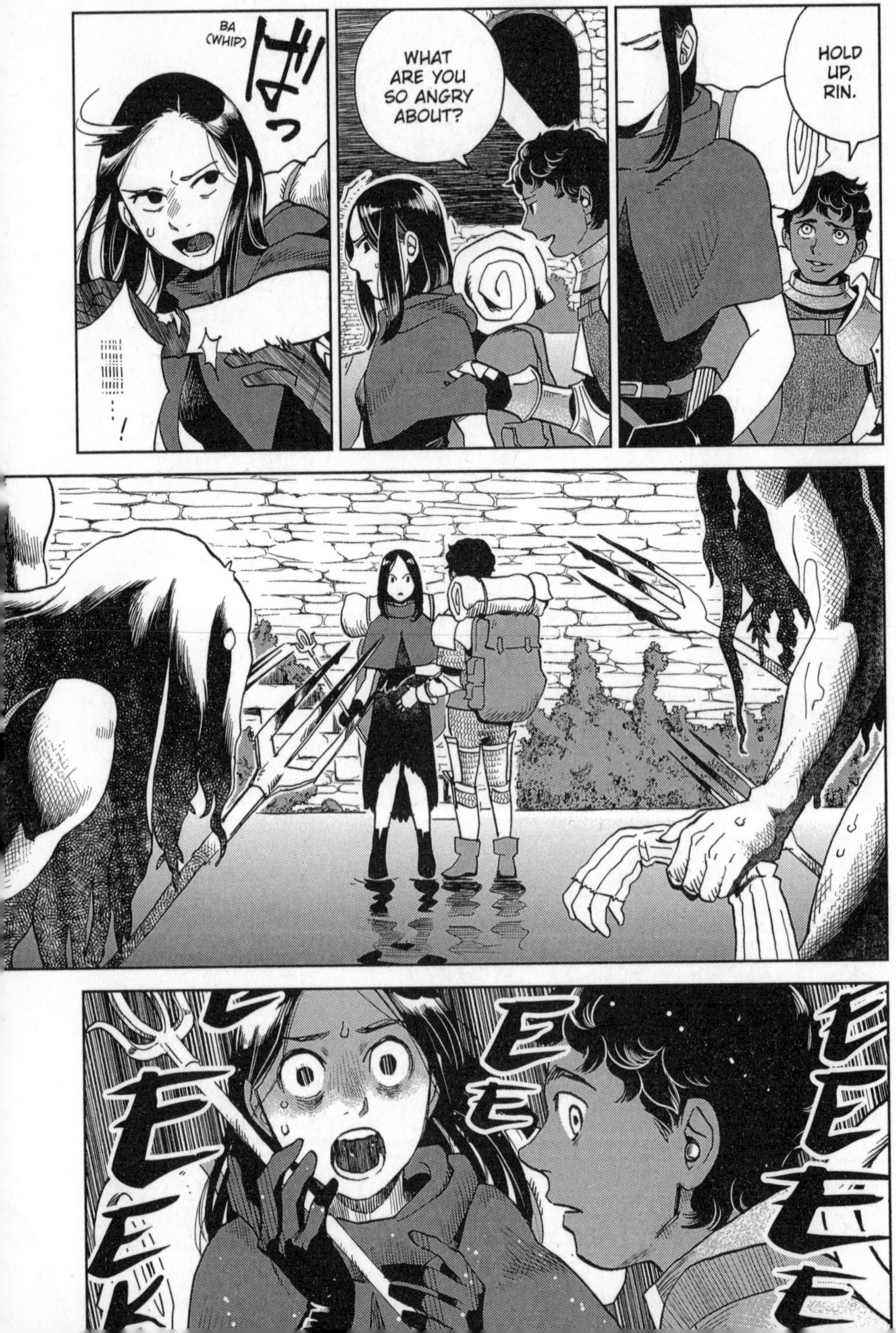
HOLD UP, RIN.
WHAT ARE YOU SO ANGRY ABOUT?
ばっ
BA (WHIP)

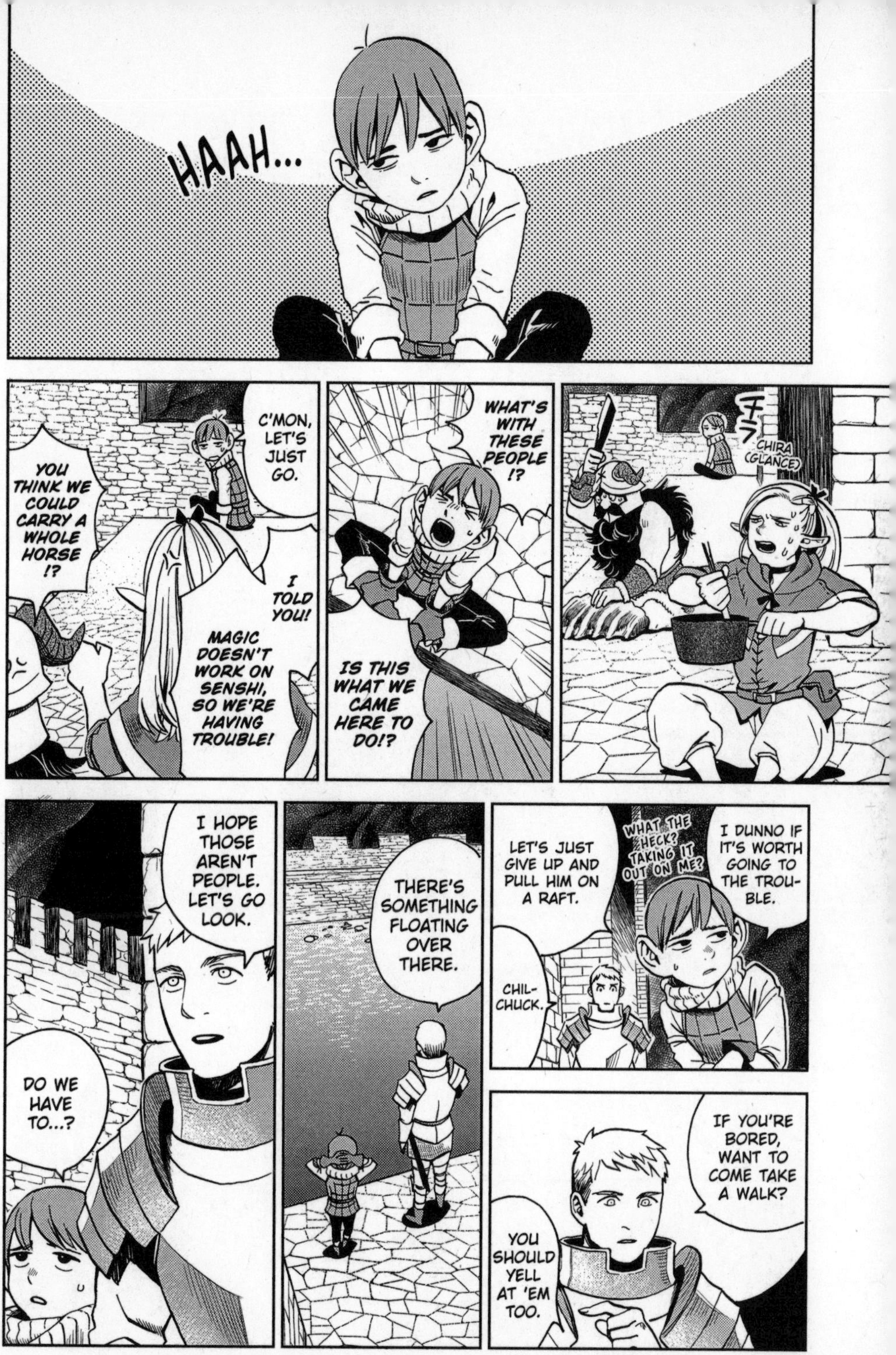
HAAH...
チラ
CHIRA (GLANCE)
WHAT'S WITH THESE PEOPLE!?
IS THIS WHAT WE CAME HERE TO DO!?
C'MON, LET'S JUST GO.
YOU THINK WE COULD CARRY A WHOLE HORSE!?
I TOLD YOU!
MAGIC DOESN'T WORK ON SENSHI, SO WE'RE HAVING TROUBLE!
I DUNNO IF IT'S WORTH GOING TO THE TROUBLE.
WHAT THE HECK? TAKING IT OUT ON ME?
LET'S JUST GIVE UP AND PULL HIM ON A RAFT.
CHILCHUCK.
IF YOU'RE BORED, WANT TO COME TAKE A WALK?
YOU SHOULD YELL AT 'EM TOO.
THERE'S SOMETHING FLOATING OVER THERE.
I HOPE THOSE AREN'T PEOPLE. LET'S GO LOOK.
DO WE HAVE TO...?

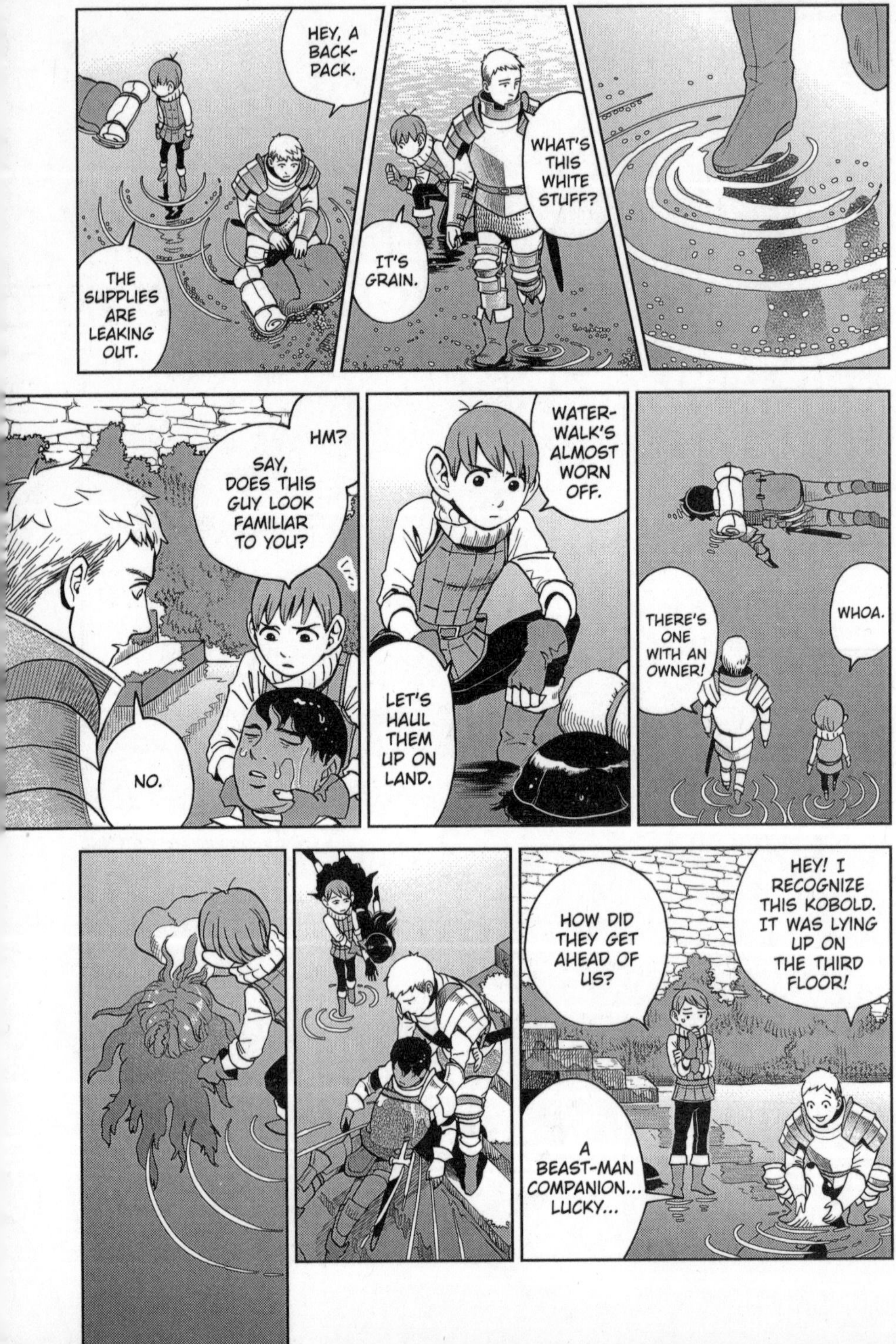
WHAT'S THIS WHITE STUFF?
IT'S GRAIN.
HEY, A BACK-PACK.
THE SUPPLIES ARE LEAKING OUT.
WHOA.
THERE'S ONE WITH AN OWNER!
WATER-WALK'S ALMOST WORN OFF.
LET'S HAUL THEM UP ON LAND.
HM?
SAY, DOES THIS GUY LOOK FAMILIAR TO YOU?
NO.
HEY! I RECOGNIZE THIS KOBOLD. IT WAS LYING UP ON THE THIRD FLOOR!
HOW DID THEY GET AHEAD OF US?
A BEAST-MAN COMPANION... LUCKY...

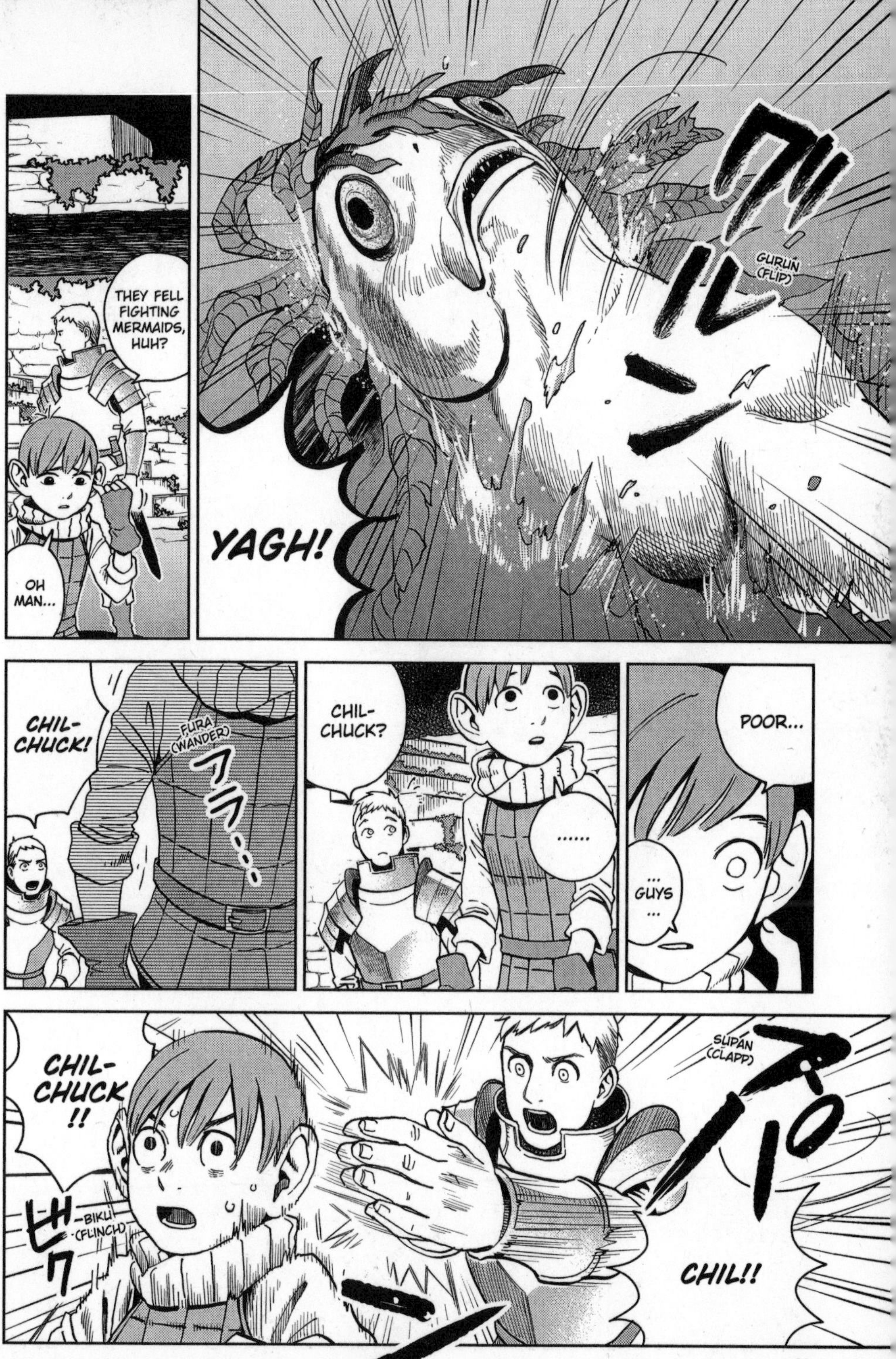
GURUN (FLIP)
YAGH!
THEY FELL FIGHTING MERMAIDS, HUH?
OH MAN...
POOR...
... GUYS ...
CHIL-CHUCK?
......
CHIL-CHUCK!
FURA (WANDER)
SUPAN (CLAPP)
CHIL!!
CHIL-CHUCK !!
BIKU (FLINCH)

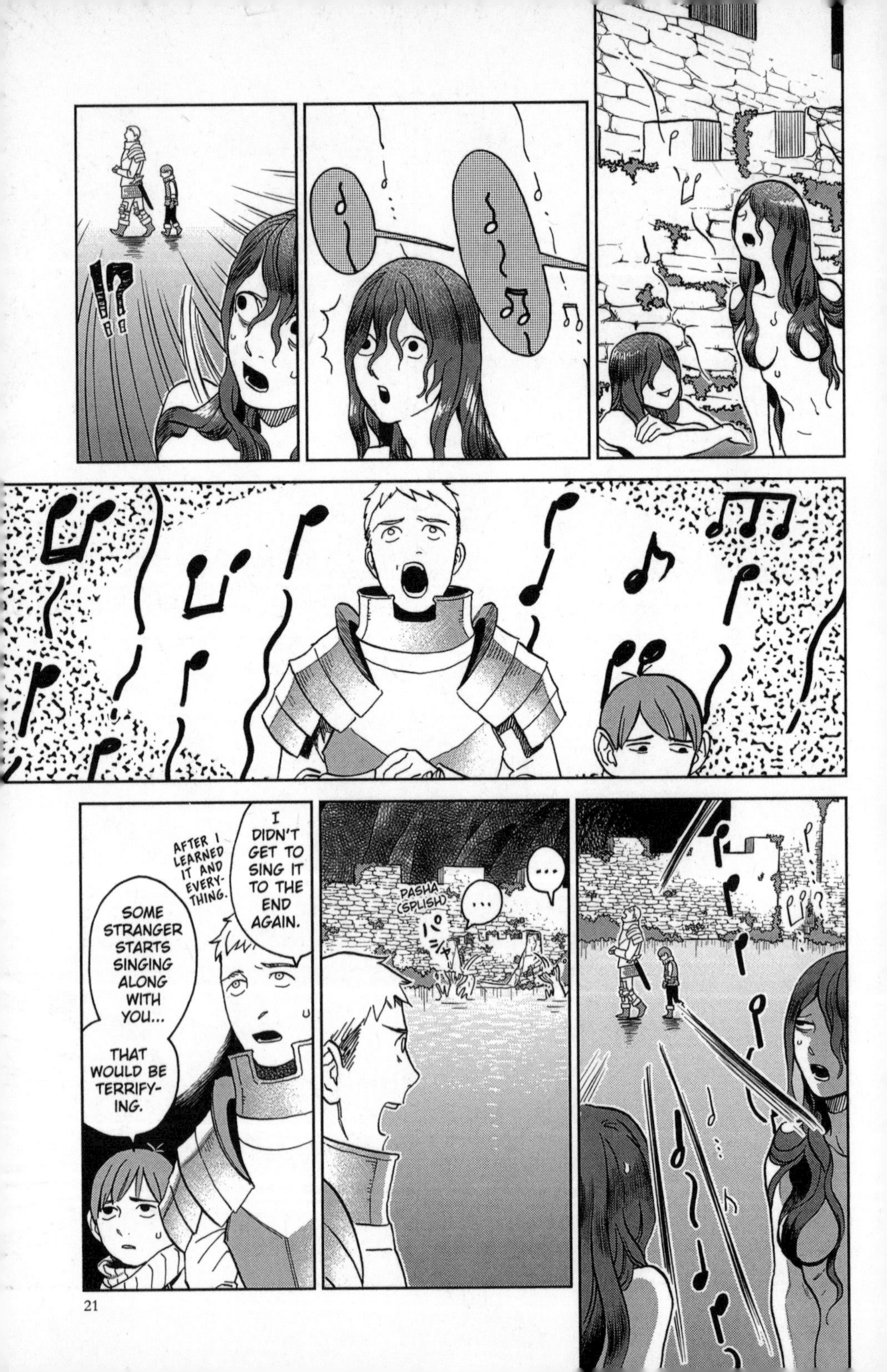
!?
...
...
PASHA (SPLISH)
パシャ
I DIDN'T GET TO SING IT TO THE END AGAIN.
AFTER I LEARNED IT AND EVERY-THING.
SOME STRANGER STARTS SINGING ALONG WITH YOU...
THAT WOULD BE TERRIFY-ING.

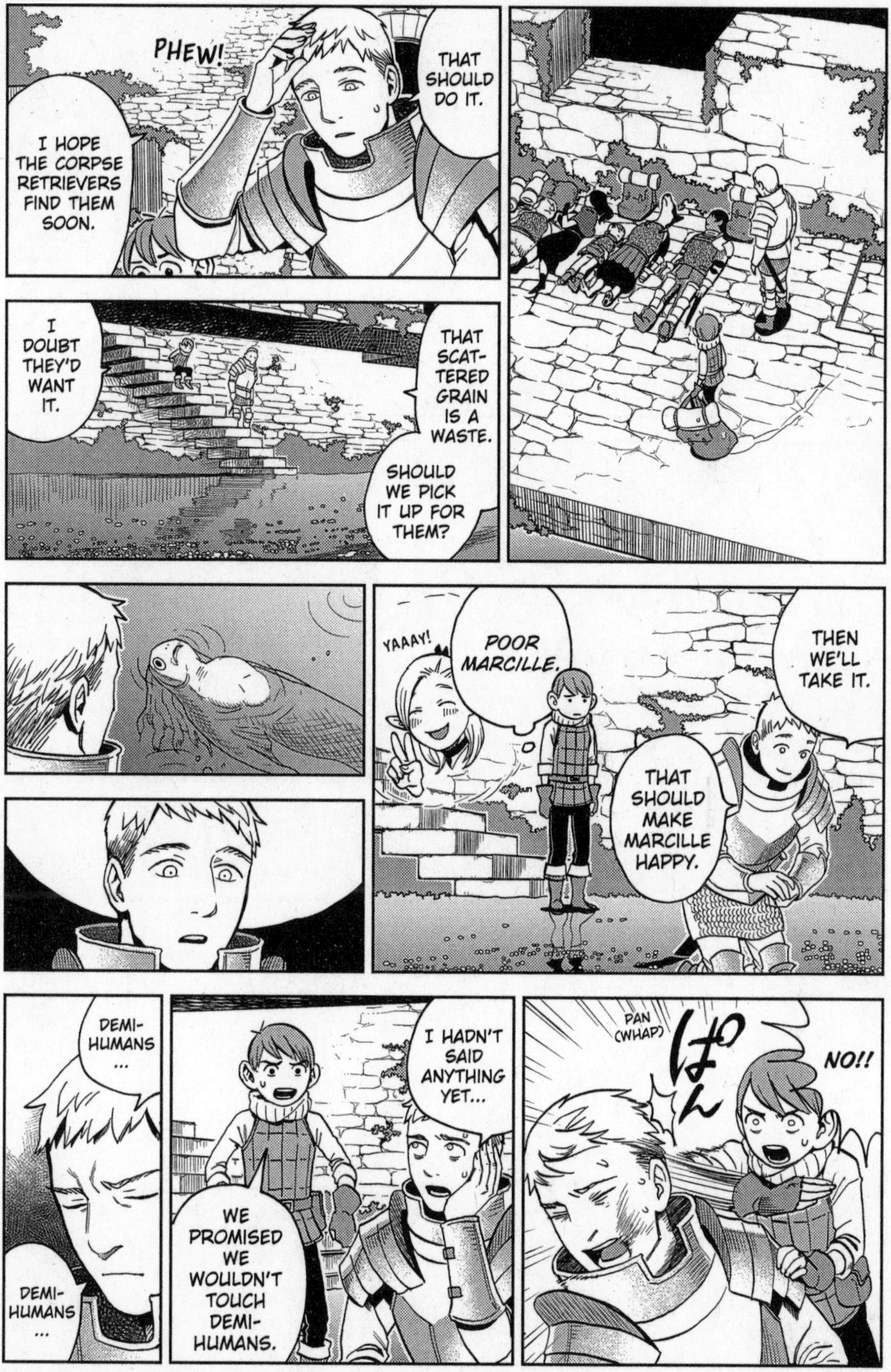
PHEW!
THAT SHOULD DO IT.
I HOPE THE CORPSE RETRIEVERS FIND THEM SOON.
THAT SCAT-TERED GRAIN IS A WASTE.
SHOULD WE PICK IT UP FOR THEM?
I DOUBT THEY'D WANT IT.
THEN WE'LL TAKE IT.
THAT SHOULD MAKE MARCILLE HAPPY.
POOR MARCILLE.
YAAAY!
NO!!
PAN (WHAP)
ぱん
I HADN'T SAID ANYTHING YET...
WE PROMISED WE WOULDN'T TOUCH DEMI-HUMANS.
DEMI-HUMANS ...
DEMI-HUMANS ...

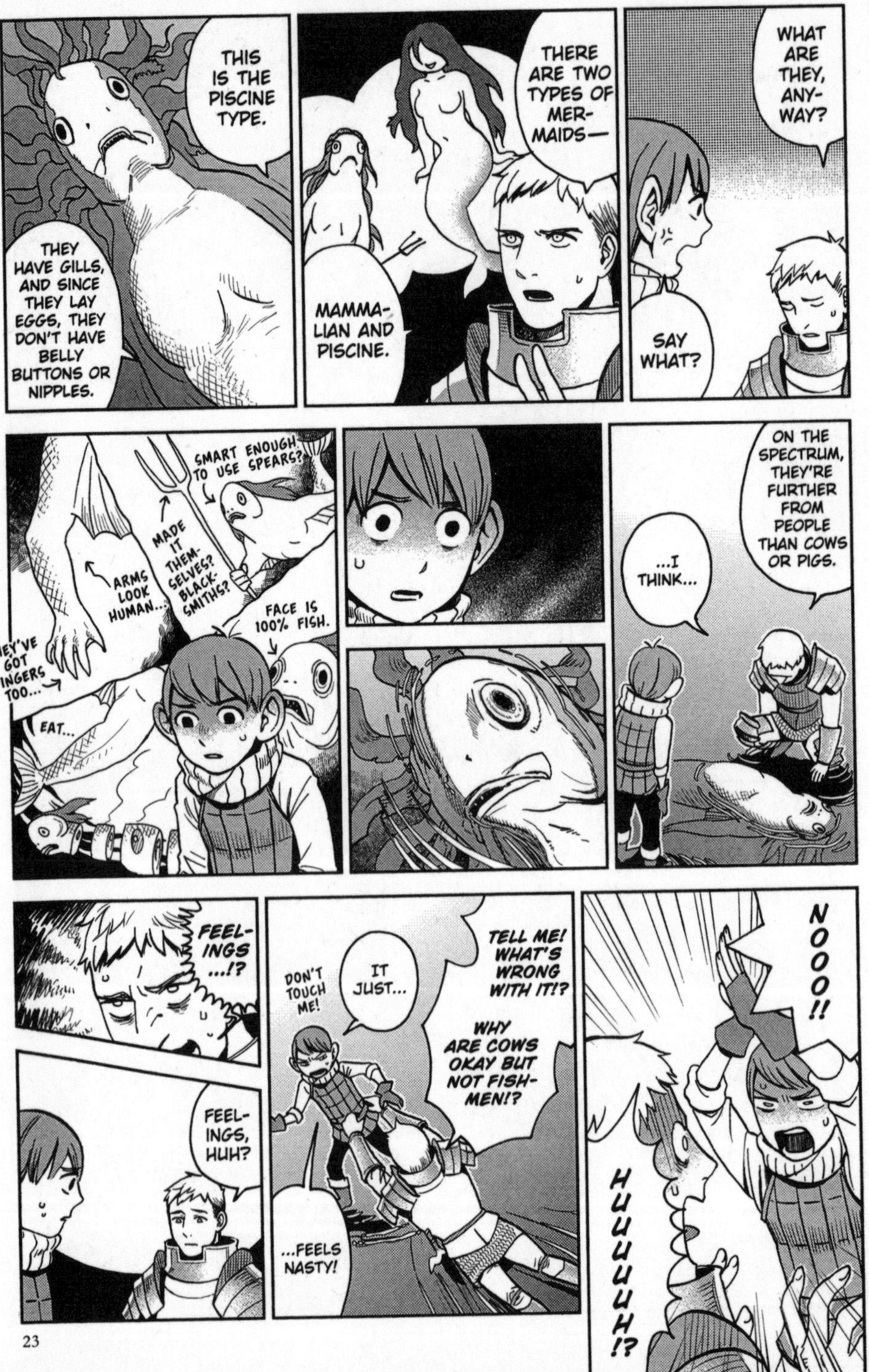
WHAT ARE THEY, ANYWAY?
SAY WHAT?
THERE ARE TWO TYPES OF MERMAIDS—
MAMMALIAN AND PISCINE.
THIS IS THE PISCINE TYPE.
THEY HAVE GILLS, AND SINCE THEY LAY EGGS, THEY DON'T HAVE BELLY BUTTONS OR NIPPLES.
ON THE SPECTRUM, THEY'RE FURTHER FROM PEOPLE THAN COWS OR PIGS.
...I THINK...
SMART ENOUGH TO USE SPEARS?
MADE IT THEMSELVES? BLACKSMITHS?
ARMS LOOK HUMAN...
FACE IS 100% FISH.
THEY'VE GOT FINGERS TOO...
EAT...
NOOOO!!
HUUUUUH!?
TELL ME! WHAT'S WRONG WITH IT!?
WHY ARE COWS OKAY BUT NOT FISHMEN!?
IT JUST...
DON'T TOUCH ME!
...FEELS NASTY!
FEELINGS...!?
FEELINGS, HUH?

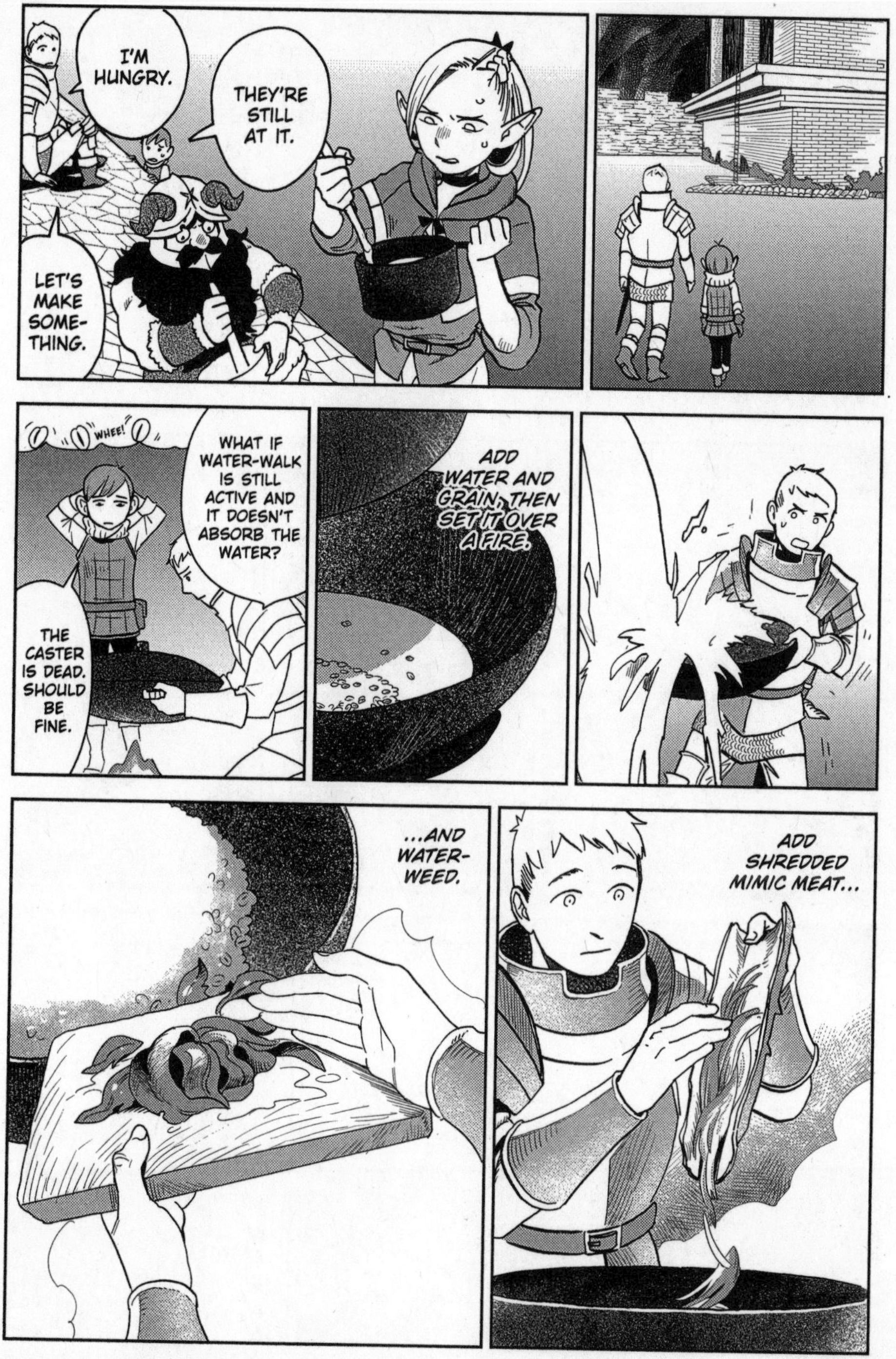
THEY'RE STILL AT IT.
I'M HUNGRY.
LET'S MAKE SOME-THING.
ADD WATER AND GRAIN, THEN SET IT OVER A FIRE.
WHAT IF WATER-WALK IS STILL ACTIVE AND IT DOESN'T ABSORB THE WATER?
WHEE!
THE CASTER IS DEAD. SHOULD BE FINE.
ADD SHREDDED MIMIC MEAT...
...AND WATER-WEED.

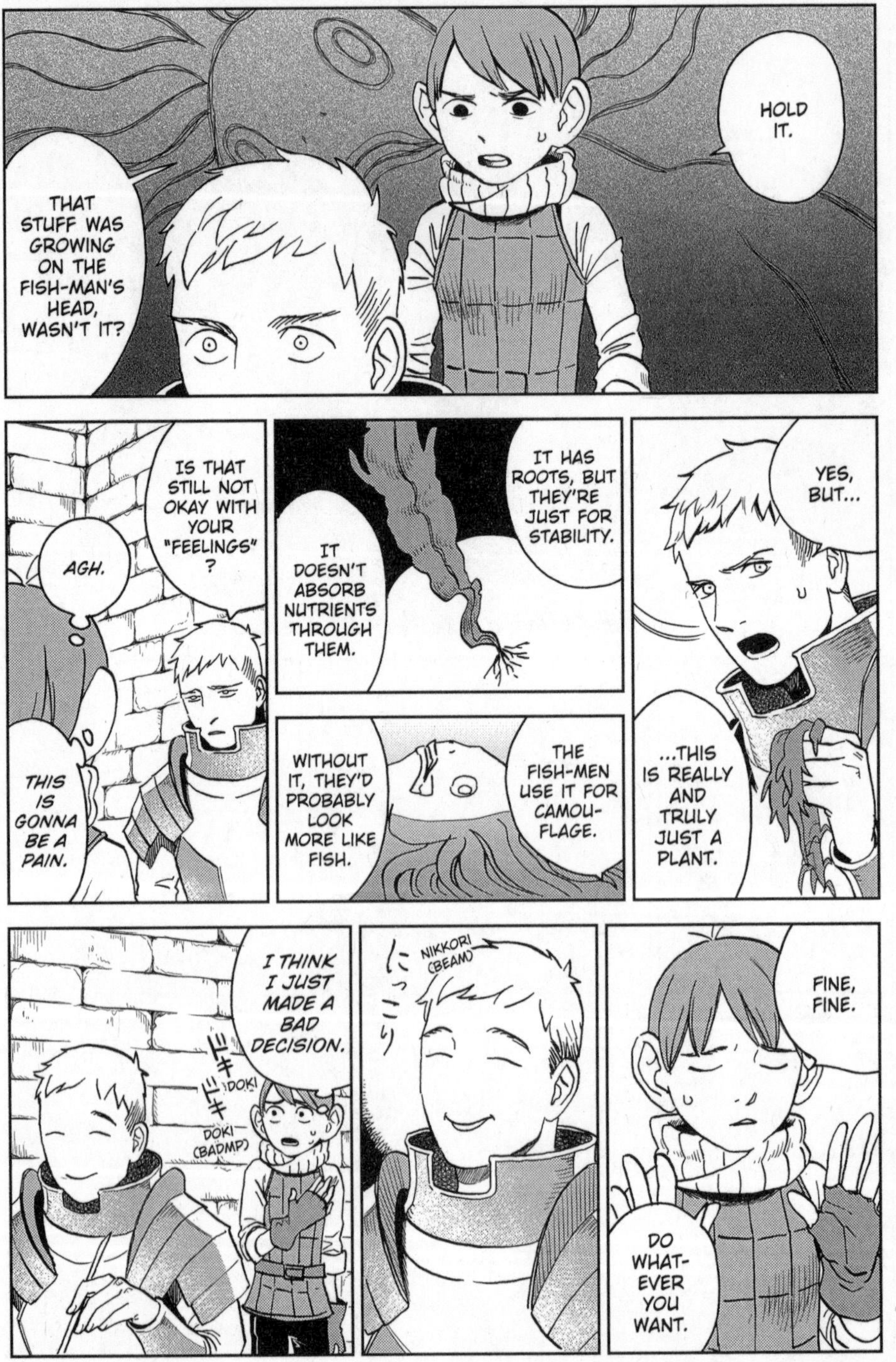
HOLD IT.
THAT STUFF WAS GROWING ON THE FISH-MAN'S HEAD, WASN'T IT?
YES, BUT...
...THIS IS REALLY AND TRULY JUST A PLANT.
IT HAS ROOTS, BUT THEY'RE JUST FOR STABILITY.
IT DOESN'T ABSORB NUTRIENTS THROUGH THEM.
THE FISH-MEN USE IT FOR CAMOUFLAGE.
WITHOUT IT, THEY'D PROBABLY LOOK MORE LIKE FISH.
IS THAT STILL NOT OKAY WITH YOUR "FEELINGS"?
AGH.
THIS IS GONNA BE A PAIN.
FINE, FINE.
DO WHATEVER YOU WANT.
にっこり
NIKKORI (BEAM)
I THINK I JUST MADE A BAD DECISION.
ドキドキ
DOKI DOKI (BADMP)

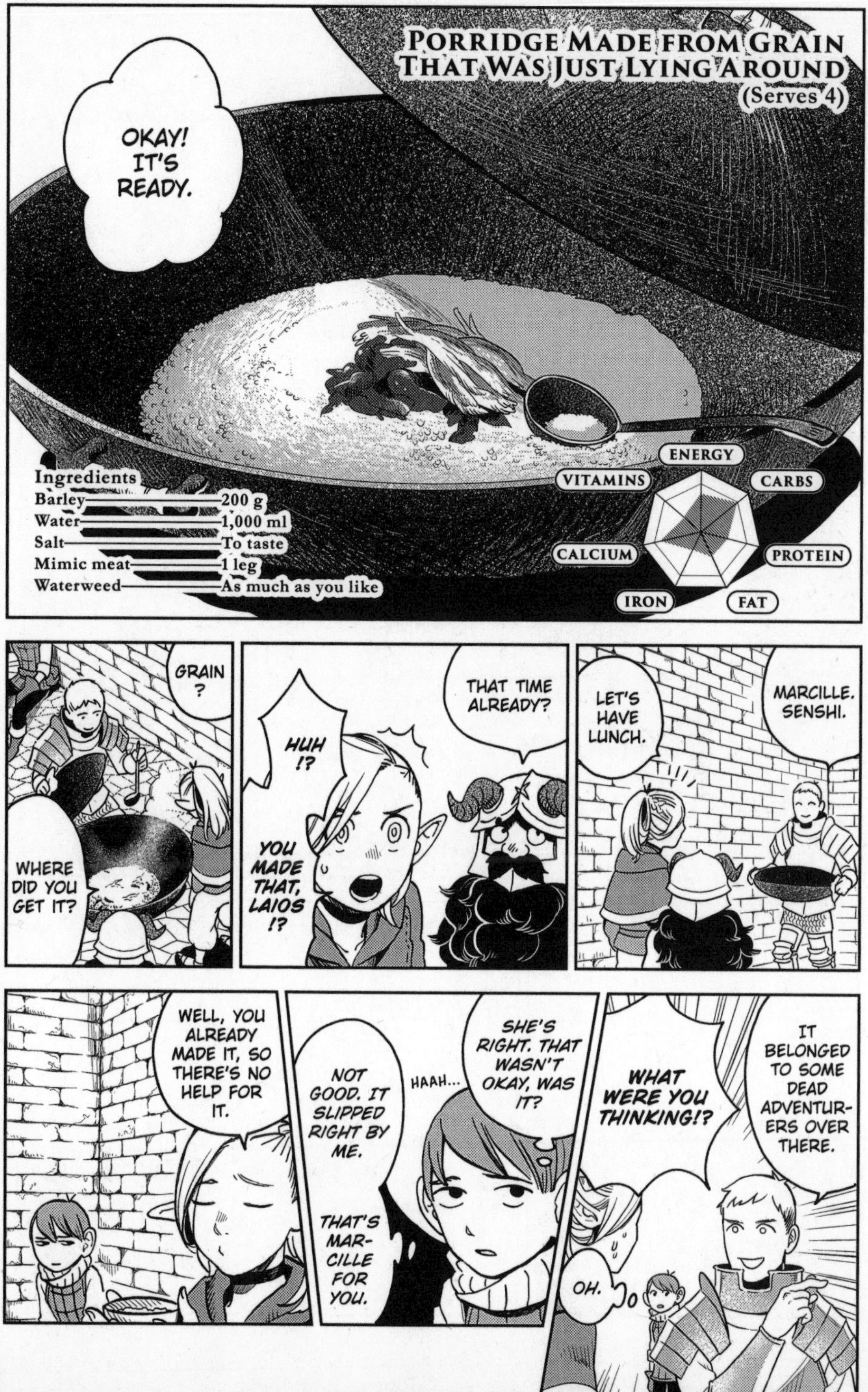
PORRIDGE MADE FROM GRAIN THAT WAS JUST LYING AROUND
(Serves 4)
OKAY! IT'S READY.
Ingredients
Barley—200 g
Water—1,000 ml
Salt—To taste
Mimic meat—1 leg
Waterweed—As much as you like
ENERGY
CARBS
PROTEIN
FAT
IRON
CALCIUM
VITAMINS
MARCILLE. SENSHI.
LET'S HAVE LUNCH.
THAT TIME ALREADY?
HUH!?
YOU MADE THAT, LAIOS!?
GRAIN?
WHERE DID YOU GET IT?
IT BELONGED TO SOME DEAD ADVENTURERS OVER THERE.
WHAT WERE YOU THINKING!?
OH.
SHE'S RIGHT. THAT WASN'T OKAY, WAS IT?
HAAH...
NOT GOOD. IT SLIPPED RIGHT BY ME.
THAT'S MARCILLE FOR YOU.
WELL, YOU ALREADY MADE IT, SO THERE'S NO HELP FOR IT.

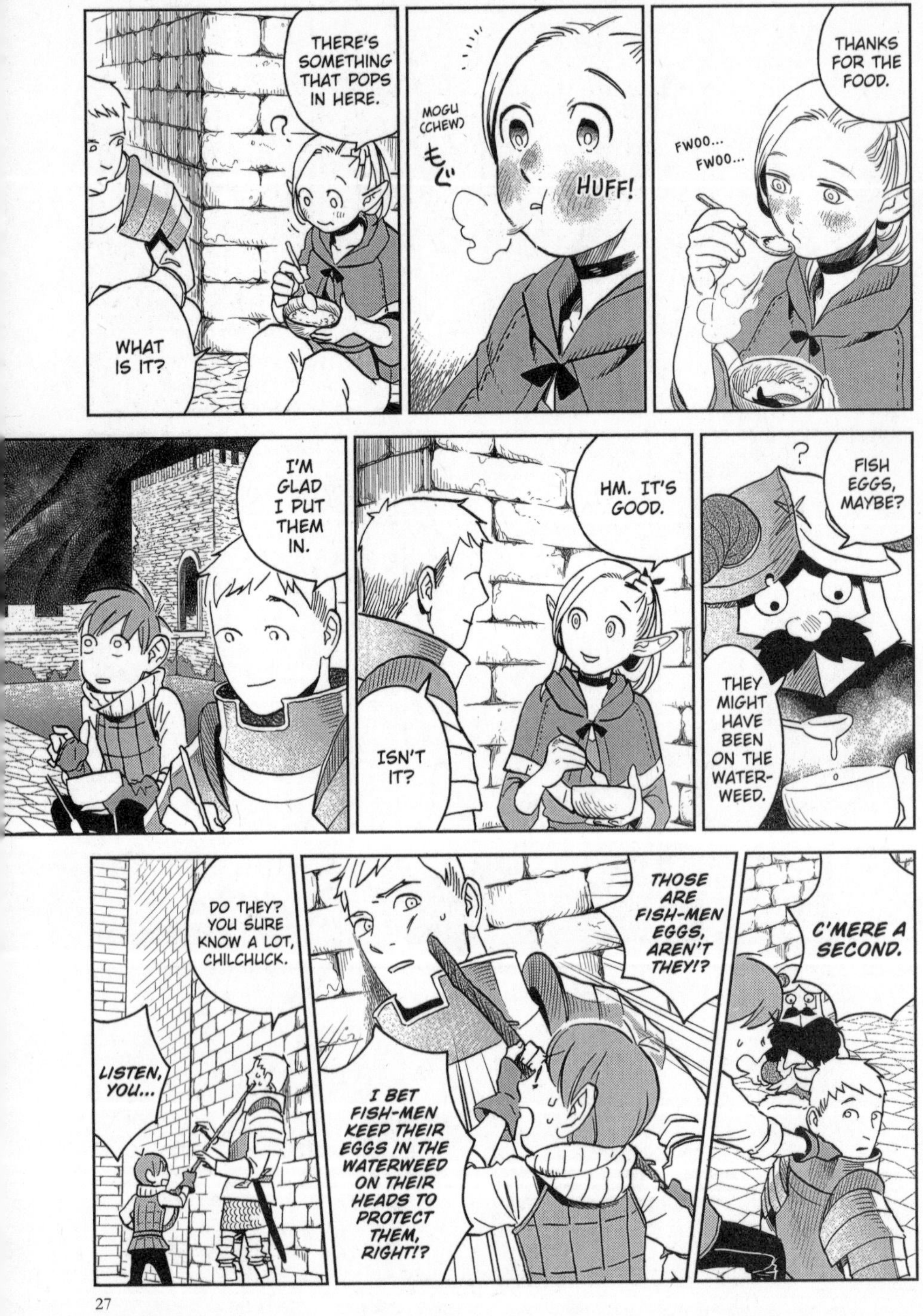
THANKS FOR THE FOOD.
FWOO... FWOO...
MOGU (CHEW)
もぐ
HUFF!
THERE'S SOMETHING THAT POPS IN HERE.
WHAT IS IT?
FISH EGGS, MAYBE?
THEY MIGHT HAVE BEEN ON THE WATER-WEED.
HM. IT'S GOOD.
ISN'T IT?
I'M GLAD I PUT THEM IN.
C'MERE A SECOND.
THOSE ARE FISH-MEN EGGS, AREN'T THEY!?
I BET FISH-MEN KEEP THEIR EGGS IN THE WATERWEED ON THEIR HEADS TO PROTECT THEM, RIGHT!?
DO THEY? YOU SURE KNOW A LOT, CHILCHUCK.
LISTEN, YOU...

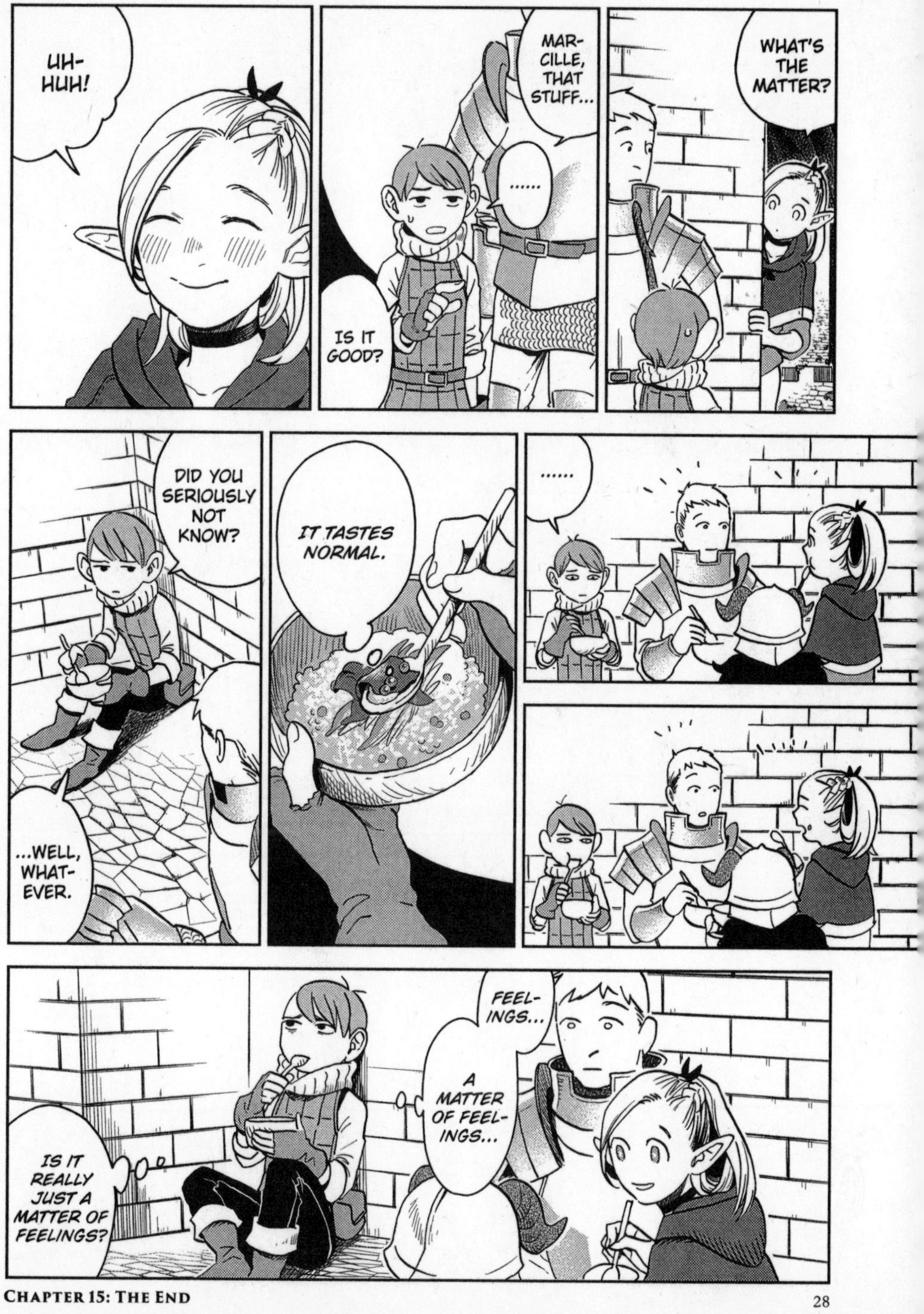
WHAT'S THE MATTER?
MAR-CILLE, THAT STUFF...
......
IS IT GOOD?
UH-HUH!
......
WHAT'S
IT TASTES NORMAL.
DID YOU SERIOUSLY NOT KNOW?
...WELL, WHAT-EVER.
FEEL-INGS...
A MATTER OF FEEL-INGS...
IS IT REALLY JUST A MATTER OF FEELINGS?

Chapter 15: The End

16. Broiled with Sauce

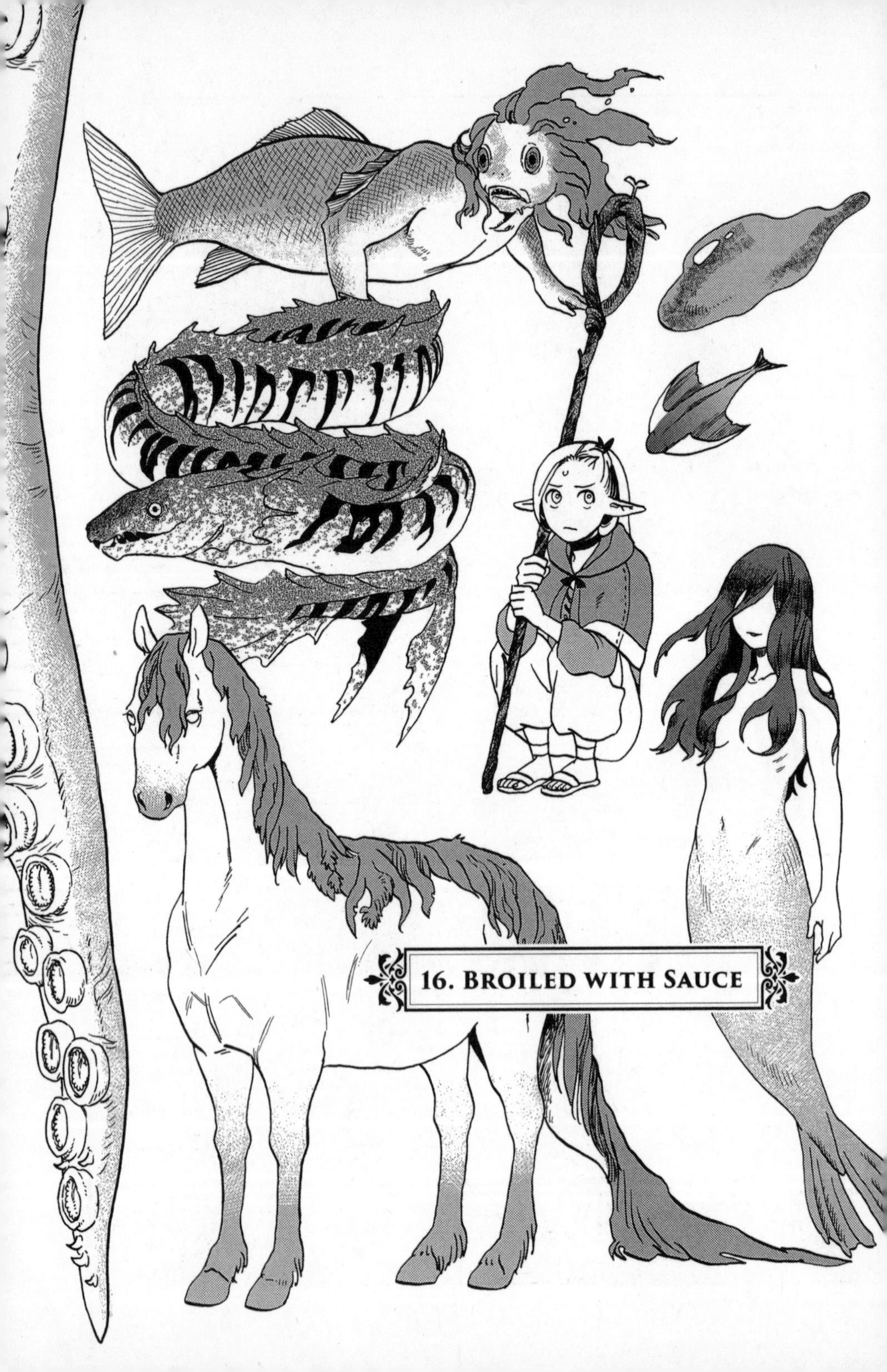

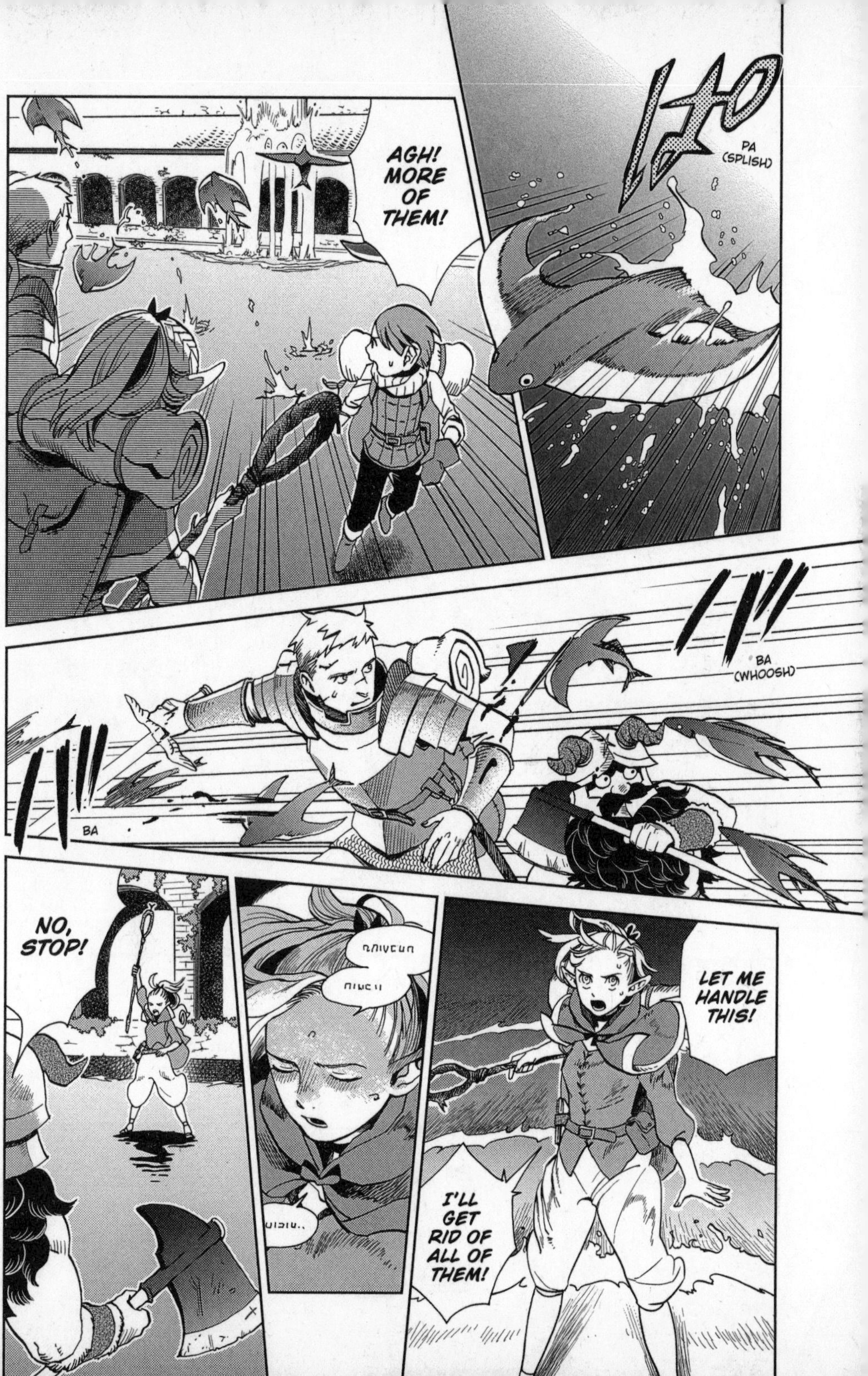
PA (SPLISH)
AGH! MORE OF THEM!
BA (WHOOSH)
BA
LET ME HANDLE THIS!
I'LL GET RID OF ALL OF THEM!
NO, STOP!

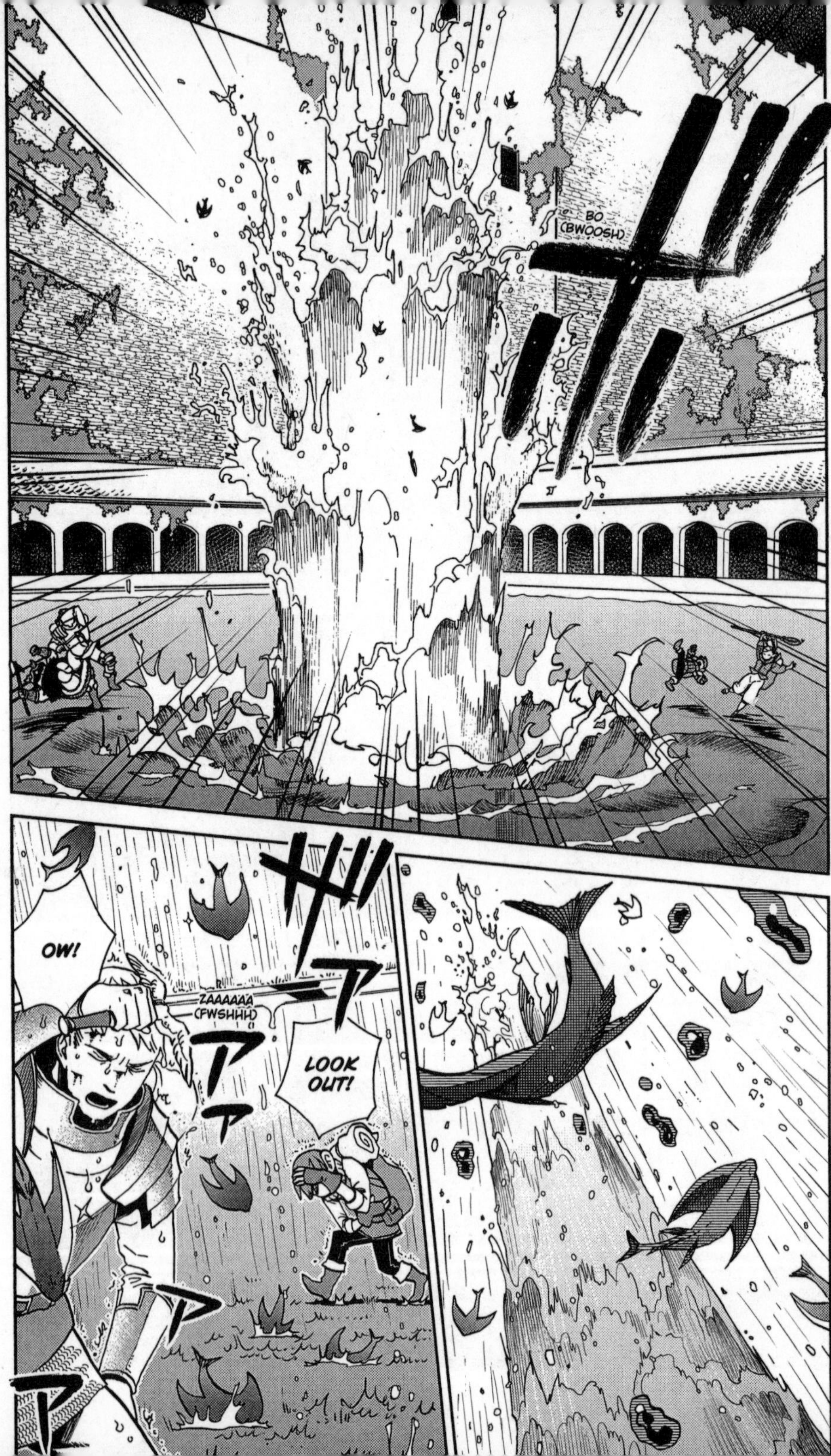
BO
(BWOOSH)
LOOK OUT!
OW!
ZAAAAAA
(FWSHHH)

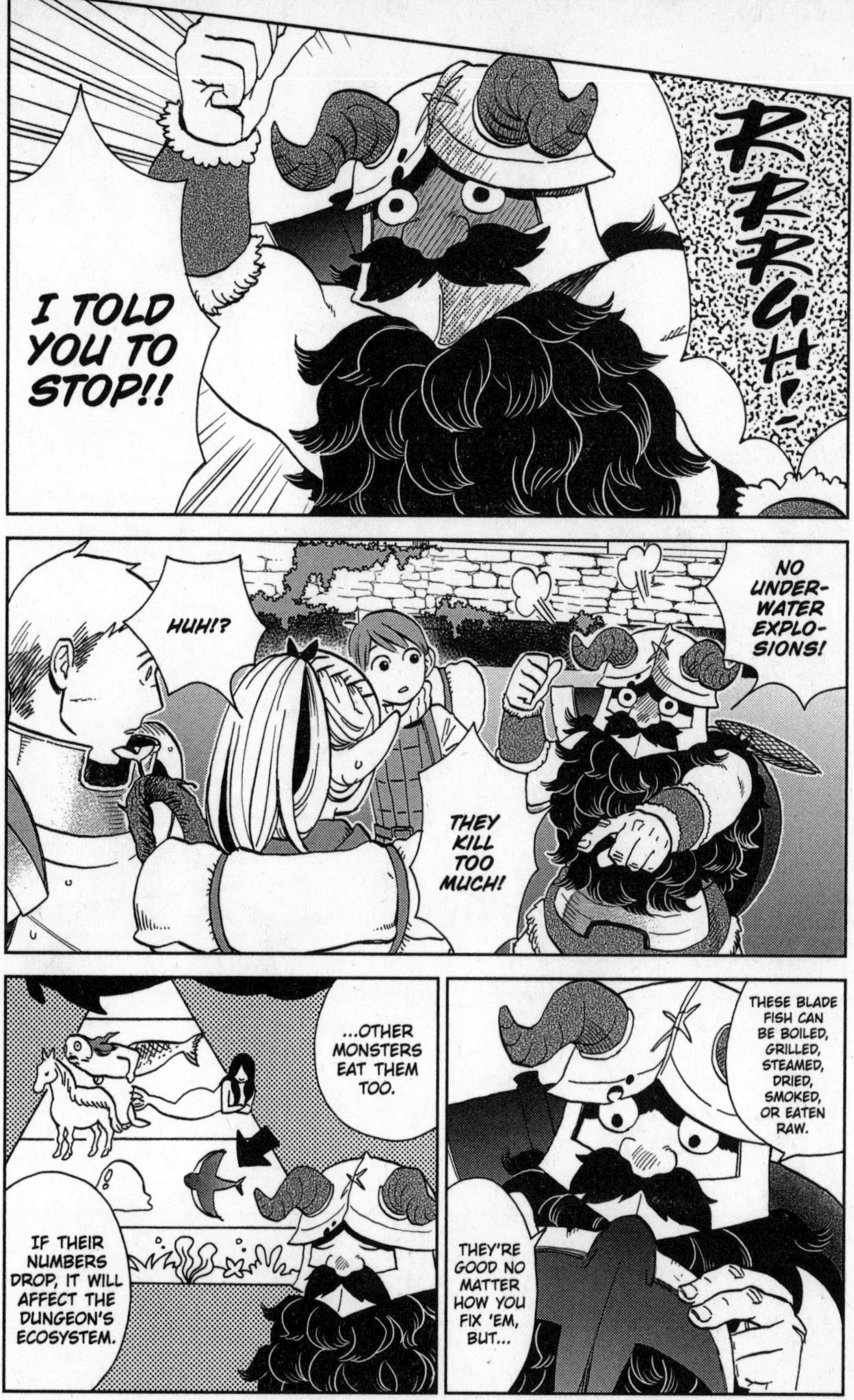
I TOLD YOU TO STOP!!
NO UNDER-WATER EXPLO-SIONS!
THEY KILL TOO MUCH!
HUH!?
THESE BLADE FISH CAN BE BOILED, GRILLED, STEAMED, DRIED, SMOKED, OR EATEN RAW.
THEY'RE GOOD NO MATTER HOW YOU FIX 'EM, BUT...
...OTHER MONSTERS EAT THEM TOO.
IF THEIR NUMBERS DROP, IT WILL AFFECT THE DUNGEON'S ECOSYSTEM.

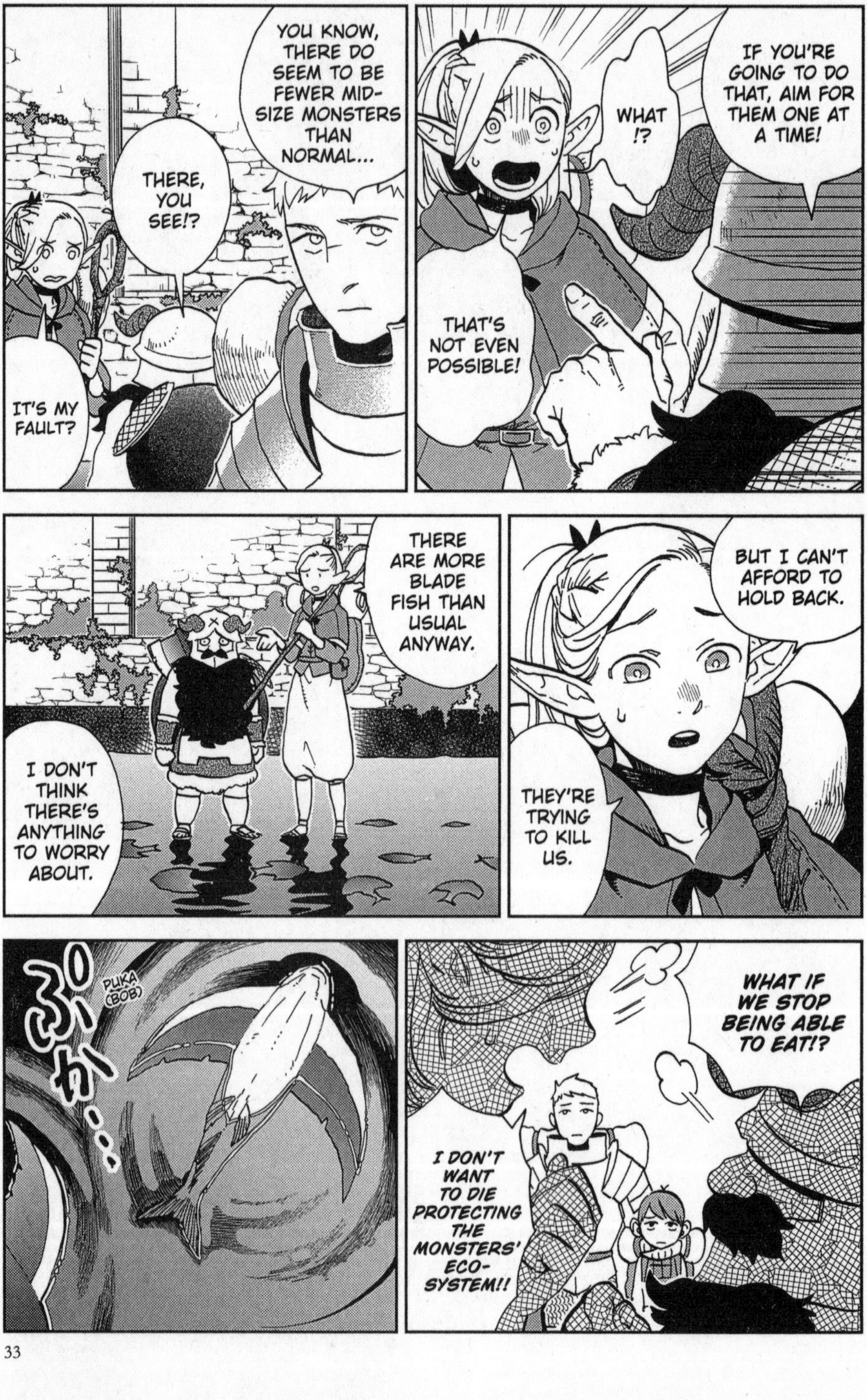
IF YOU'RE GOING TO DO THAT, AIM FOR THEM ONE AT A TIME!
WHAT !?
THAT'S NOT EVEN POSSIBLE!
YOU KNOW, THERE DO SEEM TO BE FEWER MID-SIZE MONSTERS THAN NORMAL...
THERE, YOU SEE!?
IT'S MY FAULT?
BUT I CAN'T AFFORD TO HOLD BACK.
THEY'RE TRYING TO KILL US.
THERE ARE MORE BLADE FISH THAN USUAL ANYWAY.
I DON'T THINK THERE'S ANYTHING TO WORRY ABOUT.
WHAT IF WE STOP BEING ABLE TO EAT!?
I DON'T WANT TO DIE PROTECTING THE MONSTERS' ECO-SYSTEM!!
ぷか…
PUKA (BOB)

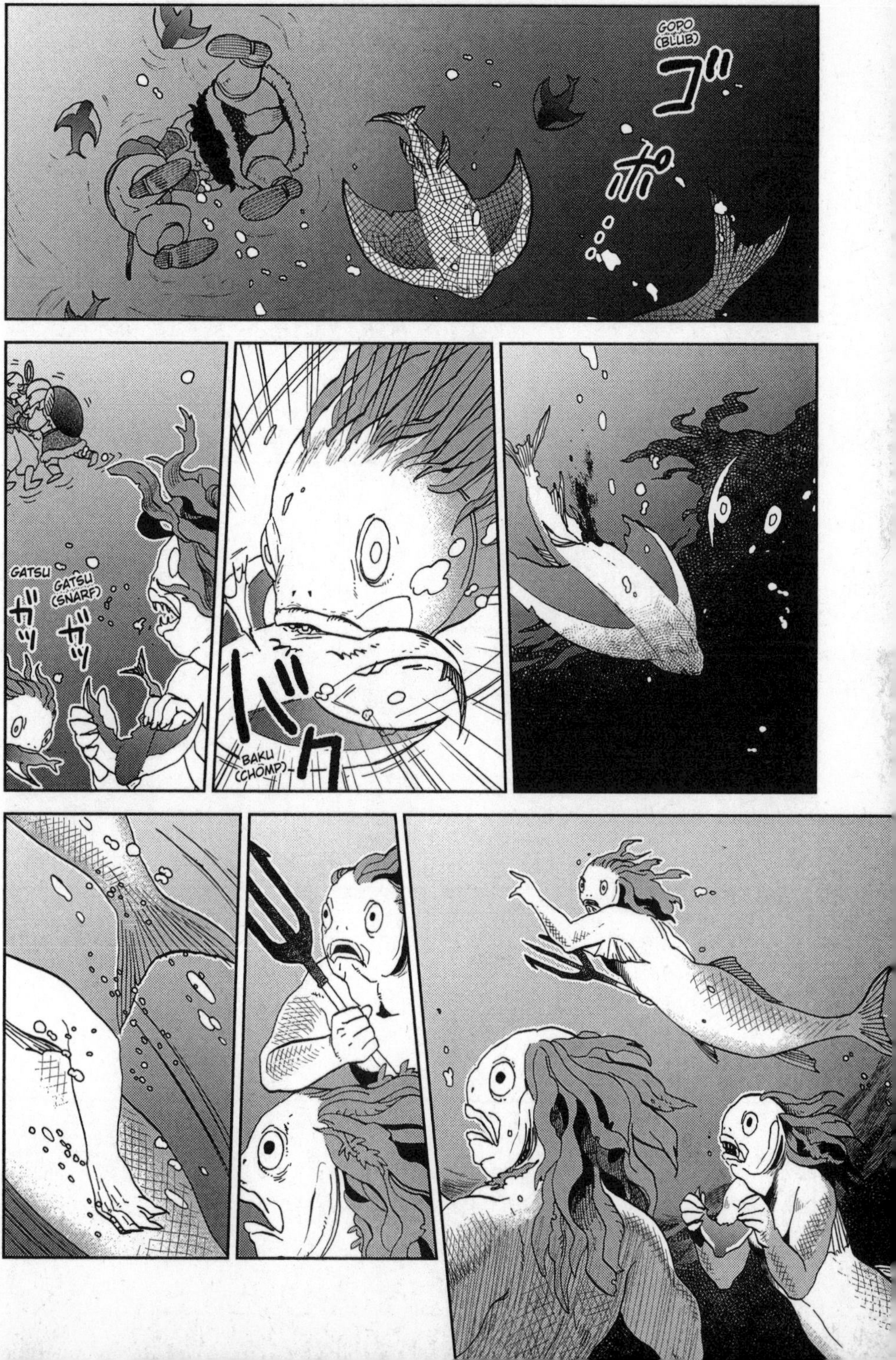
GOPO (BLUB)
ゴポ
BAKU (CHOMP)
バク
GATSU GATSU (SNARF)
ガツガツ

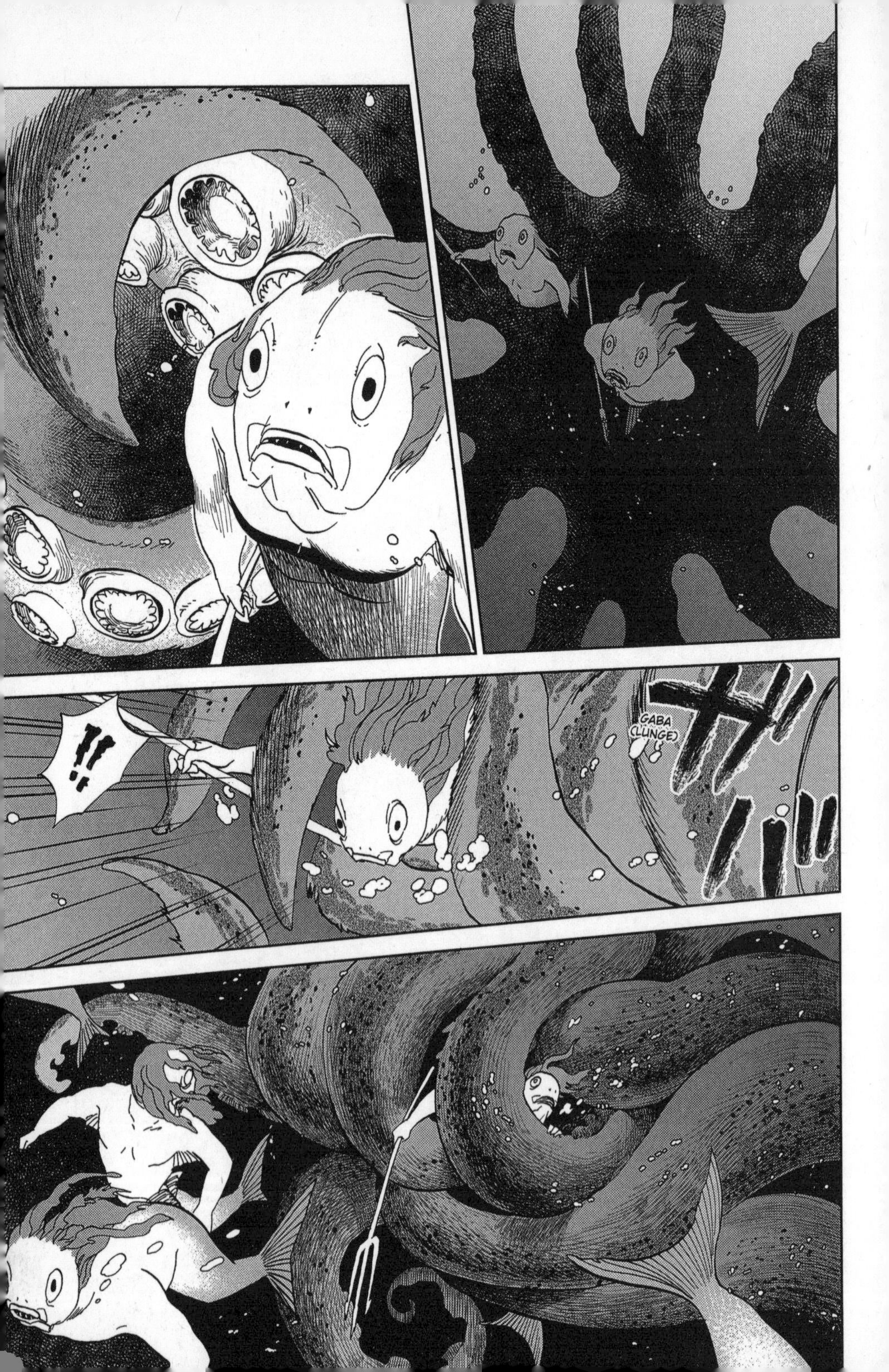

!!
GABA (LUNGE)

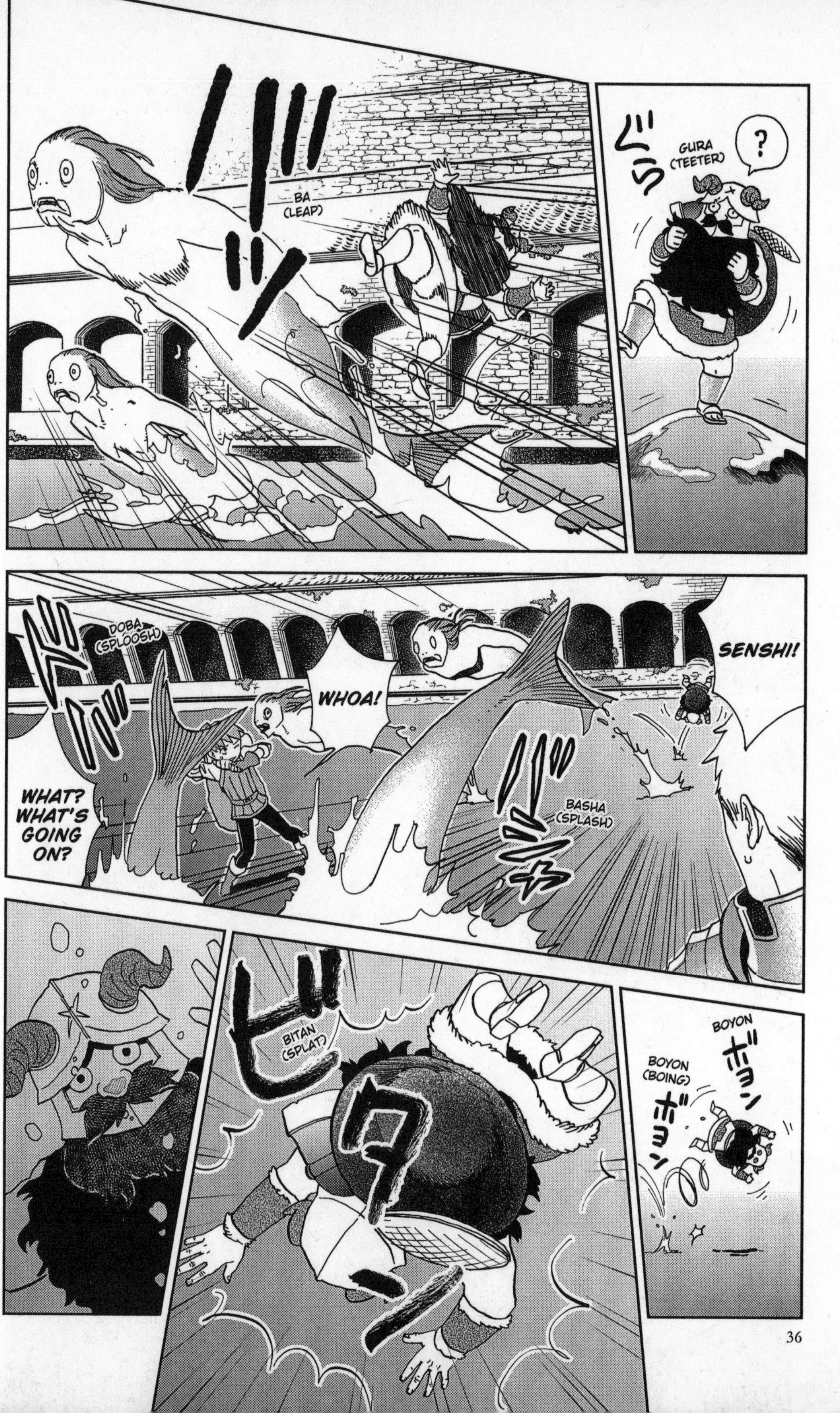

GURA (TEETER)
?
BA (LEAP)
SENSHI!
BASHA (SPLASH)
WHOA!
DOBA (SPLOOSH)
WHAT? WHAT'S GOING ON?
BOYON
BOYON (BOING)
BITAN (SPLAT)

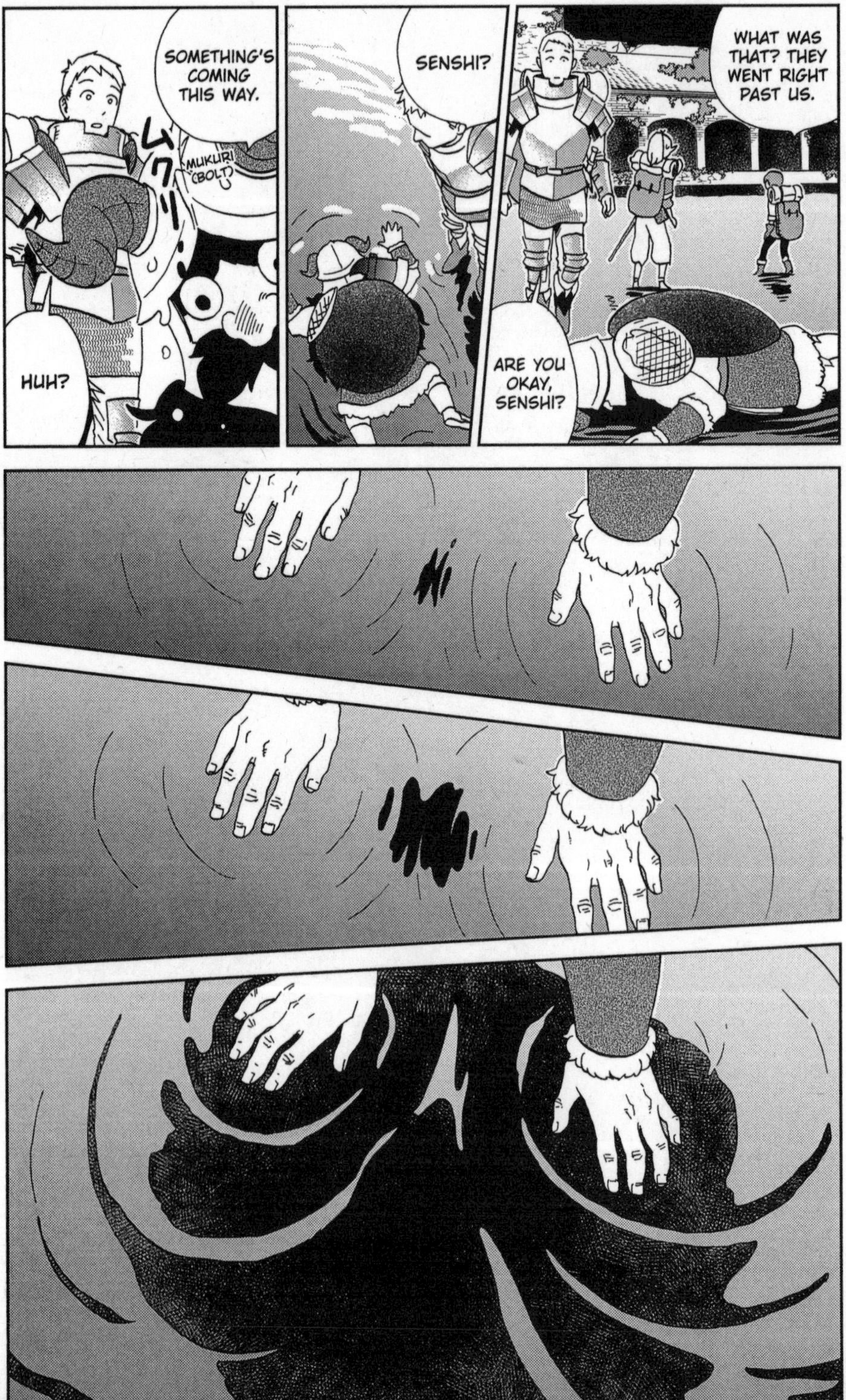
WHAT WAS THAT? THEY WENT RIGHT PAST US.
ARE YOU OKAY, SENSHI?
SENSHI?
SOMETHING'S COMING THIS WAY.
ムクリ
MUKURI (BOLT)
HUH?

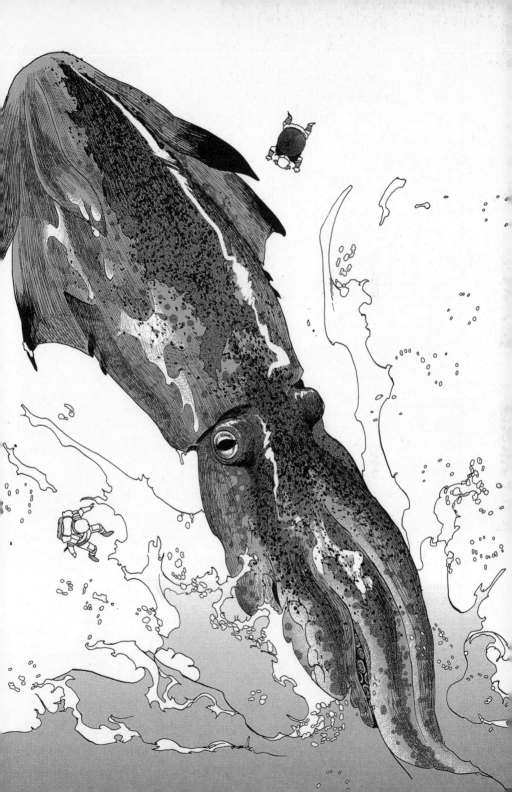

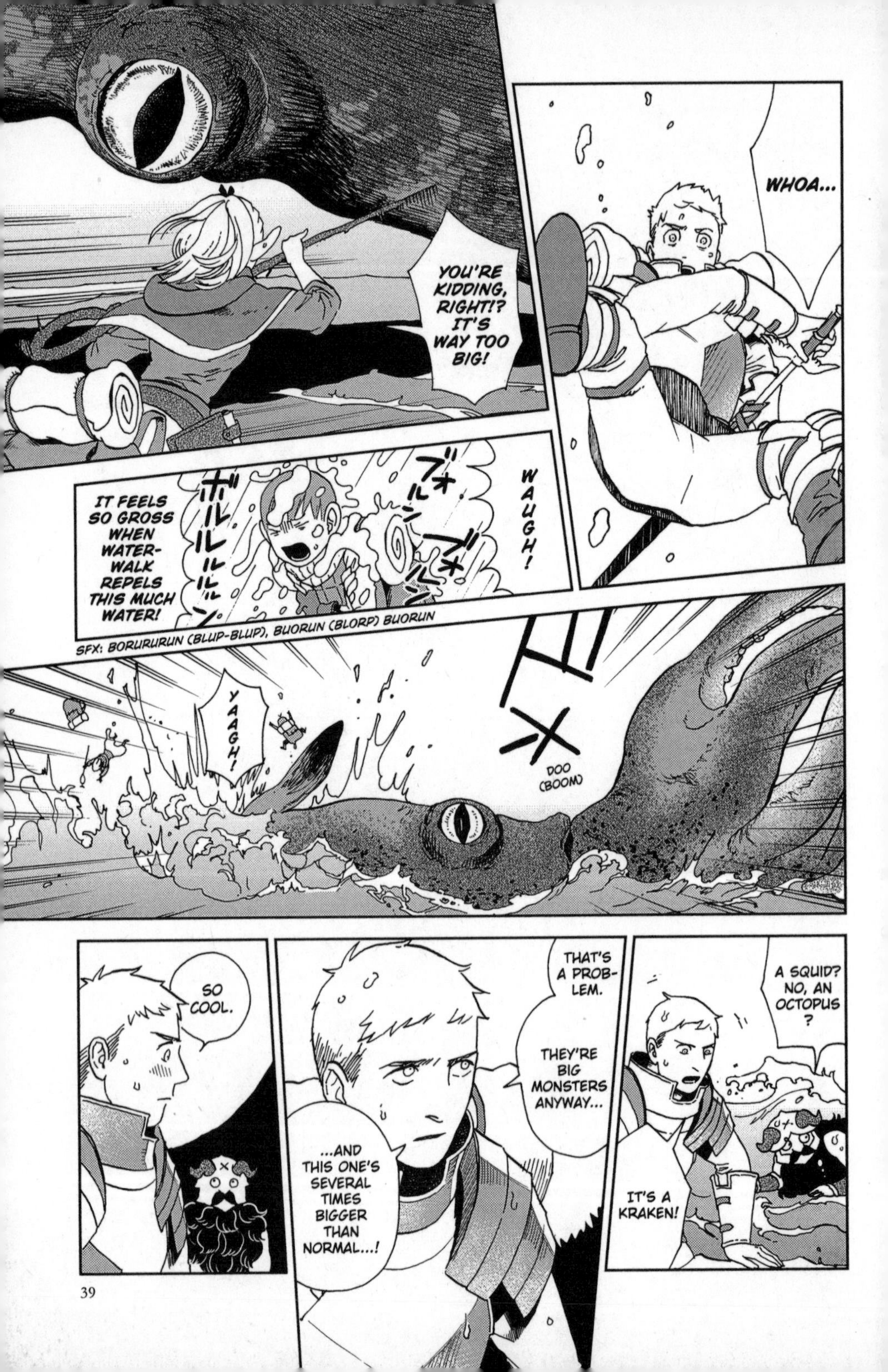
WHOA...
YOU'RE KIDDING, RIGHT!? IT'S WAY TOO BIG!
WAUGH!
IT FEELS SO GROSS WHEN WATER-WALK REPELS THIS MUCH WATER!
SFX: BORURURUN (BLUP-BLUP), BUORUN (BLORP) BUORUN
YAAGH!
DOO (BOOM)
A SQUID? NO, AN OCTOPUS?
IT'S A KRAKEN!
THAT'S A PROB-LEM.
THEY'RE BIG MONSTERS ANYWAY...
...AND THIS ONE'S SEVERAL TIMES BIGGER THAN NORMAL...!
SO COOL.

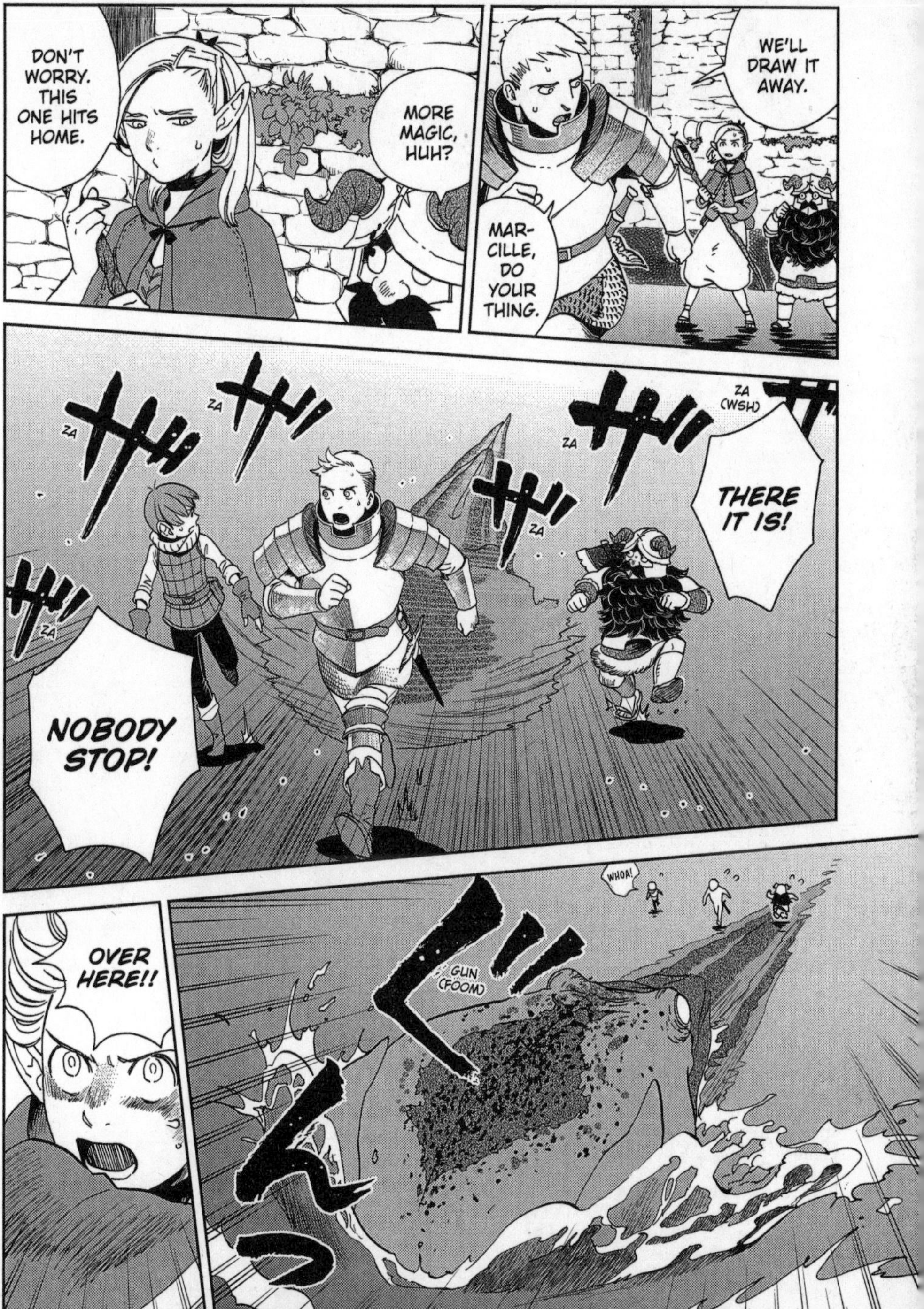
WE'LL DRAW IT AWAY.
MARCILLE, DO YOUR THING.
MORE MAGIC, HUH?
DON'T WORRY. THIS ONE HITS HOME.
ZA (WSH)
ZA
ZA
ZA
ZA
ZA
THERE IT IS!
NOBODY STOP!
WHOA!
GUN (FOOM)
OVER HERE!!

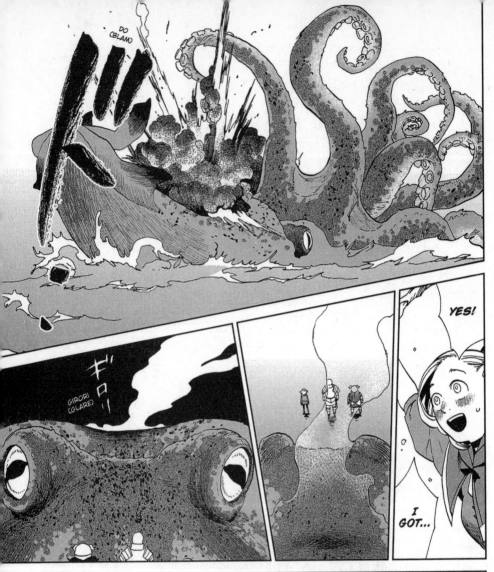

DO
(BLAM)

GIRORI
(GLARE)

YES!

I
GOT...

AAAAH!

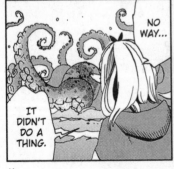

NO
WAY...

IT
DIDN'T
DO A
THING.

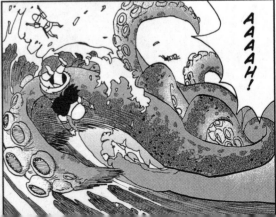

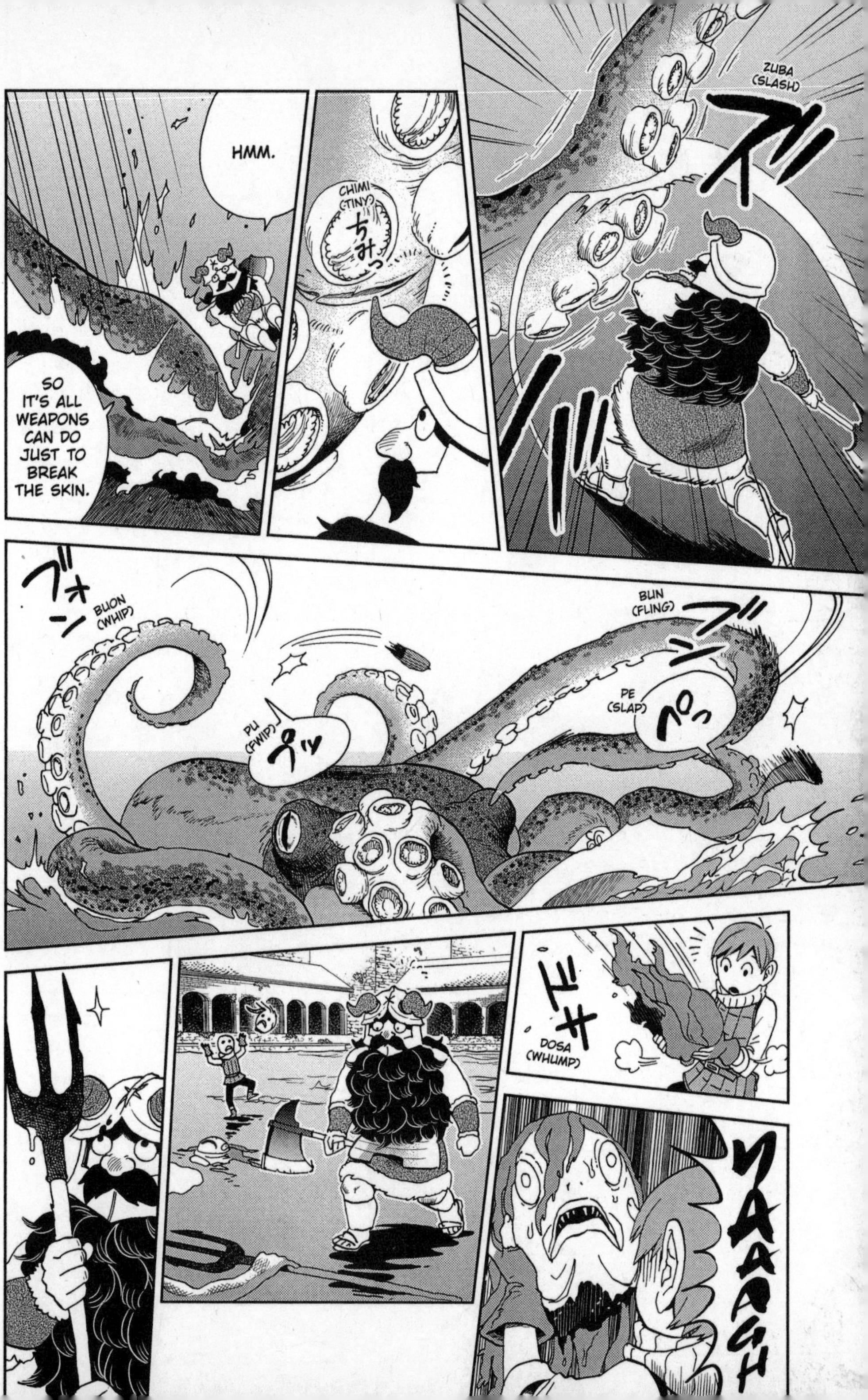

ZUBA (SLASH)
ズバ
CHIMI (TINY)
ちみっ
HMM.
SO IT'S ALL WEAPONS CAN DO JUST TO BREAK THE SKIN.
BUN (FLING)
ブン
PE (SLAP)
ぺっ
PU (FWIP)
プッ
BUON (WHIP)
ブォン
DOSA (WHUMP)
ドサ
YAAAGH

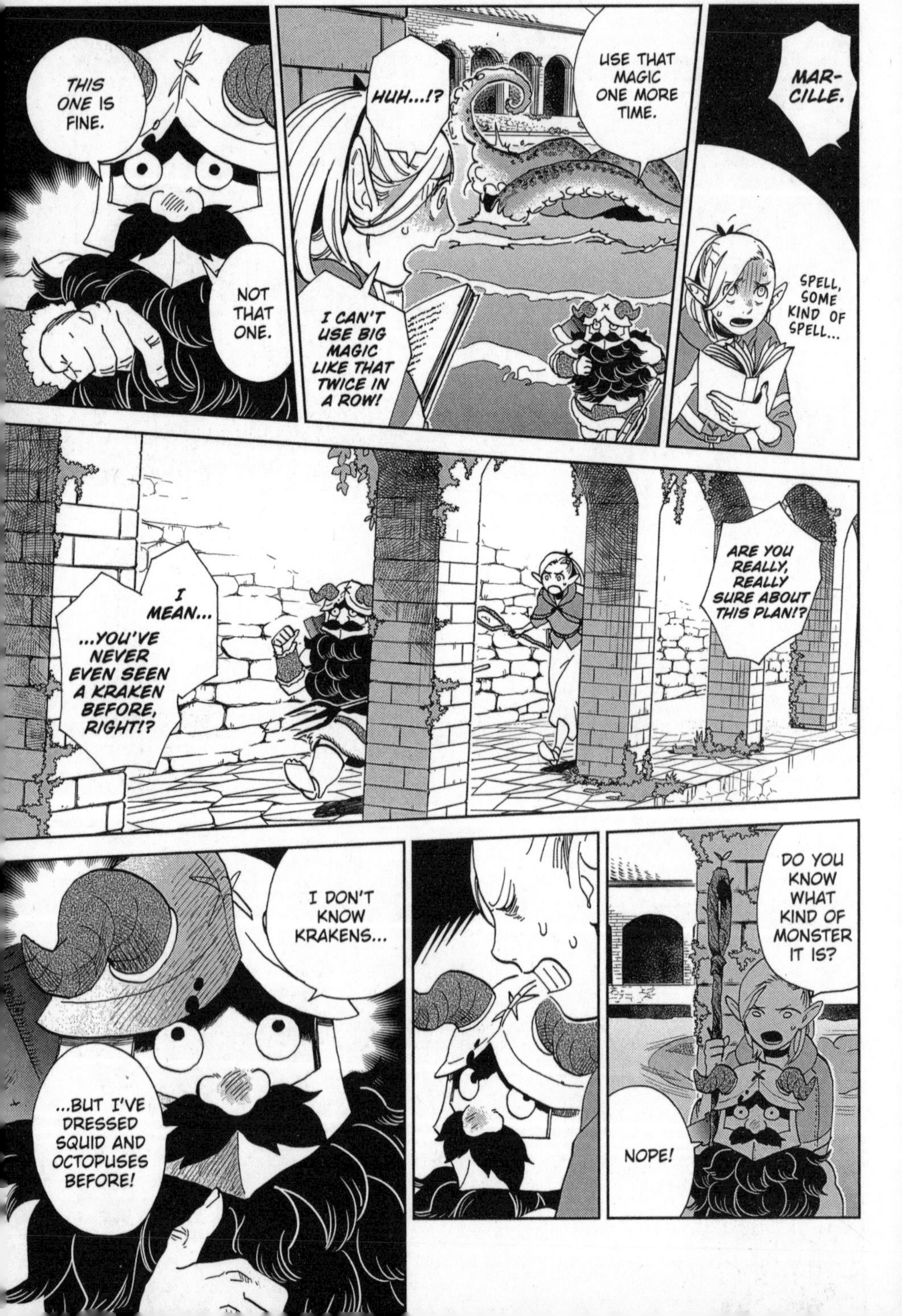
MAR-CILLE.
SPELL, SOME KIND OF SPELL...
USE THAT MAGIC ONE MORE TIME.
HUH...!?
I CAN'T USE BIG MAGIC LIKE THAT TWICE IN A ROW!
THIS ONE IS FINE.
NOT THAT ONE.
ARE YOU REALLY, REALLY SURE ABOUT THIS PLAN!?
I MEAN...
...YOU'VE NEVER EVEN SEEN A KRAKEN BEFORE, RIGHT!?
DO YOU KNOW WHAT KIND OF MONSTER IT IS?
NOPE!
I DON'T KNOW KRAKENS...
...BUT I'VE DRESSED SQUID AND OCTOPUSES BEFORE!

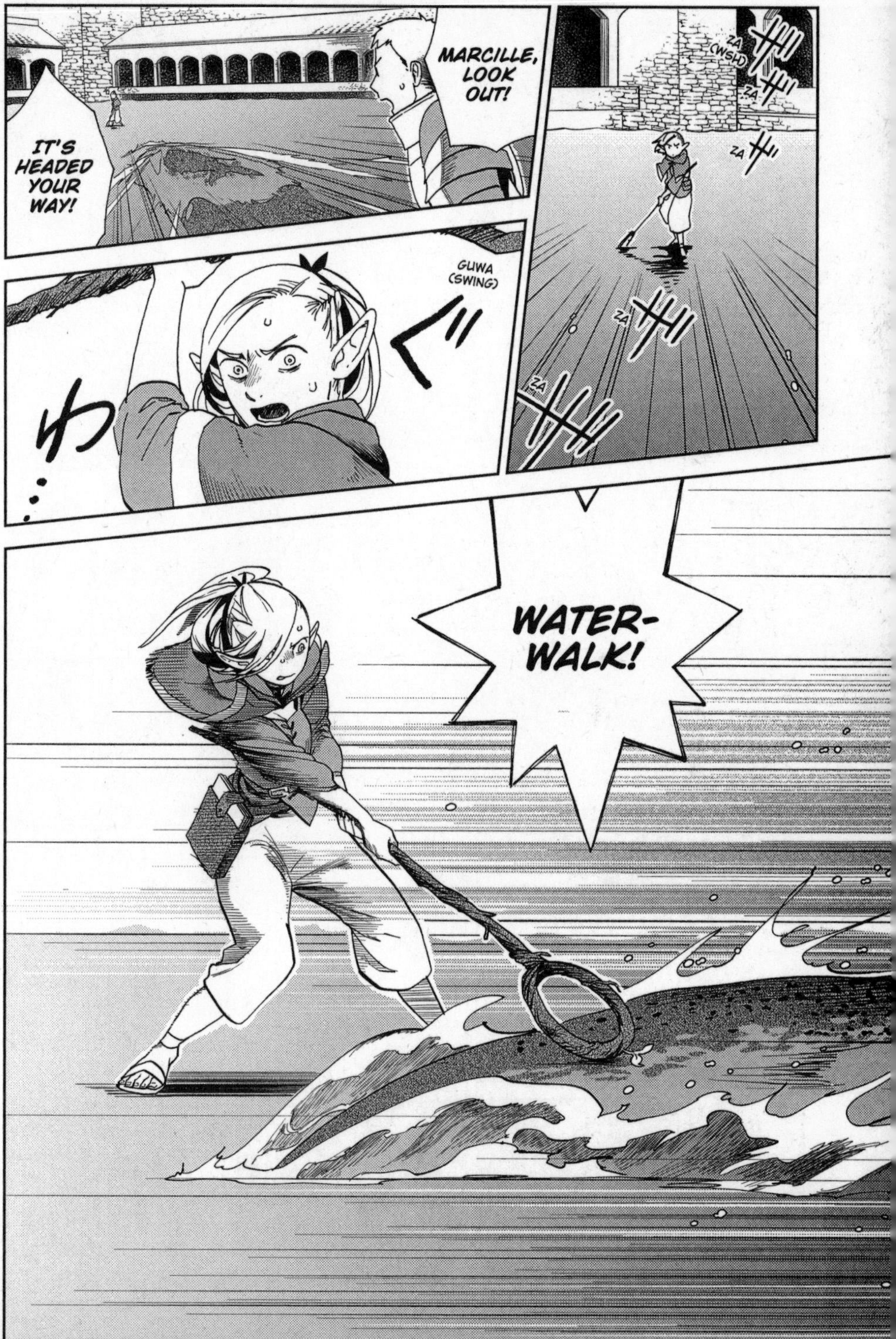
ZA (WSH)
ZA
ZA
ZA
ZA
MARCILLE, LOOK OUT!
IT'S HEADED YOUR WAY!
GUWA (SWING)
WATER-WALK!

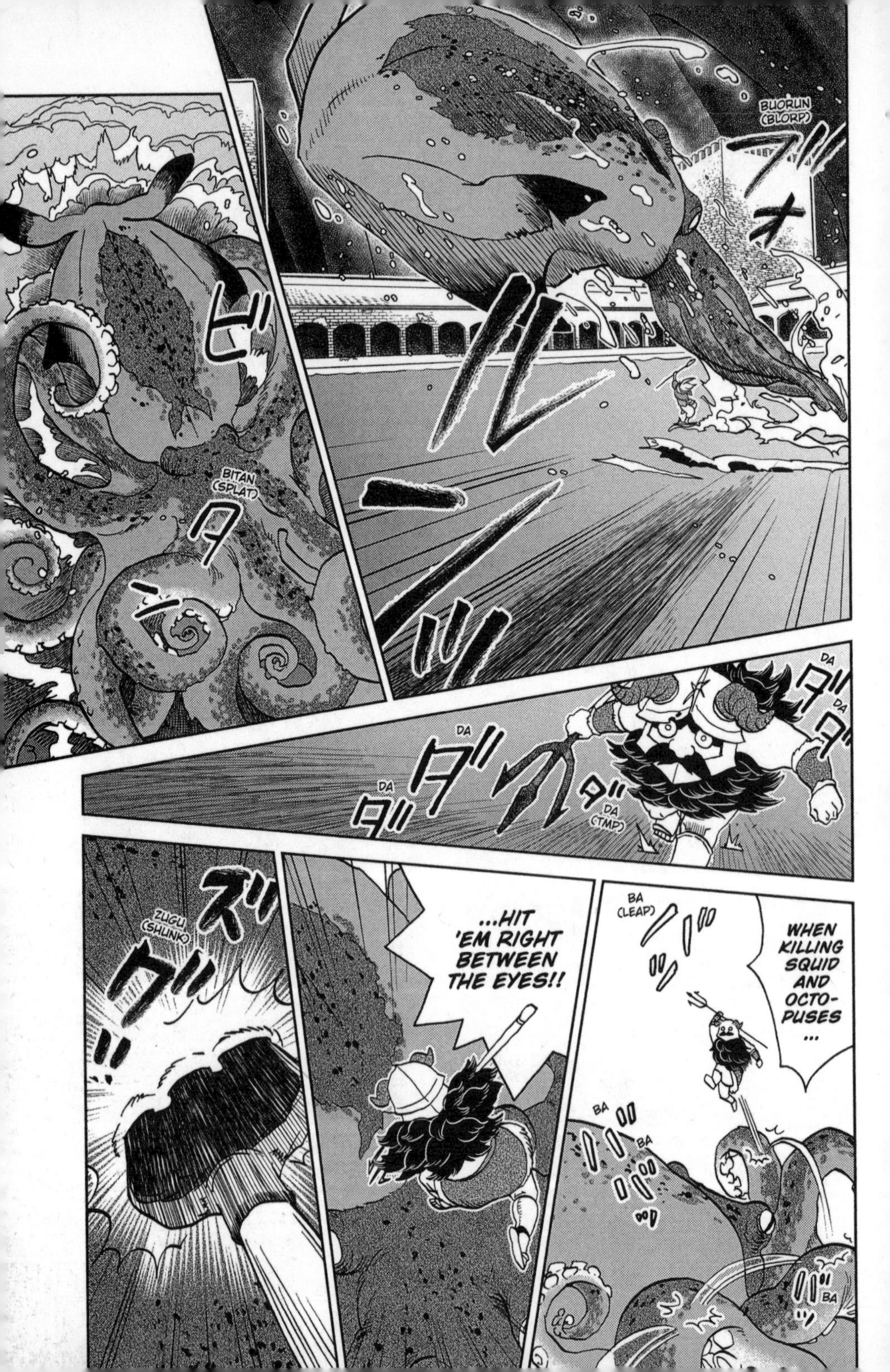
BUORUN (BLORP)
BITAN (SPLAT)
DA
DA
DA
DA (TMP)
BA (LEAP)
WHEN KILLING SQUID AND OCTOPUSES...
BA
BA
BA
...HIT 'EM RIGHT BETWEEN THE EYES!!
ZUGU (SHUNK)

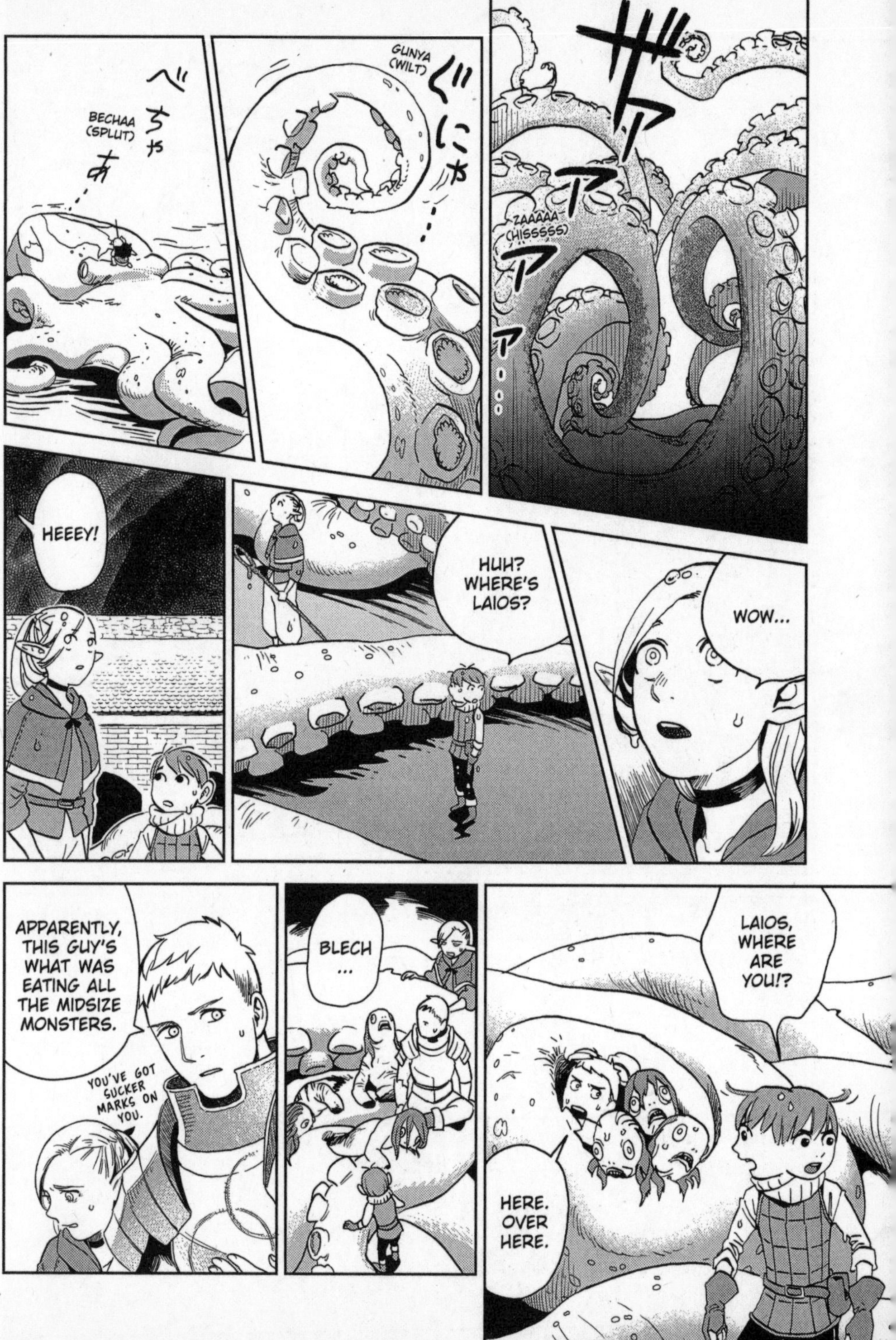
ザァァァ…
ZAAAAA
(HISSSSS)
ぐにゃ…
GUNYA
(WILT)
べちゃあ…
BECHAA
(SPLUT)
WOW...
HUH? WHERE'S LAIOS?
HEEEY!
LAIOS, WHERE ARE YOU!?
HERE. OVER HERE.
BLECH ...
APPARENTLY, THIS GUY'S WHAT WAS EATING ALL THE MIDSIZE MONSTERS.
YOU'VE GOT SUCKER MARKS ON YOU.

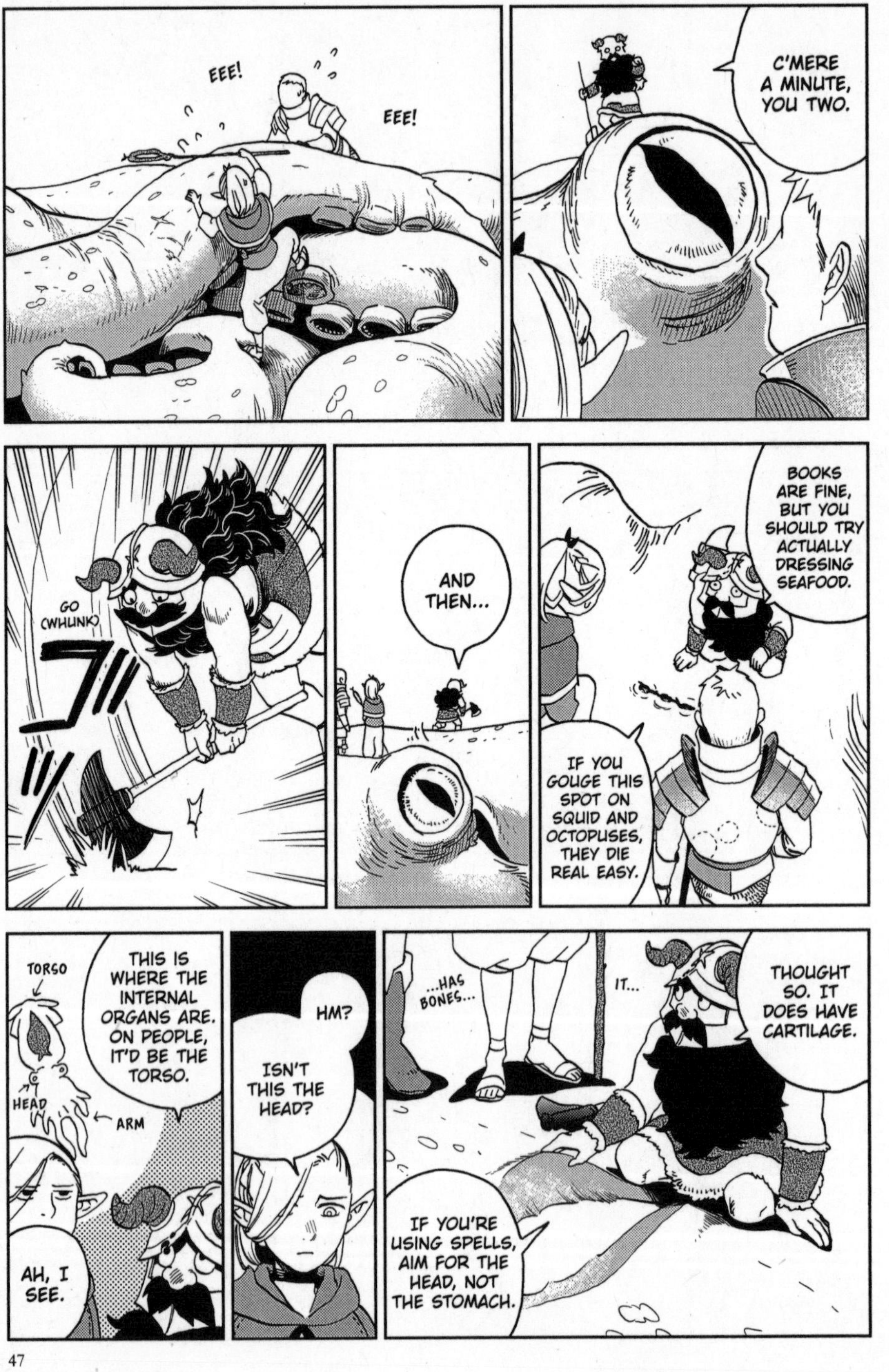
C'MERE A MINUTE, YOU TWO.
EEE!
EEE!
BOOKS ARE FINE, BUT YOU SHOULD TRY ACTUALLY DRESSING SEAFOOD.
IF YOU GOUGE THIS SPOT ON SQUID AND OCTOPUSES, THEY DIE REAL EASY.
AND THEN...
GO (WHUNK)
THOUGHT SO. IT DOES HAVE CARTILAGE.
IT...
...HAS BONES...
IF YOU'RE USING SPELLS, AIM FOR THE HEAD, NOT THE STOMACH.
HM?
ISN'T THIS THE HEAD?
THIS IS WHERE THE INTERNAL ORGANS ARE. ON PEOPLE, IT'D BE THE TORSO.
TORSO
HEAD
ARM
AH, I SEE.

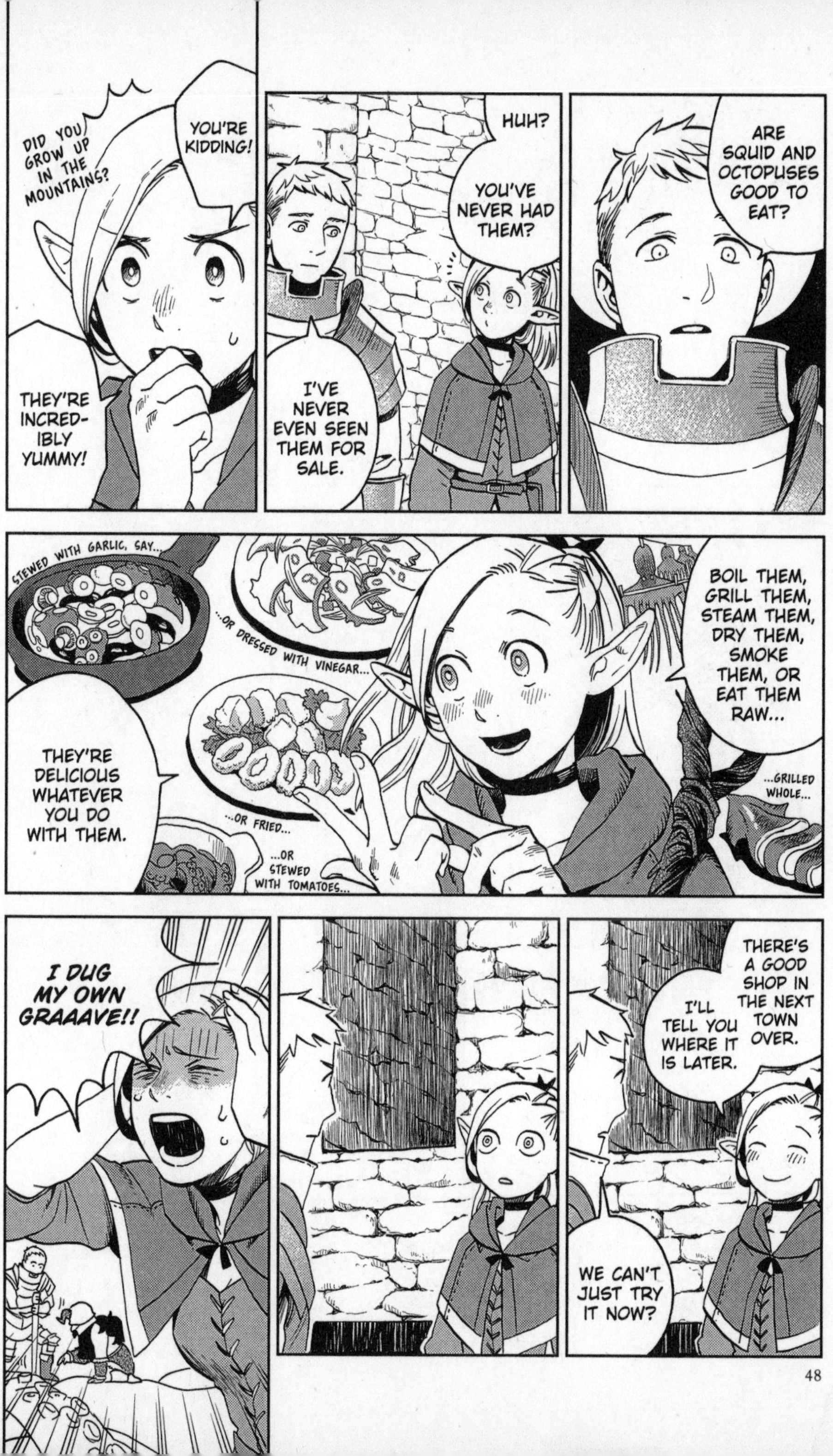
ARE SQUID AND OCTOPUSES GOOD TO EAT?
HUH?
YOU'VE NEVER HAD THEM?
I'VE NEVER EVEN SEEN THEM FOR SALE.
YOU'RE KIDDING!
DID YOU GROW UP IN THE MOUNTAINS?
THEY'RE INCRED-IBLY YUMMY!
BOIL THEM, GRILL THEM, STEAM THEM, DRY THEM, SMOKE THEM, OR EAT THEM RAW...
...GRILLED WHOLE...
...OR DRESSED WITH VINEGAR...
STEWED WITH GARLIC, SAY...
...OR FRIED...
...OR STEWED WITH TOMATOES...
THEY'RE DELICIOUS WHATEVER YOU DO WITH THEM.
THERE'S A GOOD SHOP IN THE NEXT TOWN OVER.
I'LL TELL YOU WHERE IT IS LATER.
WE CAN'T JUST TRY IT NOW?
I DUG MY OWN GRAAAVE!!

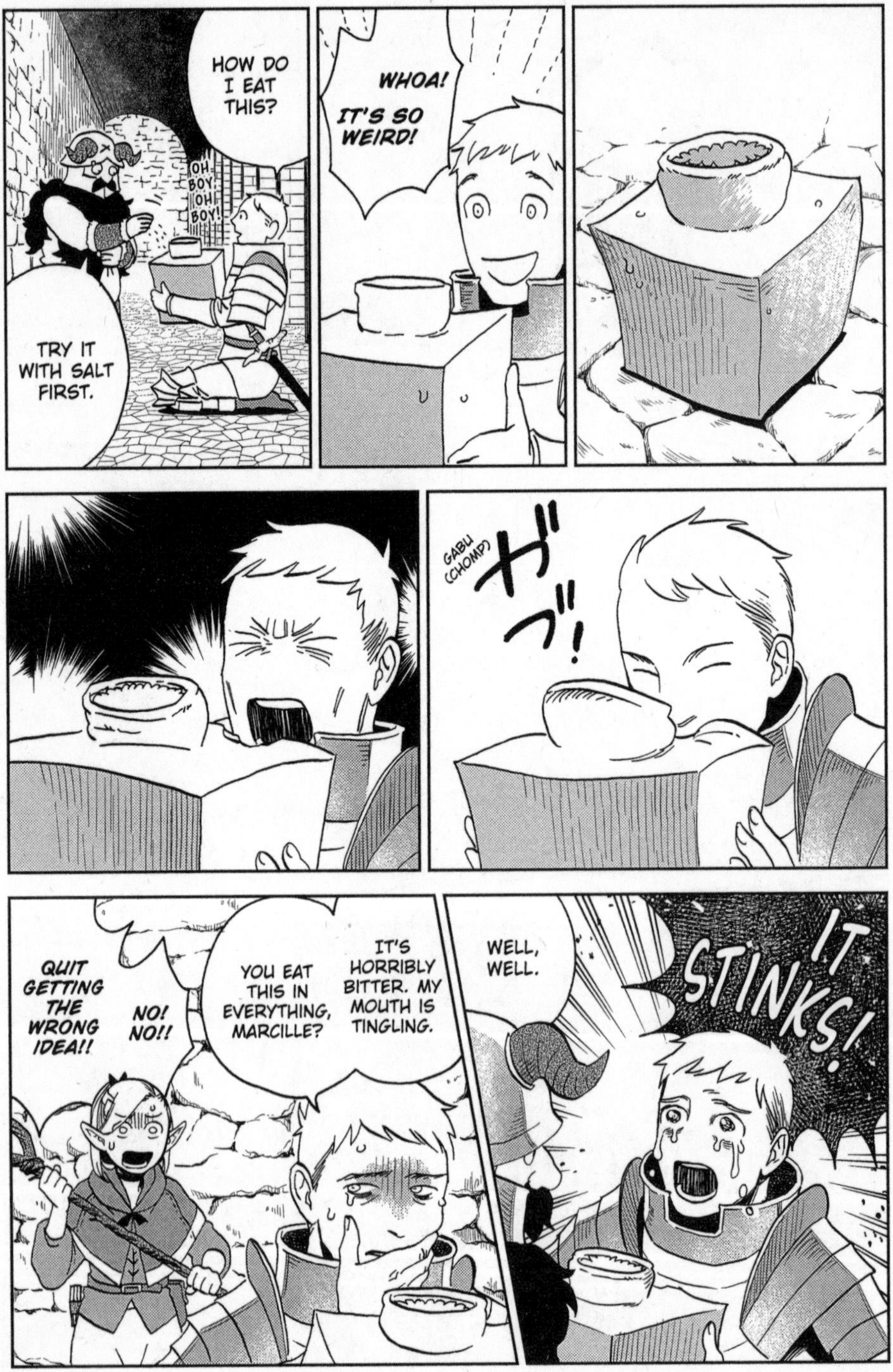
WHOA!
IT'S SO WEIRD!
HOW DO I EAT THIS?
OH BOY OH BOY!
TRY IT WITH SALT FIRST.
ガブ!
GABU (CHOMP)
IT STINKS!
WELL, WELL.
IT'S HORRIBLY BITTER. MY MOUTH IS TINGLING.
YOU EAT THIS IN EVERYTHING, MARCILLE?
NO! NO!!
QUIT GETTING THE WRONG IDEA!!

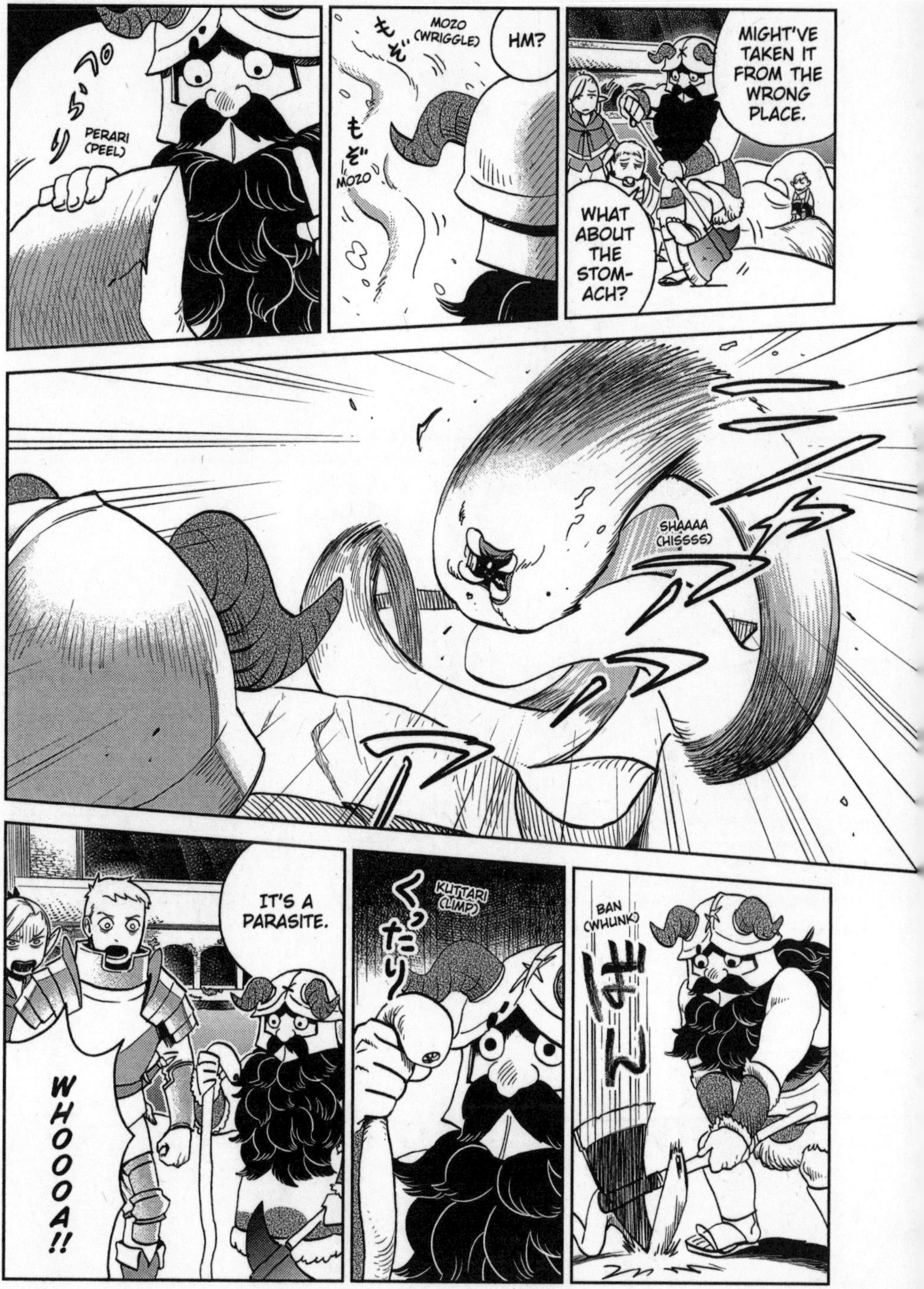
MIGHT'VE TAKEN IT FROM THE WRONG PLACE.
WHAT ABOUT THE STOMACH?
HM?
もぞ
MOZO (WRIGGLE)
もぞ
MOZO
PERARI (PEEL)
SHAAAA (HISSSS)
ばん
BAN (WHUNK)
くったり
KUTTARI (LIMP)
IT'S A PARASITE.
WHOOOOA!!

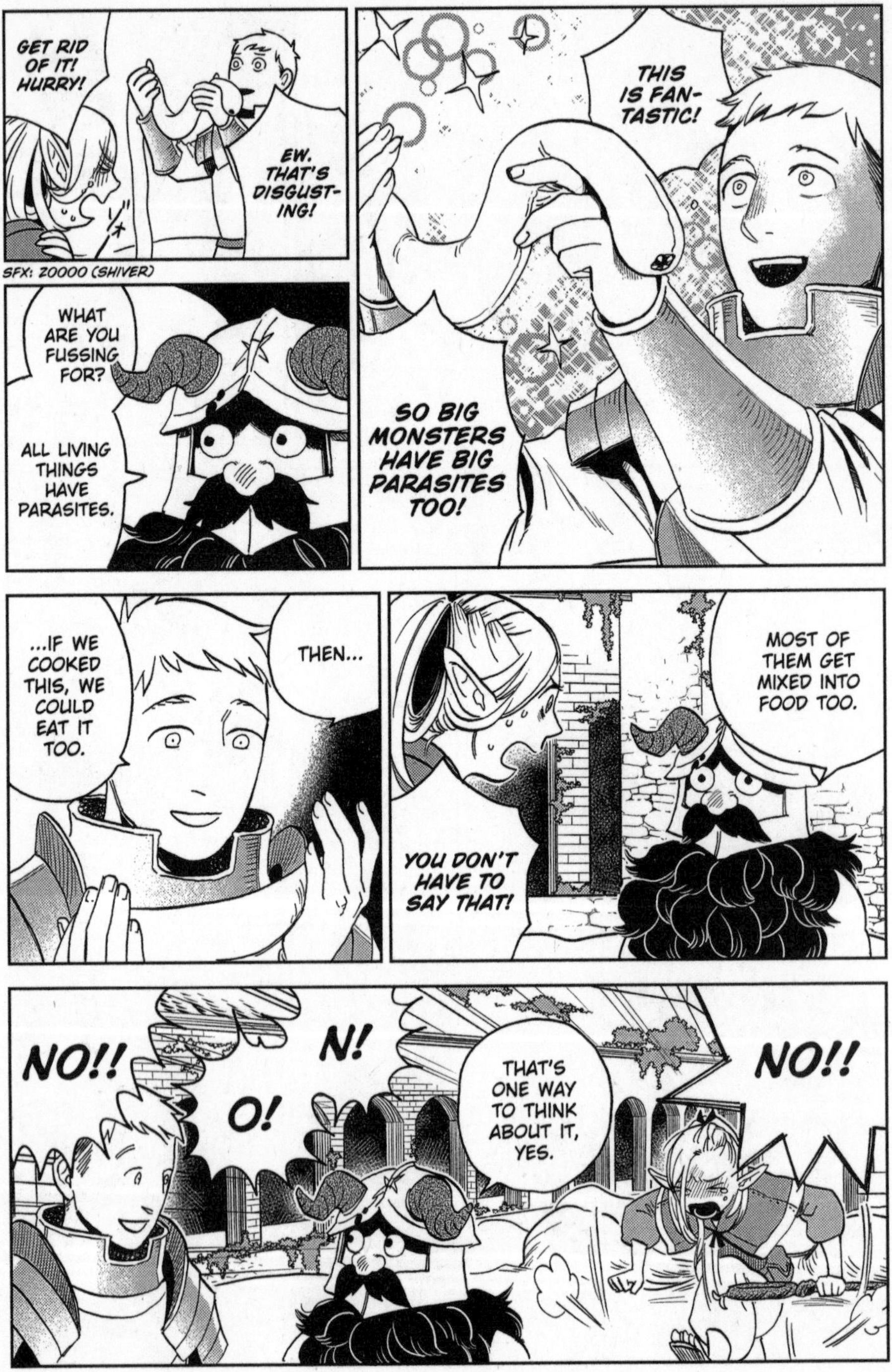
THIS IS FAN-TASTIC!
SO BIG MONSTERS HAVE BIG PARASITES TOO!
GET RID OF IT! HURRY!
EW. THAT'S DISGUST-ING!
SFX: ZOOOO (SHIVER)
WHAT ARE YOU FUSSING FOR?
ALL LIVING THINGS HAVE PARASITES.
MOST OF THEM GET MIXED INTO FOOD TOO.
YOU DON'T HAVE TO SAY THAT!
THEN...
...IF WE COOKED THIS, WE COULD EAT IT TOO.
NO!!
THAT'S ONE WAY TO THINK ABOUT IT, YES.
N!
O!
NO!!

DO (SHUNK)
ド
JYOGU
ジョグ
JYOGU (SLIT)
ジョグ
ZORIRIRIRI (SLIIIICE)
ぞりりりり
SU (SHWIP)
ズッ
SU
ズッ
SU
ズッ
PUSU (POKE)
プス
ポン
PON (TMP)

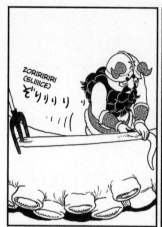

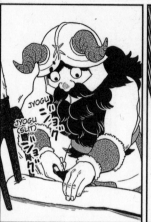

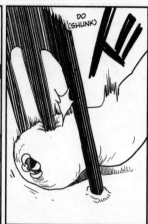

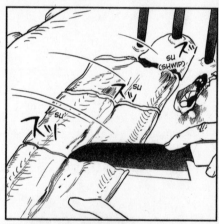

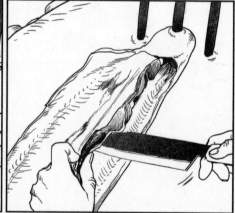

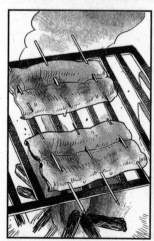

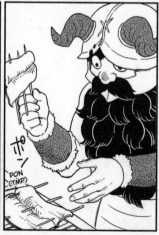

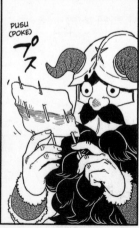

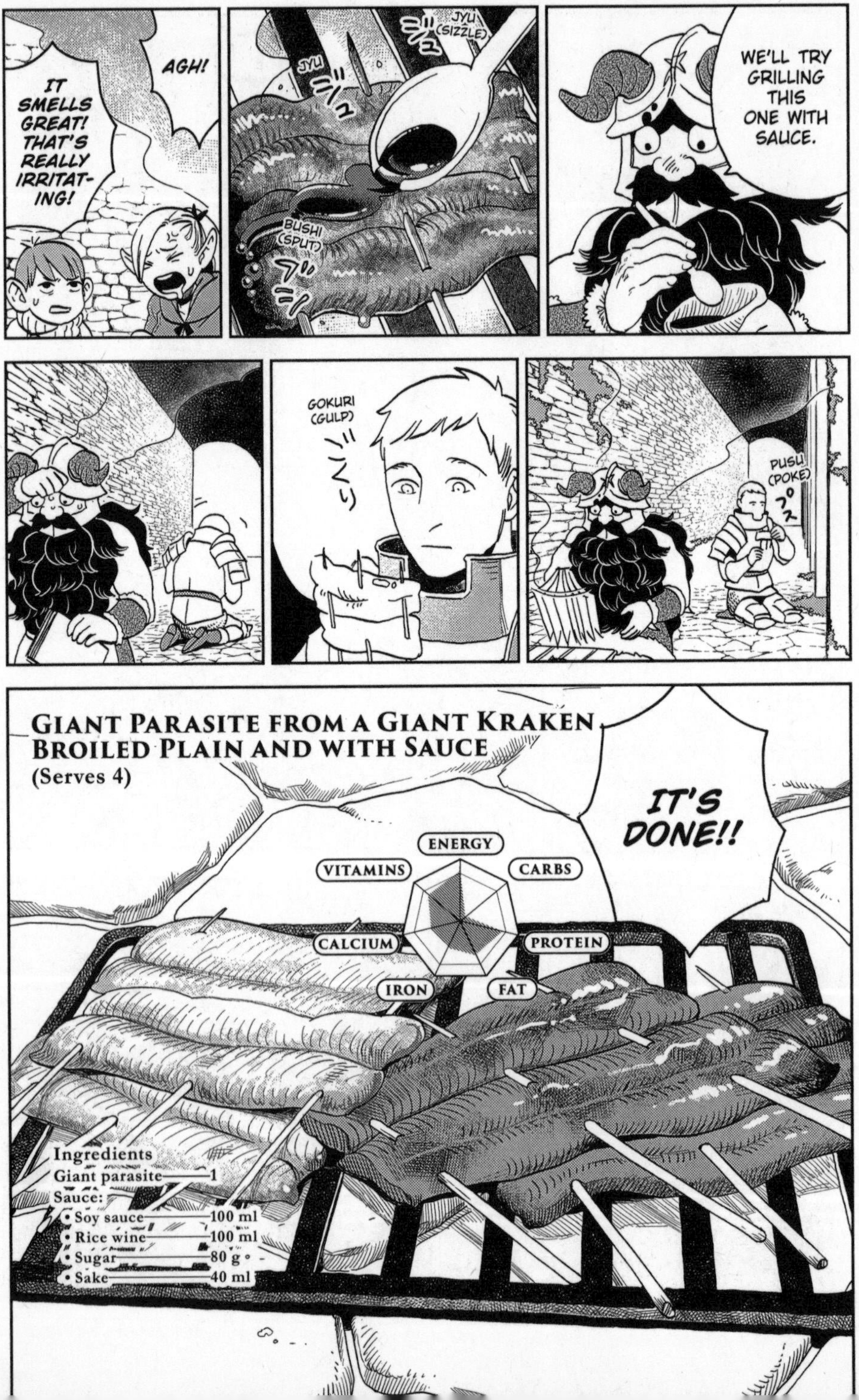
WE'LL TRY GRILLING THIS ONE WITH SAUCE.
JYU (SIZZLE)
ジュ
JYU
ジュ
BUSHI (SPUT)
ブシ
AGH!
IT SMELLS GREAT! THAT'S REALLY IRRITAT-ING!
PUSU (POKE)
プス
GOKURI (GULP)
ゴくり
GIANT PARASITE FROM A GIANT KRAKEN BROILED PLAIN AND WITH SAUCE
(Serves 4)
IT'S DONE!!
ENERGY
CARBS
PROTEIN
FAT
IRON
CALCIUM
VITAMINS
Ingredients
Giant parasite——1
Sauce:
• Soy sauce——100 ml
• Rice wine——100 ml
• Sugar——80 g
• Sake——40 ml

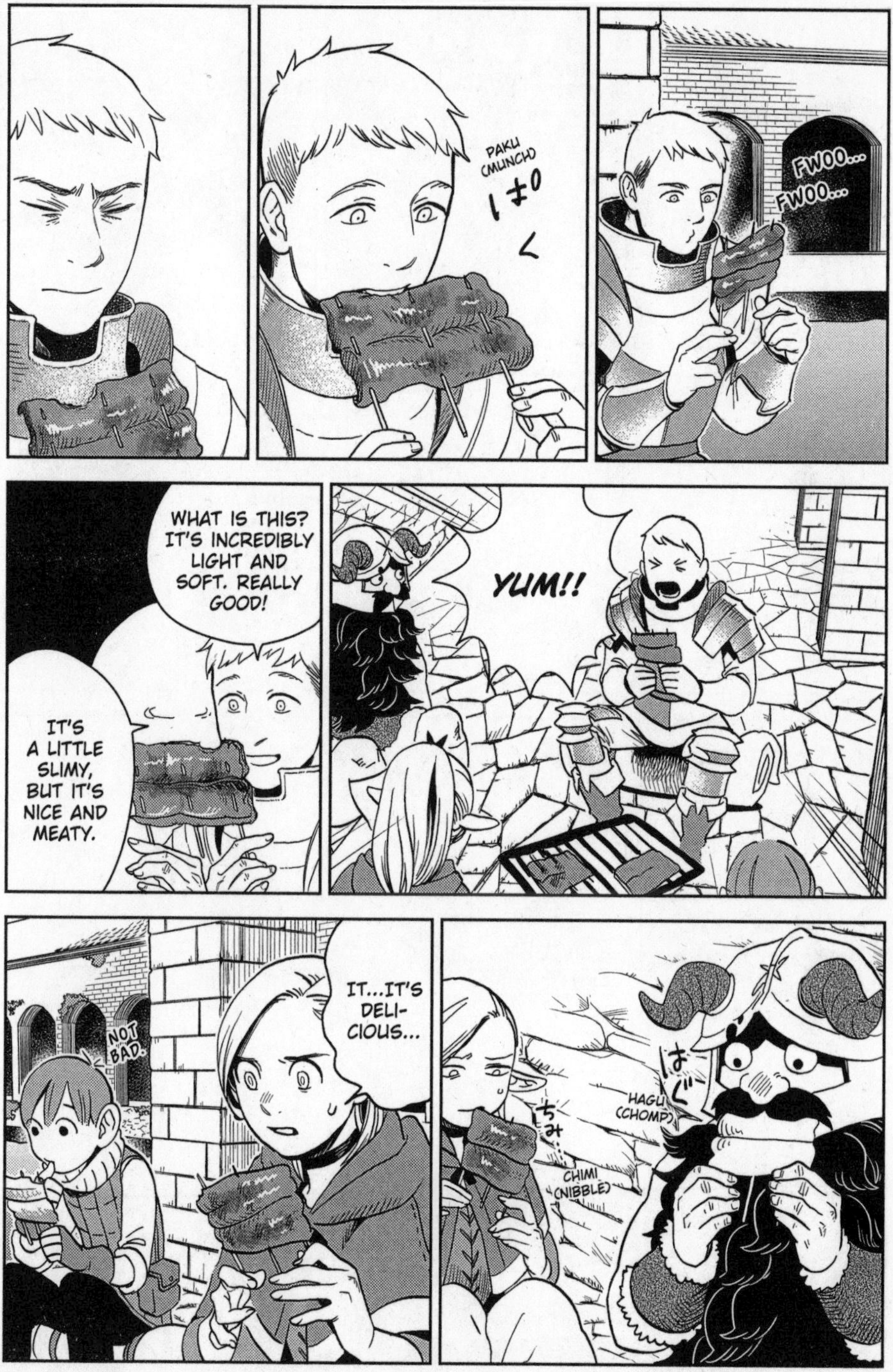
FWOO...
FWOO...
PAKU (MUNCH)
ぱく
YUM!!
WHAT IS THIS? IT'S INCREDIBLY LIGHT AND SOFT. REALLY GOOD!
IT'S A LITTLE SLIMY, BUT IT'S NICE AND MEATY.
はぐ
HAGU (CHOMP)
ちみ…
CHIMI (NIBBLE)
IT...IT'S DELICIOUS...
NOT BAD.

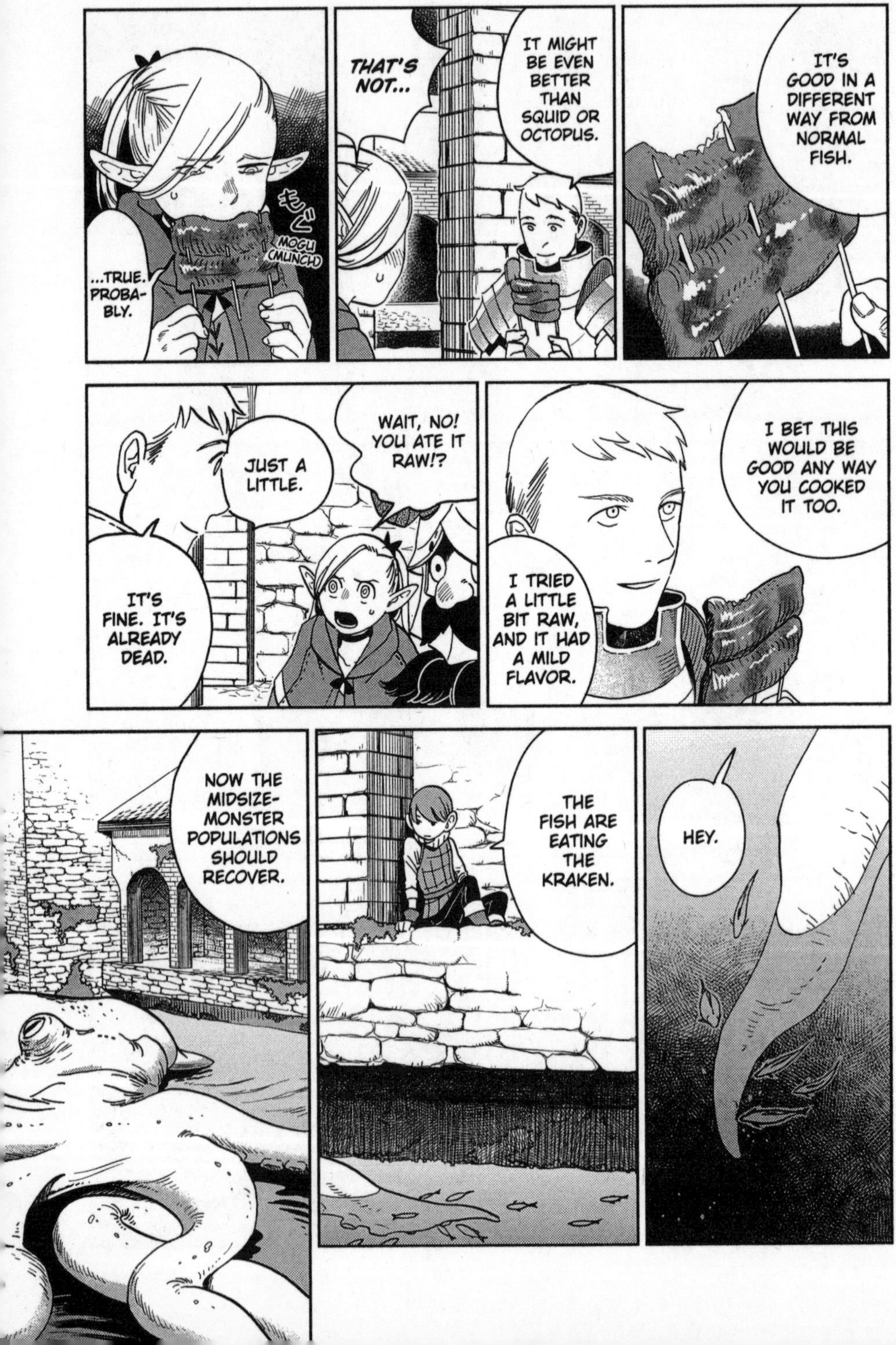
IT'S GOOD IN A DIFFERENT WAY FROM NORMAL FISH.
IT MIGHT BE EVEN BETTER THAN SQUID OR OCTOPUS.
THAT'S NOT...
もぐ
MOGU (MUNCH)
...TRUE. PROBABLY.
I BET THIS WOULD BE GOOD ANY WAY YOU COOKED IT TOO.
I TRIED A LITTLE BIT RAW, AND IT HAD A MILD FLAVOR.
WAIT, NO! YOU ATE IT RAW!?
JUST A LITTLE.
IT'S FINE. IT'S ALREADY DEAD.
HEY.
THE FISH ARE EATING THE KRAKEN.
NOW THE MIDSIZE-MONSTER POPULATIONS SHOULD RECOVER.

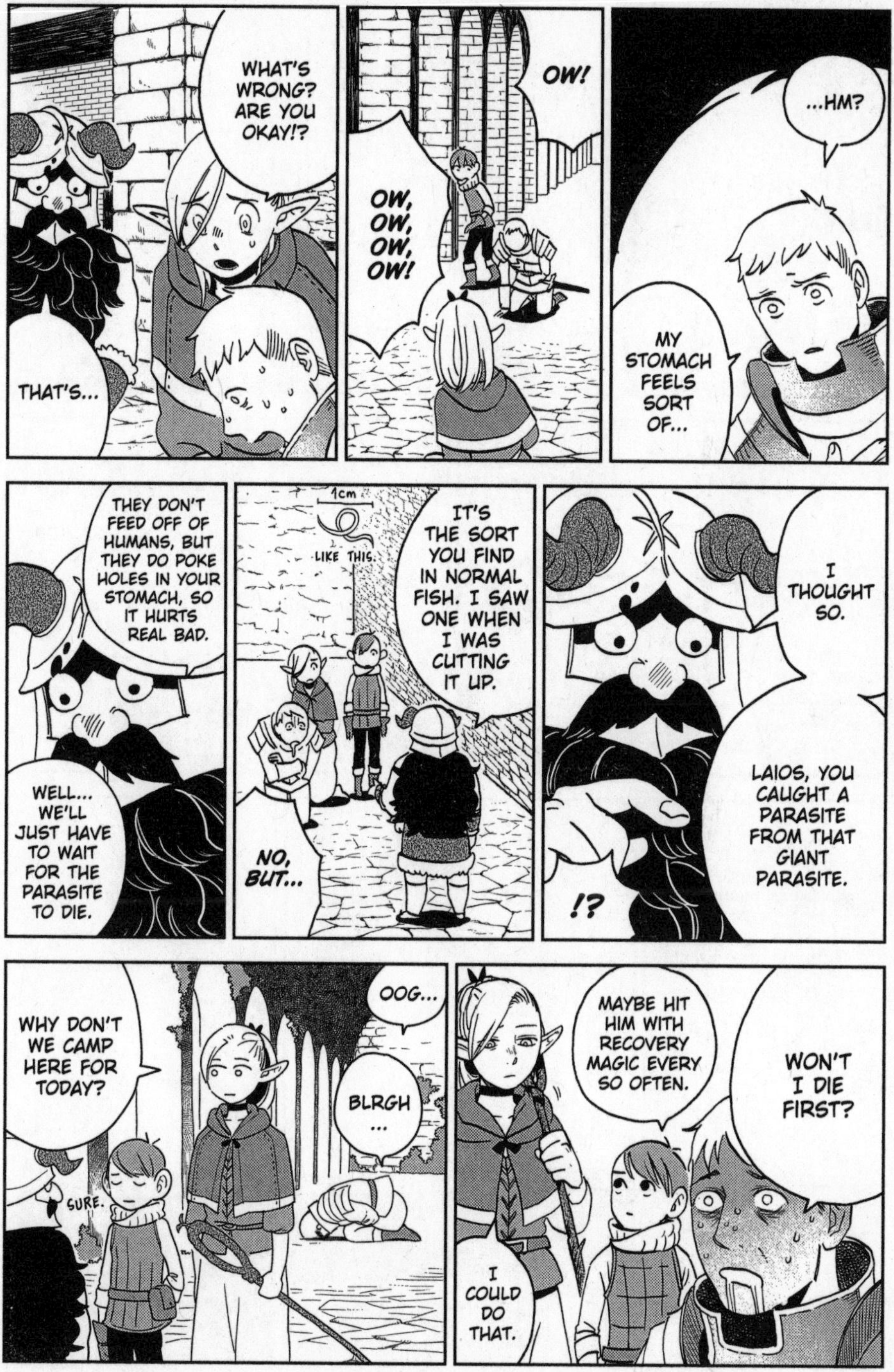
...HM?
MY STOMACH FEELS SORT OF...
OW!
OW, OW, OW, OW!
WHAT'S WRONG? ARE YOU OKAY!?
THAT'S...
I THOUGHT SO.
LAIOS, YOU CAUGHT A PARASITE FROM THAT GIANT PARASITE.
!?
IT'S THE SORT YOU FIND IN NORMAL FISH. I SAW ONE WHEN I WAS CUTTING IT UP.
1cm
LIKE THIS.
NO, BUT...
THEY DON'T FEED OFF OF HUMANS, BUT THEY DO POKE HOLES IN YOUR STOMACH, SO IT HURTS REAL BAD.
WELL... WE'LL JUST HAVE TO WAIT FOR THE PARASITE TO DIE.
WON'T I DIE FIRST?
MAYBE HIT HIM WITH RECOVERY MAGIC EVERY SO OFTEN.
I COULD DO THAT.
OOG...
WHY DON'T WE CAMP HERE FOR TODAY?
BLRGH ...
SURE.

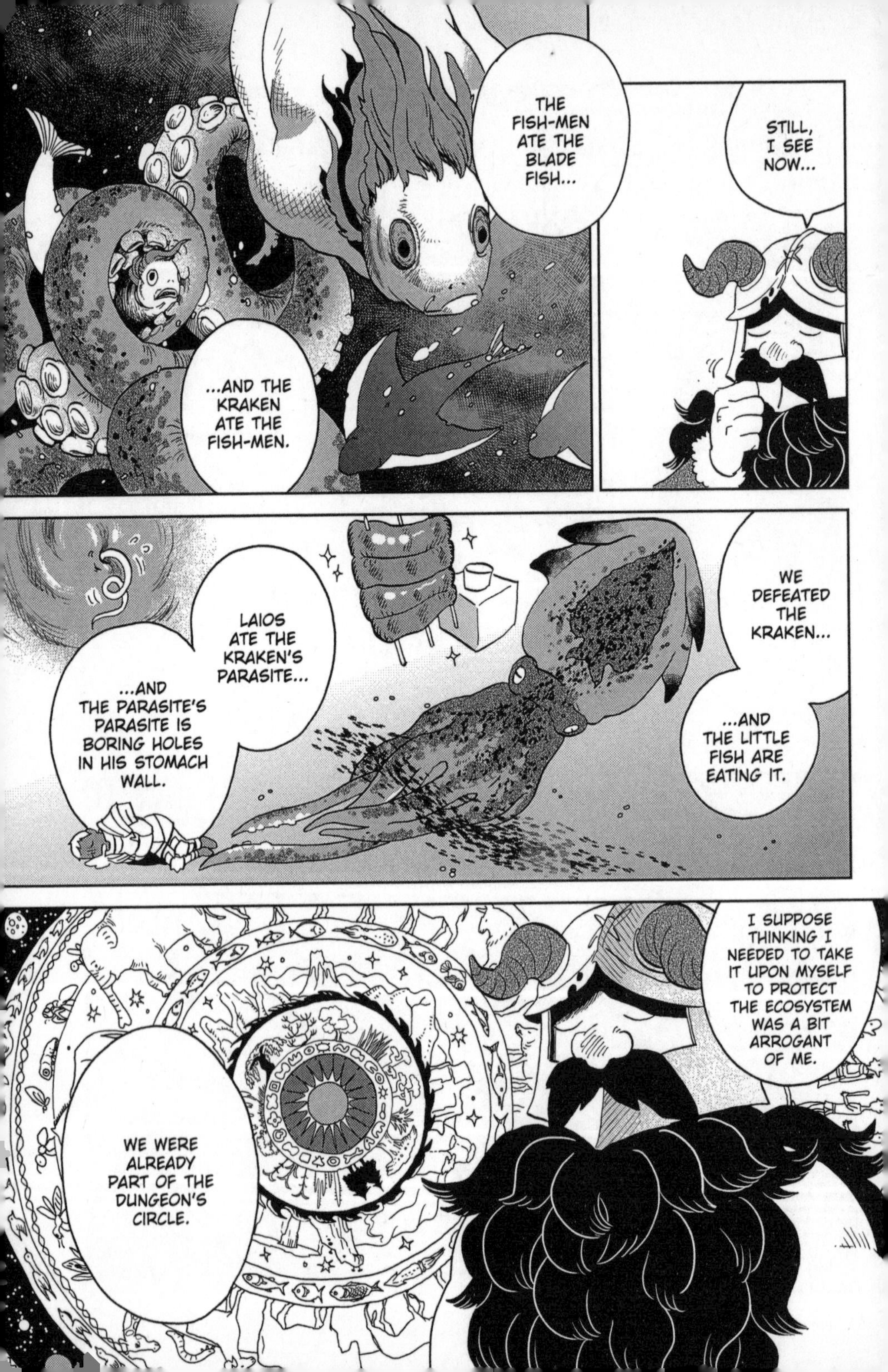
STILL, I SEE NOW...
THE FISH-MEN ATE THE BLADE FISH...
...AND THE KRAKEN ATE THE FISH-MEN.
WE DEFEATED THE KRAKEN...
...AND THE LITTLE FISH ARE EATING IT.
LAIOS ATE THE KRAKEN'S PARASITE...
...AND THE PARASITE'S PARASITE IS BORING HOLES IN HIS STOMACH WALL.
I SUPPOSE THINKING I NEEDED TO TAKE IT UPON MYSELF TO PROTECT THE ECOSYSTEM WAS A BIT ARROGANT OF ME.
WE WERE ALREADY PART OF THE DUNGEON'S CIRCLE.

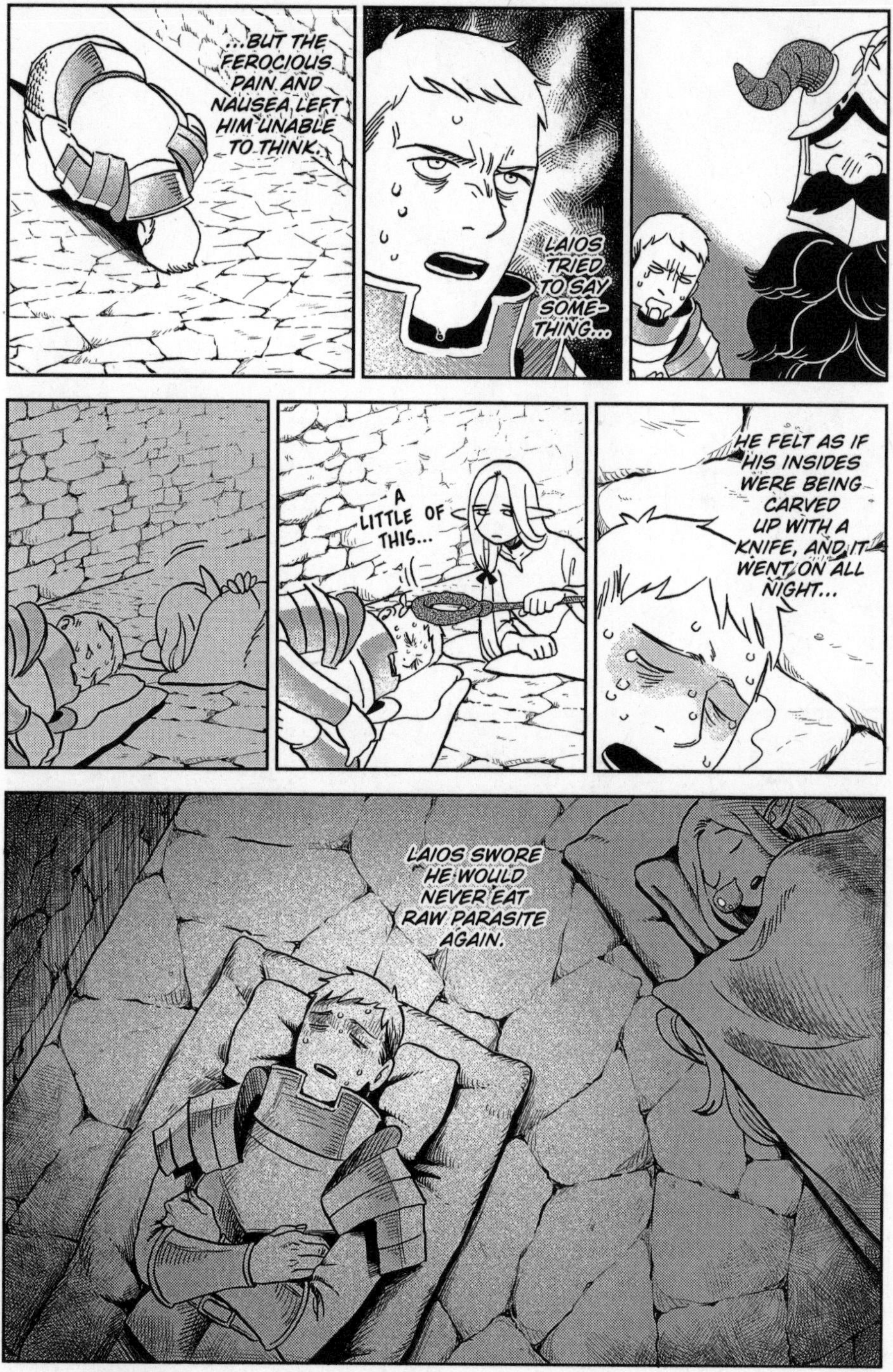
LAIOS TRIED TO SAY SOME-THING...
...BUT THE FEROCIOUS PAIN AND NAUSEA LEFT HIM UNABLE TO THINK.
HE FELT AS IF HIS INSIDES WERE BEING CARVED UP WITH A KNIFE, AND IT WENT ON ALL NIGHT...
A LITTLE OF THIS...
LAIOS SWORE HE WOULD NEVER EAT RAW PARASITE AGAIN.

Chapter 16: The End

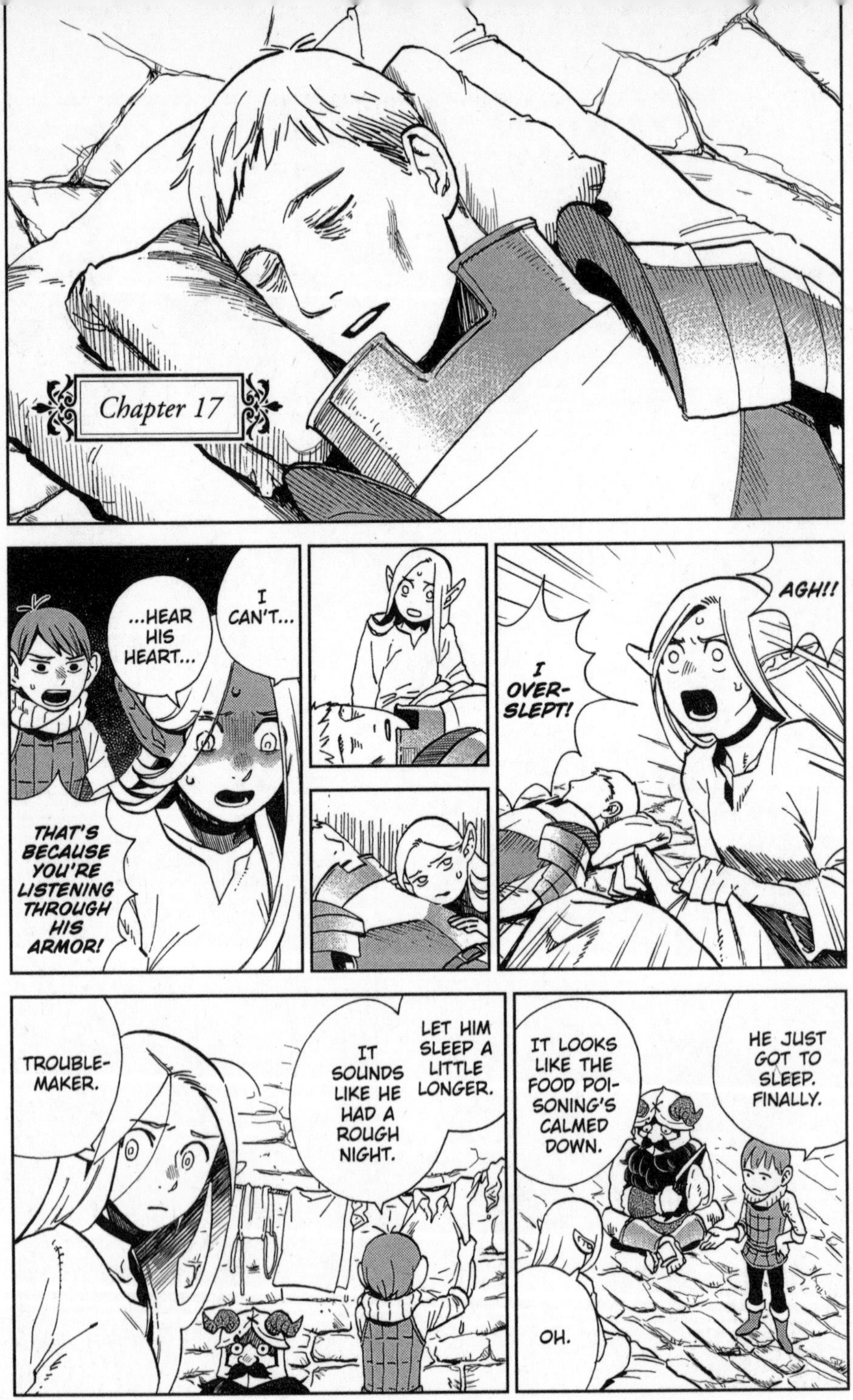
Chapter 17
AGH!!
I OVERSLEPT!
I CAN'T...
...HEAR HIS HEART...
THAT'S BECAUSE YOU'RE LISTENING THROUGH HIS ARMOR!
HE JUST GOT TO SLEEP. FINALLY.
IT LOOKS LIKE THE FOOD POISONING'S CALMED DOWN.
OH.
LET HIM SLEEP A LITTLE LONGER.
IT SOUNDS LIKE HE HAD A ROUGH NIGHT.
TROUBLEMAKER.

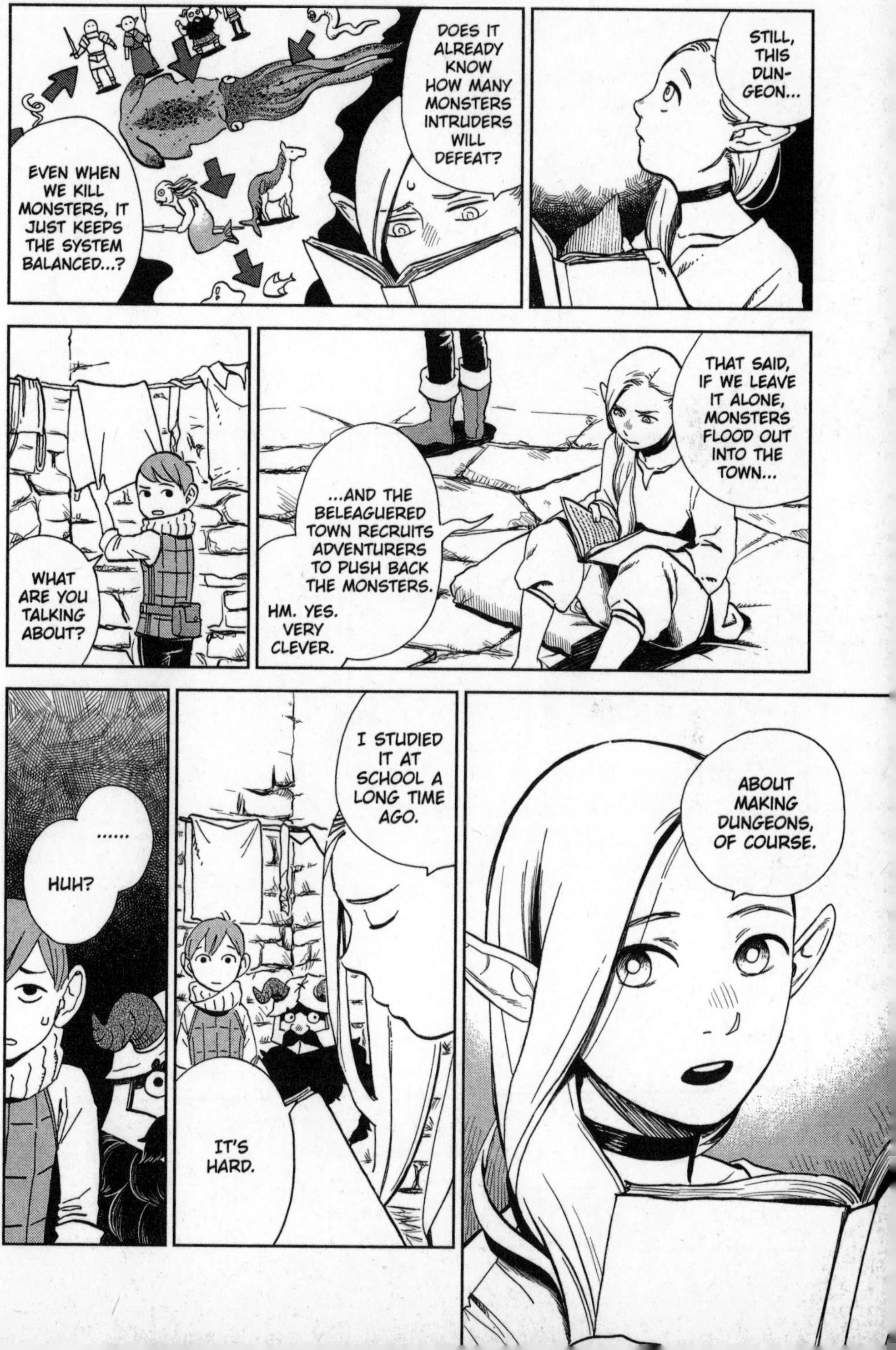
STILL, THIS DUN-GEON...
DOES IT ALREADY KNOW HOW MANY MONSTERS INTRUDERS WILL DEFEAT?
EVEN WHEN WE KILL MONSTERS, IT JUST KEEPS THE SYSTEM BALANCED...?
THAT SAID, IF WE LEAVE IT ALONE, MONSTERS FLOOD OUT INTO THE TOWN...
...AND THE BELEAGUERED TOWN RECRUITS ADVENTURERS TO PUSH BACK THE MONSTERS.
HM. YES. VERY CLEVER.
WHAT ARE YOU TALKING ABOUT?
ABOUT MAKING DUNGEONS, OF COURSE.
I STUDIED IT AT SCHOOL A LONG TIME AGO.
IT'S HARD.
......
HUH?

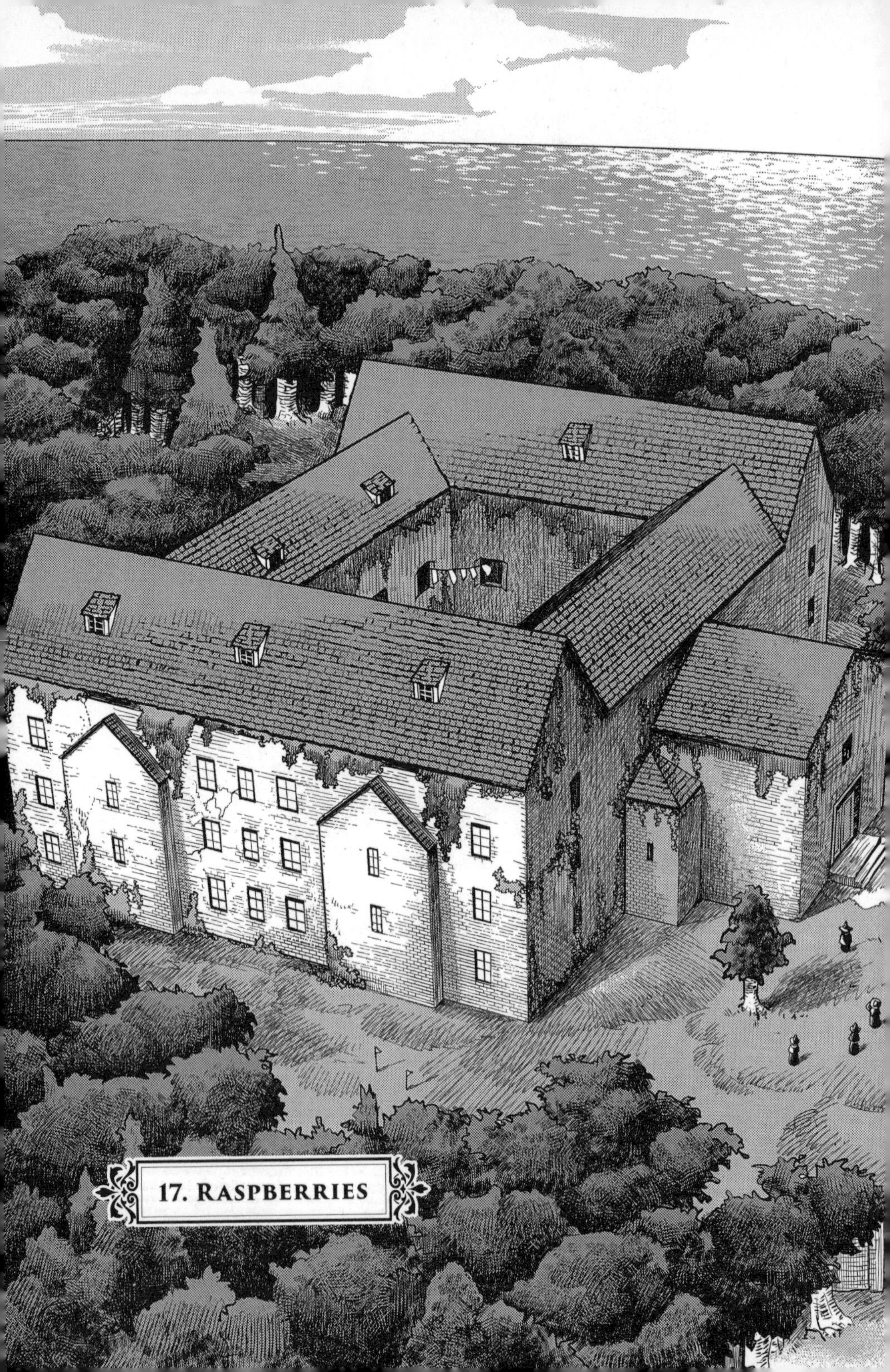

17. Raspberries

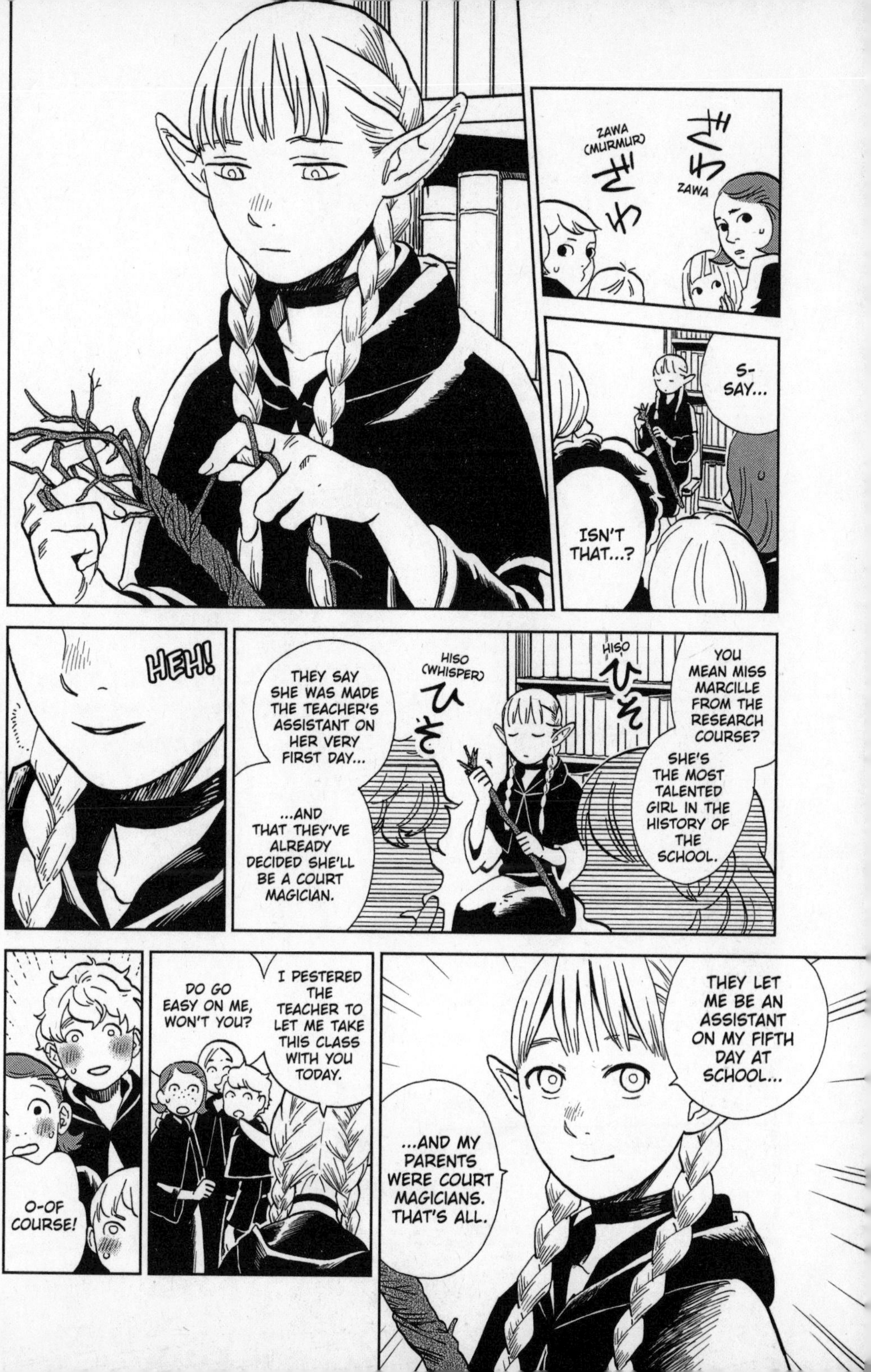

ざわ
ZAWA
ZAWA (MURMUR)
ざわ
S-SAY...
ISN'T THAT...?
ひそ
HISO
YOU MEAN MISS MARCILLE FROM THE RESEARCH COURSE?
SHE'S THE MOST TALENTED GIRL IN THE HISTORY OF THE SCHOOL.
HISO (WHISPER)
ひそ
THEY SAY SHE WAS MADE THE TEACHER'S ASSISTANT ON HER VERY FIRST DAY...
...AND THAT THEY'VE ALREADY DECIDED SHE'LL BE A COURT MAGICIAN.
HEH!
THEY LET ME BE AN ASSISTANT ON MY FIFTH DAY AT SCHOOL...
...AND MY PARENTS WERE COURT MAGICIANS. THAT'S ALL.
I PESTERED THE TEACHER TO LET ME TAKE THIS CLASS WITH YOU TODAY.
DO GO EASY ON ME, WON'T YOU?
O-OF COURSE!

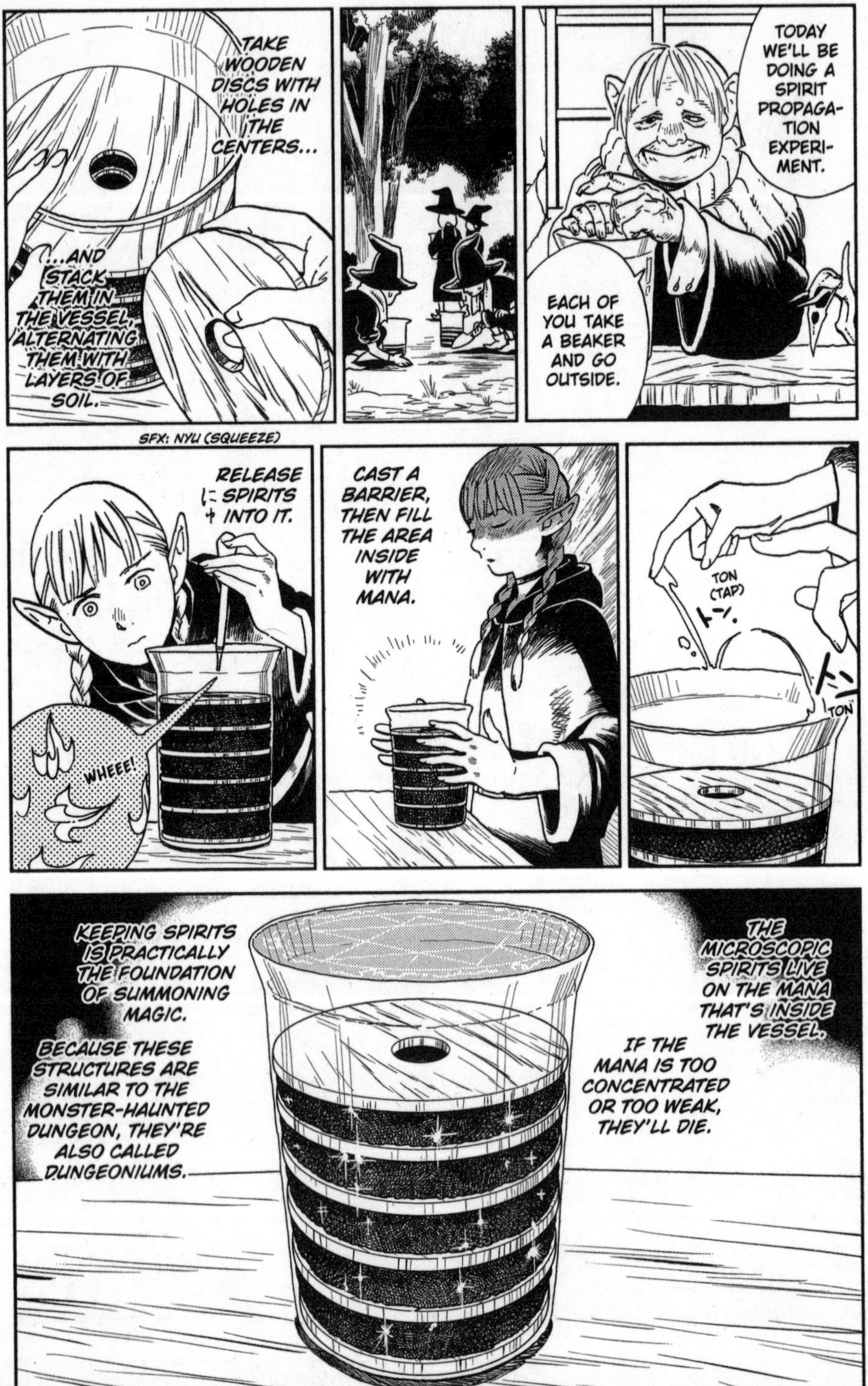
TODAY WE'LL BE DOING A SPIRIT PROPAGATION EXPERIMENT.
EACH OF YOU TAKE A BEAKER AND GO OUTSIDE.
TAKE WOODEN DISCS WITH HOLES IN THE CENTERS...
...AND STACK THEM IN THE VESSEL, ALTERNATING THEM WITH LAYERS OF SOIL.
SFX: NYU (SQUEEZE)
TON (TAP)
TON
CAST A BARRIER, THEN FILL THE AREA INSIDE WITH MANA.
RELEASE SPIRITS INTO IT.
WHEEE!
THE MICROSCOPIC SPIRITS LIVE ON THE MANA THAT'S INSIDE THE VESSEL.
IF THE MANA IS TOO CONCENTRATED OR TOO WEAK, THEY'LL DIE.
KEEPING SPIRITS IS PRACTICALLY THE FOUNDATION OF SUMMONING MAGIC.
BECAUSE THESE STRUCTURES ARE SIMILAR TO THE MONSTER-HAUNTED DUNGEON, THEY'RE ALSO CALLED DUNGEONIUMS.

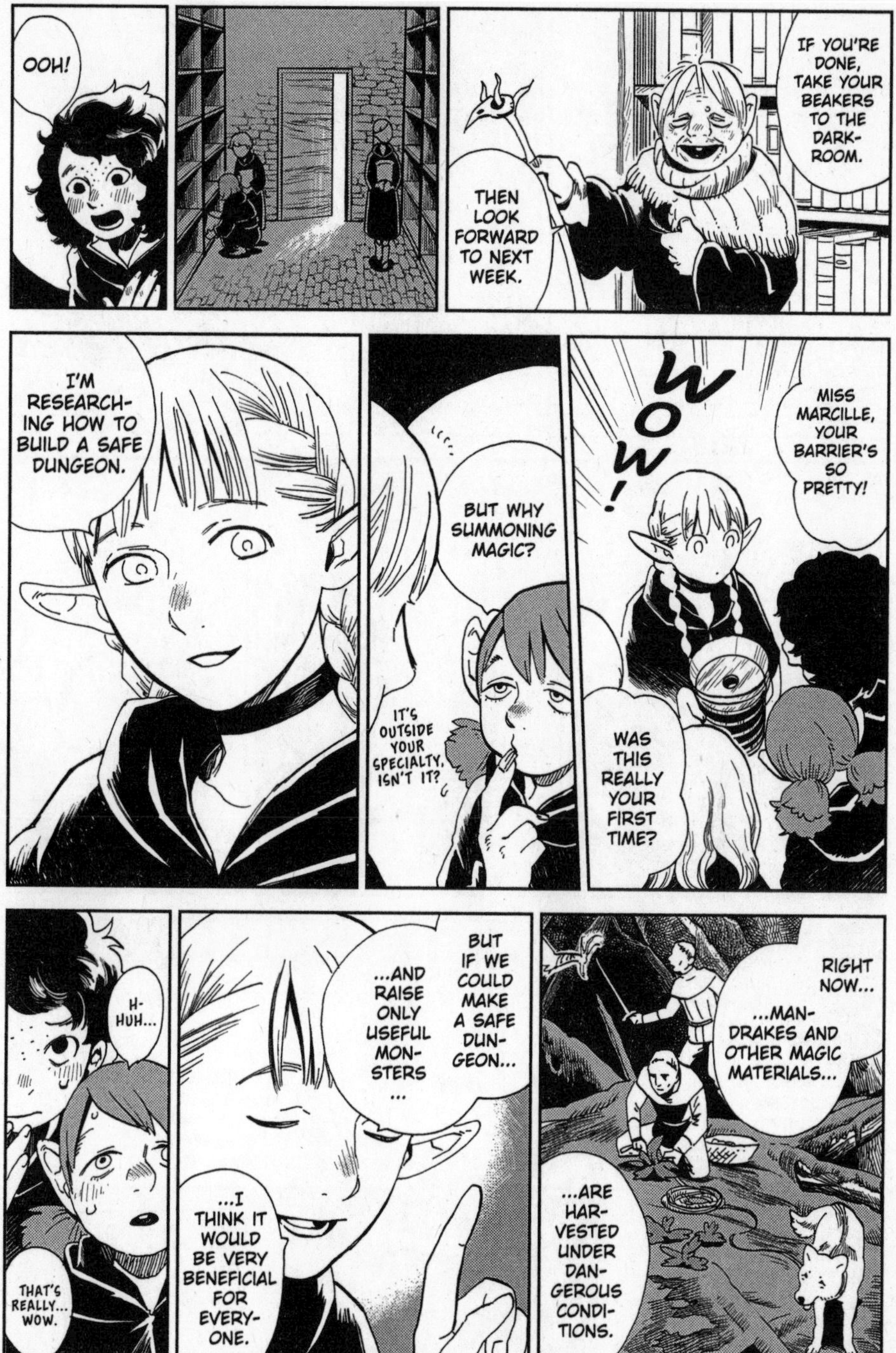
IF YOU'RE DONE, TAKE YOUR BEAKERS TO THE DARKROOM.
THEN LOOK FORWARD TO NEXT WEEK.
OOH!
WOW!
MISS MARCILLE, YOUR BARRIER'S SO PRETTY!
WAS THIS REALLY YOUR FIRST TIME?
BUT WHY SUMMONING MAGIC?
IT'S OUTSIDE YOUR SPECIALTY, ISN'T IT?
I'M RESEARCHING HOW TO BUILD A SAFE DUNGEON.
RIGHT NOW...
...MANDRAKES AND OTHER MAGIC MATERIALS...
...ARE HARVESTED UNDER DANGEROUS CONDITIONS.
BUT IF WE COULD MAKE A SAFE DUNGEON...
...AND RAISE ONLY USEFUL MONSTERS...
...I THINK IT WOULD BE VERY BENEFICIAL FOR EVERYONE.
H-HUH...
THAT'S REALLY... WOW.

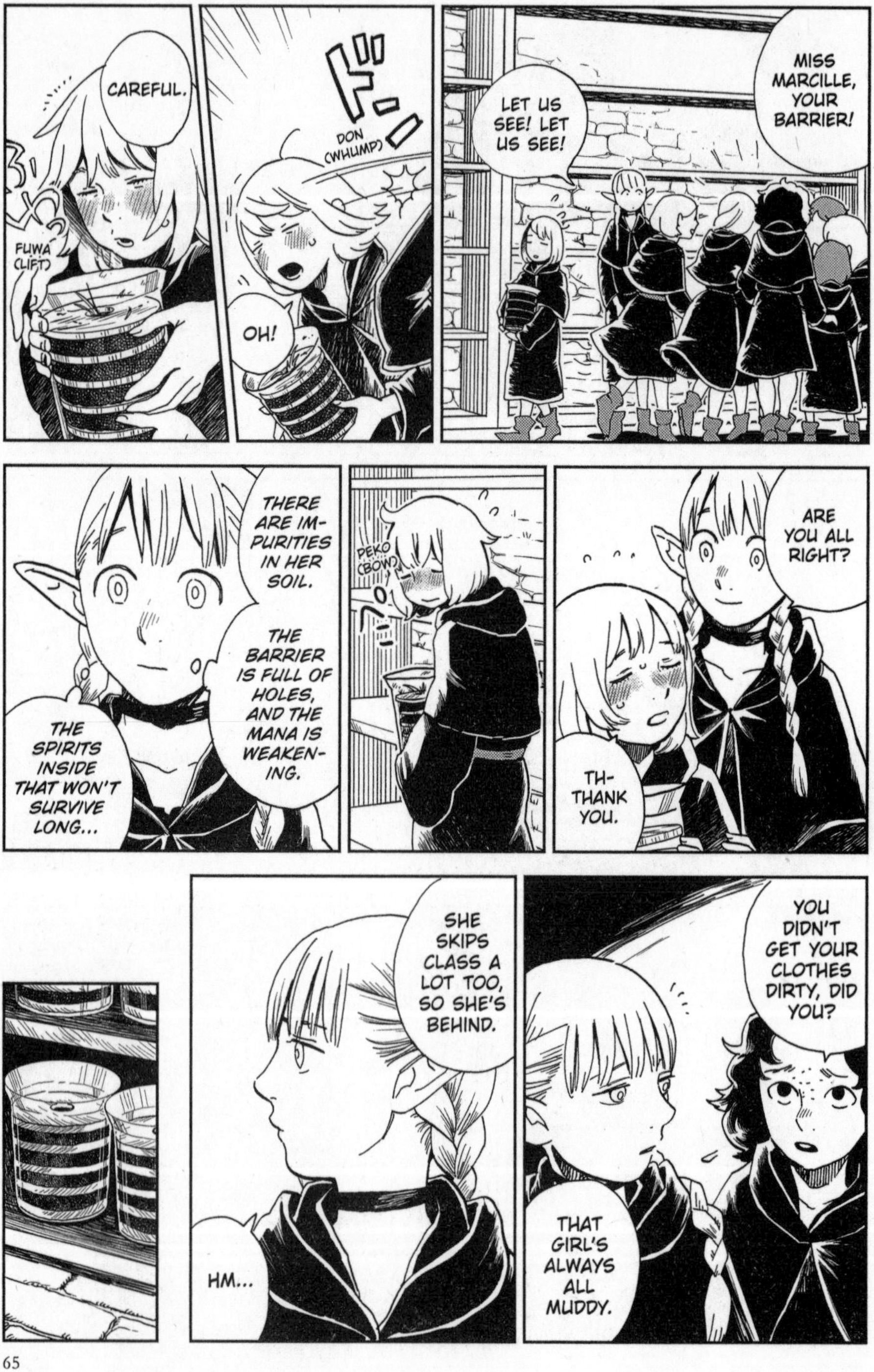
MISS MARCILLE, YOUR BARRIER!
LET US SEE! LET US SEE!
DON (WHUMP)
OH!
CAREFUL.
FUWA (LIFT)
ARE YOU ALL RIGHT?
TH-THANK YOU.
PEKO (BOW)
THERE ARE IM-PURITIES IN HER SOIL.
THE BARRIER IS FULL OF HOLES, AND THE MANA IS WEAKEN-ING.
THE SPIRITS INSIDE THAT WON'T SURVIVE LONG...
YOU DIDN'T GET YOUR CLOTHES DIRTY, DID YOU?
THAT GIRL'S ALWAYS ALL MUDDY.
SHE SKIPS CLASS A LOT TOO, SO SHE'S BEHIND.
HM...

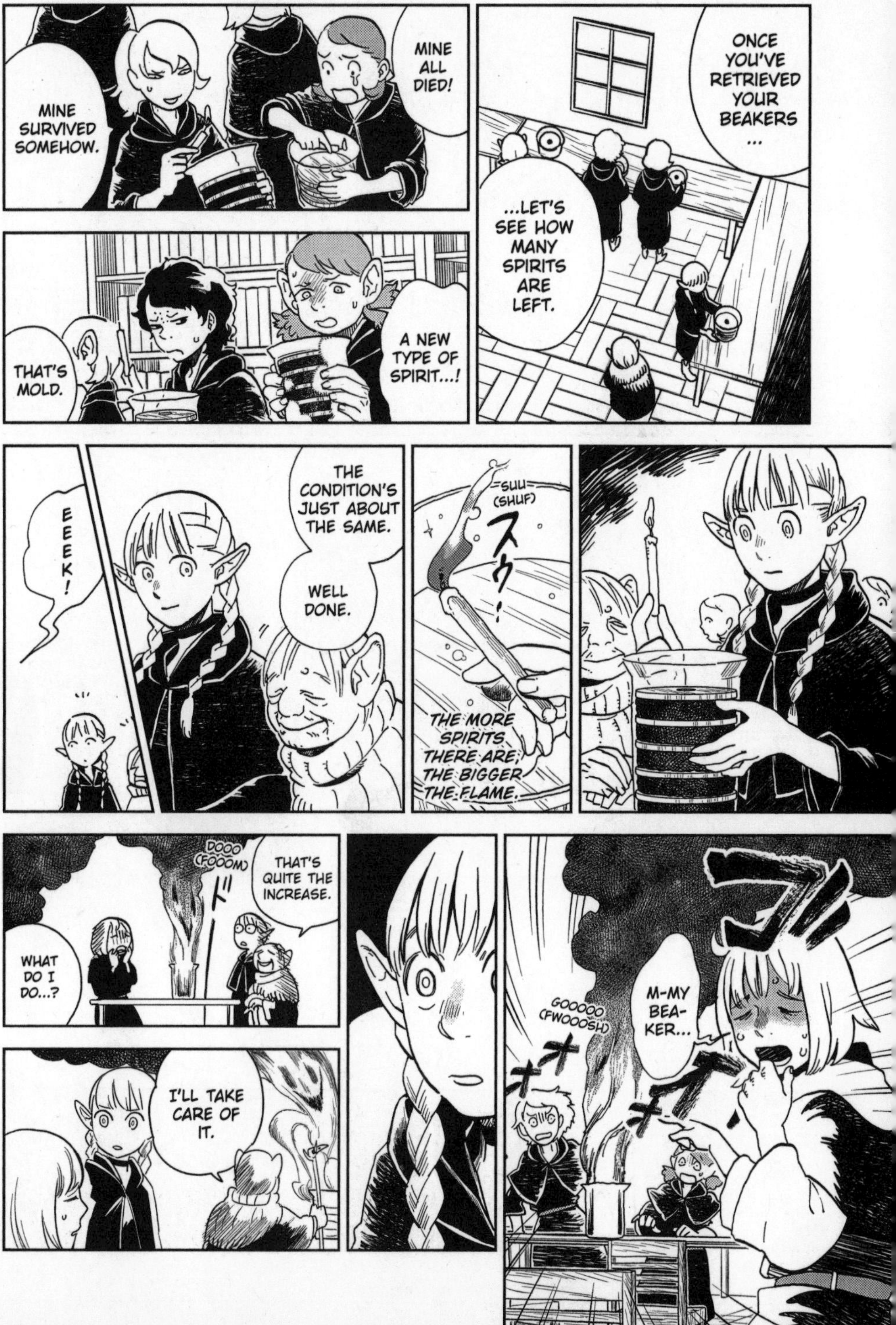
ONCE YOU'VE RETRIEVED YOUR BEAKERS ...
...LET'S SEE HOW MANY SPIRITS ARE LEFT.
MINE ALL DIED!
MINE SURVIVED SOMEHOW.
A NEW TYPE OF SPIRIT...!
THAT'S MOLD.
SUU (SHUF)
スゥ
THE MORE SPIRITS THERE ARE, THE BIGGER THE FLAME.
THE CONDITION'S JUST ABOUT THE SAME.
WELL DONE.
EEEK!
ゴオ
GOOOOO (FWOOOSH)
M-MY BEA-KER...
DOOO (FOOOM)
ド
THAT'S QUITE THE INCREASE.
WHAT DO I DO...?
I'LL TAKE CARE OF IT.

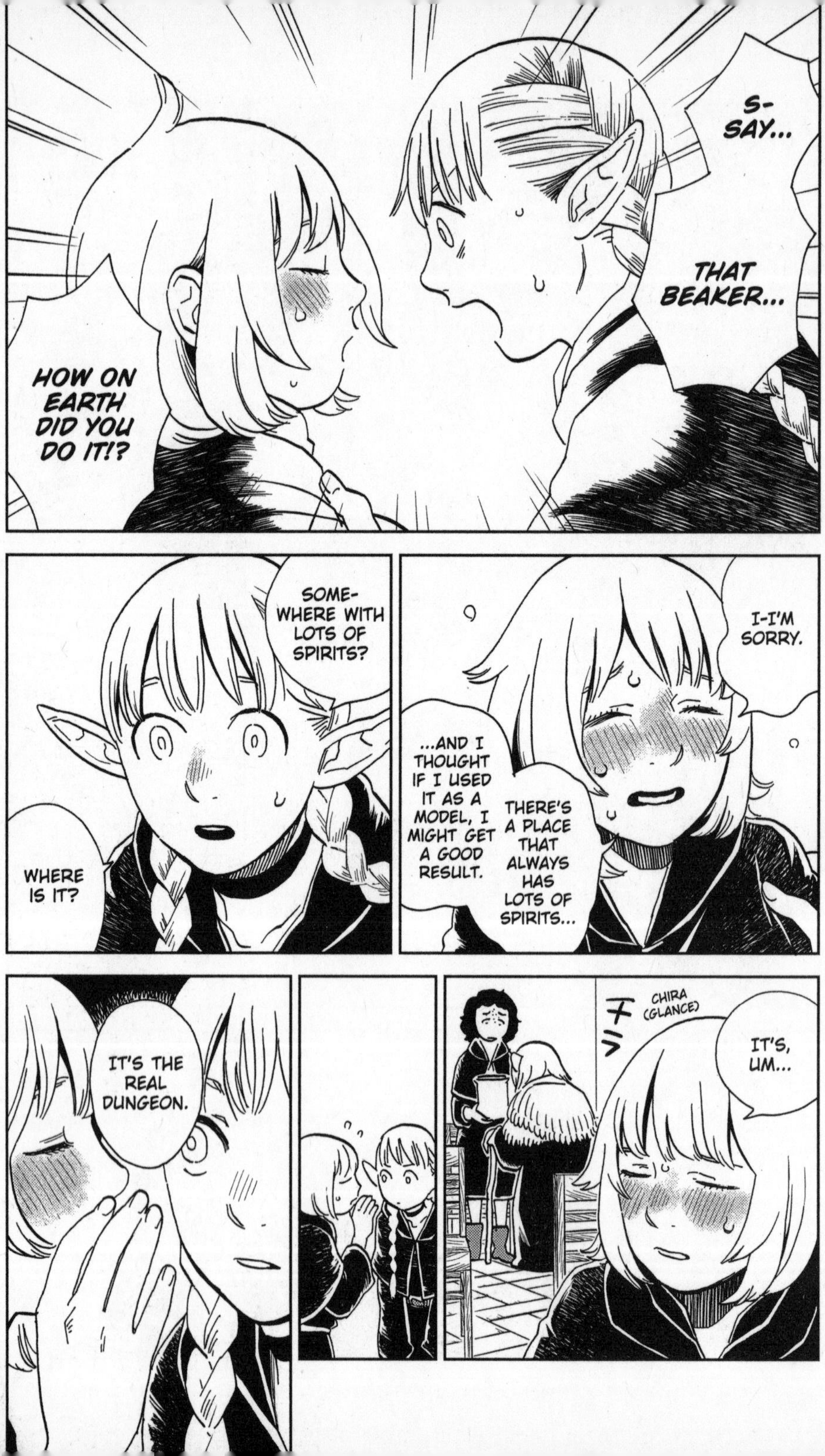
S-SAY...
THAT BEAKER...
HOW ON EARTH DID YOU DO IT!?
I-I'M SORRY.
THERE'S A PLACE THAT ALWAYS HAS LOTS OF SPIRITS...
...AND I THOUGHT IF I USED IT AS A MODEL, I MIGHT GET A GOOD RESULT.
SOME-WHERE WITH LOTS OF SPIRITS?
WHERE IS IT?
チラ
CHIRA (GLANCE)
IT'S, UM...
IT'S THE REAL DUNGEON.

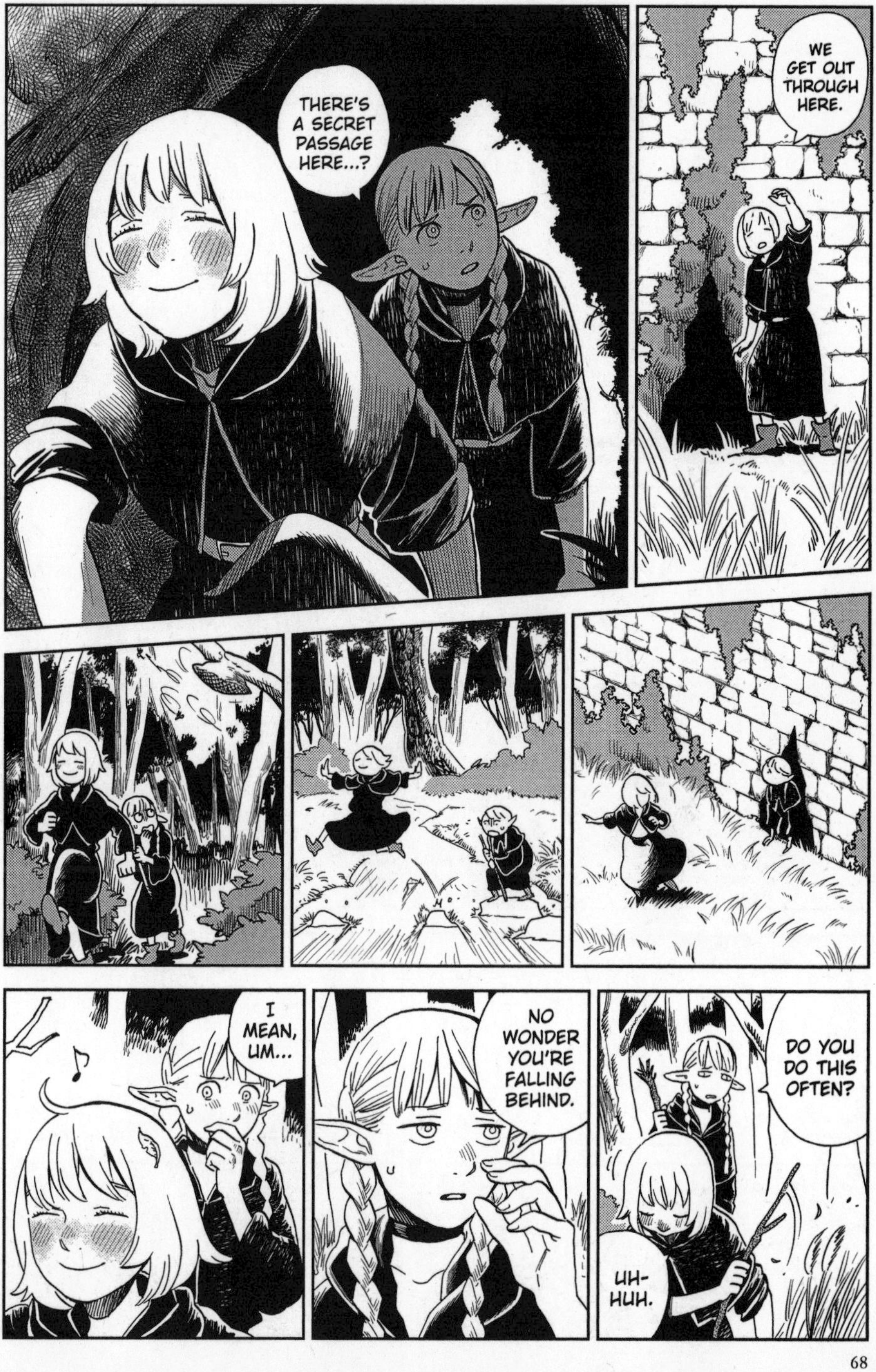
WE GET OUT THROUGH HERE.
THERE'S A SECRET PASSAGE HERE...?
DO YOU DO THIS OFTEN?
UH-HUH.
NO WONDER YOU'RE FALLING BEHIND.
I MEAN, UM...

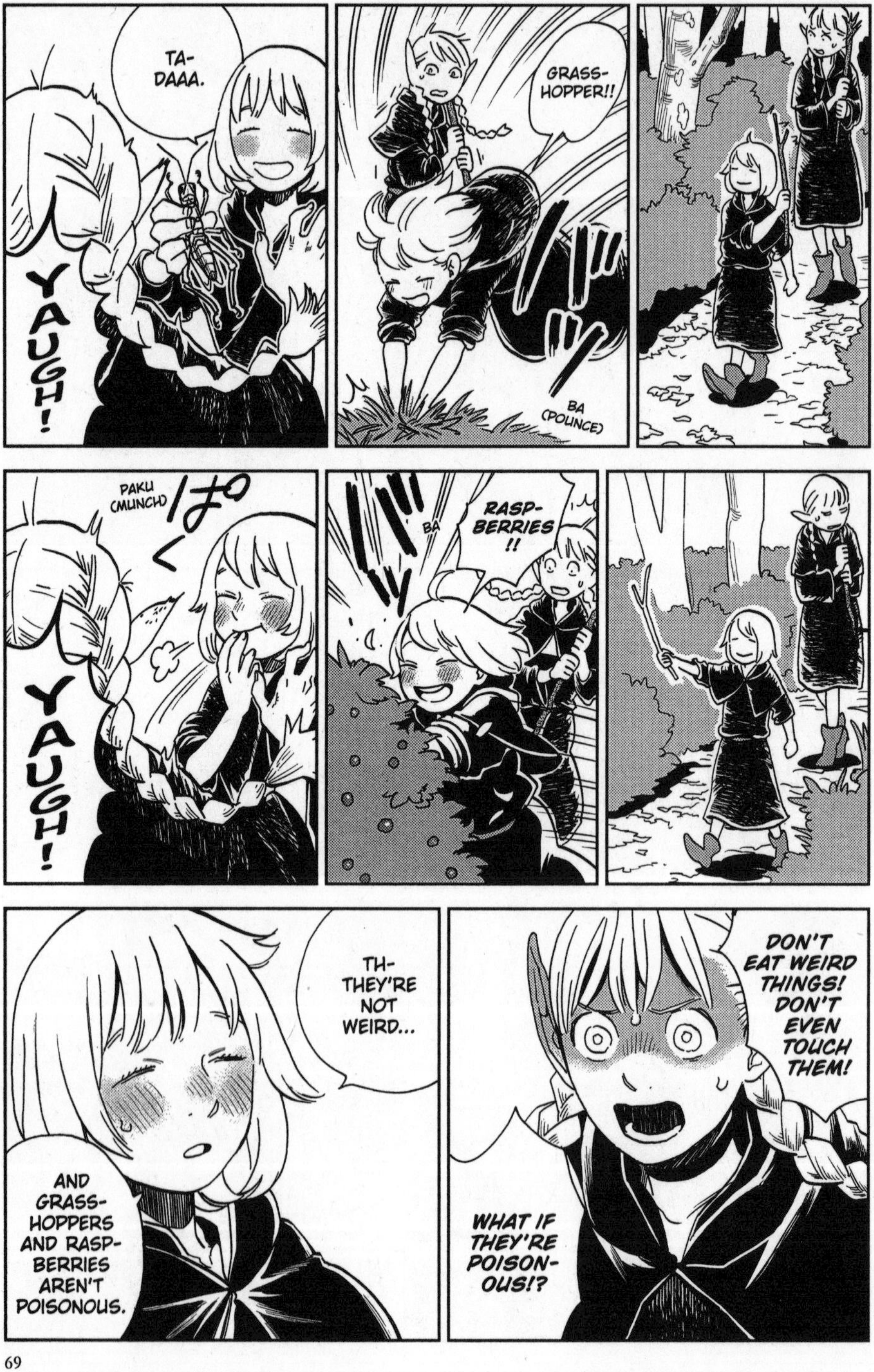
GRASS-HOPPER!!
BA (POUNCE)
TA-DAAA.
YAUGH!
RASP-BERRIES!!
BA
PAKU (MUNCH)
ぱく
YAUGH!
DON'T EAT WEIRD THINGS! DON'T EVEN TOUCH THEM!
WHAT IF THEY'RE POISON-OUS!?
TH-THEY'RE NOT WEIRD...
AND GRASS-HOPPERS AND RASP-BERRIES AREN'T POISONOUS.

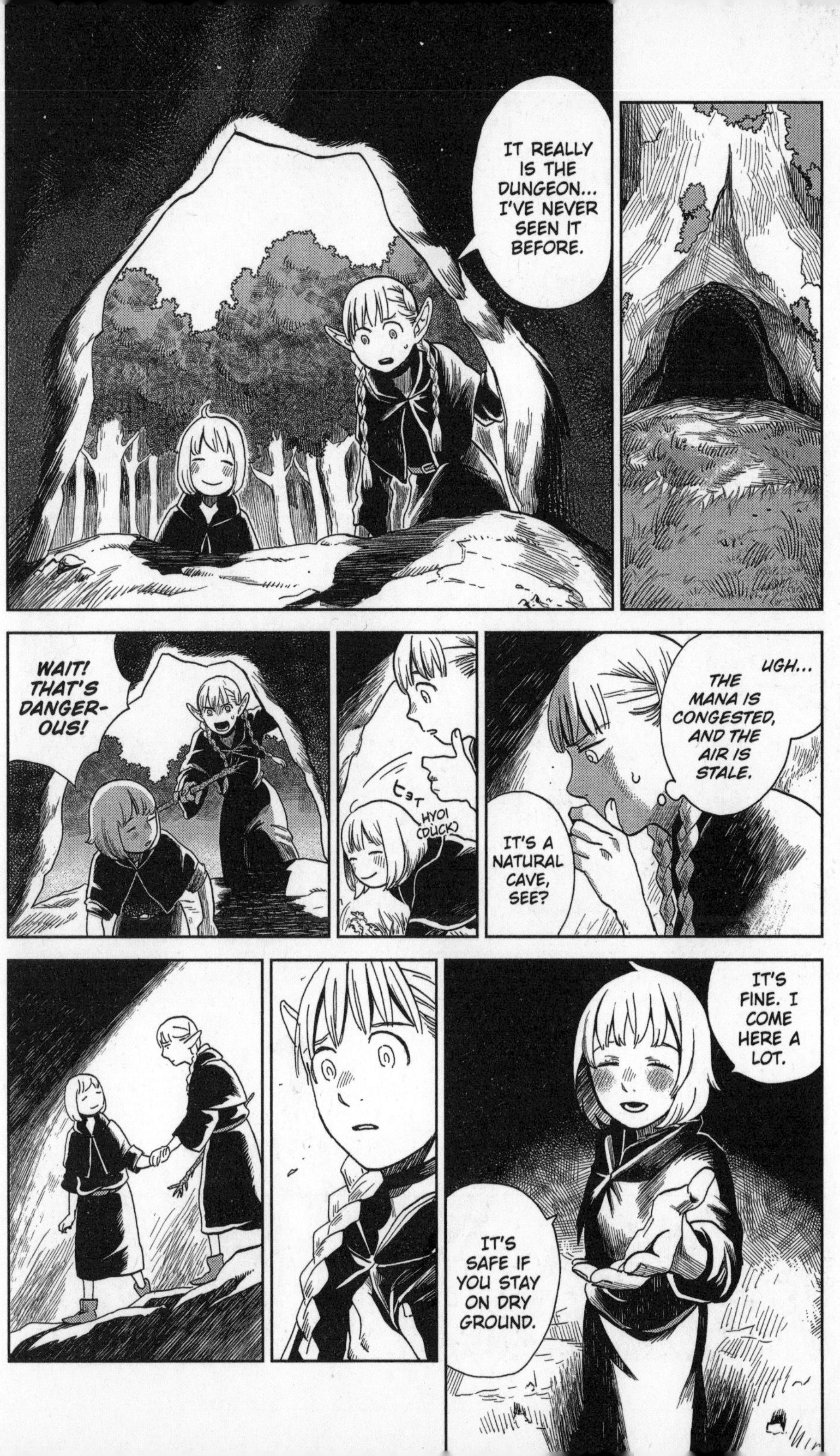
IT REALLY IS THE DUNGEON... I'VE NEVER SEEN IT BEFORE.
UGH...
THE MANA IS CONGESTED, AND THE AIR IS STALE.
IT'S A NATURAL CAVE, SEE?
ヒョイ
HYOI (DUCK)
WAIT! THAT'S DANGER-OUS!
IT'S FINE. I COME HERE A LOT.
IT'S SAFE IF YOU STAY ON DRY GROUND.

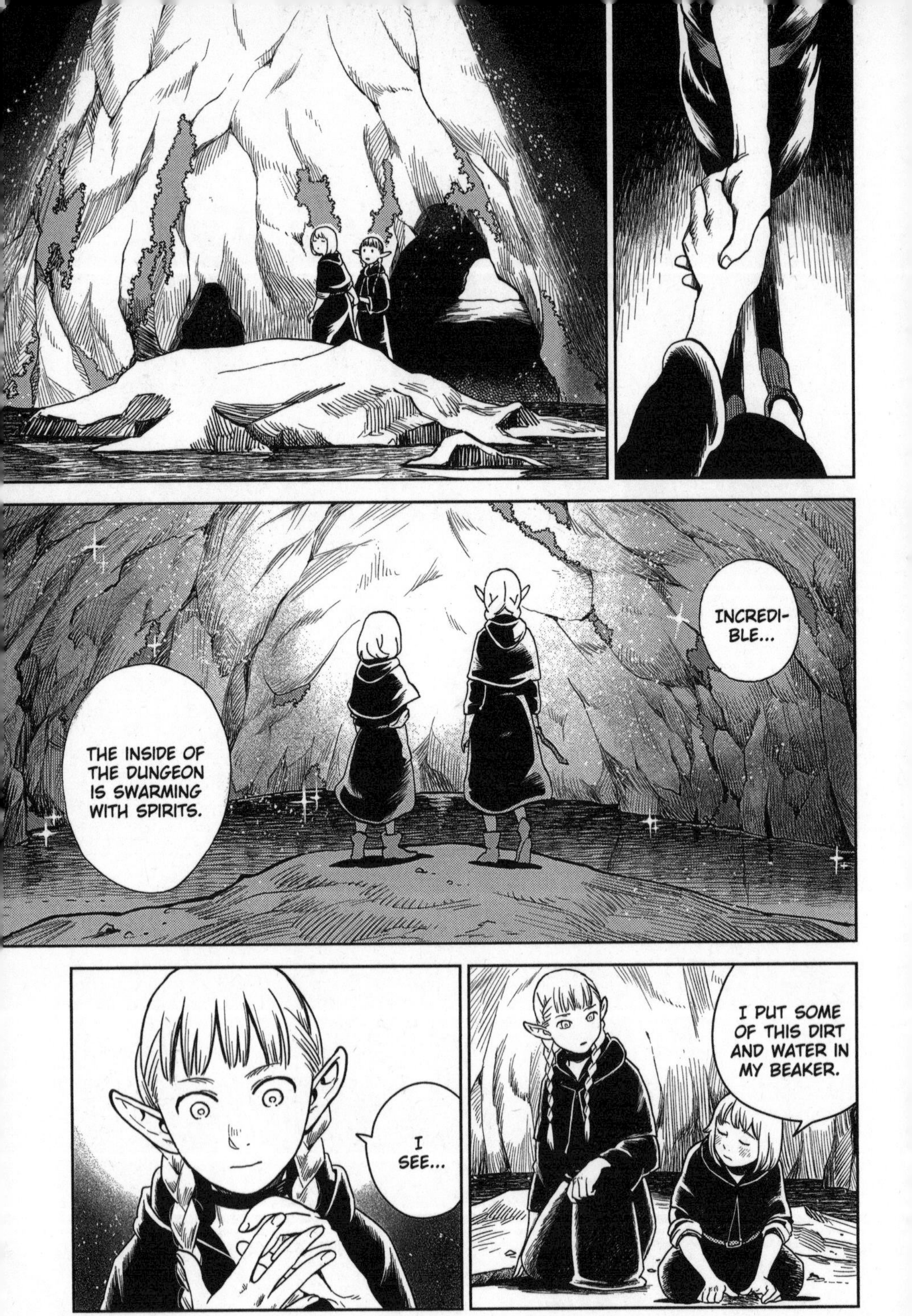
INCREDI-BLE...
THE INSIDE OF THE DUNGEON IS SWARMING WITH SPIRITS.
I PUT SOME OF THIS DIRT AND WATER IN MY BEAKER.
I SEE...

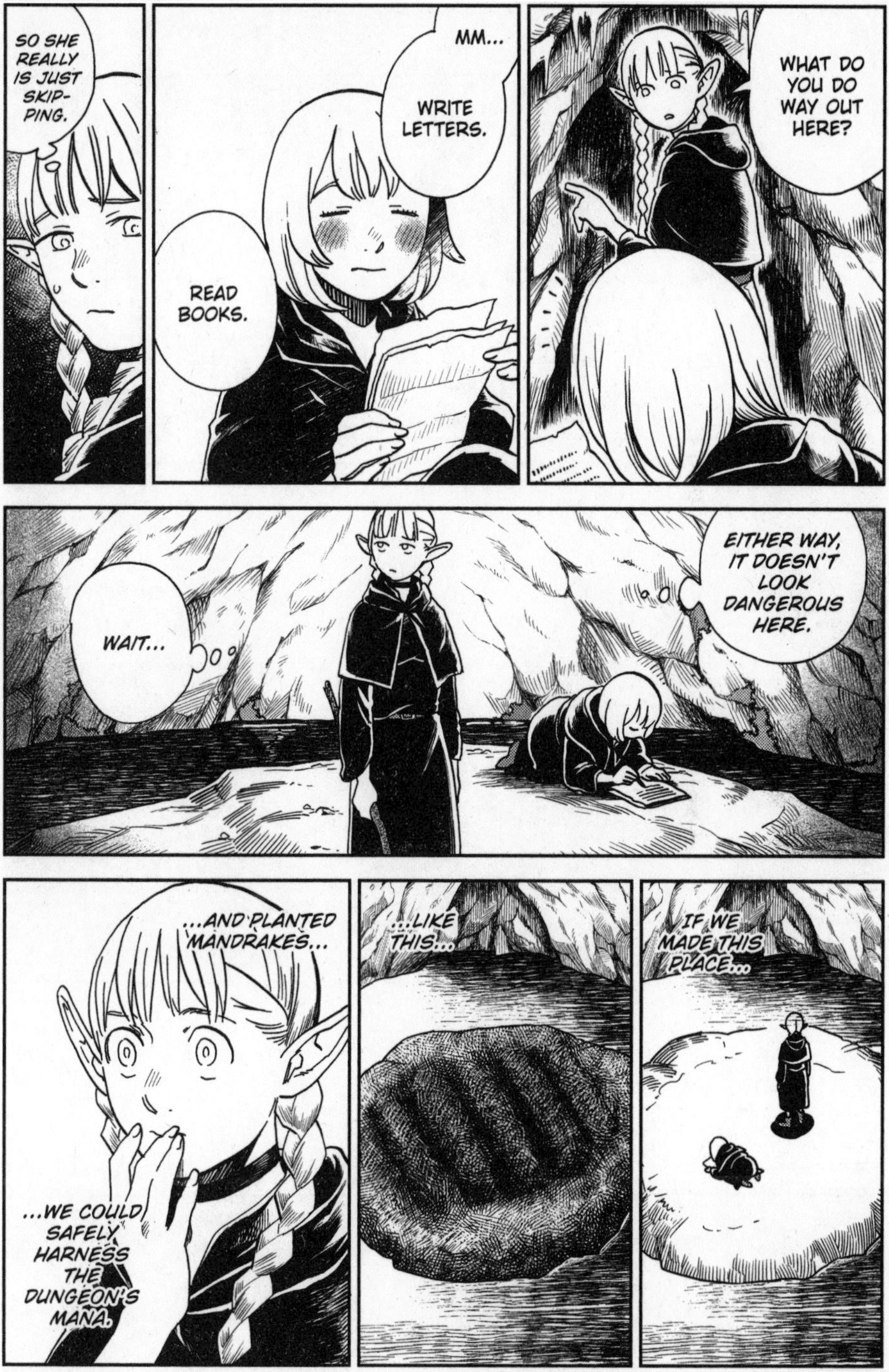
WHAT DO YOU DO WAY OUT HERE?
MM...
WRITE LETTERS.
READ BOOKS.
SO SHE REALLY IS JUST SKIP-PING.
EITHER WAY, IT DOESN'T LOOK DANGEROUS HERE.
WAIT...
IF WE MADE THIS PLACE...
...LIKE THIS...
...AND PLANTED MANDRAKES...
...WE COULD SAFELY HARNESS THE DUNGEON'S MANA.

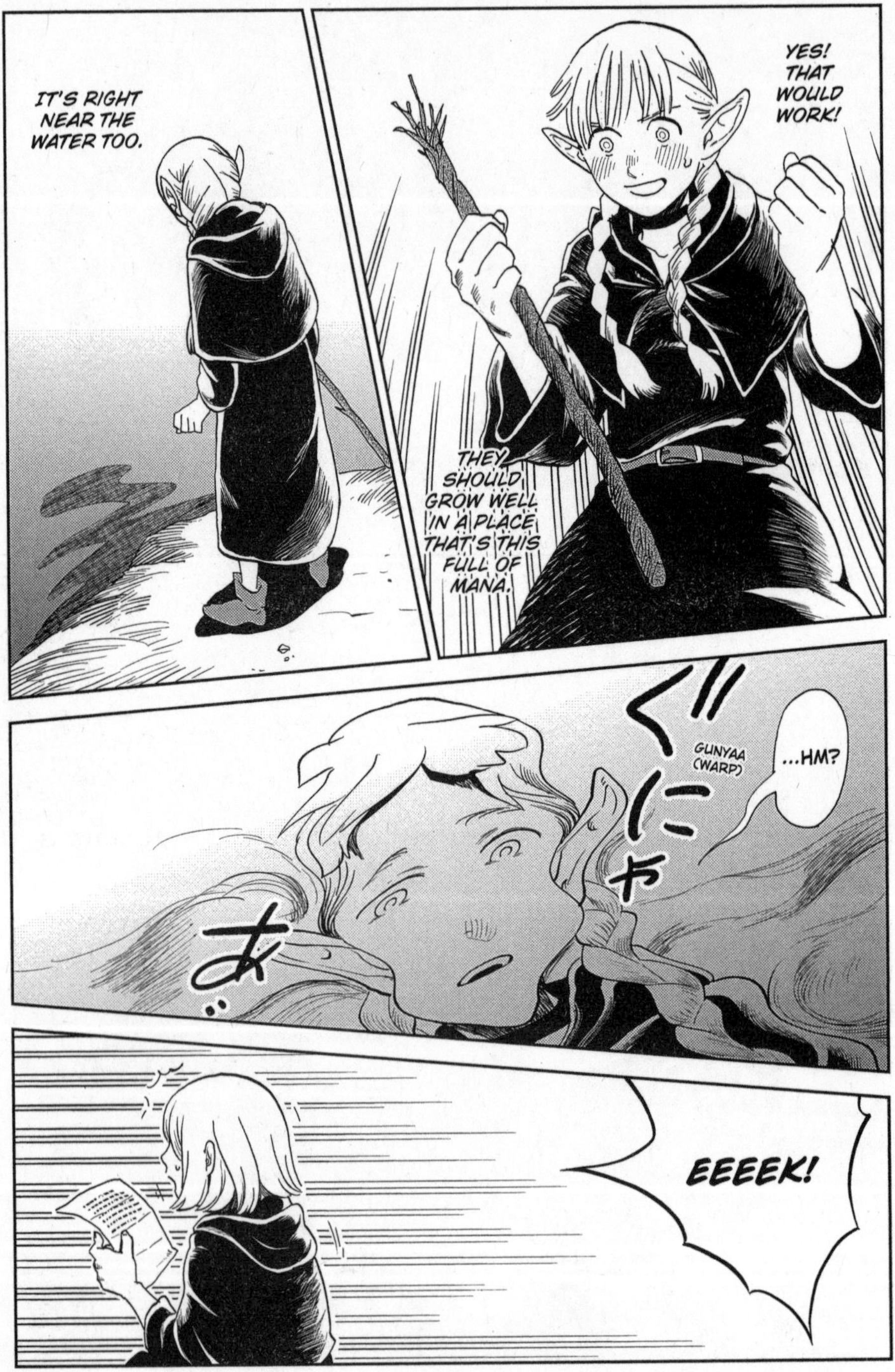
YES! THAT WOULD WORK!
THEY SHOULD GROW WELL IN A PLACE THAT'S THIS FULL OF MANA.
IT'S RIGHT NEAR THE WATER TOO.
...HM?
ぐにゃ
GUNYAA (WARP)
あ
EEEEK!

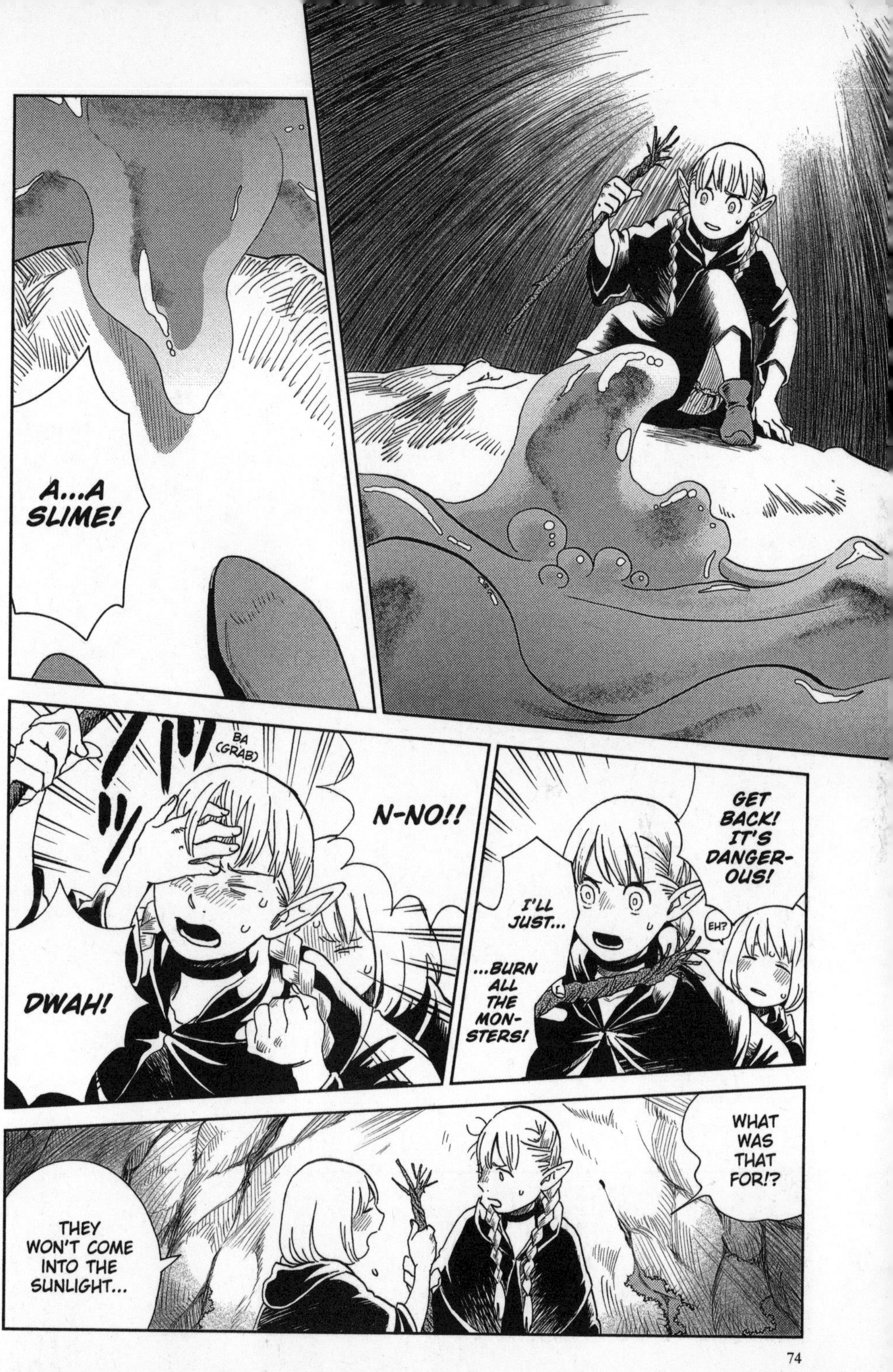
A...A SLIME!
GET BACK! IT'S DANGER-OUS!
I'LL JUST...
...BURN ALL THE MON-STERS!
EH?
BA (GRAB)
N-NO!!
DWAH!
WHAT WAS THAT FOR!?
THEY WON'T COME INTO THE SUNLIGHT...

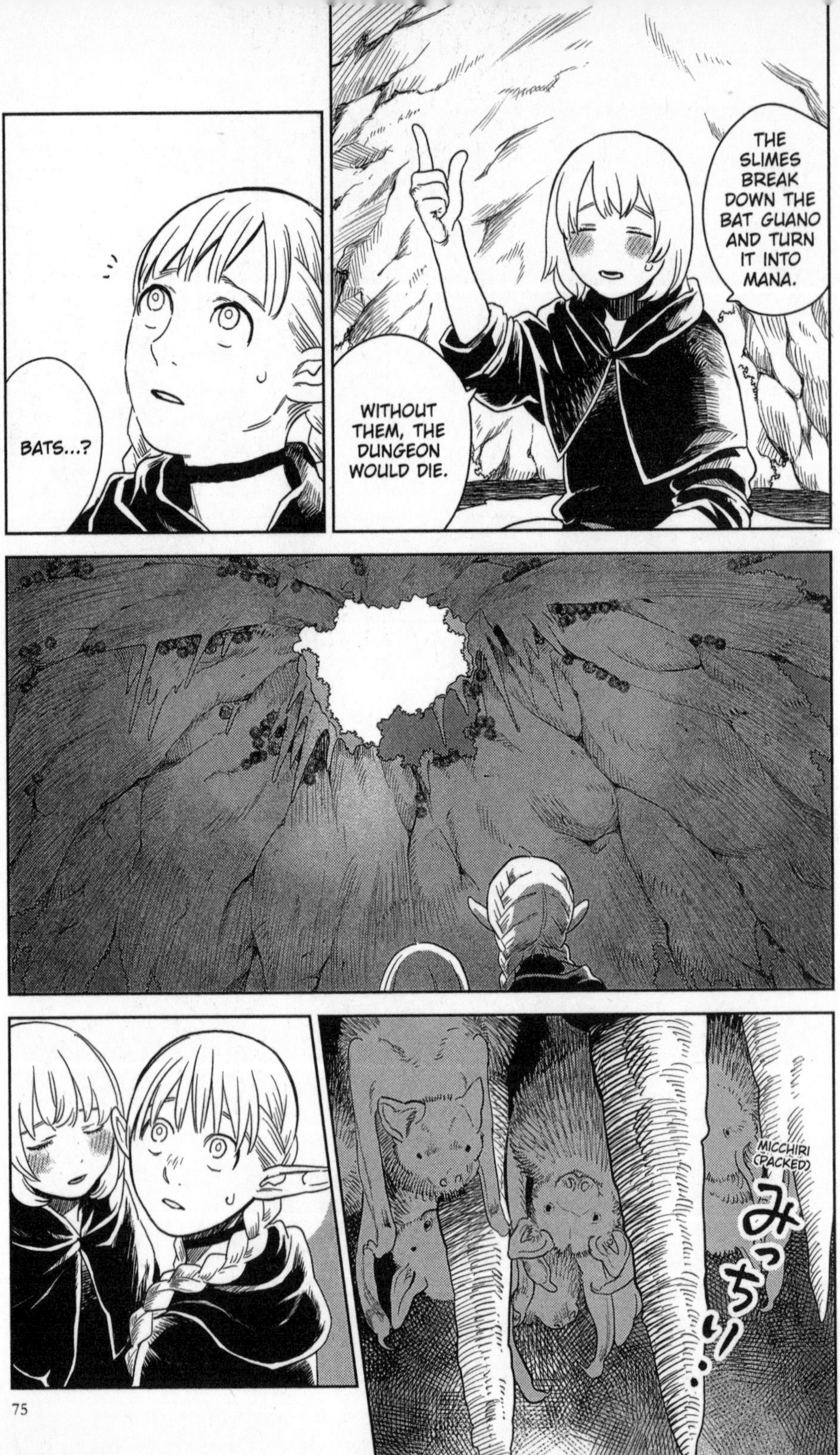
THE SLIMES BREAK DOWN THE BAT GUANO AND TURN IT INTO MANA.
WITHOUT THEM, THE DUNGEON WOULD DIE.
BATS...?
MICCHIRI (PACKED)
みっちり…

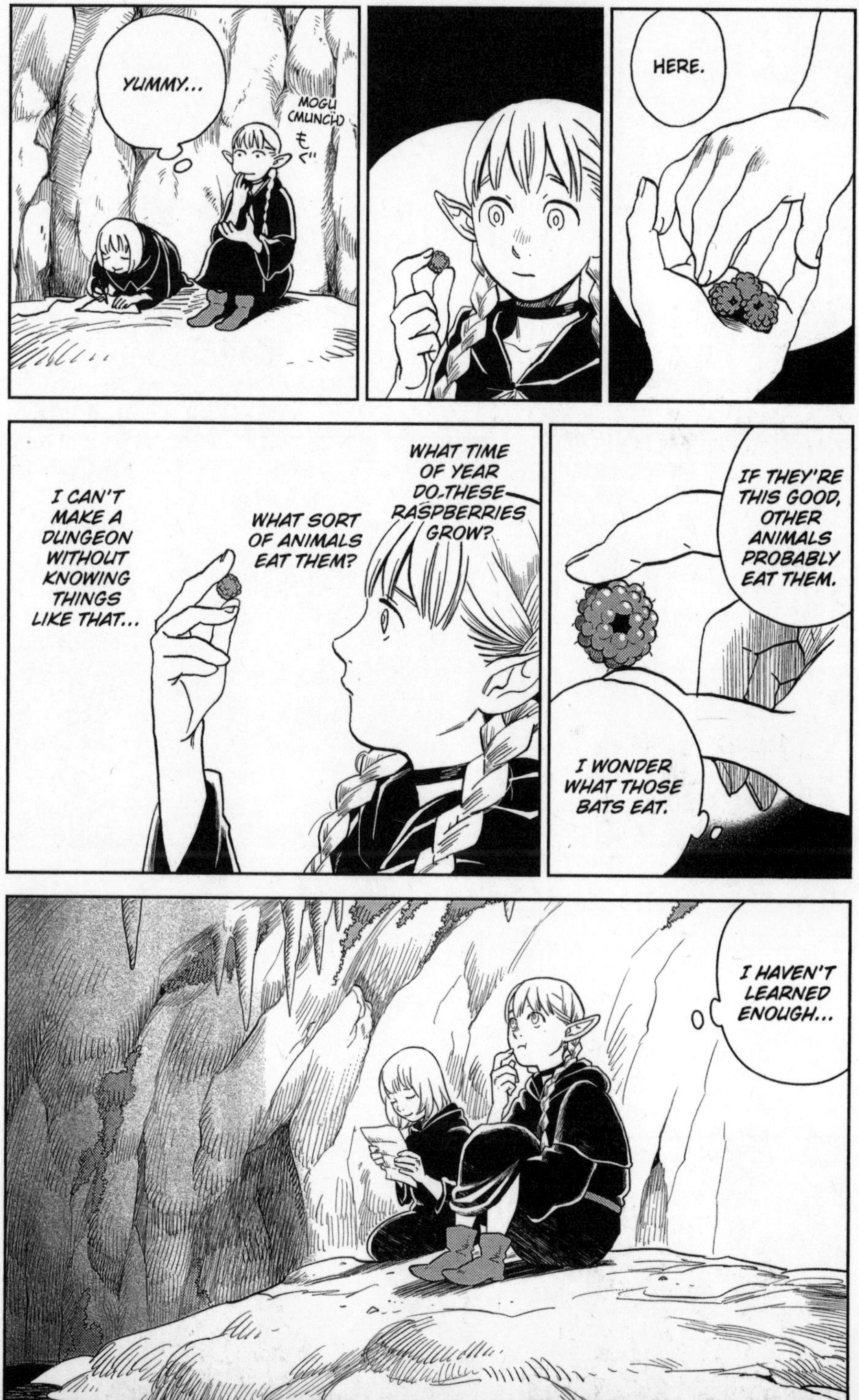
HERE.
MOGU (MUNCH)
もぐ
YUMMY...
IF THEY'RE THIS GOOD, OTHER ANIMALS PROBABLY EAT THEM.
I WONDER WHAT THOSE BATS EAT.
WHAT TIME OF YEAR DO THESE RASPBERRIES GROW?
WHAT SORT OF ANIMALS EAT THEM?
I CAN'T MAKE A DUNGEON WITHOUT KNOWING THINGS LIKE THAT...
I HAVEN'T LEARNED ENOUGH...

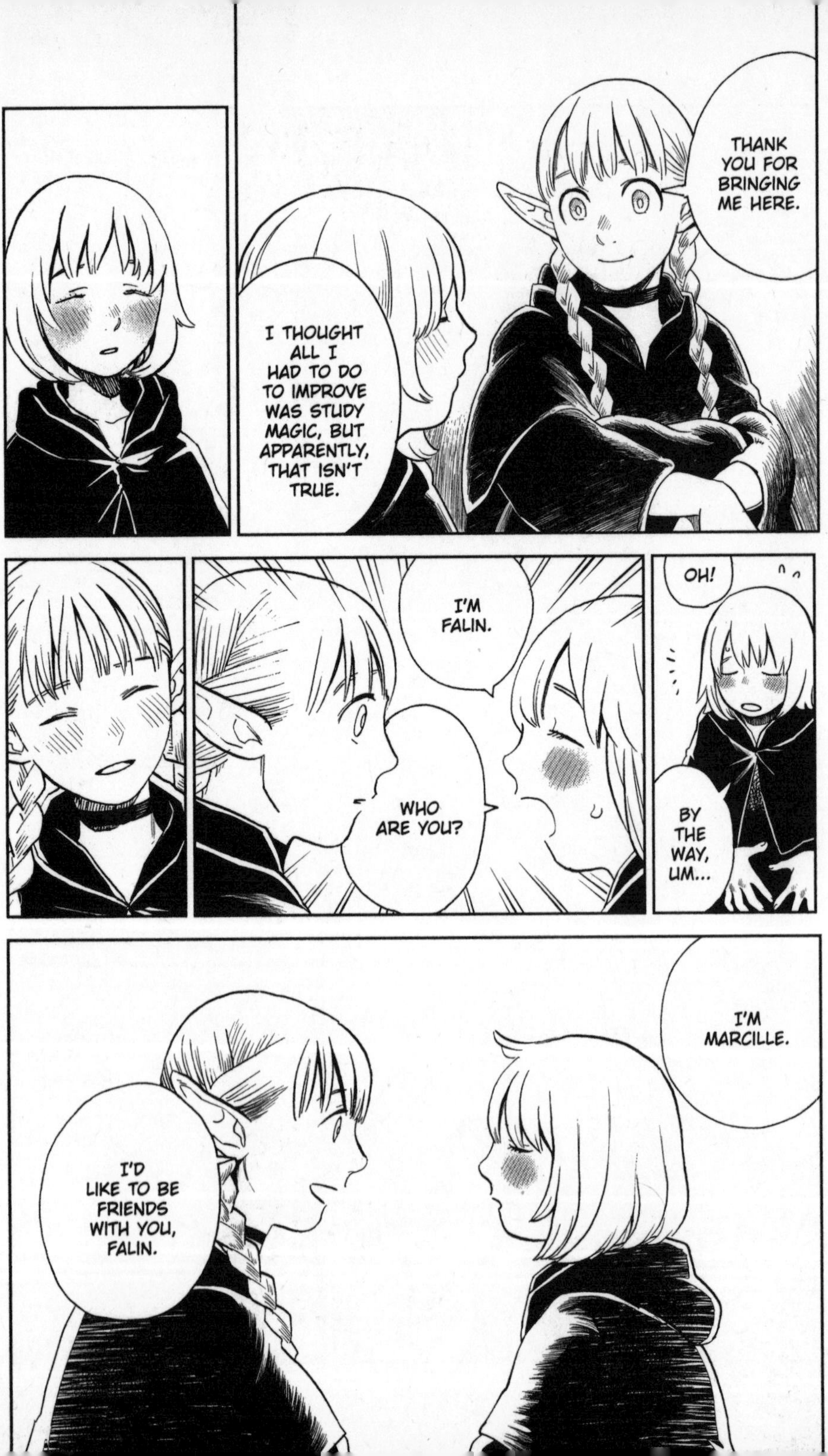
THANK YOU FOR BRINGING ME HERE.
I THOUGHT ALL I HAD TO DO TO IMPROVE WAS STUDY MAGIC, BUT APPARENTLY, THAT ISN'T TRUE.
OH!
BY THE WAY, UM...
I'M FALIN.
WHO ARE YOU?
I'M MARCILLE.
I'D LIKE TO BE FRIENDS WITH YOU, FALIN.

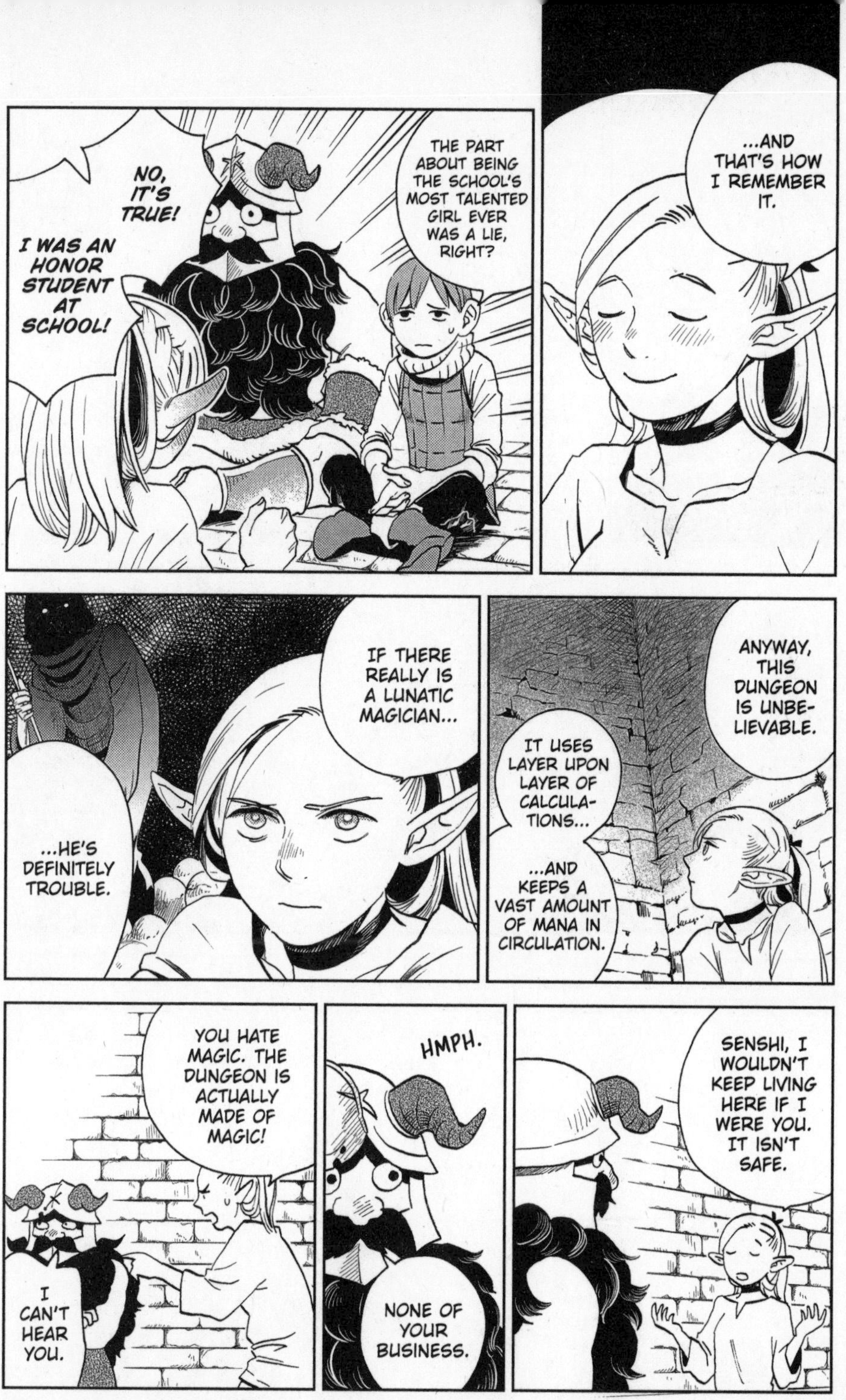
...AND THAT'S HOW I REMEMBER IT.
THE PART ABOUT BEING THE SCHOOL'S MOST TALENTED GIRL EVER WAS A LIE, RIGHT?
NO, IT'S TRUE!
I WAS AN HONOR STUDENT AT SCHOOL!
ANYWAY, THIS DUNGEON IS UNBE-LIEVABLE.
IT USES LAYER UPON LAYER OF CALCULA-TIONS...
...AND KEEPS A VAST AMOUNT OF MANA IN CIRCULATION.
IF THERE REALLY IS A LUNATIC MAGICIAN...
...HE'S DEFINITELY TROUBLE.
SENSHI, I WOULDN'T KEEP LIVING HERE IF I WERE YOU. IT ISN'T SAFE.
HMPH.
NONE OF YOUR BUSINESS.
YOU HATE MAGIC. THE DUNGEON IS ACTUALLY MADE OF MAGIC!
I CAN'T HEAR YOU.

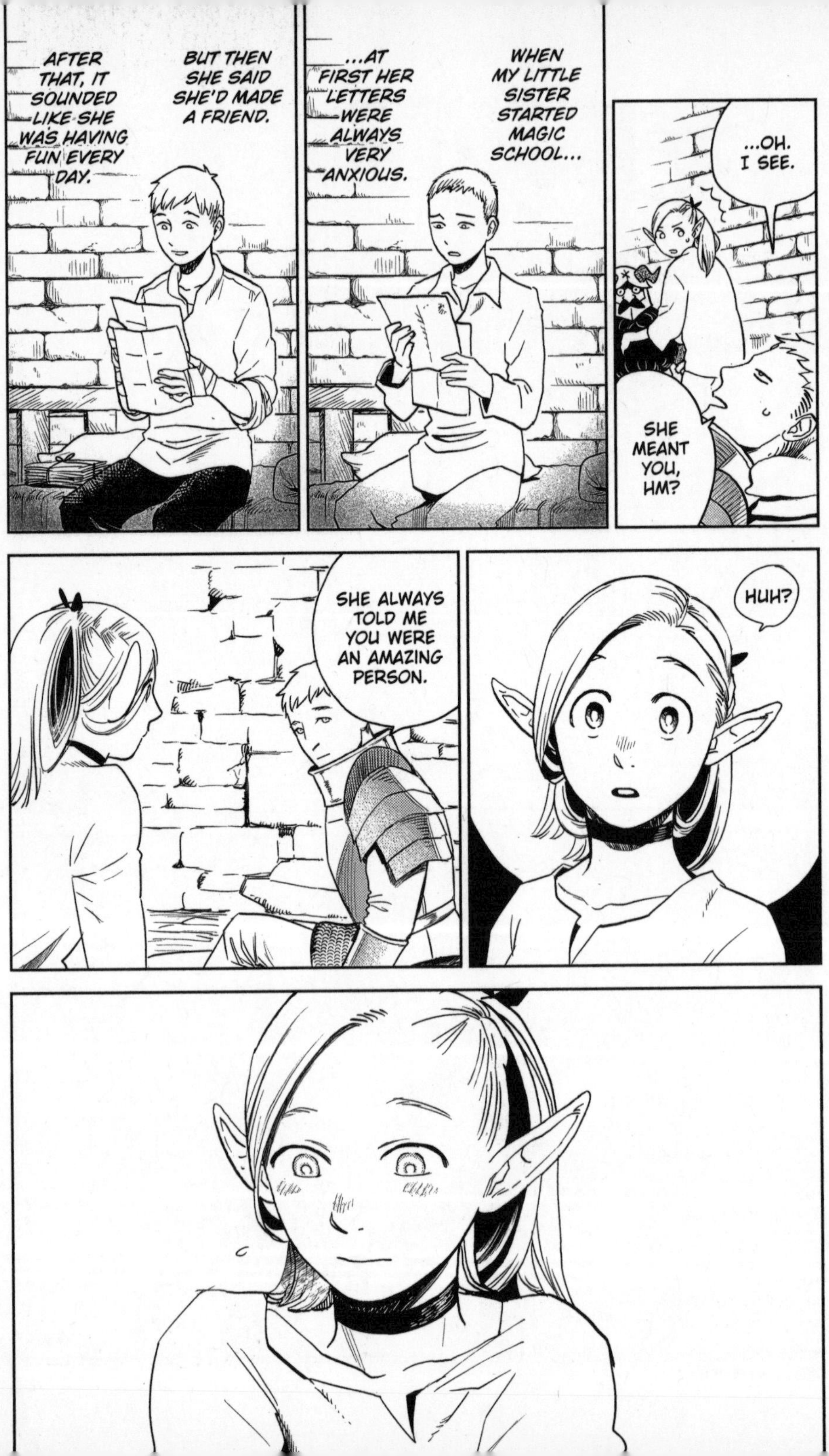
...OH. I SEE.
SHE MEANT YOU, HM?
WHEN MY LITTLE SISTER STARTED MAGIC SCHOOL...
...AT FIRST HER LETTERS WERE ALWAYS VERY ANXIOUS.
BUT THEN SHE SAID SHE'D MADE A FRIEND.
AFTER THAT, IT SOUNDED LIKE SHE WAS HAVING FUN EVERY DAY.
HUH?
SHE ALWAYS TOLD ME YOU WERE AN AMAZING PERSON.

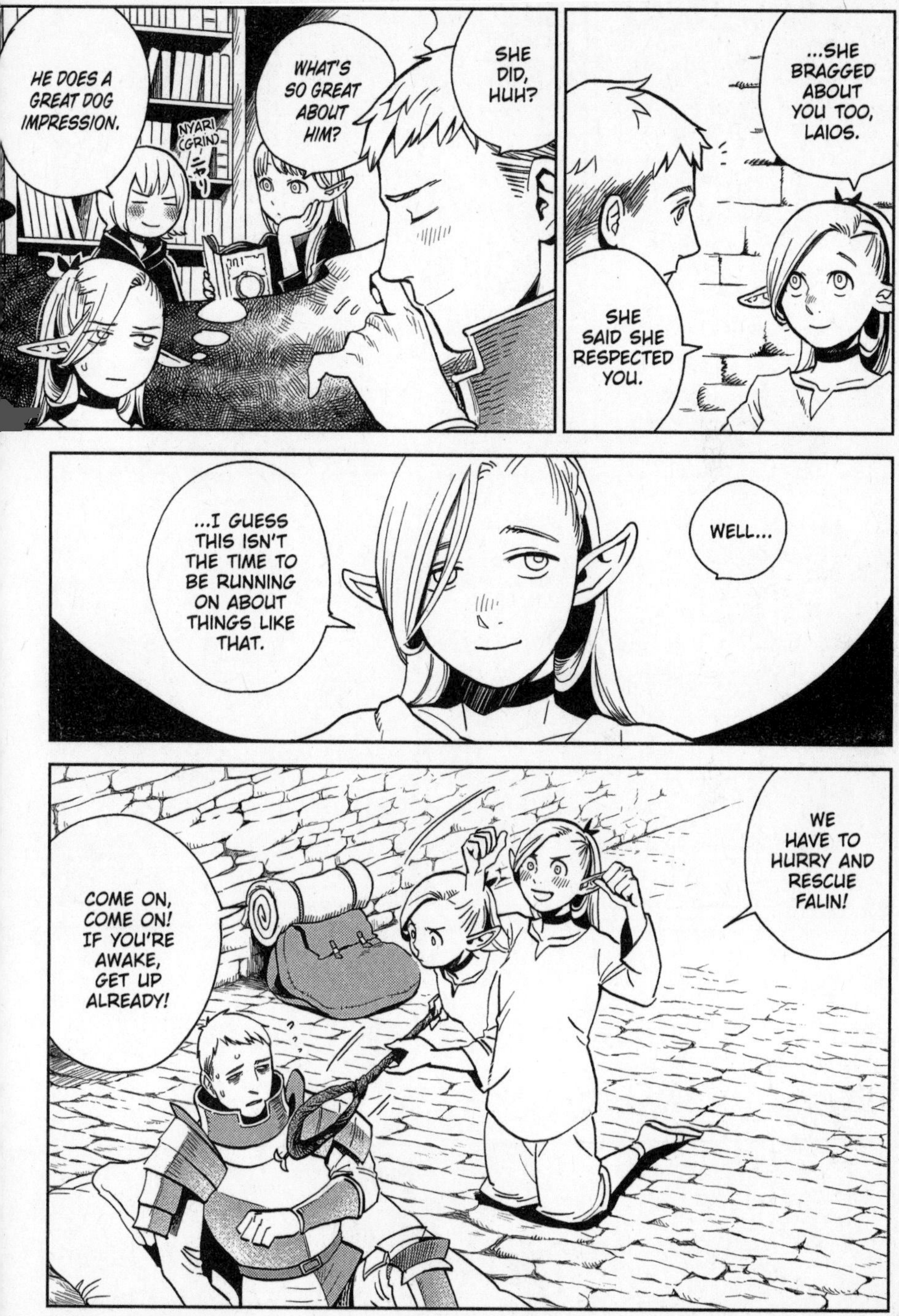
...SHE BRAGGED ABOUT YOU TOO, LAIOS.
SHE SAID SHE RESPECTED YOU.
SHE DID, HUH?
WHAT'S SO GREAT ABOUT HIM?
NYARI (GRIN)
ニヤリ
HE DOES A GREAT DOG IMPRESSION.
WELL...
...I GUESS THIS ISN'T THE TIME TO BE RUNNING ON ABOUT THINGS LIKE THAT.
WE HAVE TO HURRY AND RESCUE FALIN!
COME ON, COME ON! IF YOU'RE AWAKE, GET UP ALREADY!

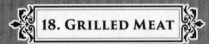

18. Grilled Meat

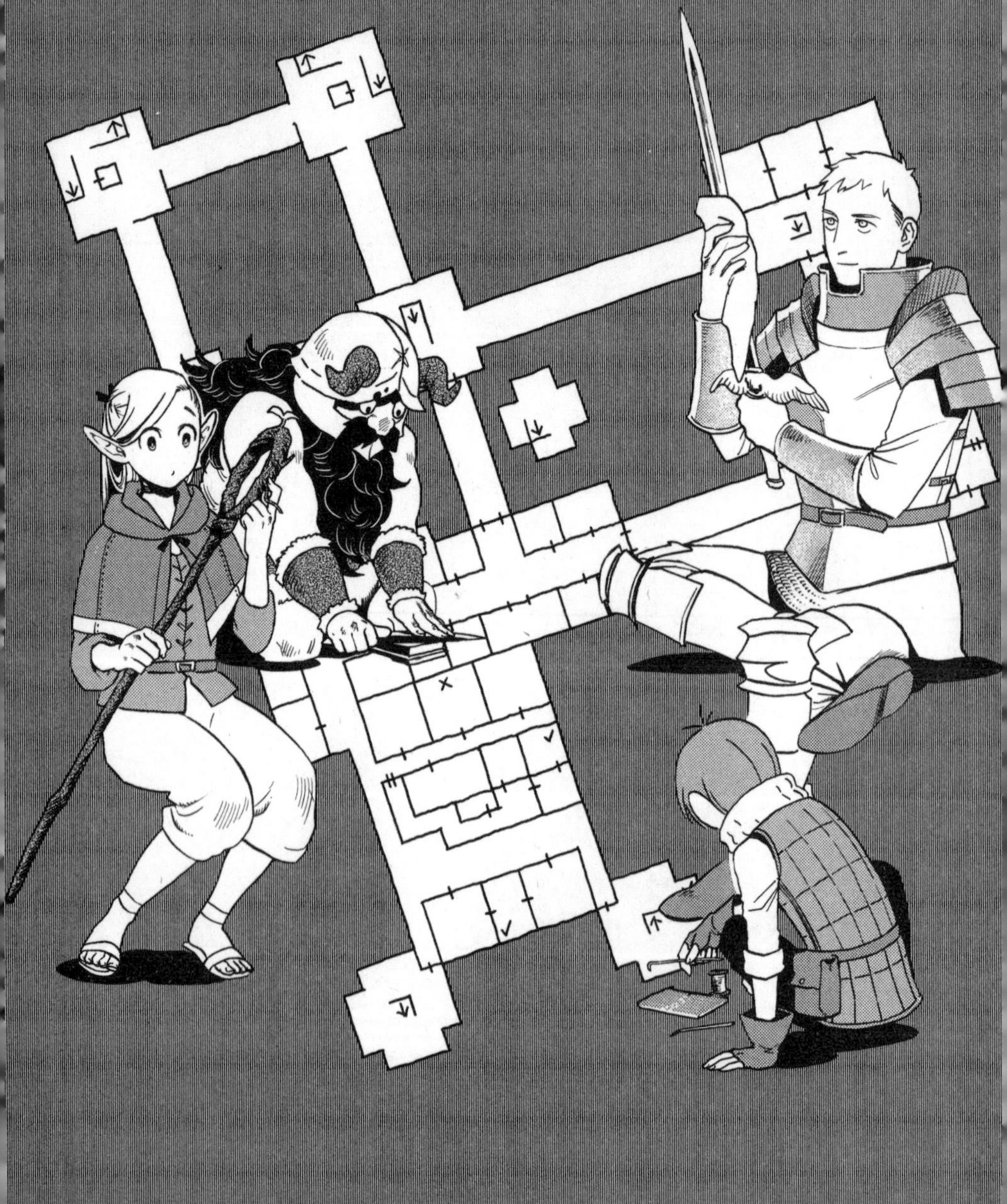

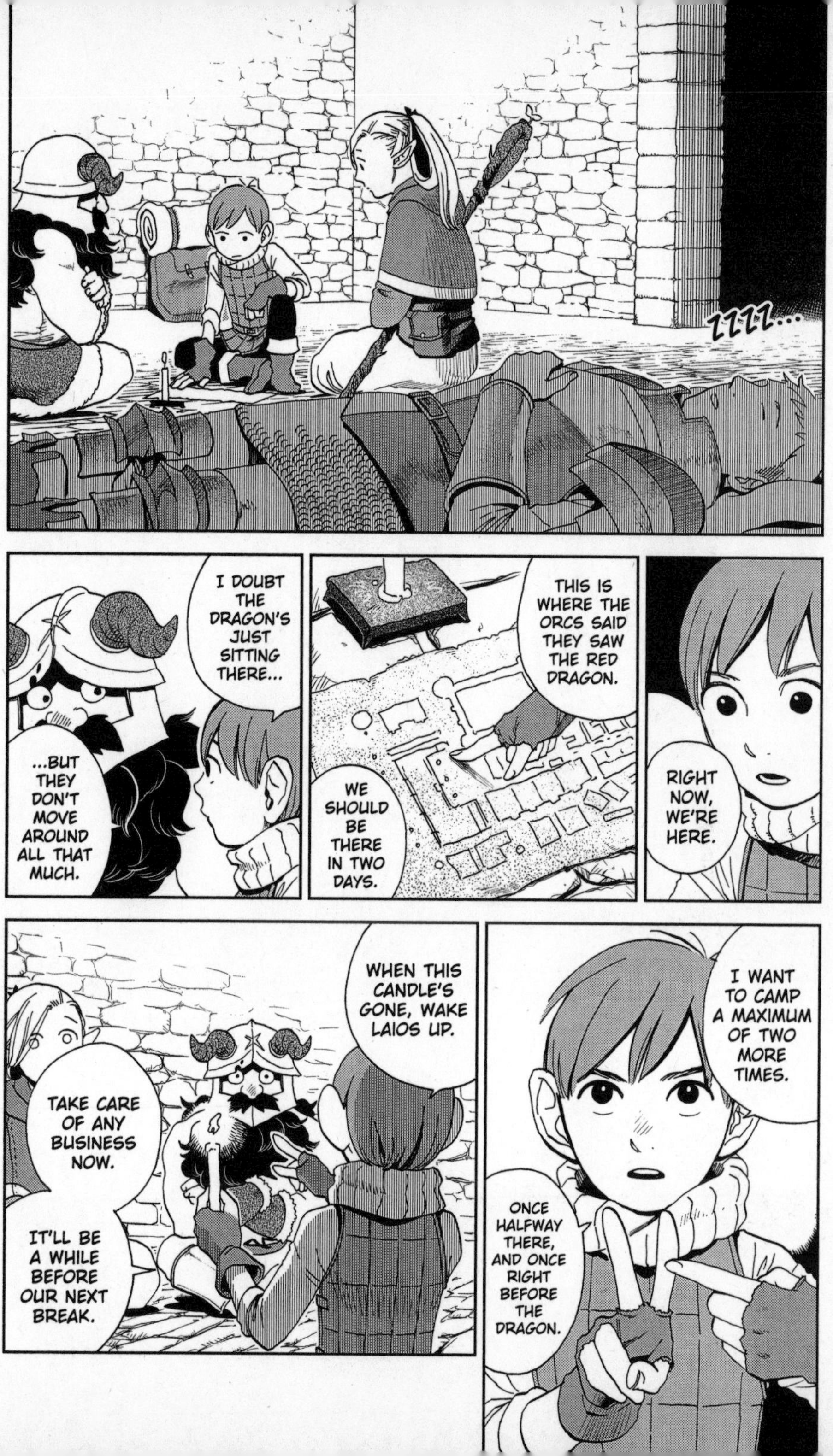
ZZZZ...
RIGHT NOW, WE'RE HERE.
THIS IS WHERE THE ORCS SAID THEY SAW THE RED DRAGON.
WE SHOULD BE THERE IN TWO DAYS.
I DOUBT THE DRAGON'S JUST SITTING THERE...
...BUT THEY DON'T MOVE AROUND ALL THAT MUCH.
I WANT TO CAMP A MAXIMUM OF TWO MORE TIMES.
ONCE HALFWAY THERE, AND ONCE RIGHT BEFORE THE DRAGON.
WHEN THIS CANDLE'S GONE, WAKE LAIOS UP.
TAKE CARE OF ANY BUSINESS NOW.
IT'LL BE A WHILE BEFORE OUR NEXT BREAK.

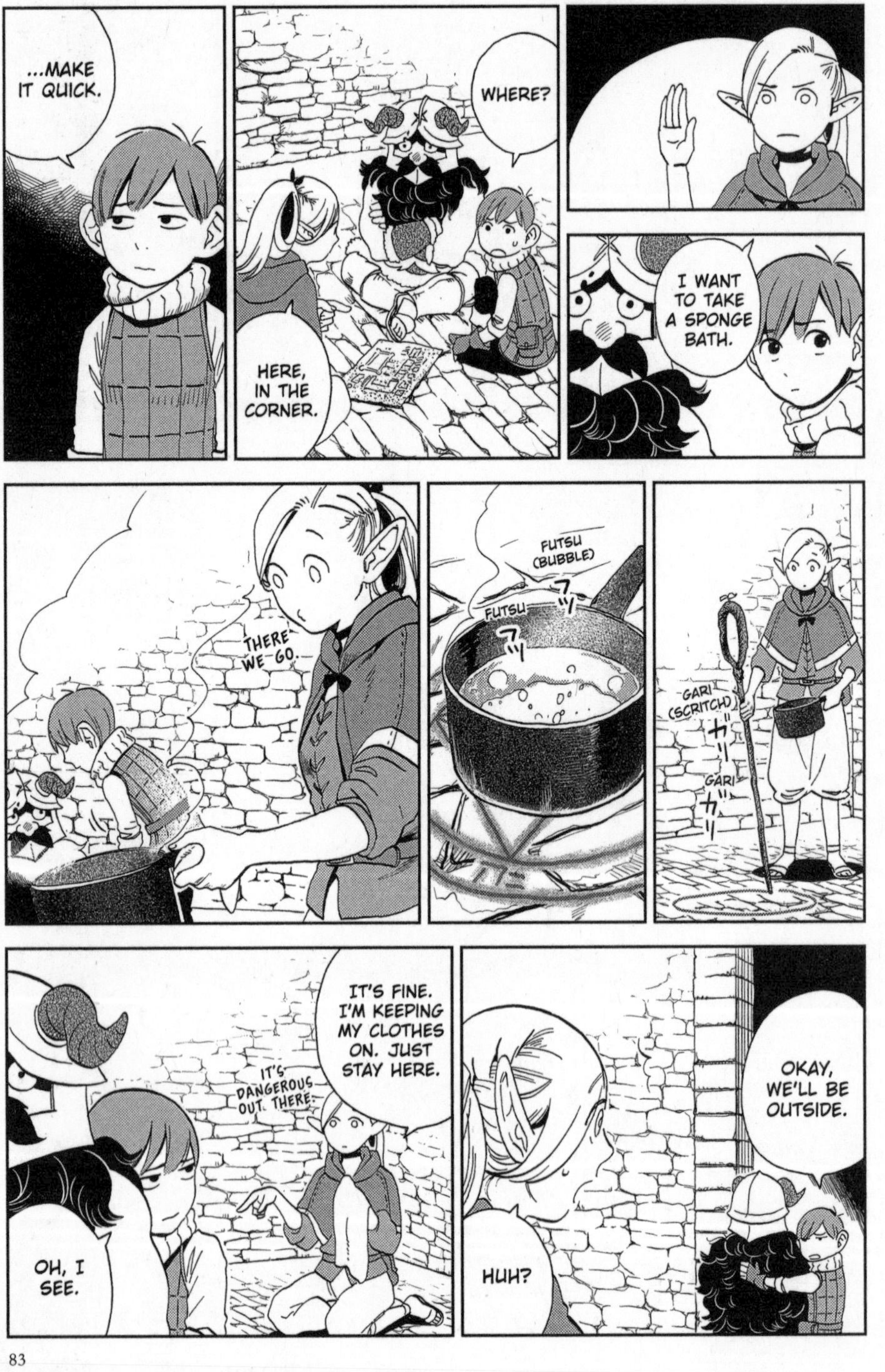
I WANT TO TAKE A SPONGE BATH.
WHERE?
HERE, IN THE CORNER.
...MAKE IT QUICK.
GARI (SCRITCH)
GARI
FUTSU (BUBBLE)
FUTSU
THERE WE GO.
OKAY, WE'LL BE OUTSIDE.
HUH?
IT'S FINE. I'M KEEPING MY CLOTHES ON. JUST STAY HERE.
IT'S DANGEROUS OUT THERE.
OH, I SEE.

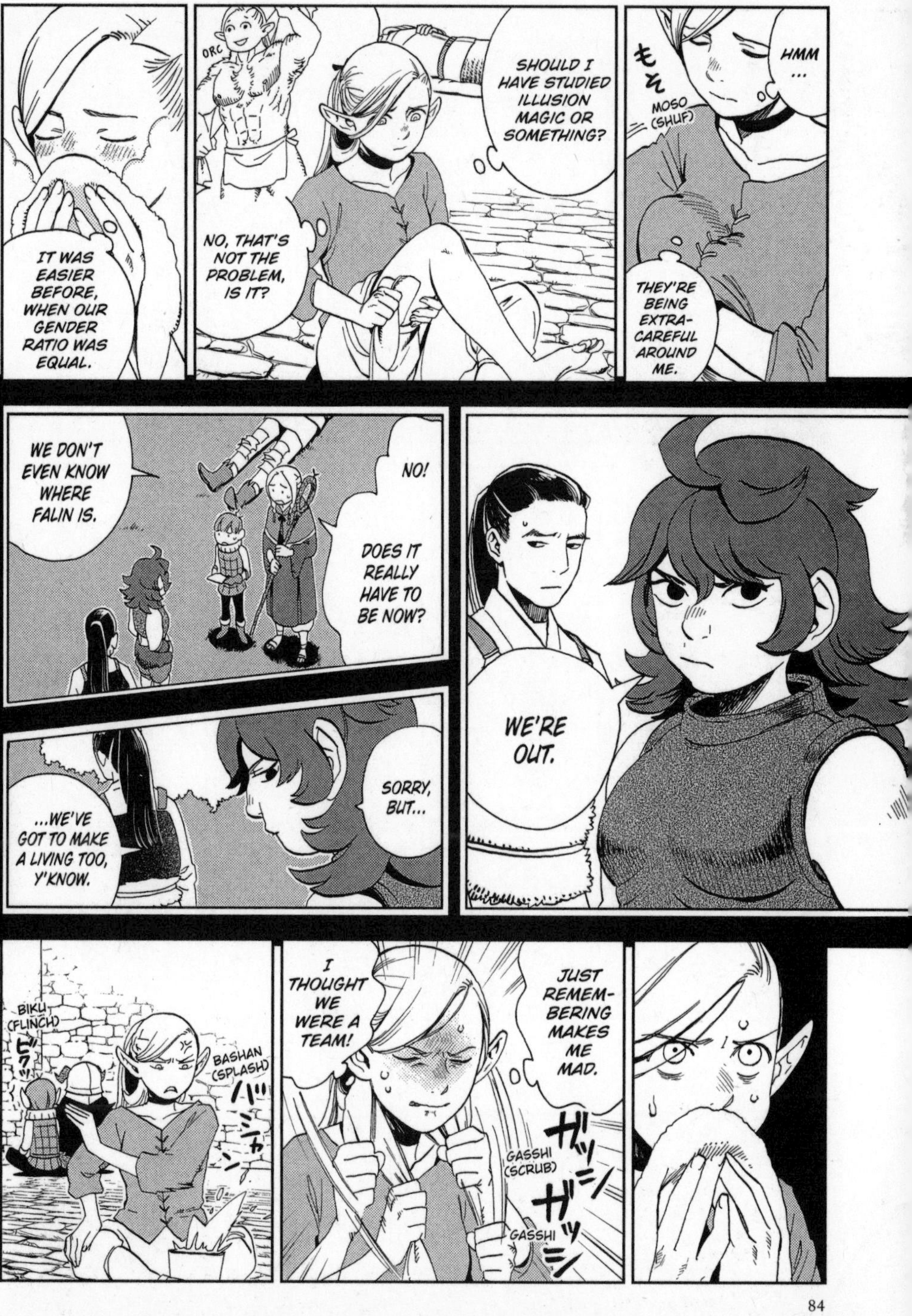
HMM...
もそ
MOSO (SHUF)
THEY'RE BEING EXTRA-CAREFUL AROUND ME.
SHOULD I HAVE STUDIED ILLUSION MAGIC OR SOMETHING?
ORC
NO, THAT'S NOT THE PROBLEM, IS IT?
IT WAS EASIER BEFORE, WHEN OUR GENDER RATIO WAS EQUAL.
WE'RE OUT.
NO!
DOES IT REALLY HAVE TO BE NOW?
WE DON'T EVEN KNOW WHERE FALIN IS.
SORRY, BUT...
...WE'VE GOT TO MAKE A LIVING TOO, Y'KNOW.
JUST REMEM-BERING MAKES ME MAD.
ガッシ
GASSHI (SCRUB)
ガッシ
GASSHI
I THOUGHT WE WERE A TEAM!
バシャン
BASHAN (SPLASH)
ビクッ
BIKU (FLINCH)

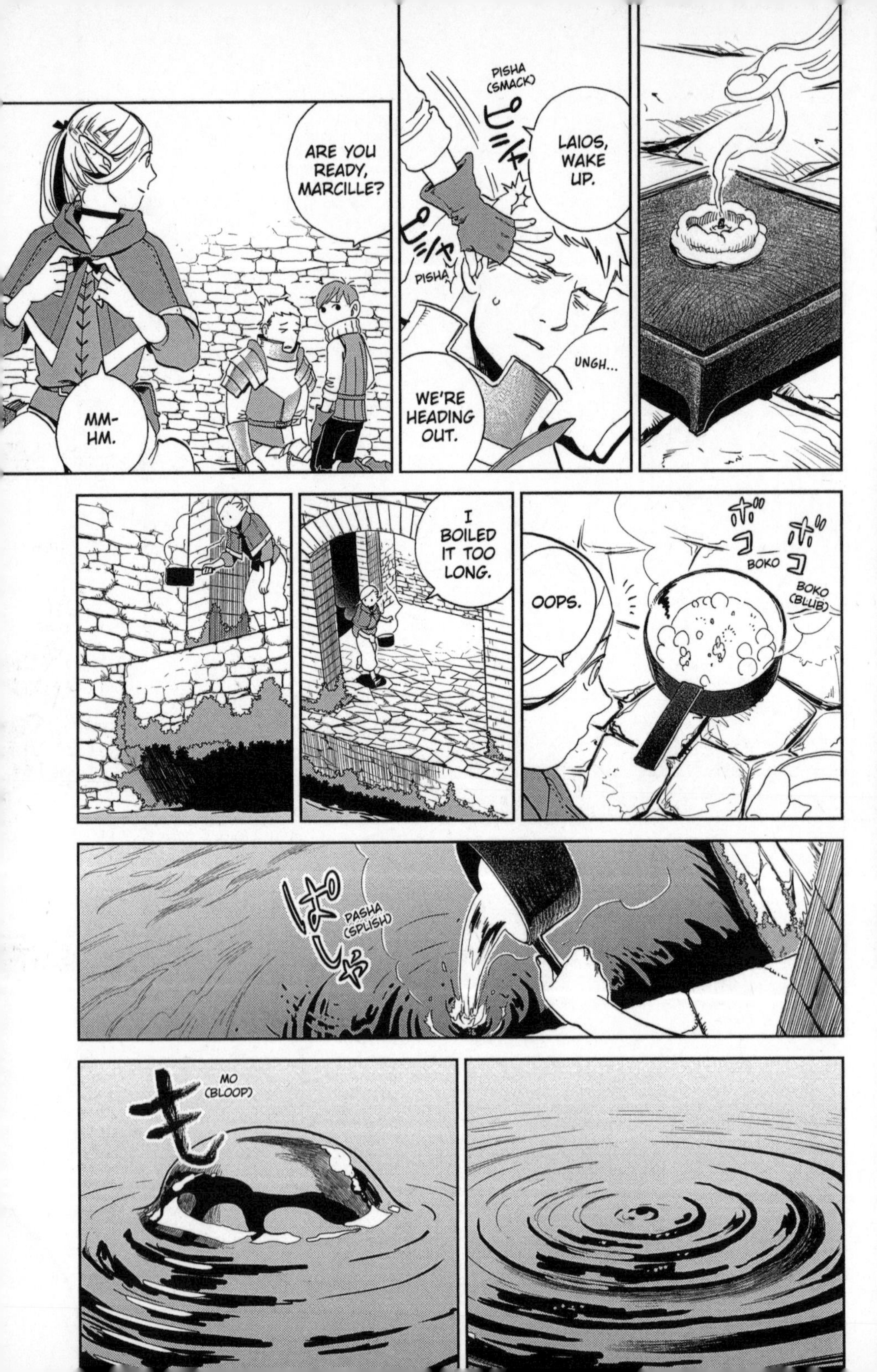
PISHA (SMACK)
ピシャ
LAIOS, WAKE UP.
ピシャ
PISHA
UNGH...
WE'RE HEADING OUT.
ARE YOU READY, MARCILLE?
MM-HM.
ボコ
ボコ
BOKO
BOKO (BLUB)
OOPS.
I BOILED IT TOO LONG.
ぱしゃ
PASHA (SPLISH)
も
MO (BLOOP)

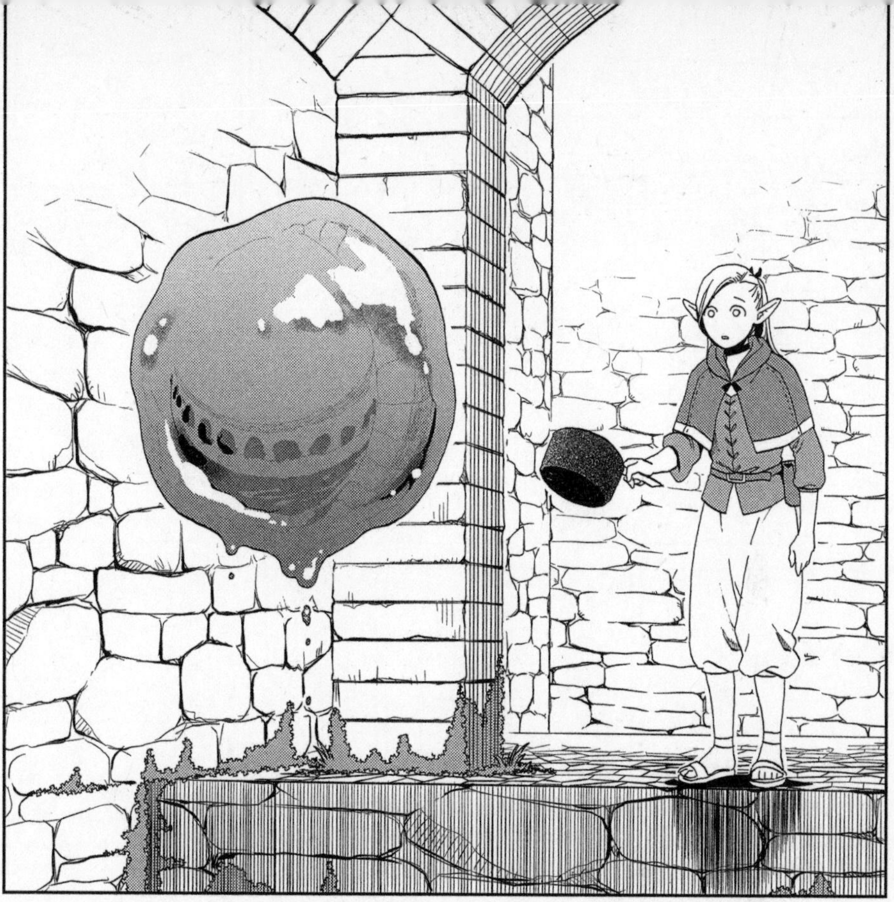

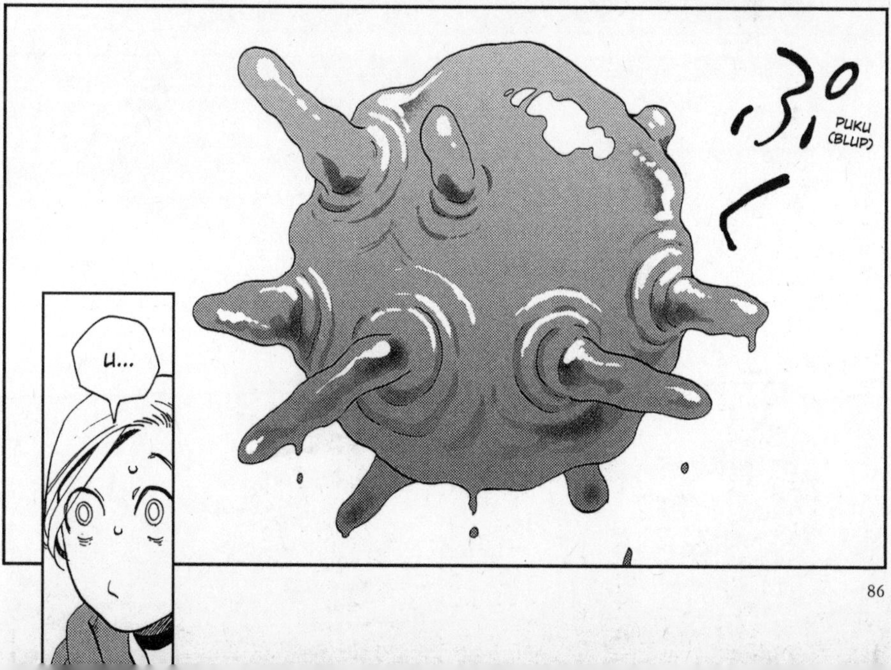
PUKU
(BLUP)
U...

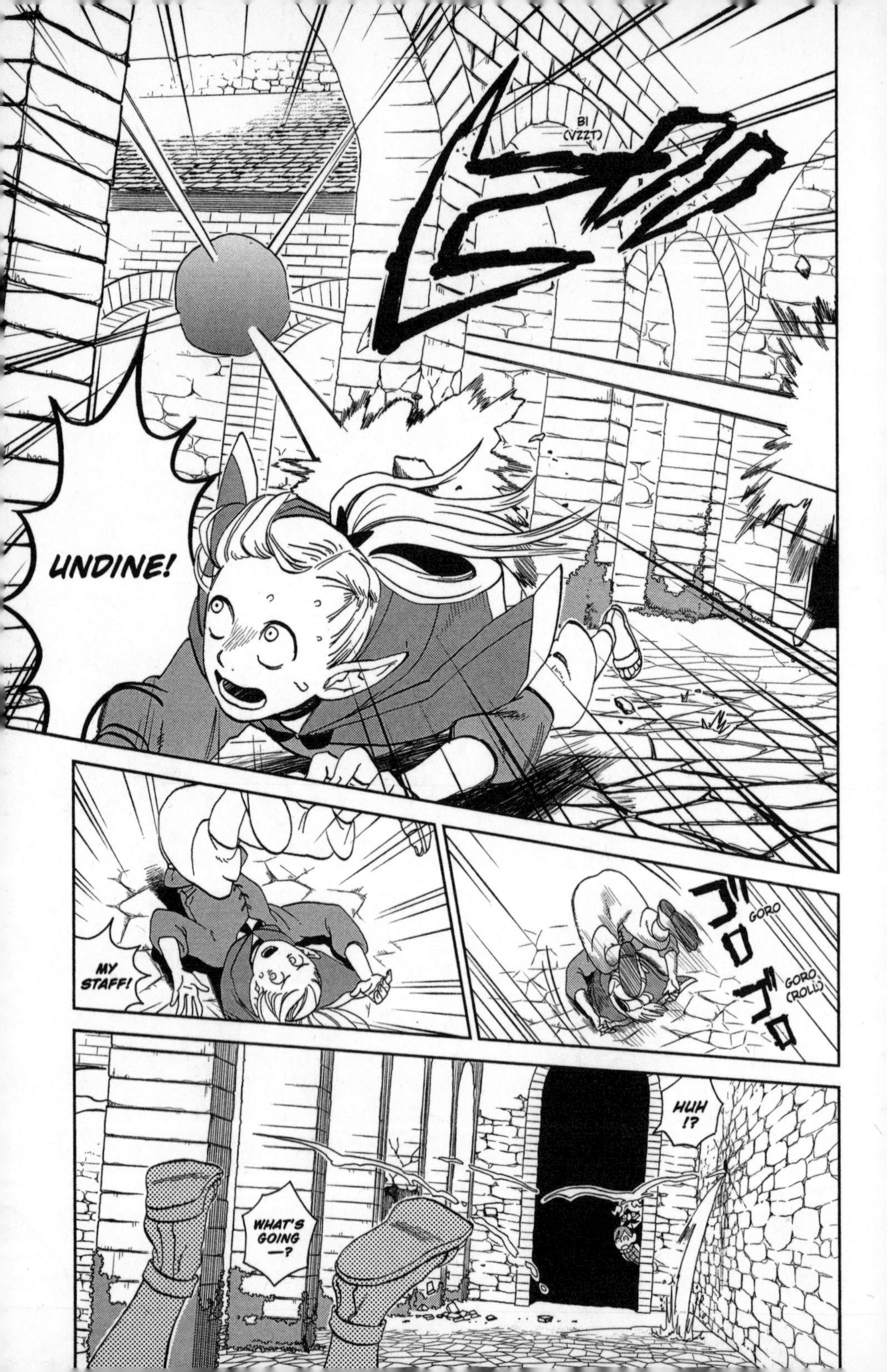
BI (VZZT)
UNDINE!
ゴロゴロ
GORO GORO (ROLL)
MY STAFF!
HUH !?
WHAT'S GOING —?

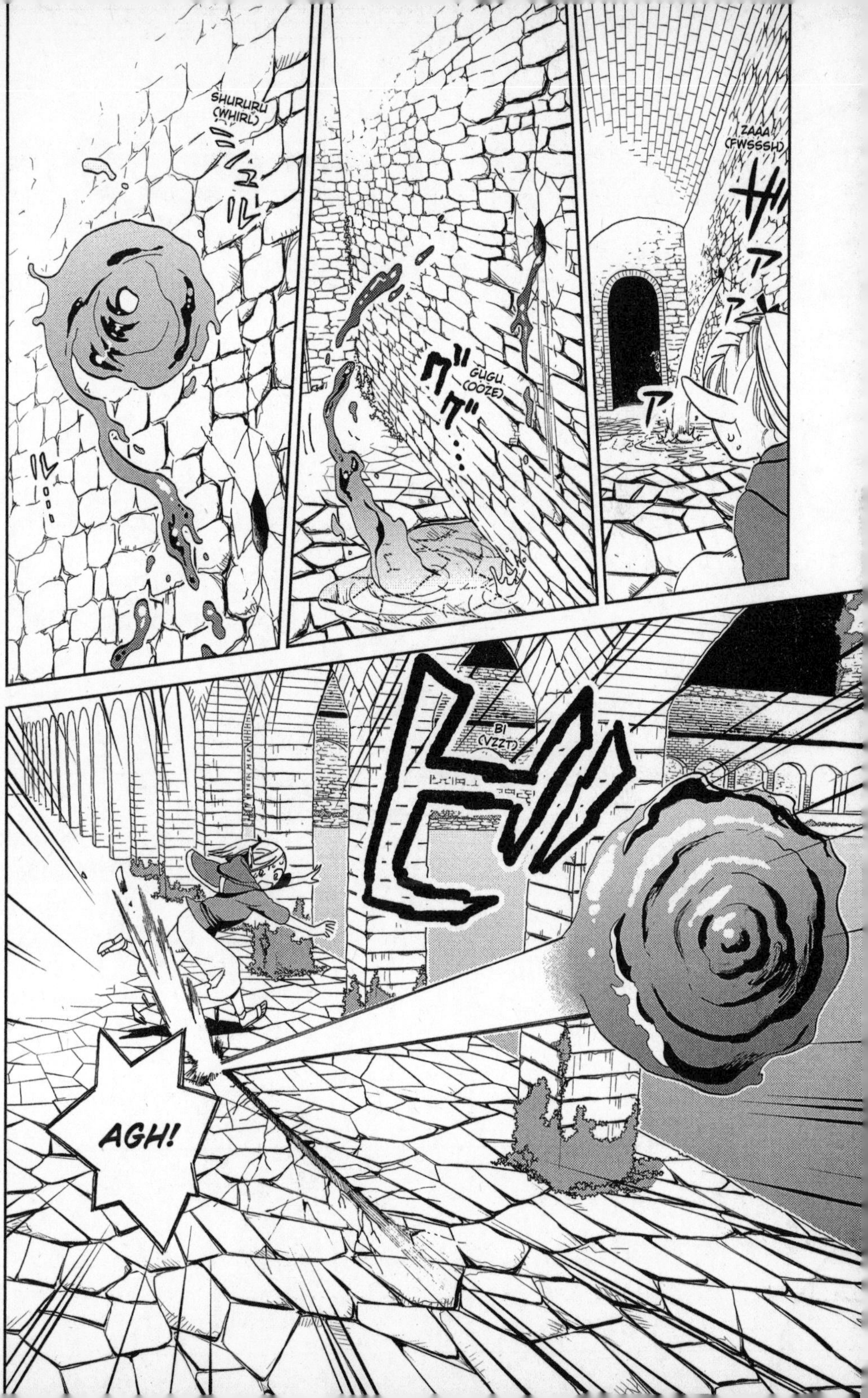
ZAAA
(FWSSSH)
GUGU
(OOZE)
SHURURU
(WHIRL)
BI
(VZZT)
AGH!

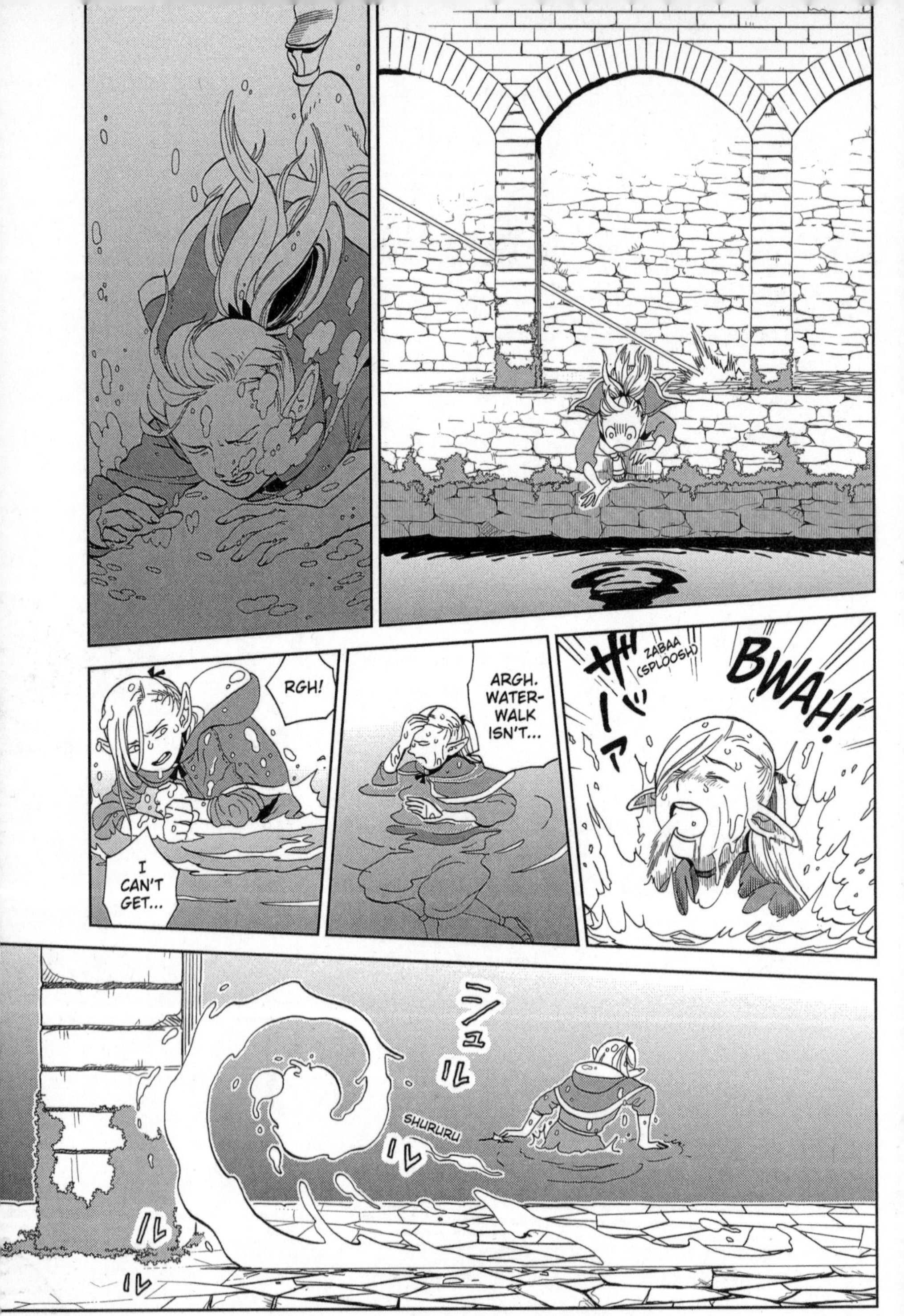
ザバァ
ZABAA (SPLOOSH)
BWAH!
ARGH. WATER-WALK ISN'T...
RGH!
I CAN'T GET...
シュルルルル
SHURURU

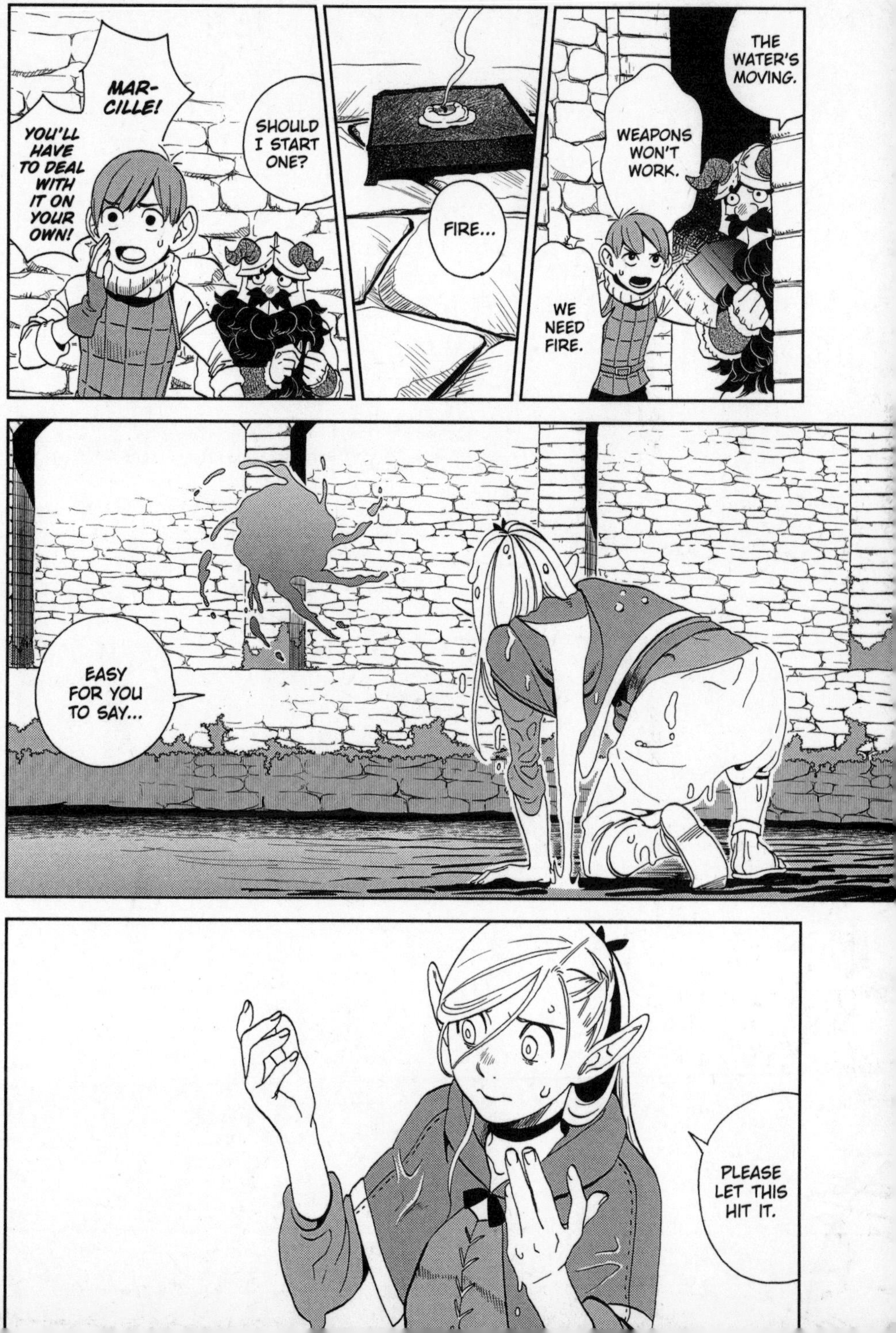
THE WATER'S MOVING.
WEAPONS WON'T WORK.
WE NEED FIRE.
FIRE...
SHOULD I START ONE?
MAR-CILLE!
YOU'LL HAVE TO DEAL WITH IT ON YOUR OWN!
EASY FOR YOU TO SAY...
PLEASE LET THIS HIT IT.

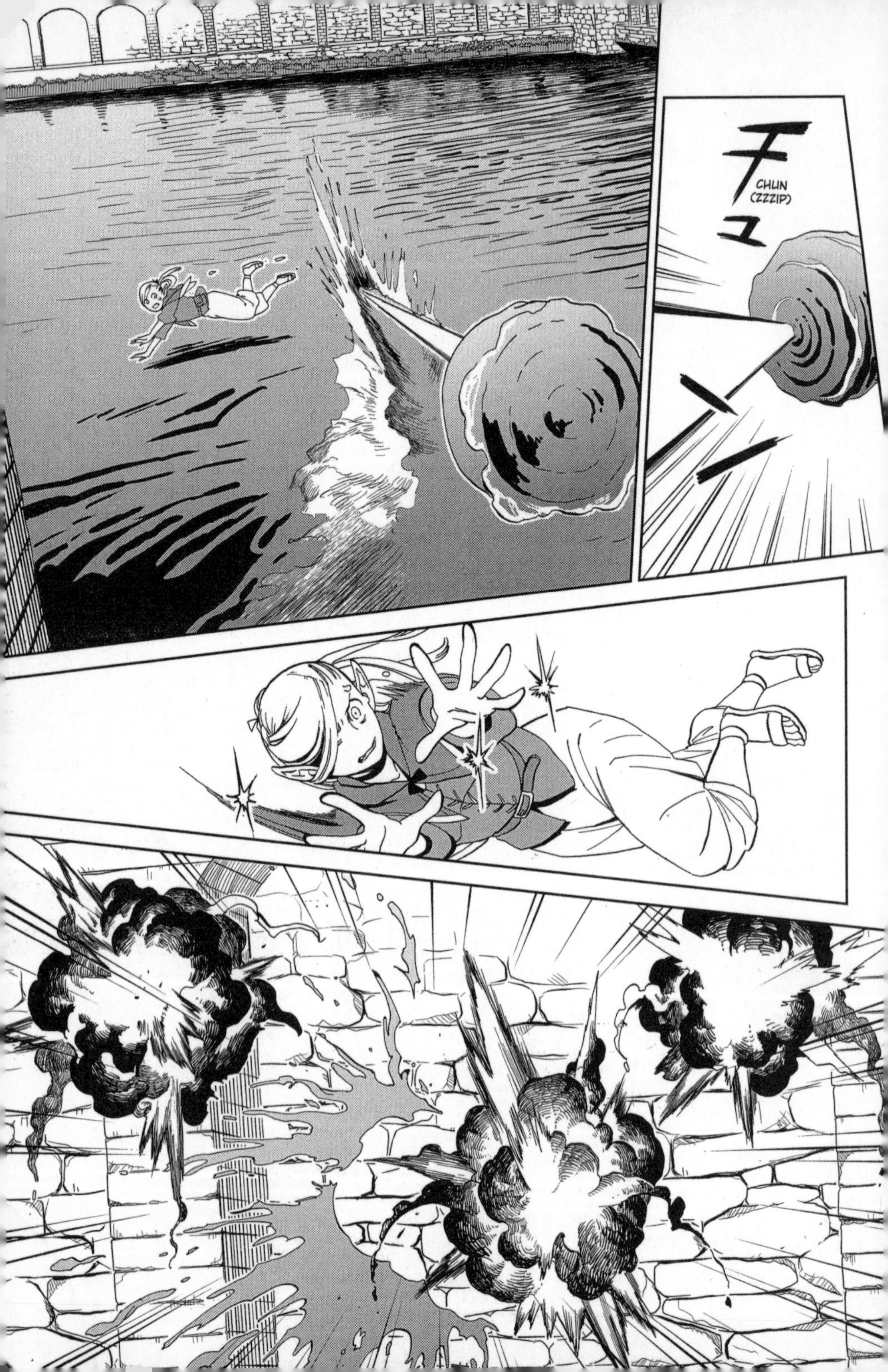
CHUN
(ZZZIP)

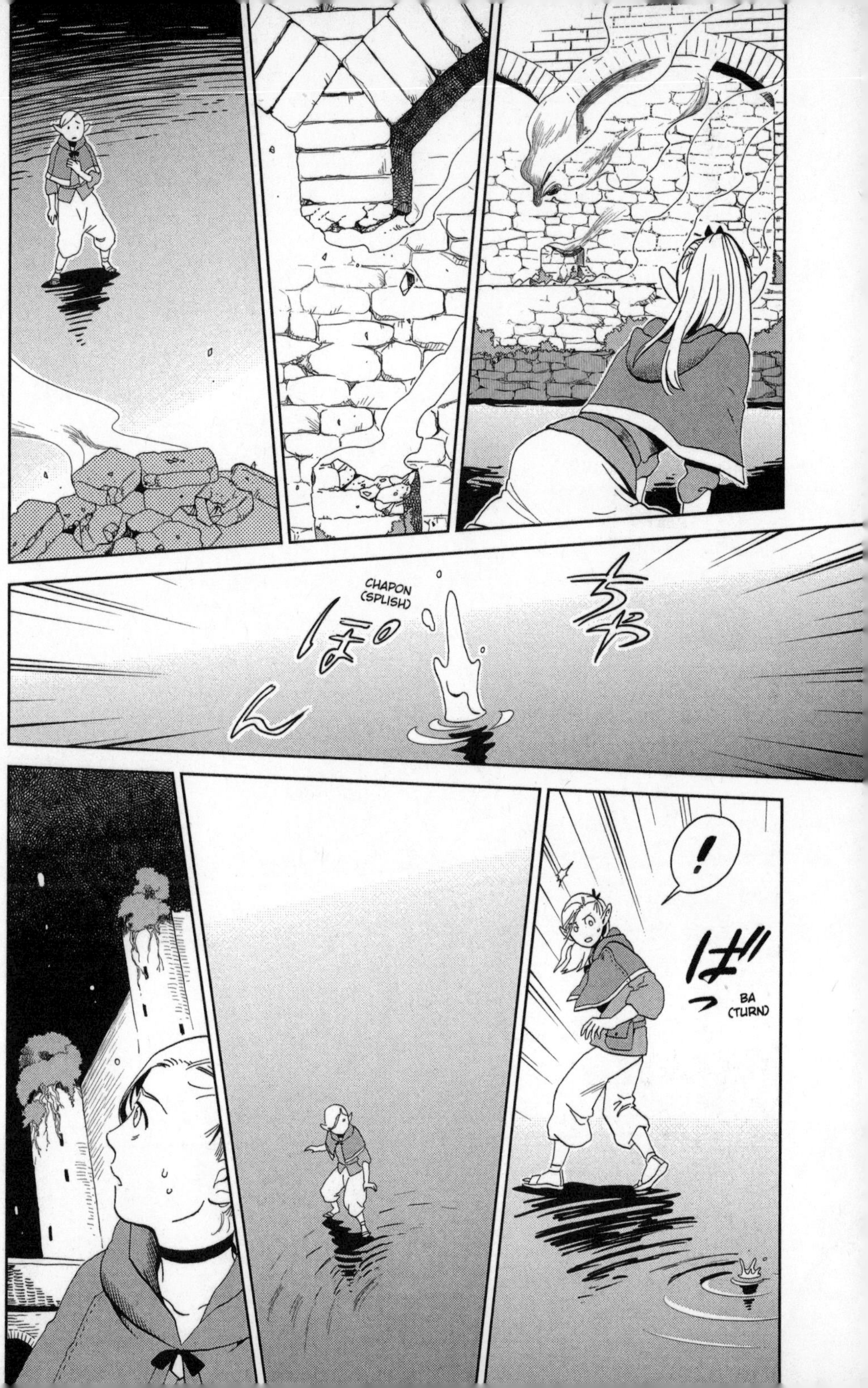
ちゃぽん
CHAPON (SPLISH)
!
ばっ
BA (TURN)

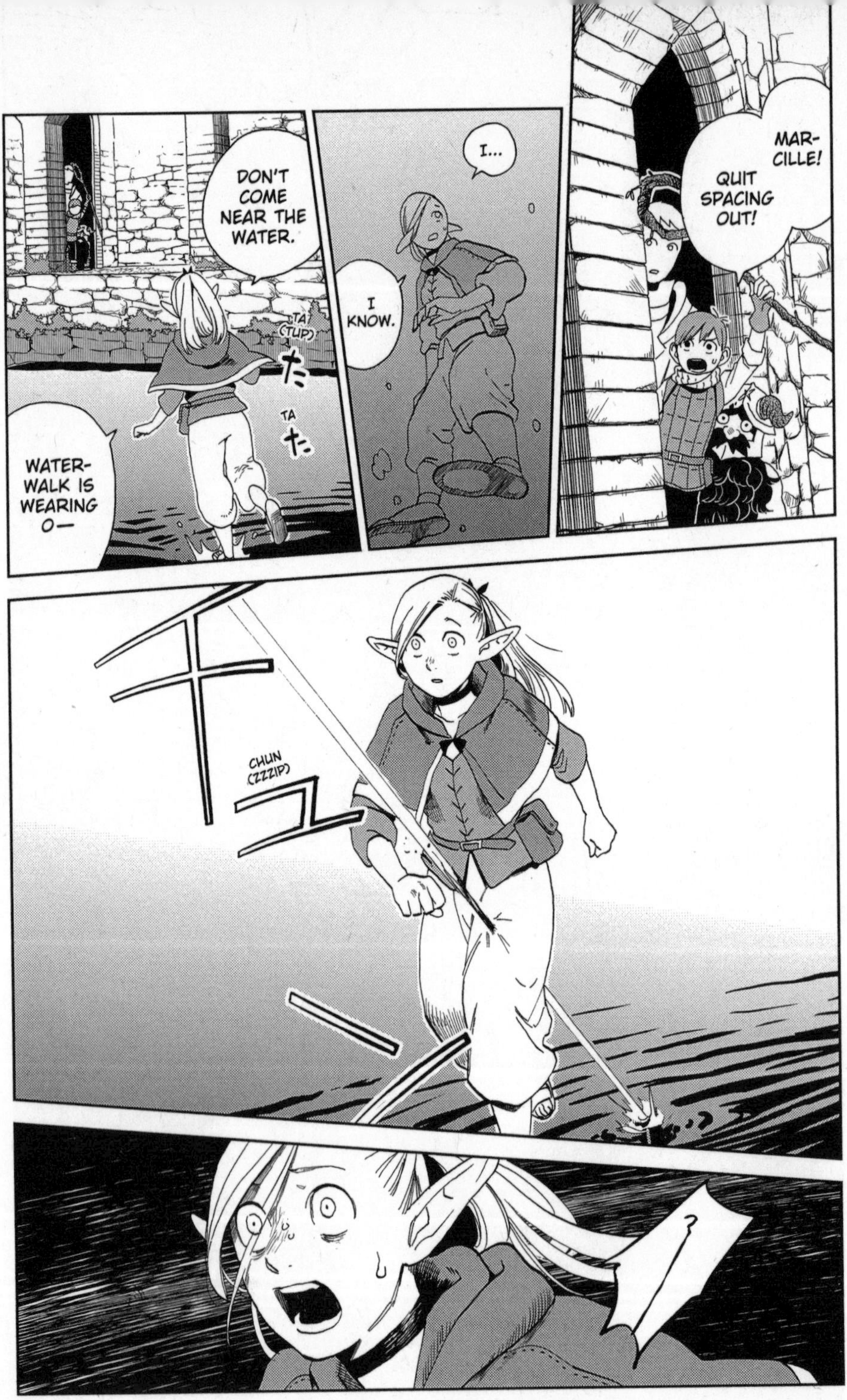
MAR-CILLE!
QUIT SPACING OUT!
I...
I KNOW.
DON'T COME NEAR THE WATER.
TA (TUP)
た
TA
た
WATER-WALK IS WEARING O—
CHUN (ZZZIP)
チュン

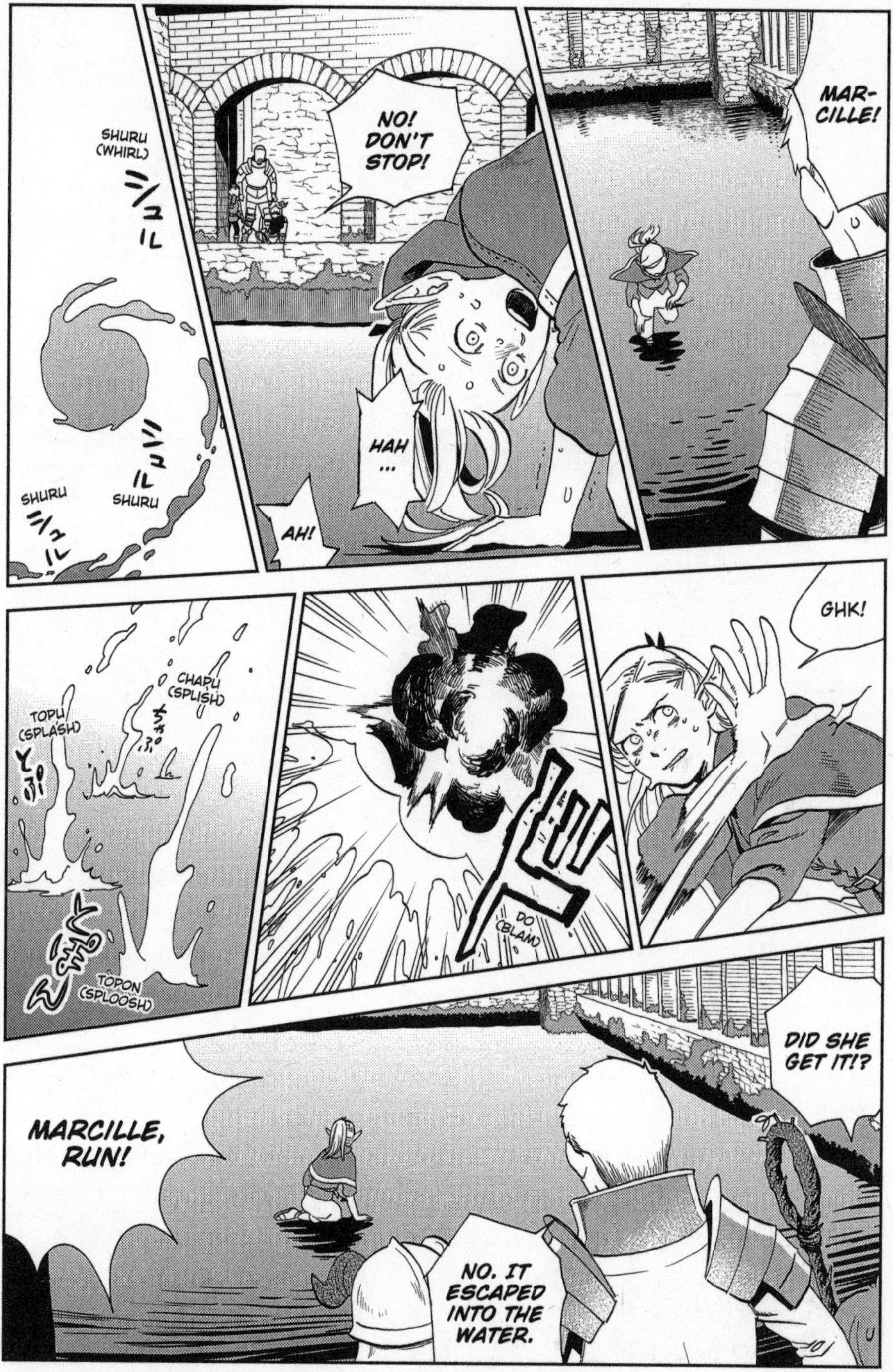
MAR-CILLE!
NO! DON'T STOP!
HAH ...
AH!
SHURU (WHIRL)
シュル
シュル
SHURU
SHURU
シュル
GHK!
DO (BLAM)
CHAPU (SPLASH)
ちゃぷ
TOPU (SPLASH)
とぷ
TOPON (SPLOOSH)
DID SHE GET IT!?
MARCILLE, RUN!
NO. IT ESCAPED INTO THE WATER.

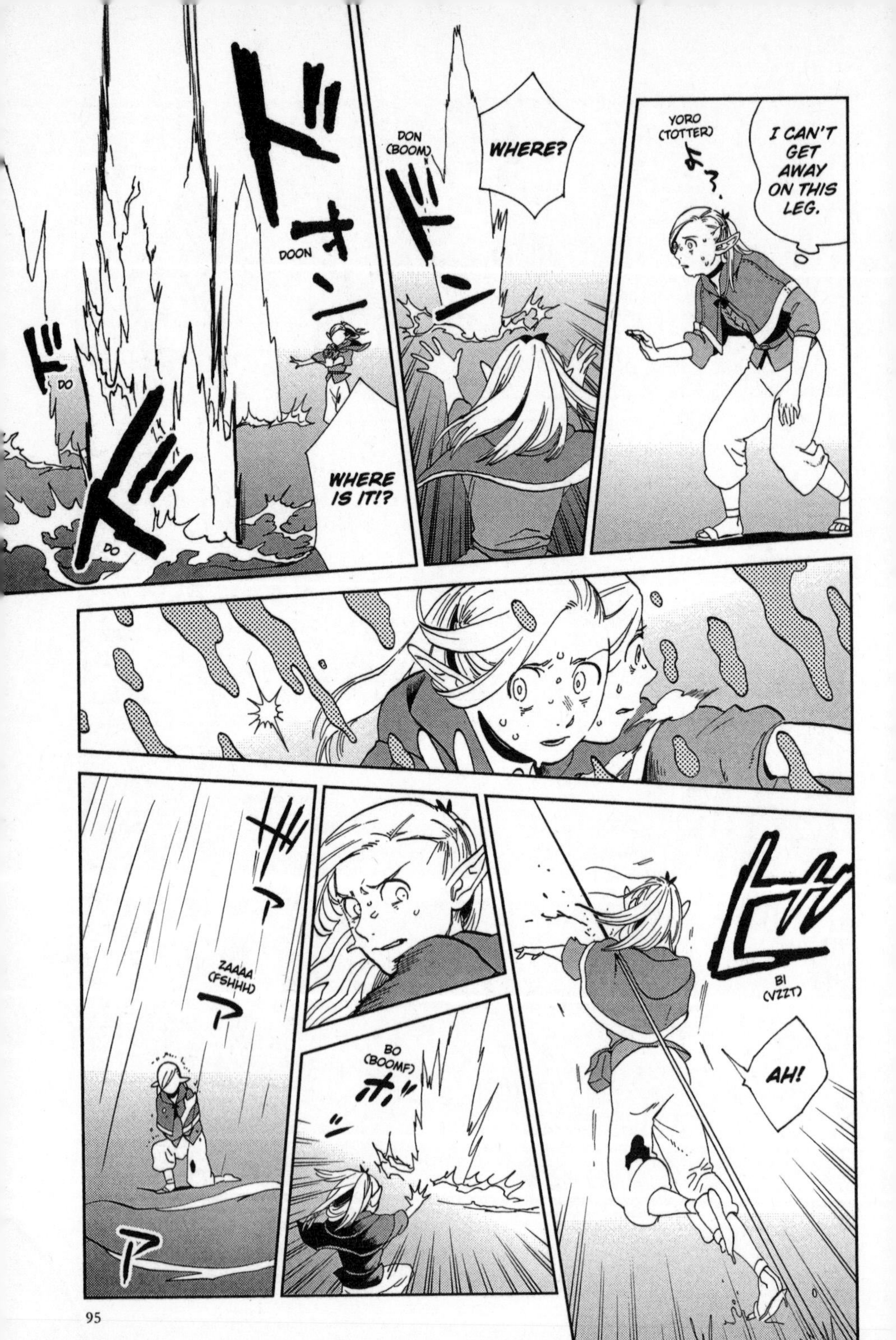
I CAN'T GET AWAY ON THIS LEG.
YORO (TOTTER)
WHERE?
DON (BOOM)
DOON
WHERE IS IT!?
DO
DO
BI (VZZT)
AH!
BO (BOOMF)
ZAAAA (FSHHH)

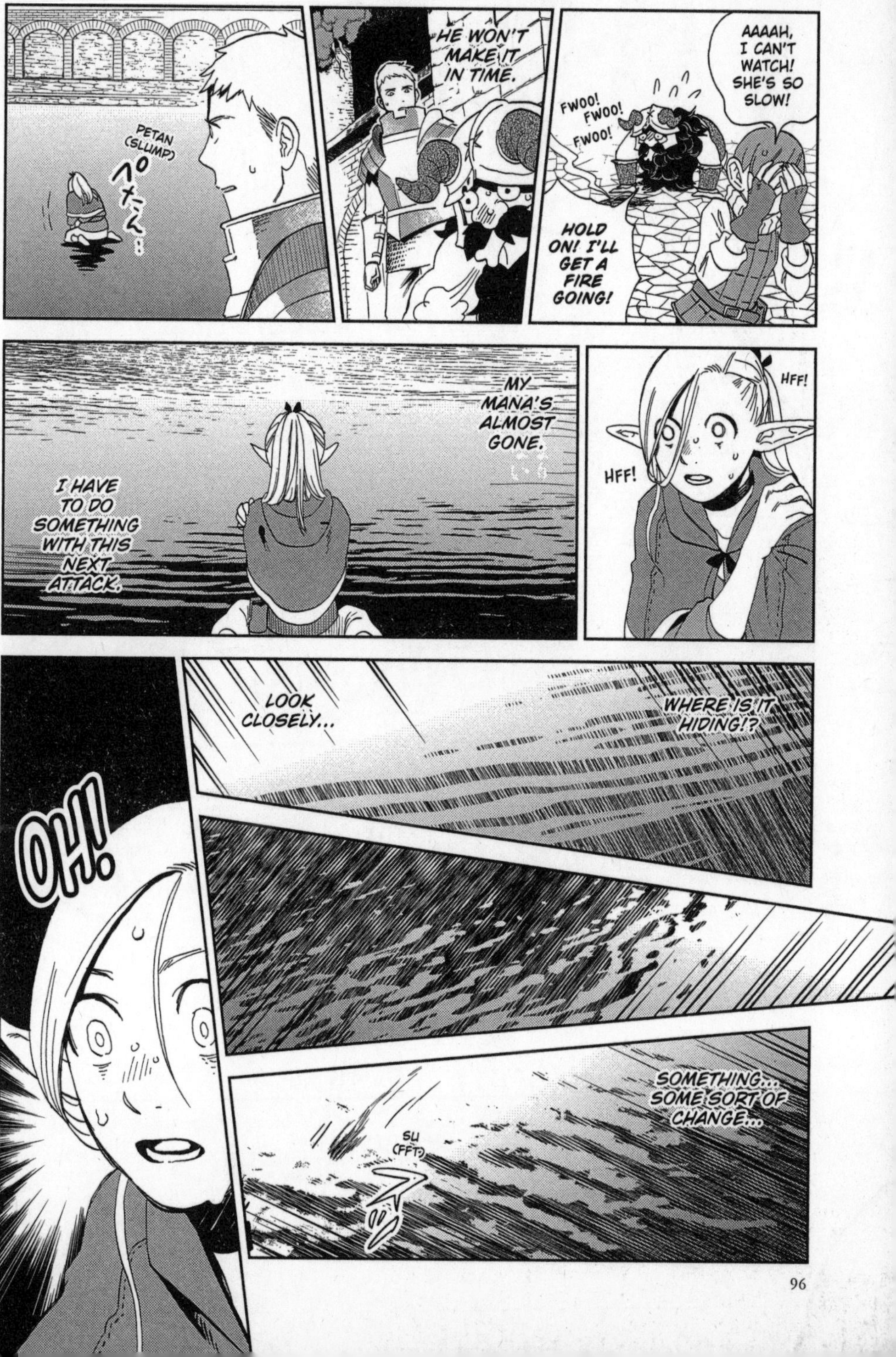
AAAAH, I CAN'T WATCH! SHE'S SO SLOW!
FWOO! FWOO! FWOO!
HOLD ON! I'LL GET A FIRE GOING!
HE WON'T MAKE IT IN TIME.
PETAN (SLUMP)
ぺたん…
HFF!
HFF!
MY MANA'S ALMOST GONE.
I HAVE TO DO SOMETHING WITH THIS NEXT ATTACK.
WHERE IS IT HIDING!?
LOOK CLOSELY...
SOMETHING... SOME SORT OF CHANGE...
SU (FFT)
OH!

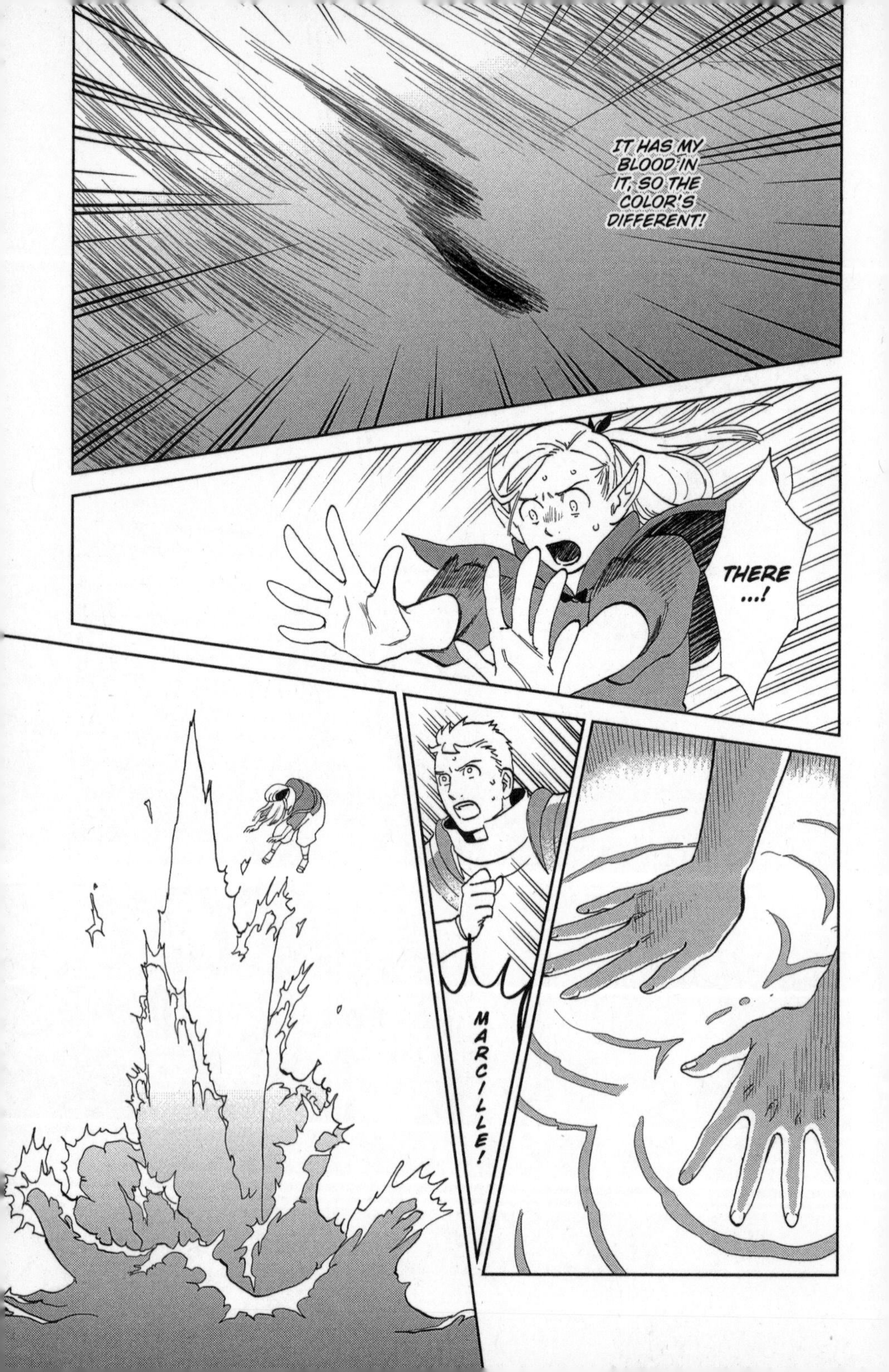
IT HAS MY BLOOD IN IT, SO THE COLOR'S DIFFERENT!
THERE ...!
MARCILLE!

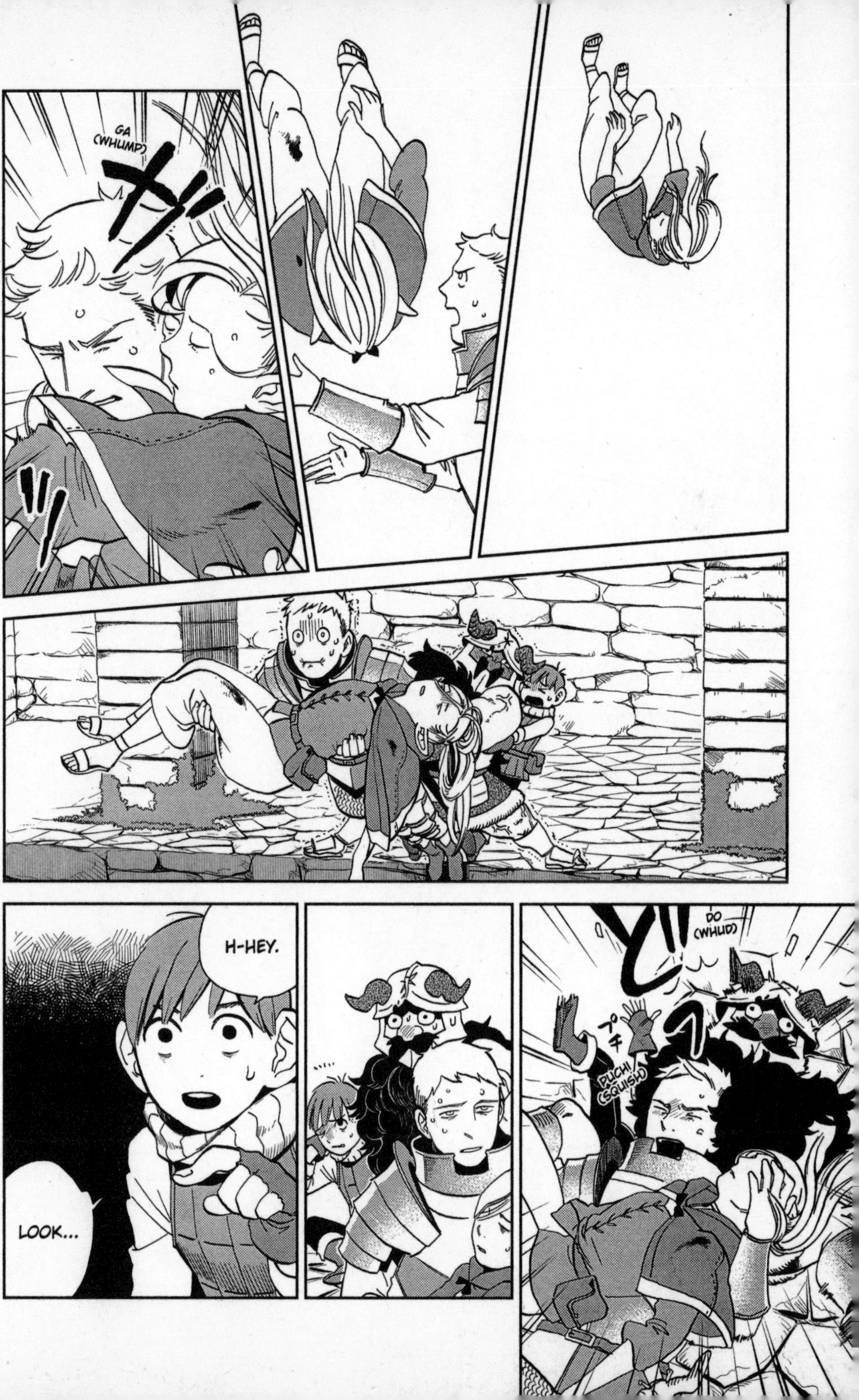
GA (WHUMP)
DO (WHUD)
PUCHI (SQUISH)
H-HEY.
LOOK...

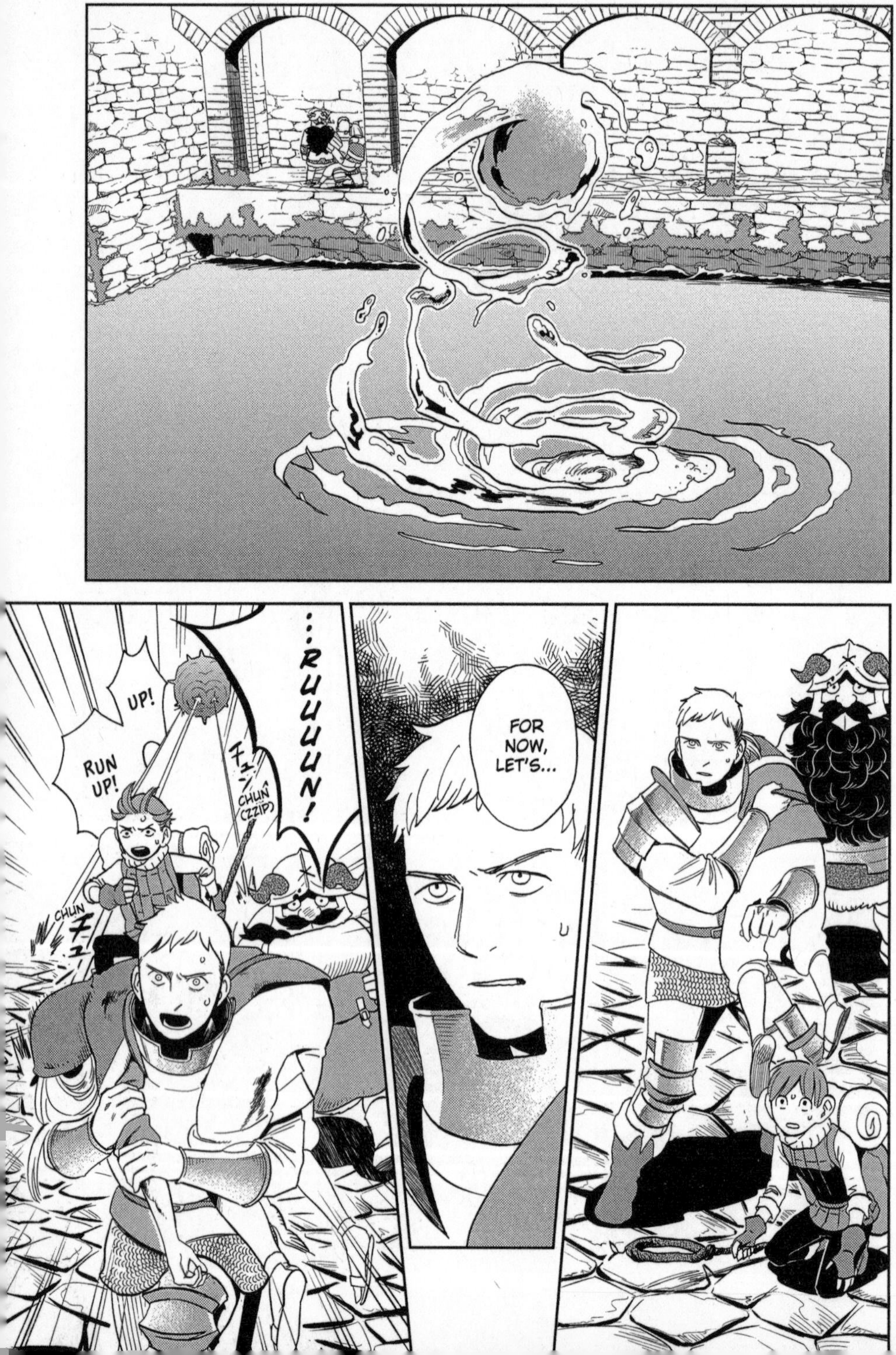
FOR NOW, LET'S...
...RUUUUUN!
UP!
RUN UP!
チュン CHUN (ZZIP)
CHUN チュ

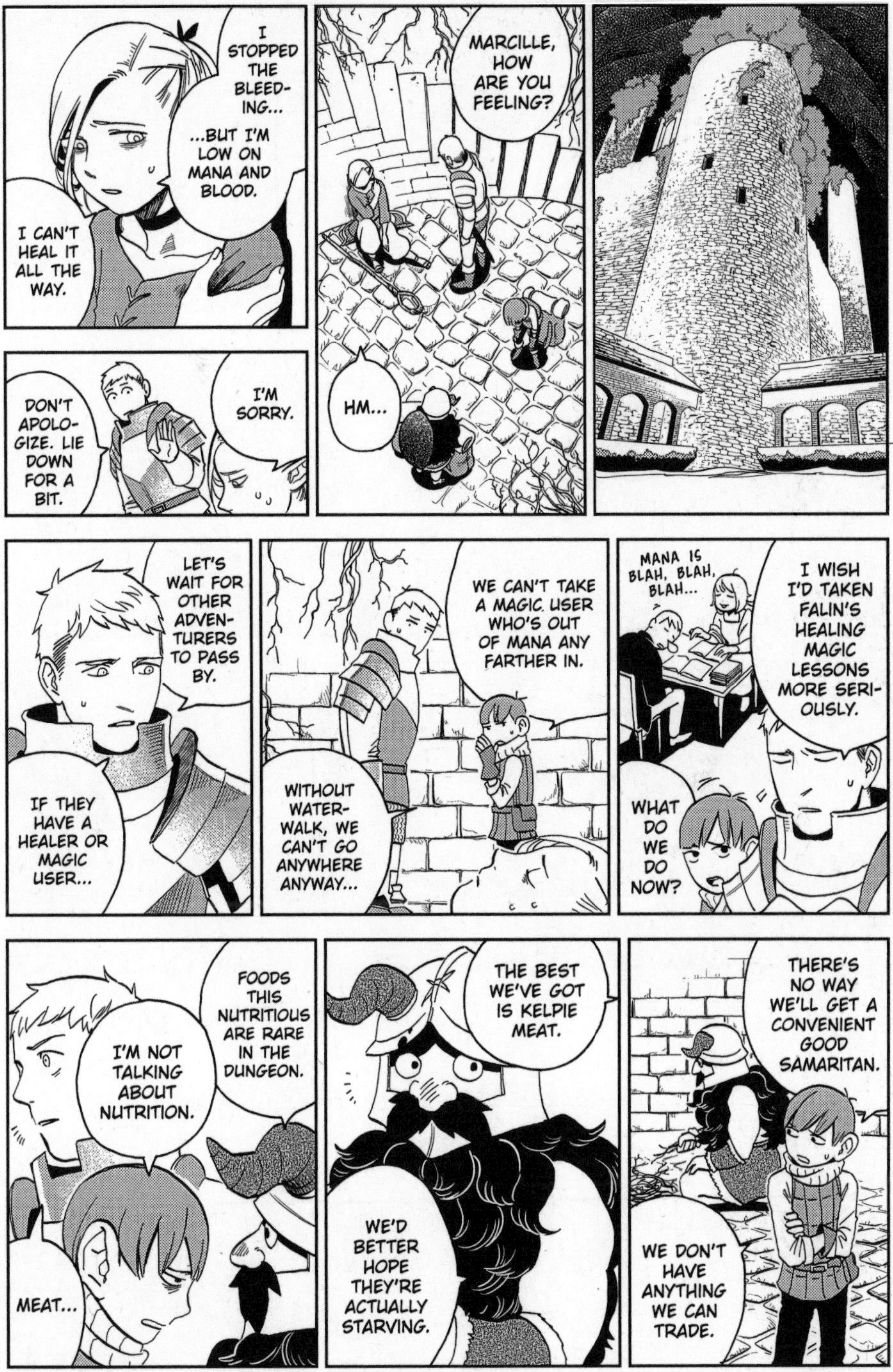
MARCILLE, HOW ARE YOU FEELING?
HM...
I STOPPED THE BLEEDING...
...BUT I'M LOW ON MANA AND BLOOD.
I CAN'T HEAL IT ALL THE WAY.
I'M SORRY.
DON'T APOLOGIZE. LIE DOWN FOR A BIT.
I WISH I'D TAKEN FALIN'S HEALING MAGIC LESSONS MORE SERIOUSLY.
MANA IS BLAH, BLAH, BLAH...
WHAT DO WE DO NOW?
WE CAN'T TAKE A MAGIC USER WHO'S OUT OF MANA ANY FARTHER IN.
WITHOUT WATER-WALK, WE CAN'T GO ANYWHERE ANYWAY...
LET'S WAIT FOR OTHER ADVENTURERS TO PASS BY.
IF THEY HAVE A HEALER OR MAGIC USER...
THERE'S NO WAY WE'LL GET A CONVENIENT GOOD SAMARITAN.
WE DON'T HAVE ANYTHING WE CAN TRADE.
THE BEST WE'VE GOT IS KELPIE MEAT.
WE'D BETTER HOPE THEY'RE ACTUALLY STARVING.
FOODS THIS NUTRITIOUS ARE RARE IN THE DUNGEON.
I'M NOT TALKING ABOUT NUTRITION.
MEAT...

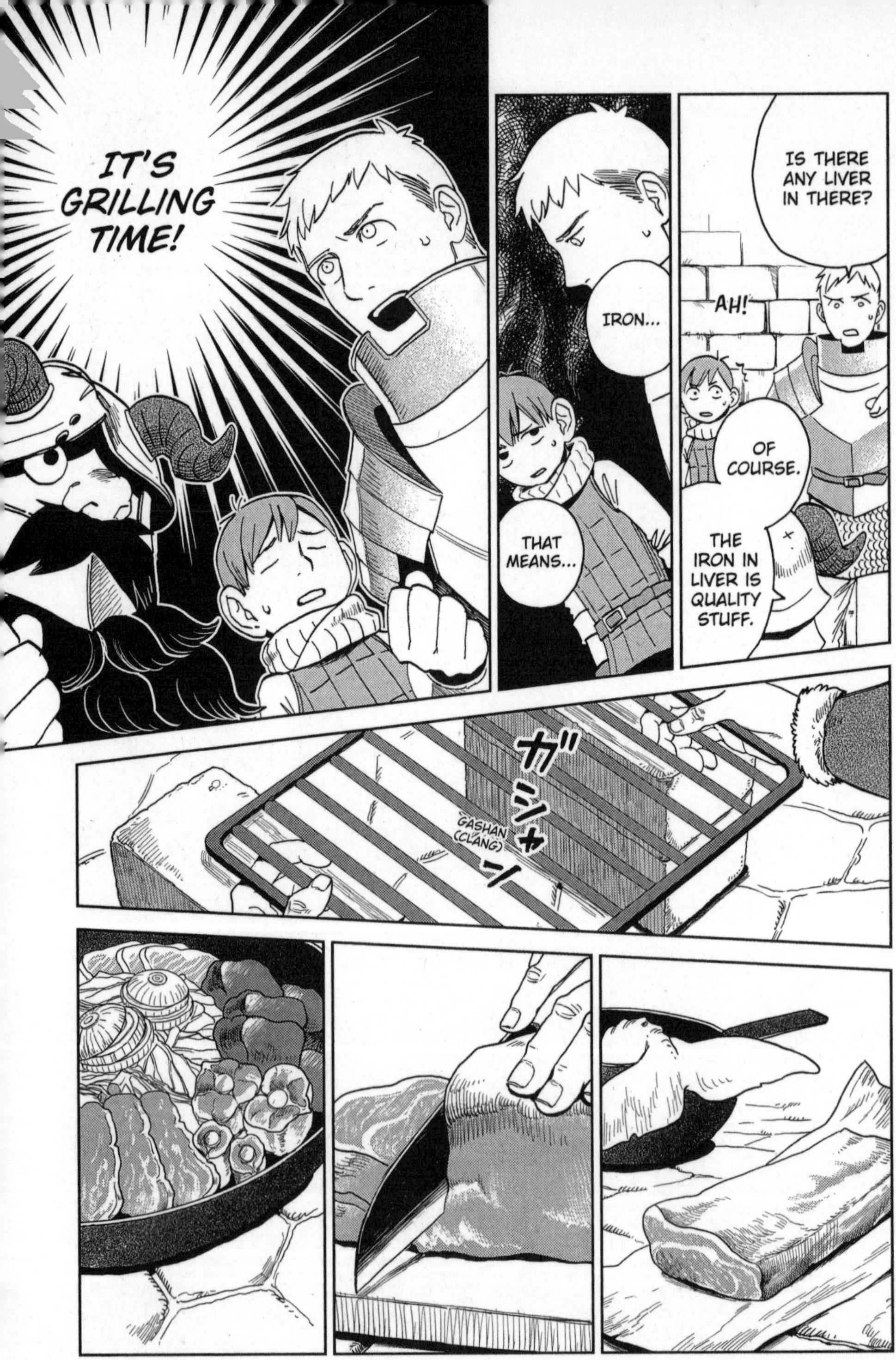
IS THERE ANY LIVER IN THERE?
AH!
OF COURSE.
THE IRON IN LIVER IS QUALITY STUFF.
IRON...
THAT MEANS...
IT'S GRILLING TIME!
ガシャン
GASHAN (CLANG)

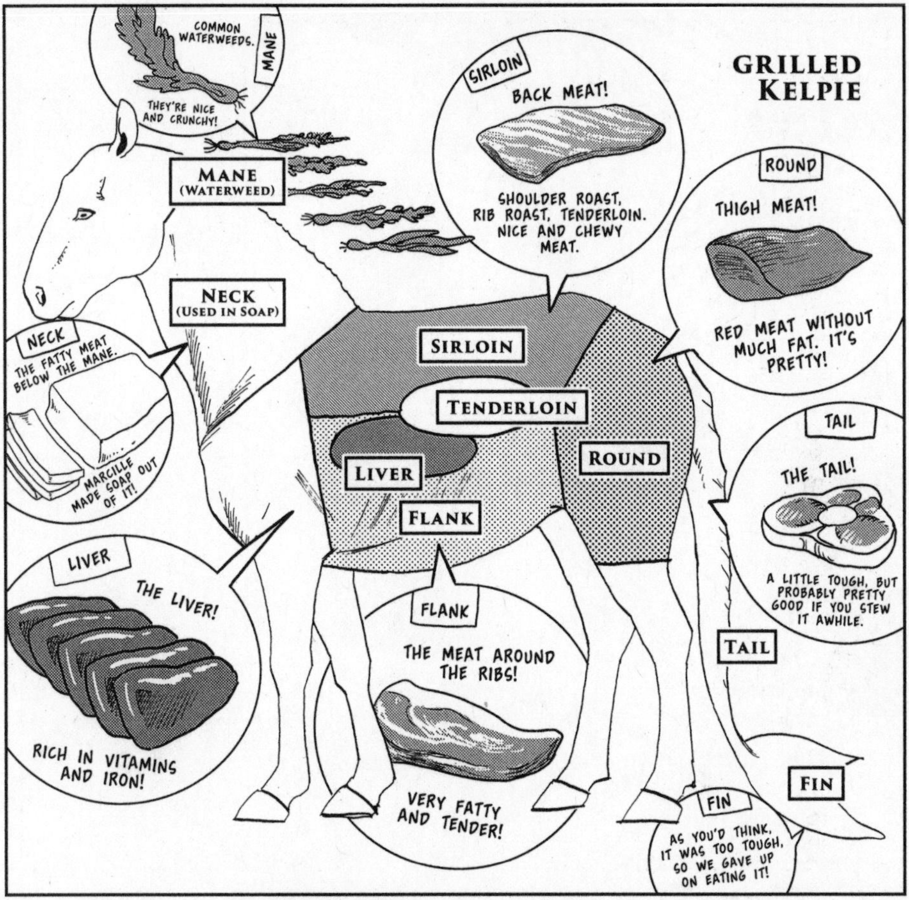
GRILLED KELPIE
SIRLOIN
BACK MEAT!
SHOULDER ROAST, RIB ROAST, TENDERLOIN. NICE AND CHEWY MEAT.
MANE
COMMON WATERWEEDS.
THEY'RE NICE AND CRUNCHY!
MANE (WATERWEED)
ROUND
THIGH MEAT!
RED MEAT WITHOUT MUCH FAT. IT'S PRETTY!
NECK (USED IN SOAP)
NECK
THE FATTY MEAT BELOW THE MANE.
MARCILLE MADE SOAP OUT OF IT!
SIRLOIN
TENDERLOIN
ROUND
LIVER
FLANK
TAIL
THE TAIL!
A LITTLE TOUGH, BUT PROBABLY PRETTY GOOD IF YOU STEW IT AWHILE.
TAIL
FLANK
THE MEAT AROUND THE RIBS!
VERY FATTY AND TENDER!
LIVER
THE LIVER!
RICH IN VITAMINS AND IRON!
FIN
FIN
AS YOU'D THINK, IT WAS TOO TOUGH, SO WE GAVE UP ON EATING IT!

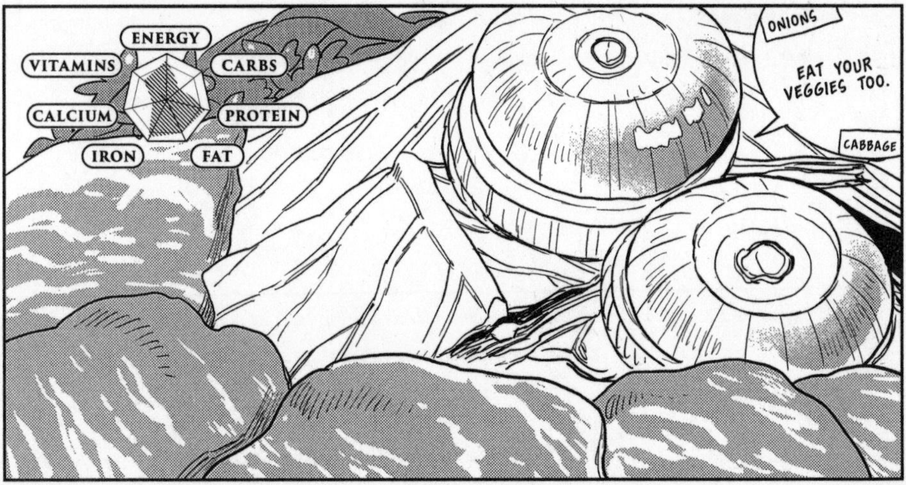
ONIONS
EAT YOUR VEGGIES TOO.
CABBAGE
ENERGY
VITAMINS
CARBS
CALCIUM
PROTEIN
IRON
FAT

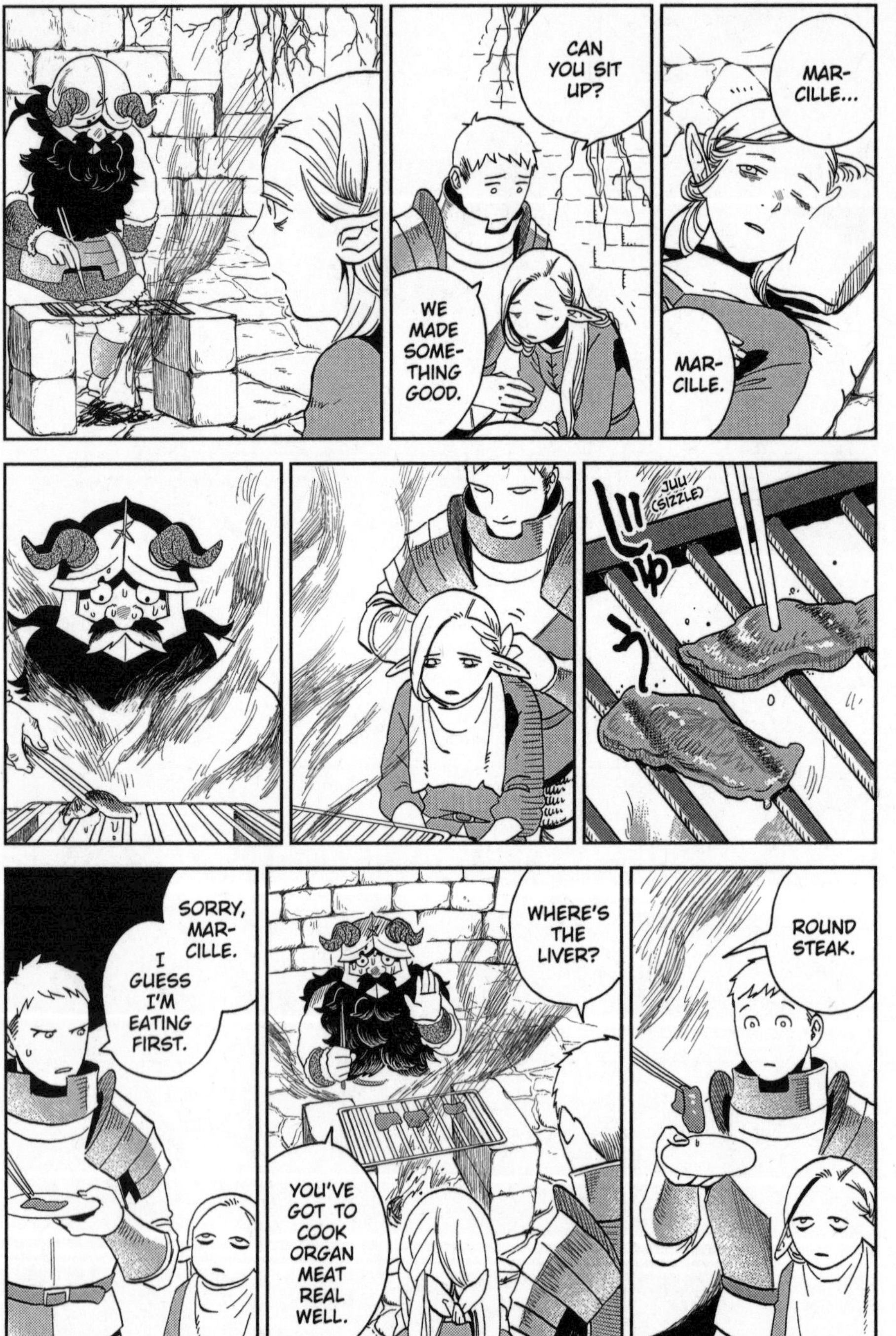
MAR-CILLE...
.....
MAR-CILLE.
CAN YOU SIT UP?
WE MADE SOME-THING GOOD.
JUU (SIZZLE)
じゅう
ROUND STEAK.
WHERE'S THE LIVER?
YOU'VE GOT TO COOK ORGAN MEAT REAL WELL.
SORRY, MAR-CILLE.
I GUESS I'M EATING FIRST.

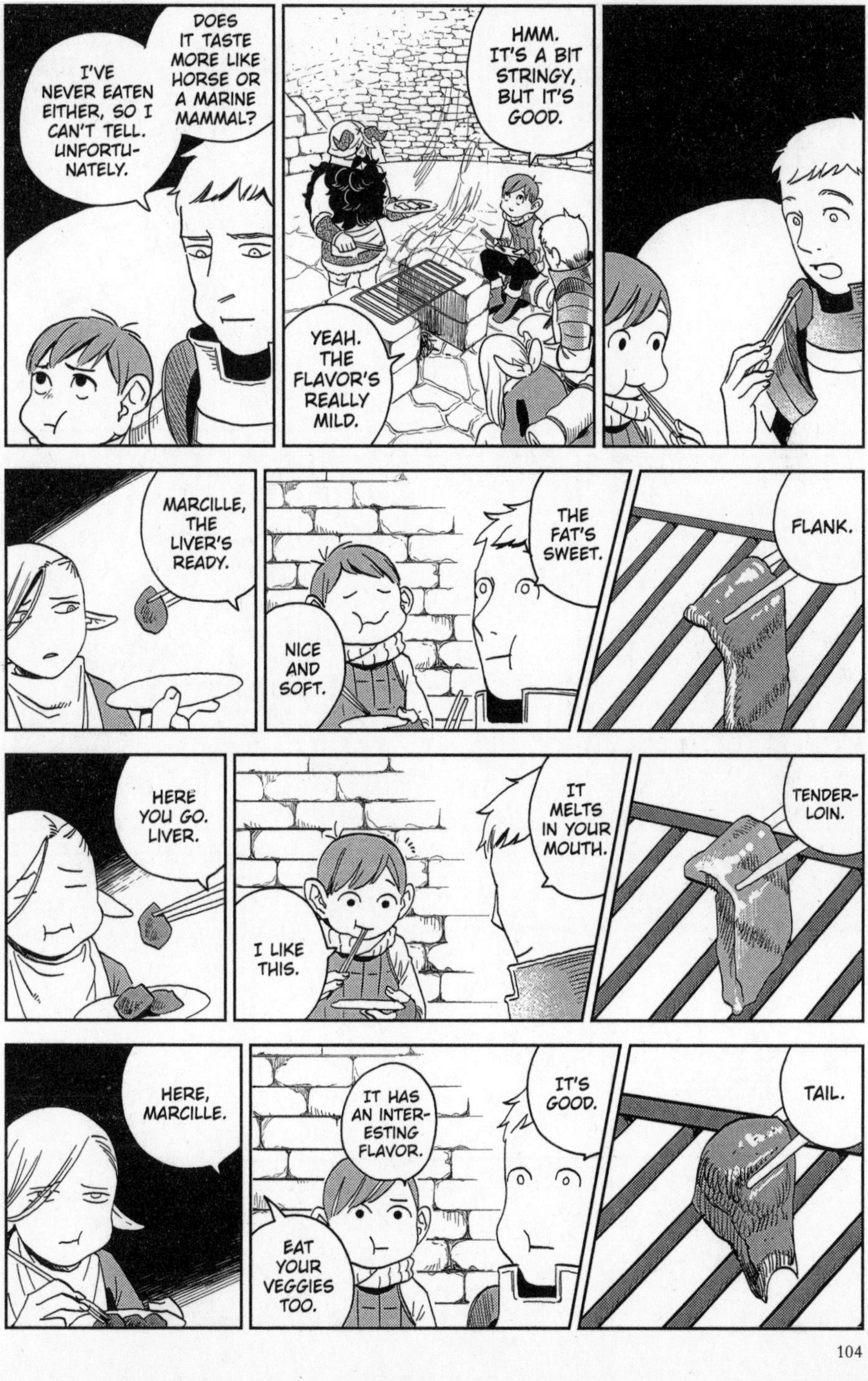
HMM. IT'S A BIT STRINGY, BUT IT'S GOOD.
YEAH. THE FLAVOR'S REALLY MILD.
DOES IT TASTE MORE LIKE HORSE OR A MARINE MAMMAL?
I'VE NEVER EATEN EITHER, SO I CAN'T TELL. UNFORTUNATELY.
FLANK.
THE FAT'S SWEET.
NICE AND SOFT.
MARCILLE, THE LIVER'S READY.
TENDERLOIN.
IT MELTS IN YOUR MOUTH.
I LIKE THIS.
HERE YOU GO. LIVER.
TAIL.
IT'S GOOD.
IT HAS AN INTERESTING FLAVOR.
EAT YOUR VEGGIES TOO.
HERE, MARCILLE.

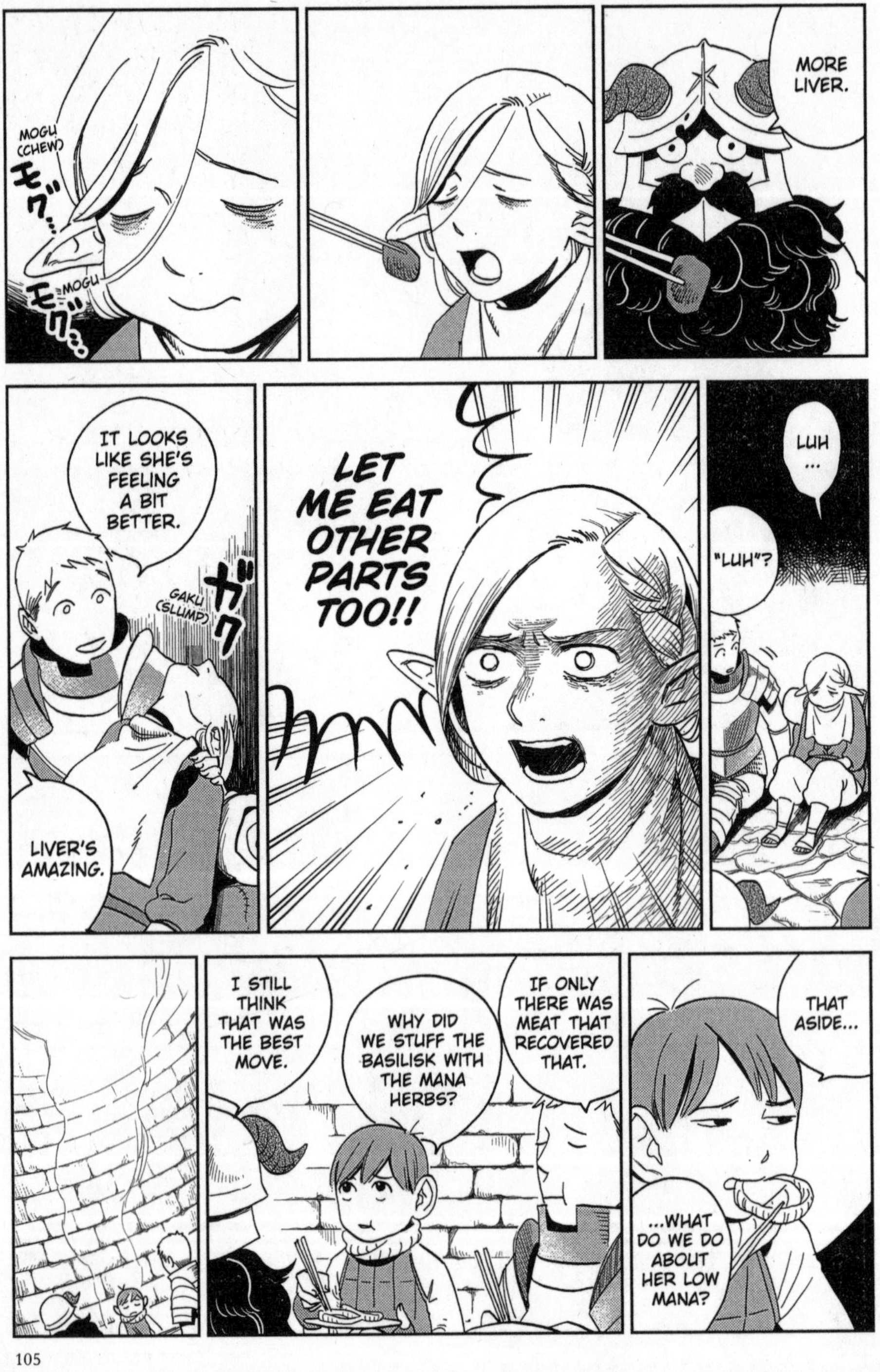
MORE LIVER.
MOGU (CHEW)
モグ…
MOGU
モグ…
LUH ...
"LUH"?
LET ME EAT OTHER PARTS TOO!!
IT LOOKS LIKE SHE'S FEELING A BIT BETTER.
GAKU (SLUMP)
ガク
LIVER'S AMAZING.
THAT ASIDE...
...WHAT DO WE DO ABOUT HER LOW MANA?
IF ONLY THERE WAS MEAT THAT RECOVERED THAT.
WHY DID WE STUFF THE BASILISK WITH THE MANA HERBS?
I STILL THINK THAT WAS THE BEST MOVE.

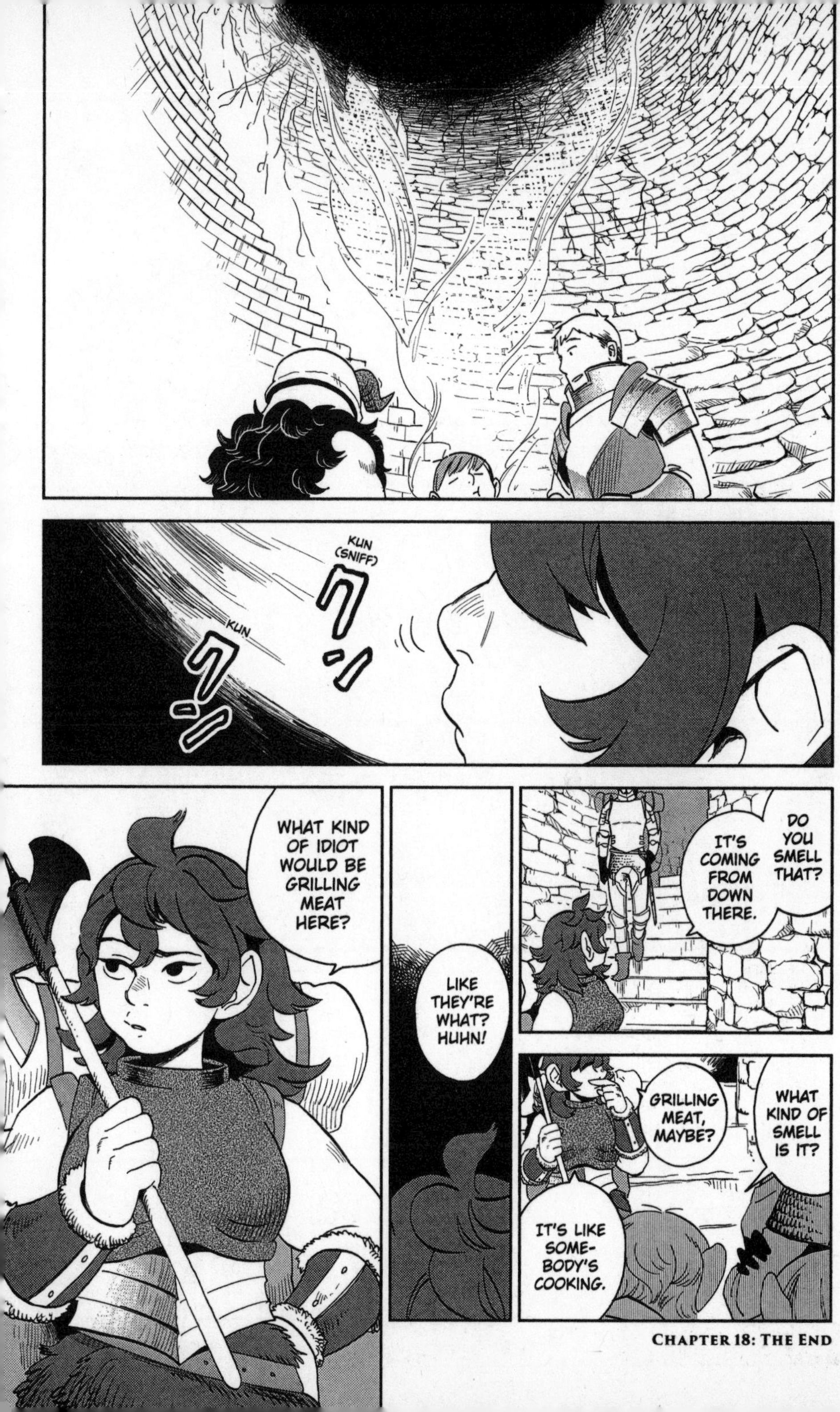
KUN (SNIFF)
KUN
DO YOU SMELL THAT?
IT'S COMING FROM DOWN THERE.
WHAT KIND OF SMELL IS IT?
GRILLING MEAT, MAYBE?
IT'S LIKE SOME-BODY'S COOKING.
LIKE THEY'RE WHAT? HUHN!
WHAT KIND OF IDIOT WOULD BE GRILLING MEAT HERE?

CHAPTER 18: THE END

19. TENTACLES

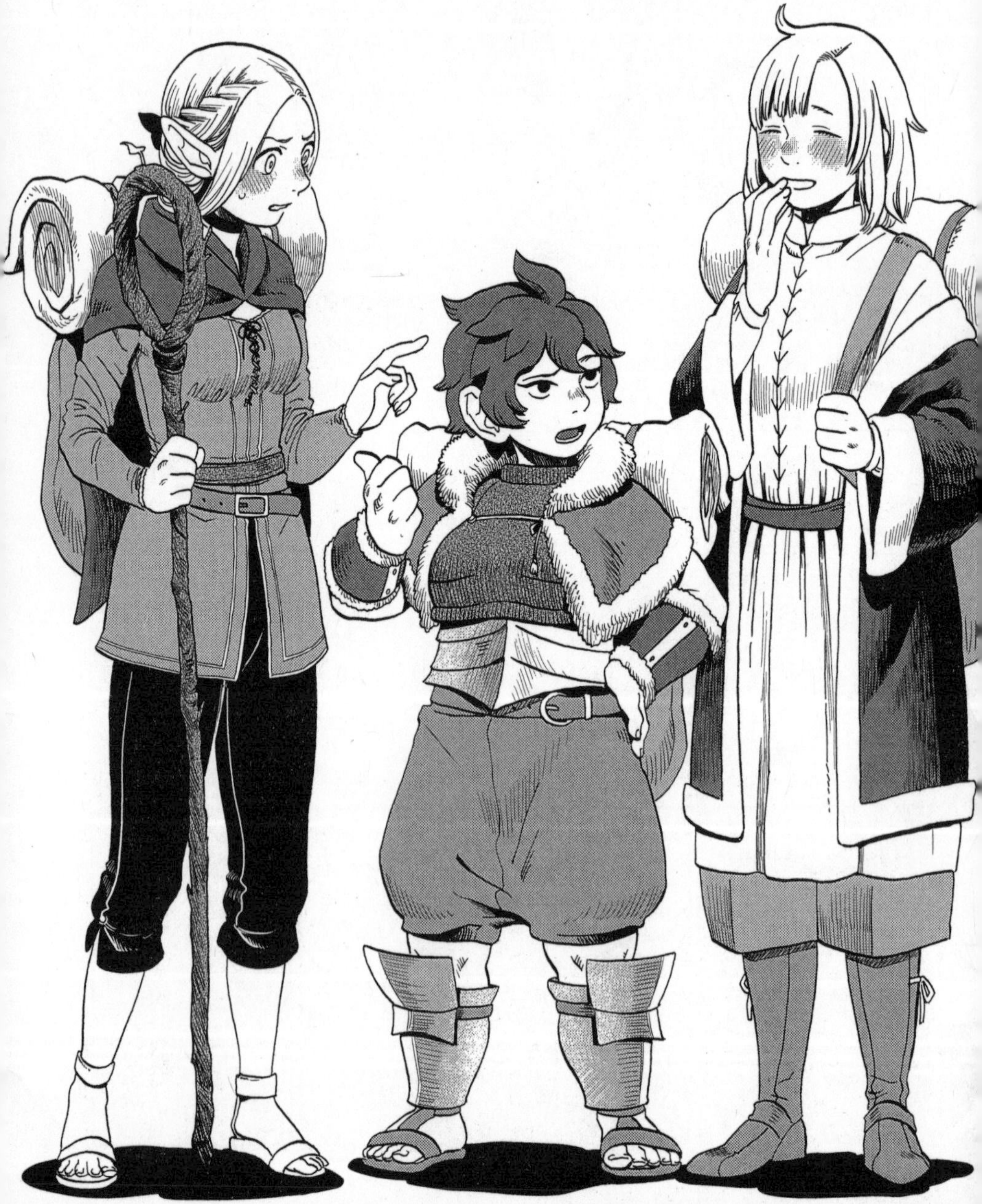

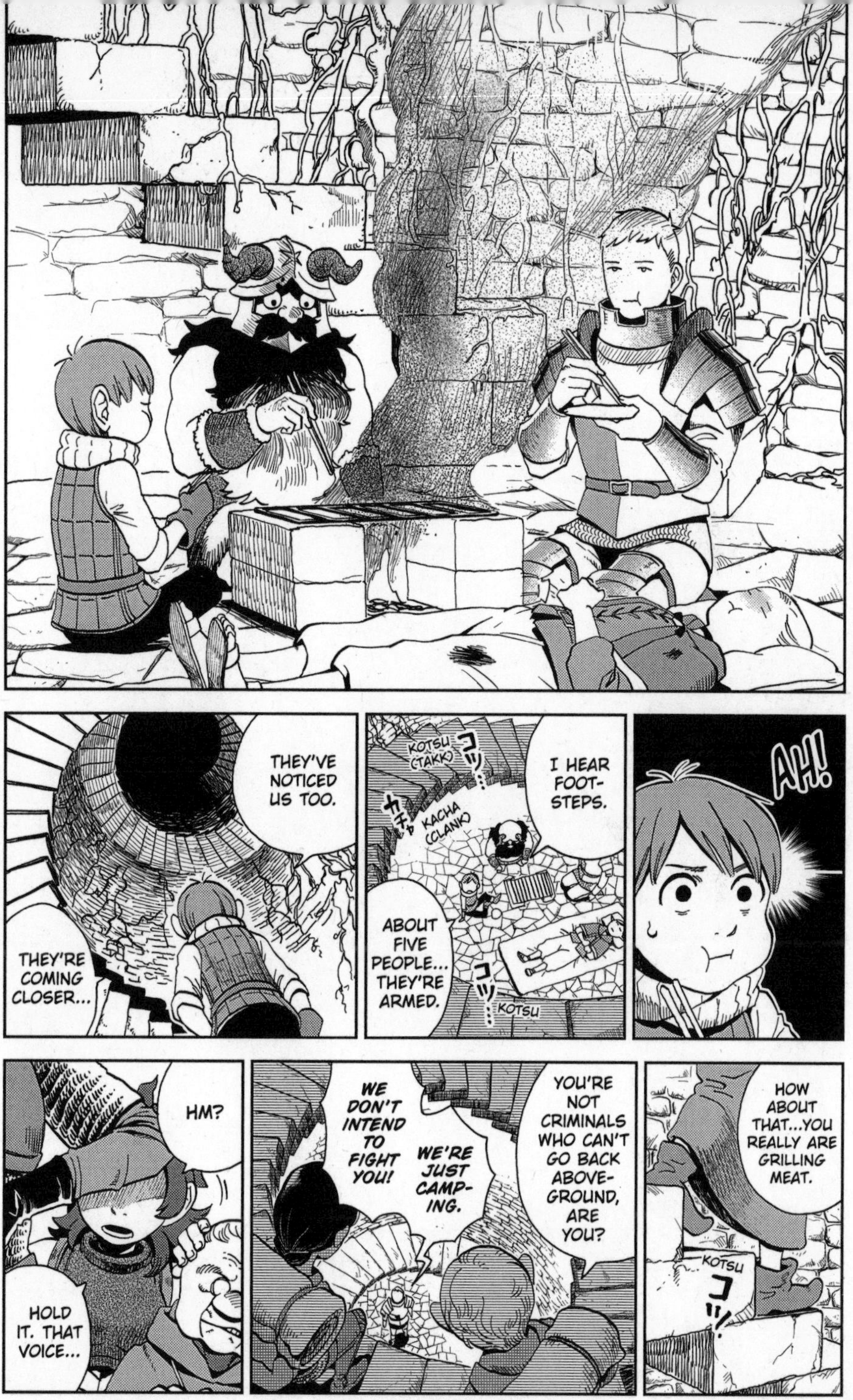
AH!
KOTSU (TAKK)
I HEAR FOOT-STEPS.
KACHA (CLANK)
ABOUT FIVE PEOPLE... THEY'RE ARMED.
KOTSU
THEY'VE NOTICED US TOO.
THEY'RE COMING CLOSER...
HOW ABOUT THAT...YOU REALLY ARE GRILLING MEAT.
KOTSU
YOU'RE NOT CRIMINALS WHO CAN'T GO BACK ABOVE-GROUND, ARE YOU?
WE'RE JUST CAMP-ING.
WE DON'T INTEND TO FIGHT YOU!
HM?
HOLD IT. THAT VOICE...

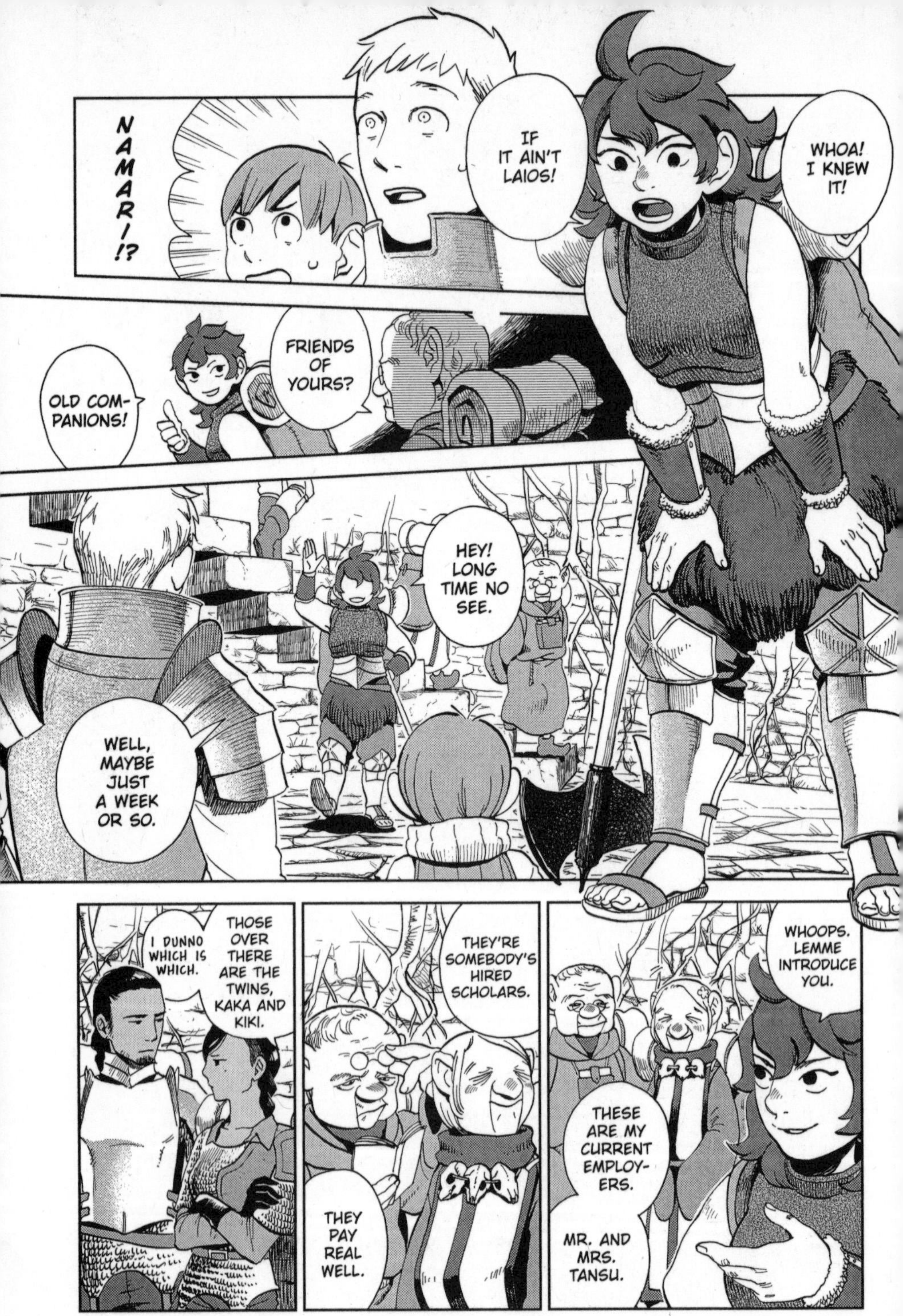
WHOA! I KNEW IT!
IF IT AIN'T LAIOS!
NAMARI!?
FRIENDS OF YOURS?
OLD COMPANIONS!
HEY! LONG TIME NO SEE.
WELL, MAYBE JUST A WEEK OR SO.
WHOOPS. LEMME INTRODUCE YOU.
THESE ARE MY CURRENT EMPLOYERS.
MR. AND MRS. TANSU.
THEY'RE SOMEBODY'S HIRED SCHOLARS.
THEY PAY REAL WELL.
THOSE OVER THERE ARE THE TWINS, KAKA AND KIKI.
I DUNNO WHICH IS WHICH.

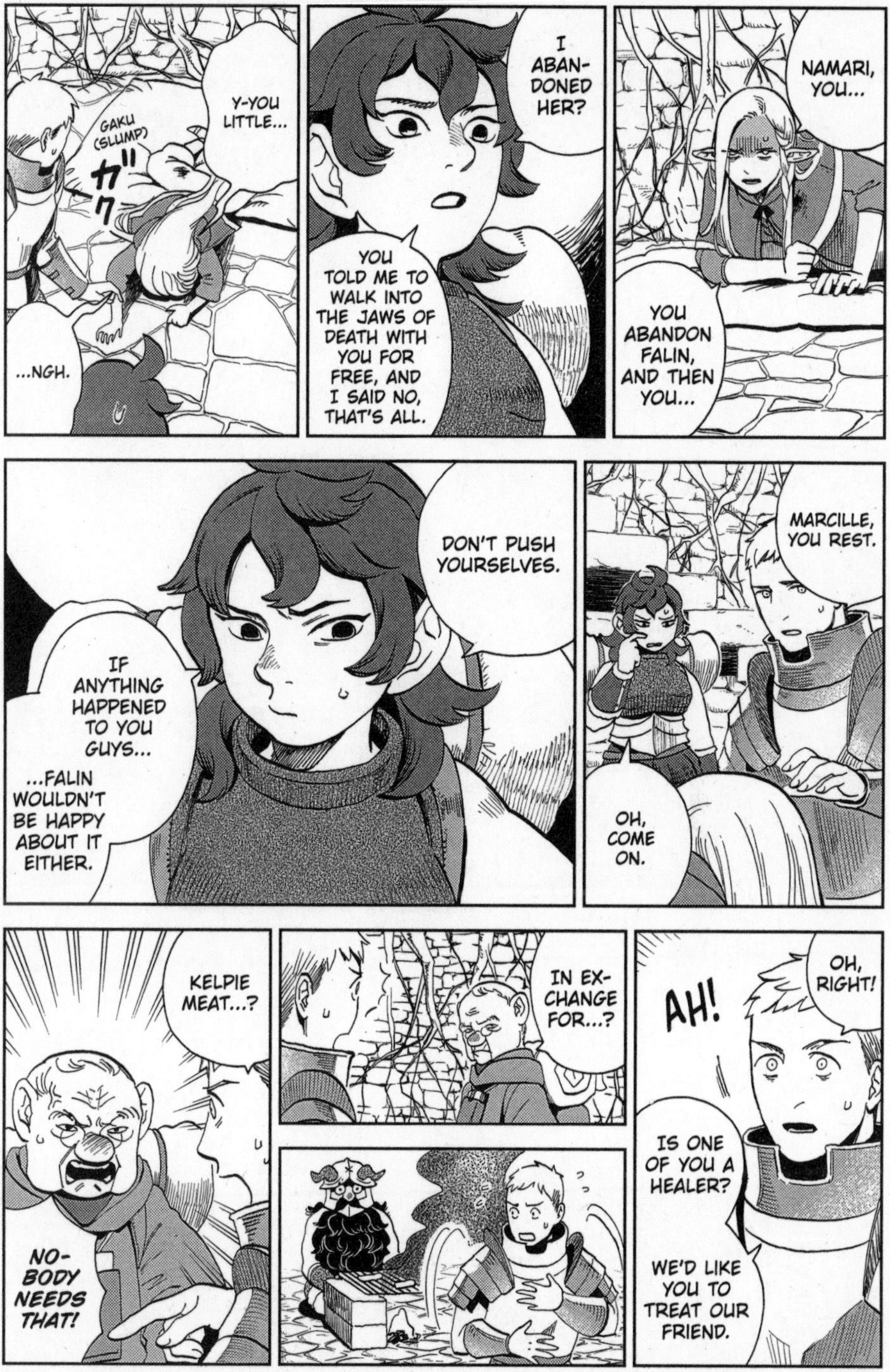
NAMARI, YOU...
YOU ABANDON FALIN, AND THEN YOU...
I ABAN-DONED HER?
YOU TOLD ME TO WALK INTO THE JAWS OF DEATH WITH YOU FOR FREE, AND I SAID NO, THAT'S ALL.
Y-YOU LITTLE...
GAKU (SLUMP)
ガク
...NGH.
MARCILLE, YOU REST.
OH, COME ON.
DON'T PUSH YOURSELVES.
IF ANYTHING HAPPENED TO YOU GUYS...
...FALIN WOULDN'T BE HAPPY ABOUT IT EITHER.
OH, RIGHT!
AH!
IS ONE OF YOU A HEALER?
WE'D LIKE YOU TO TREAT OUR FRIEND.
IN EX-CHANGE FOR...?
KELPIE MEAT...?
NO-BODY NEEDS THAT!

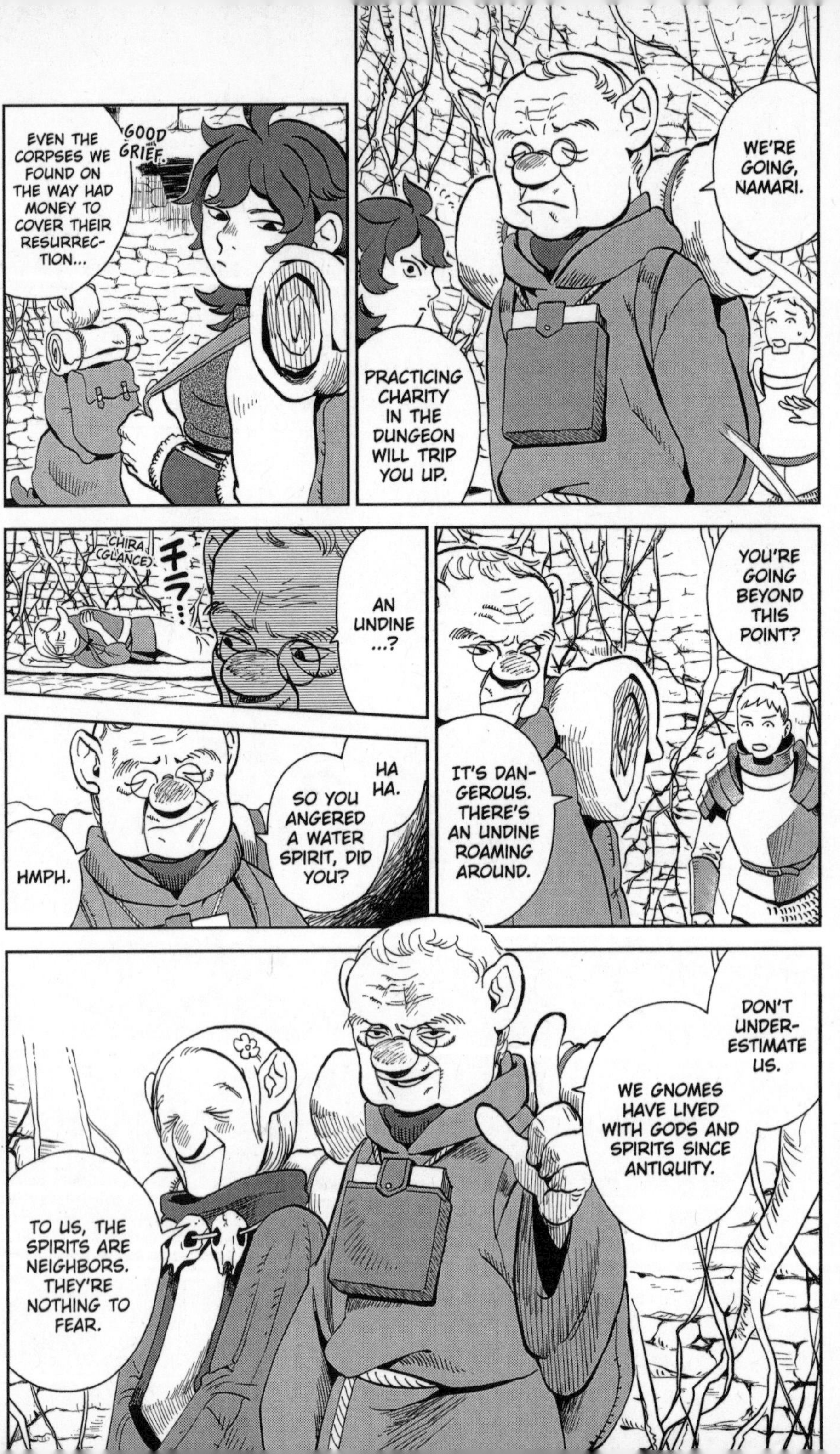
WE'RE GOING, NAMARI.
PRACTICING CHARITY IN THE DUNGEON WILL TRIP YOU UP.
GOOD GRIEF.
EVEN THE CORPSES WE FOUND ON THE WAY HAD MONEY TO COVER THEIR RESURREC-TION...
YOU'RE GOING BEYOND THIS POINT?
IT'S DAN-GEROUS. THERE'S AN UNDINE ROAMING AROUND.
チラ
CHIRA (GLANCE)
AN UNDINE ...?
HA HA.
SO YOU ANGERED A WATER SPIRIT, DID YOU?
HMPH.
DON'T UNDER-ESTIMATE US.
WE GNOMES HAVE LIVED WITH GODS AND SPIRITS SINCE ANTIQUITY.
TO US, THE SPIRITS ARE NEIGHBORS. THEY'RE NOTHING TO FEAR.

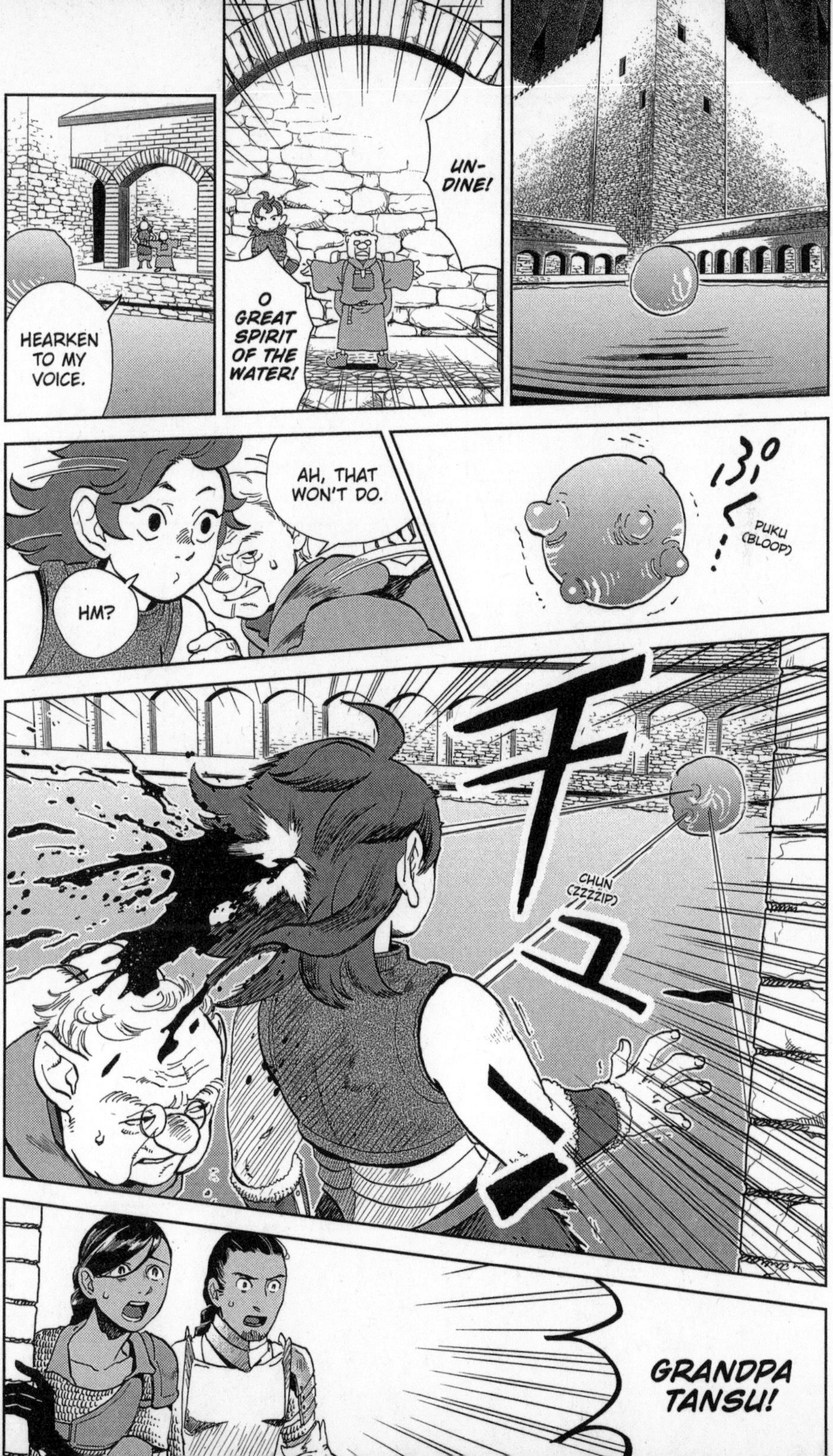
UN-DINE!
O GREAT SPIRIT OF THE WATER!
HEARKEN TO MY VOICE.
ぷく…
PUKU (BLOOP)
AH, THAT WON'T DO.
HM?
チュン
CHUN (ZZZZIP)
GRANDPA TANSU!

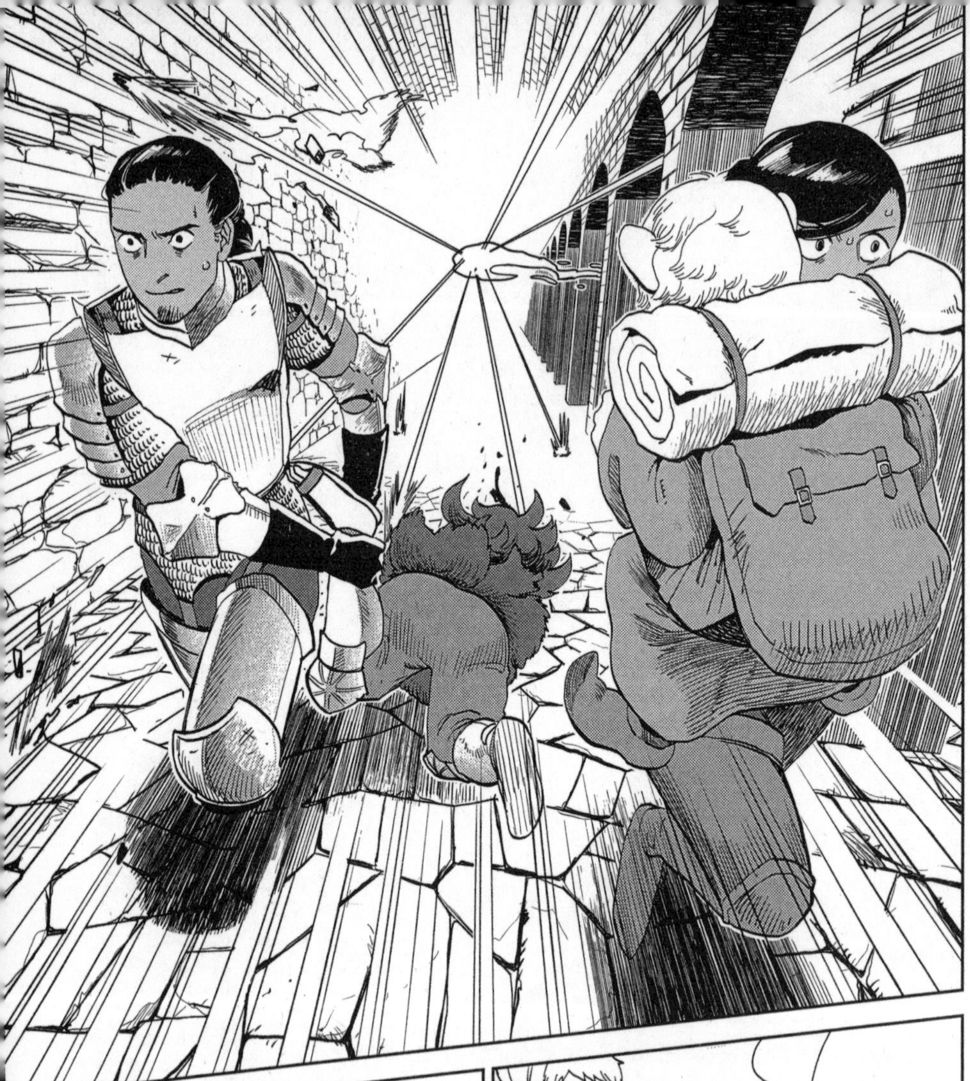

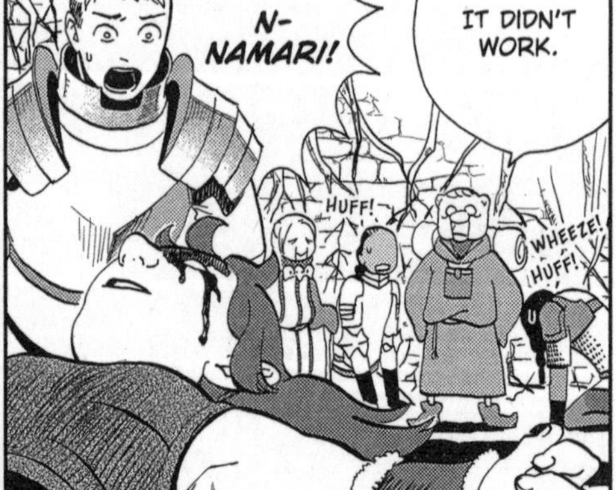
IT DIDN'T WORK.
N-NAMARI!
HUFF!
WHEEZE! HUFF!

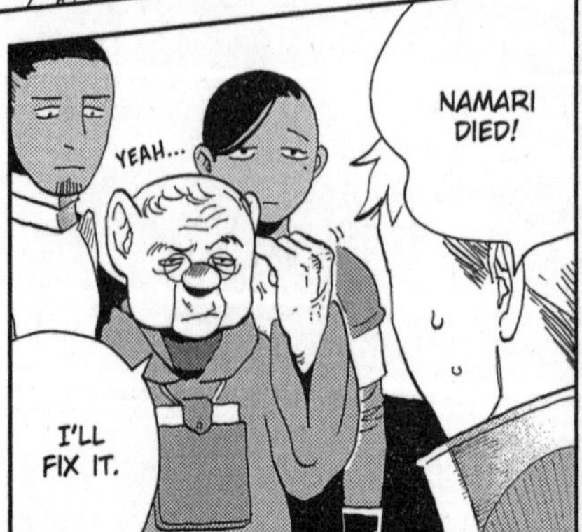
NAMARI DIED!
YEAH...
I'LL FIX IT.

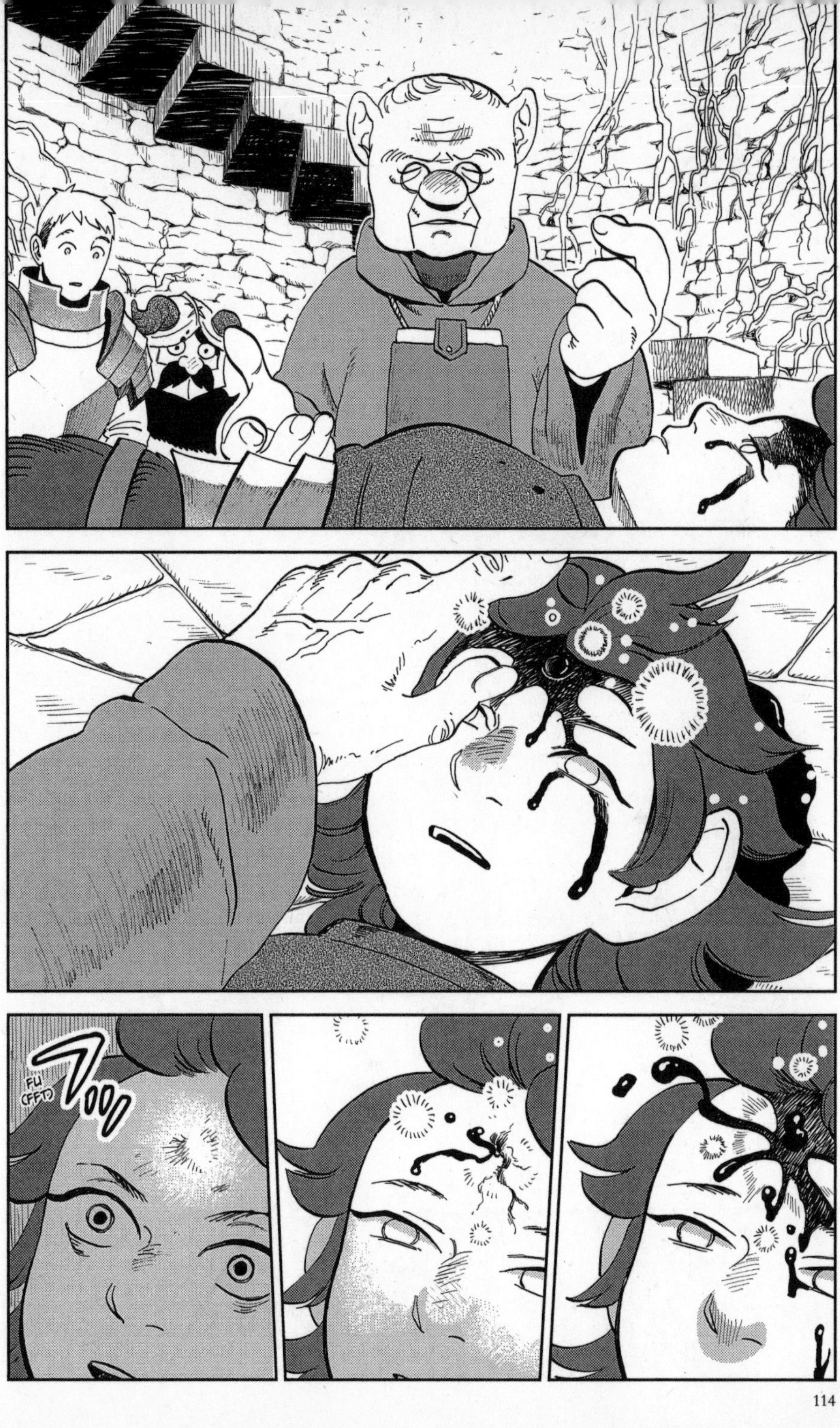
FU (FFT)

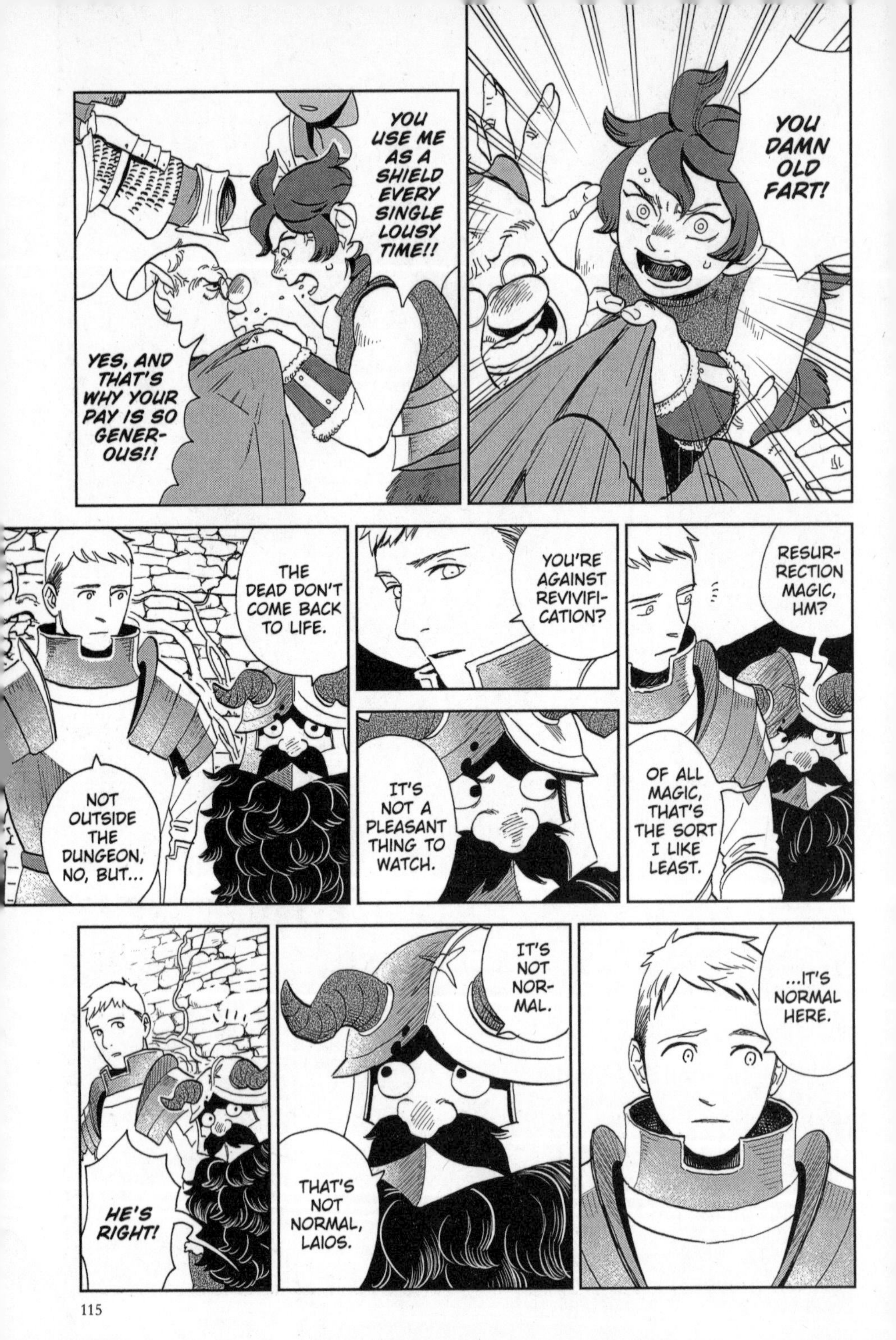
YOU DAMN OLD FART!
YOU USE ME AS A SHIELD EVERY SINGLE LOUSY TIME!!
YES, AND THAT'S WHY YOUR PAY IS SO GENER-OUS!!
RESUR-RECTION MAGIC, HM?
OF ALL MAGIC, THAT'S THE SORT I LIKE LEAST.
YOU'RE AGAINST REVIVIFI-CATION?
IT'S NOT A PLEASANT THING TO WATCH.
THE DEAD DON'T COME BACK TO LIFE.
NOT OUTSIDE THE DUNGEON, NO, BUT...
...IT'S NORMAL HERE.
IT'S NOT NOR-MAL.
THAT'S NOT NORMAL, LAIOS.
HE'S RIGHT!

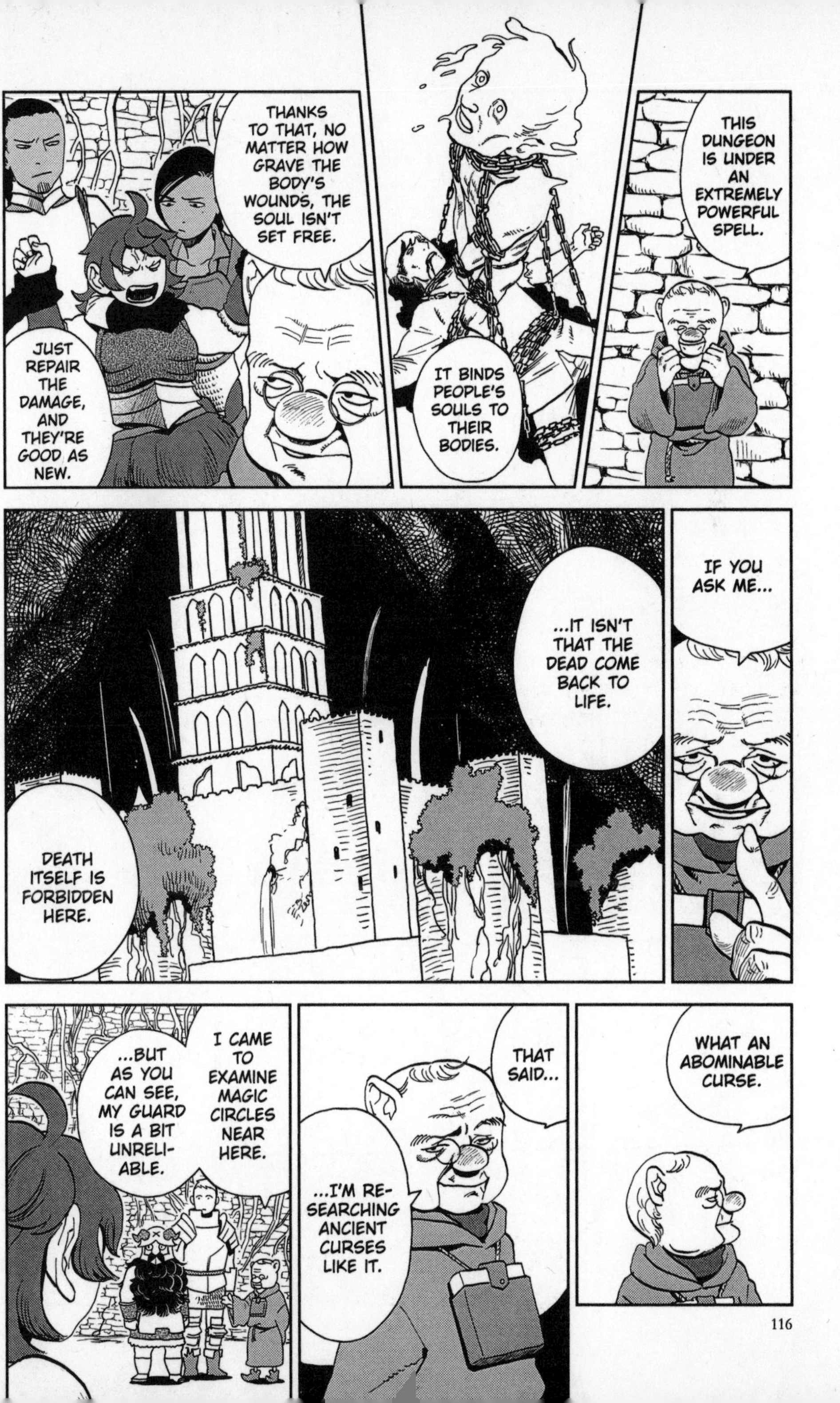
THIS DUNGEON IS UNDER AN EXTREMELY POWERFUL SPELL.
IT BINDS PEOPLE'S SOULS TO THEIR BODIES.
THANKS TO THAT, NO MATTER HOW GRAVE THE BODY'S WOUNDS, THE SOUL ISN'T SET FREE.
JUST REPAIR THE DAMAGE, AND THEY'RE GOOD AS NEW.
IF YOU ASK ME...
...IT ISN'T THAT THE DEAD COME BACK TO LIFE.
DEATH ITSELF IS FORBIDDEN HERE.
WHAT AN ABOMINABLE CURSE.
THAT SAID...
...I'M RE-SEARCHING ANCIENT CURSES LIKE IT.
I CAME TO EXAMINE MAGIC CIRCLES NEAR HERE.
...BUT AS YOU CAN SEE, MY GUARD IS A BIT UNRELI-ABLE.

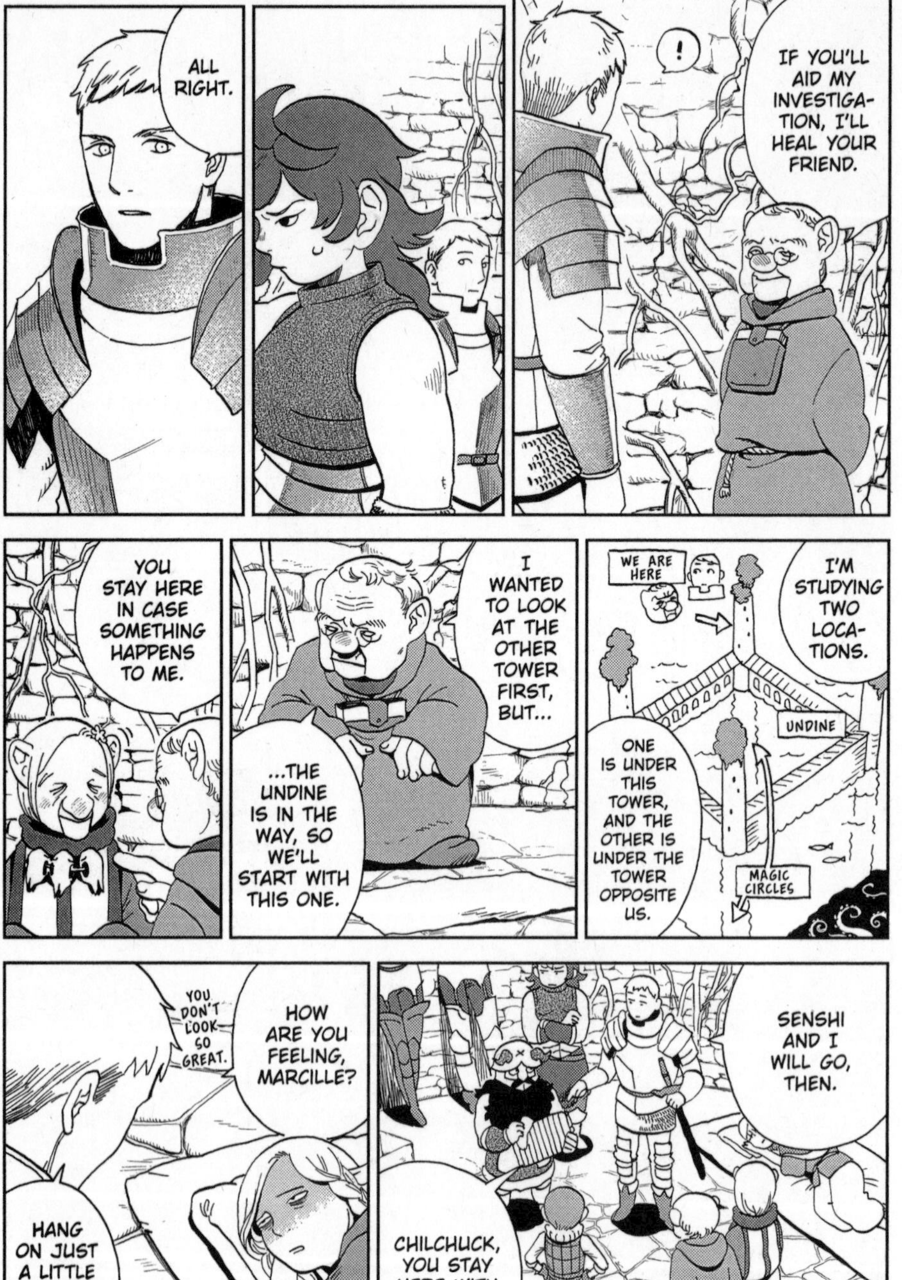
!
IF YOU'LL AID MY INVESTIGATION, I'LL HEAL YOUR FRIEND.
ALL RIGHT.
I'M STUDYING TWO LOCATIONS.
WE ARE HERE
UNDINE
ONE IS UNDER THIS TOWER, AND THE OTHER IS UNDER THE TOWER OPPOSITE US.
MAGIC CIRCLES
I WANTED TO LOOK AT THE OTHER TOWER FIRST, BUT...
...THE UNDINE IS IN THE WAY, SO WE'LL START WITH THIS ONE.
YOU STAY HERE IN CASE SOMETHING HAPPENS TO ME.
SENSHI AND I WILL GO, THEN.
CHILCHUCK, YOU STAY HERE WITH MARCILLE.
HOW ARE YOU FEELING, MARCILLE?
YOU DON'T LOOK SO GREAT.
HANG ON JUST A LITTLE LONGER, ALL RIGHT?

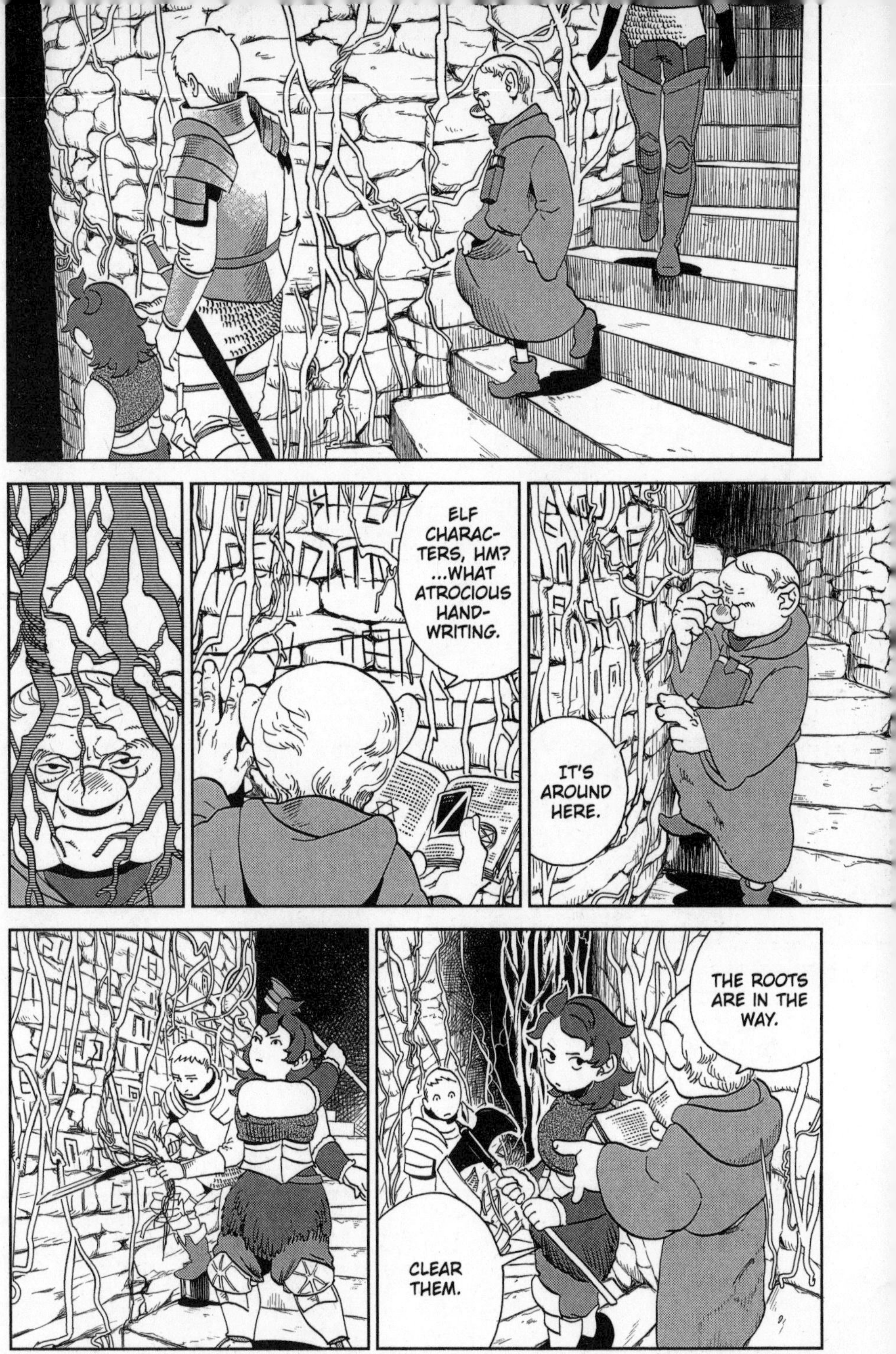
IT'S AROUND HERE.
ELF CHARACTERS, HM? ...WHAT ATROCIOUS HANDWRITING.
THE ROOTS ARE IN THE WAY.
CLEAR THEM.

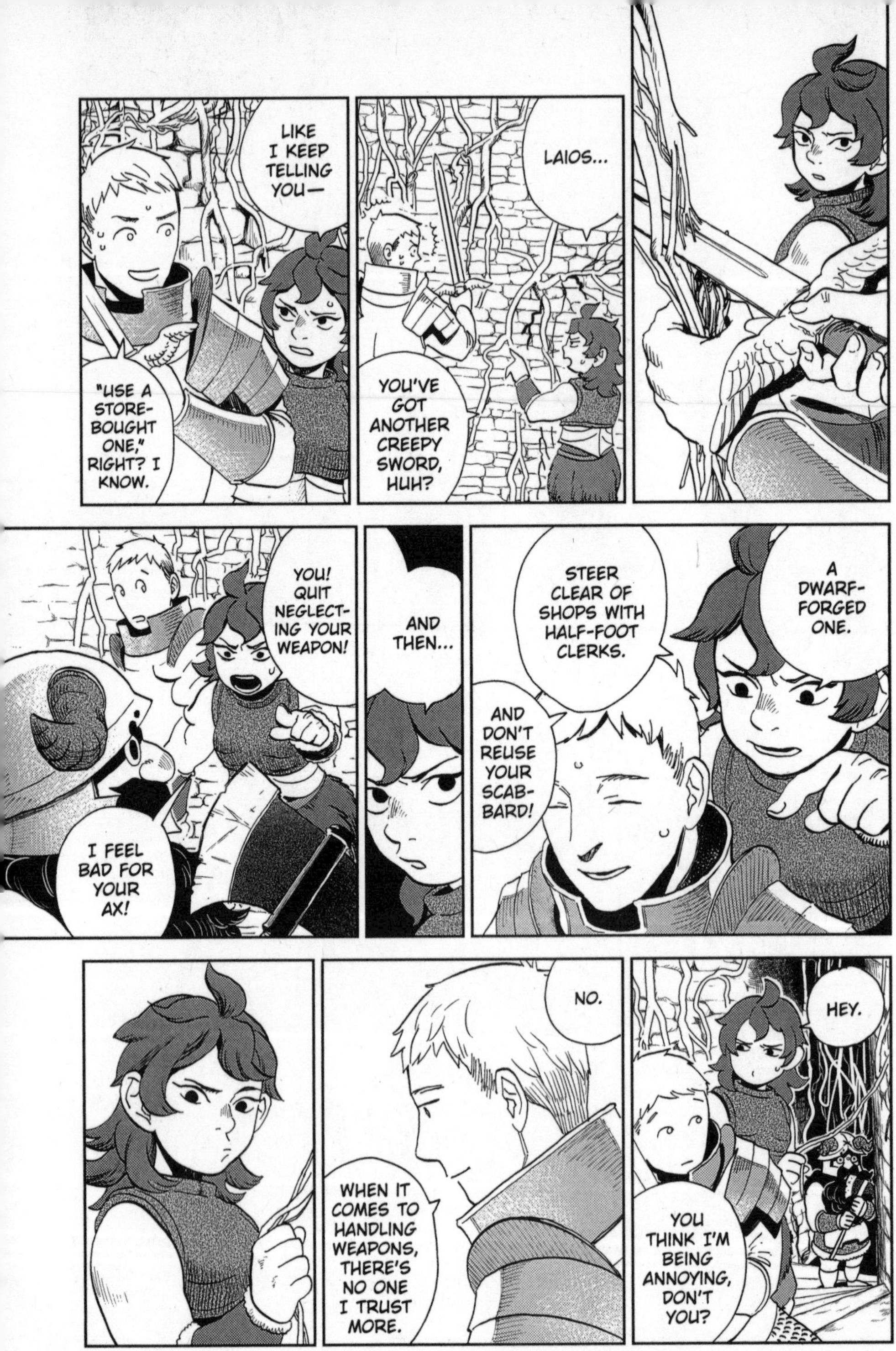
LAIOS...
YOU'VE GOT ANOTHER CREEPY SWORD, HUH?
LIKE I KEEP TELLING YOU—
"USE A STORE-BOUGHT ONE," RIGHT? I KNOW.
A DWARF-FORGED ONE.
STEER CLEAR OF SHOPS WITH HALF-FOOT CLERKS.
AND DON'T REUSE YOUR SCABBARD!
AND THEN...
YOU! QUIT NEGLECTING YOUR WEAPON!
I FEEL BAD FOR YOUR AX!
HEY.
YOU THINK I'M BEING ANNOYING, DON'T YOU?
NO.
WHEN IT COMES TO HANDLING WEAPONS, THERE'S NO ONE I TRUST MORE.

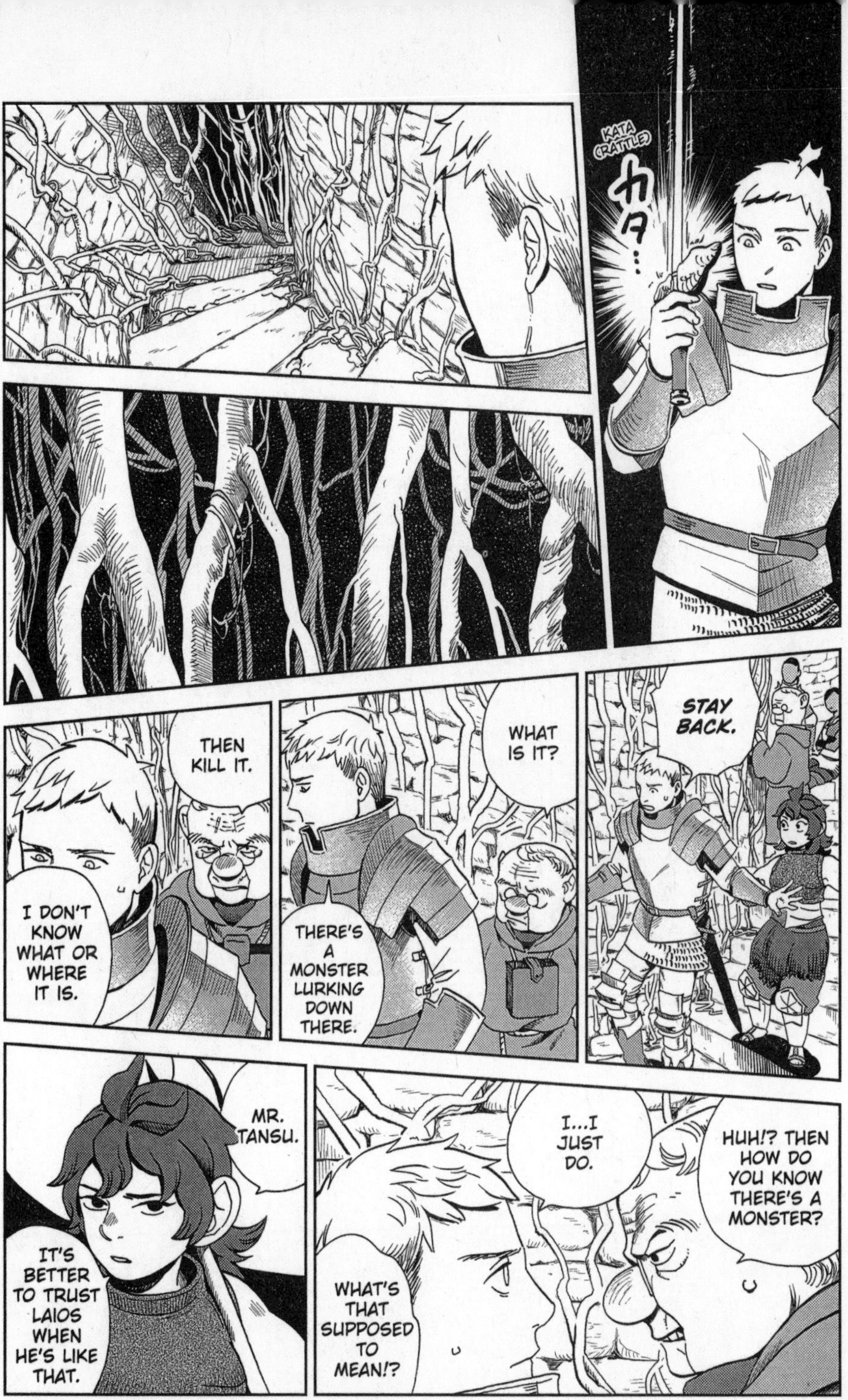
KATA (RATTLE)
カタ…
STAY BACK.
WHAT IS IT?
THERE'S A MONSTER LURKING DOWN THERE.
THEN KILL IT.
I DON'T KNOW WHAT OR WHERE IT IS.
HUH!? THEN HOW DO YOU KNOW THERE'S A MONSTER?
I...I JUST DO.
WHAT'S THAT SUPPOSED TO MEAN!?
MR. TANSU.
IT'S BETTER TO TRUST LAIOS WHEN HE'S LIKE THAT.

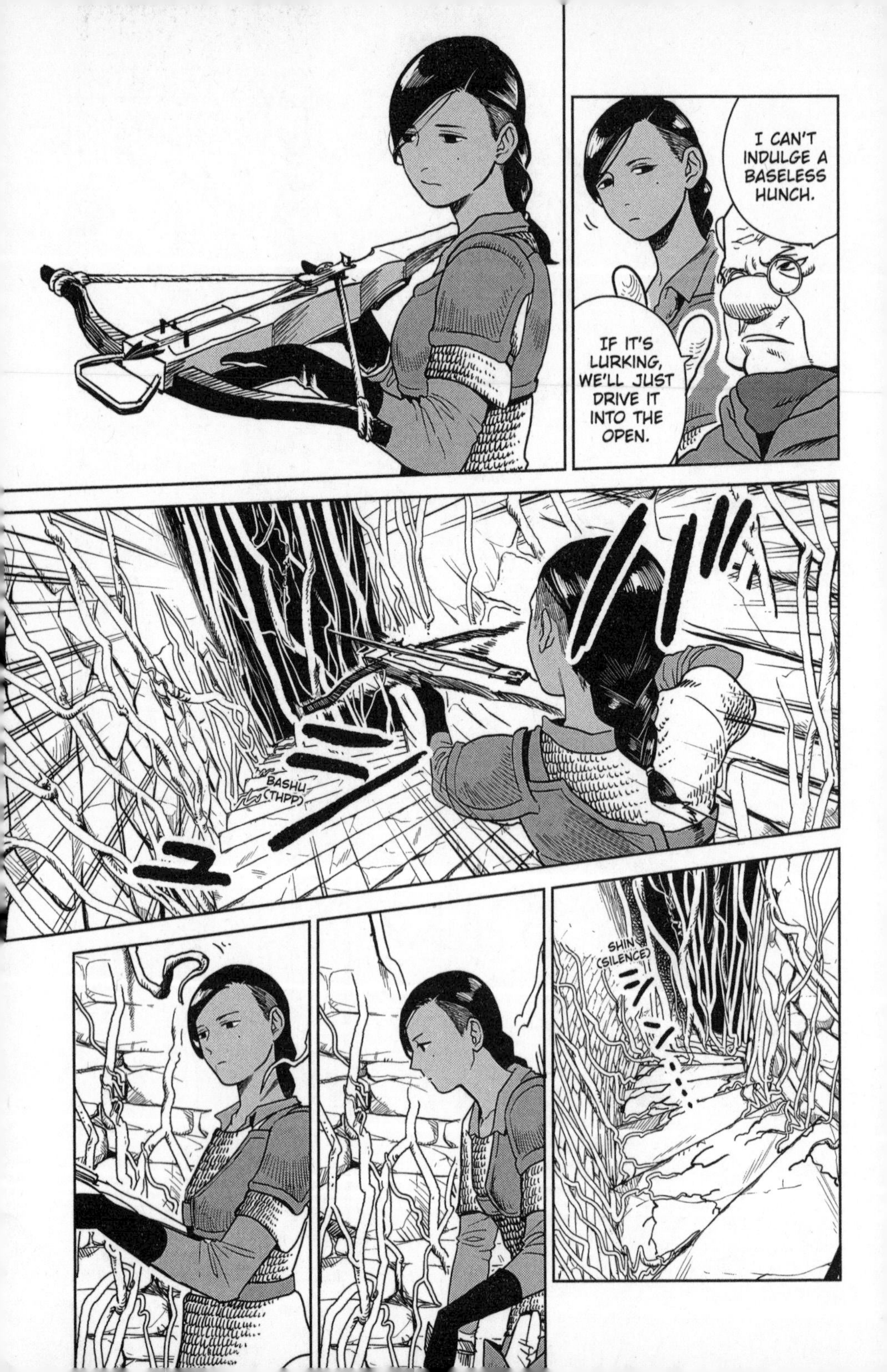
I CAN'T INDULGE A BASELESS HUNCH.
IF IT'S LURKING, WE'LL JUST DRIVE IT INTO THE OPEN.
BASHU (THPP)
SHIN (SILENCE)

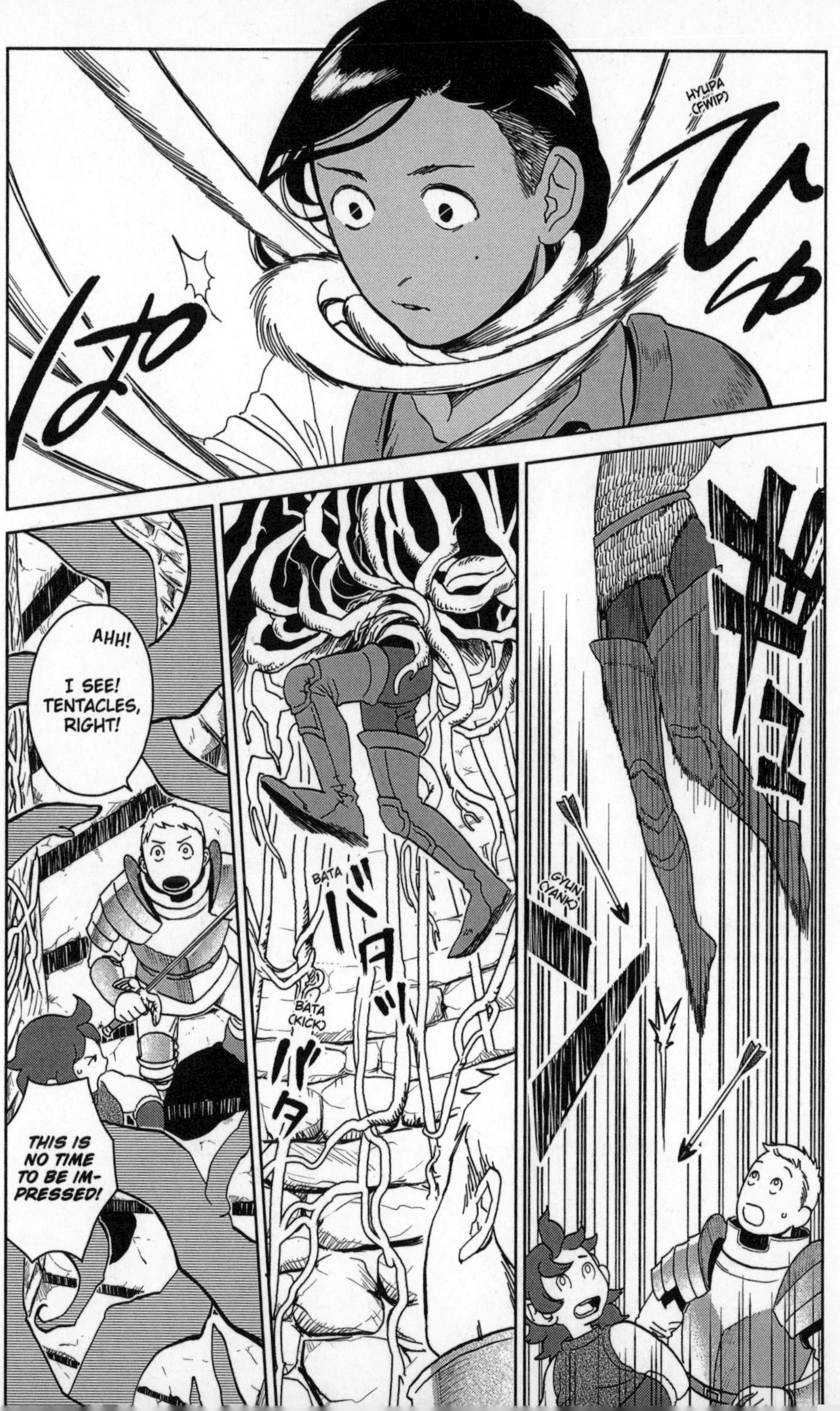
HYUPA (FWIP)
GYUN (YANK)
BATA
BATA (KICK)
AHH!
I SEE! TENTACLES, RIGHT!
THIS IS NO TIME TO BE IM-PRESSED!

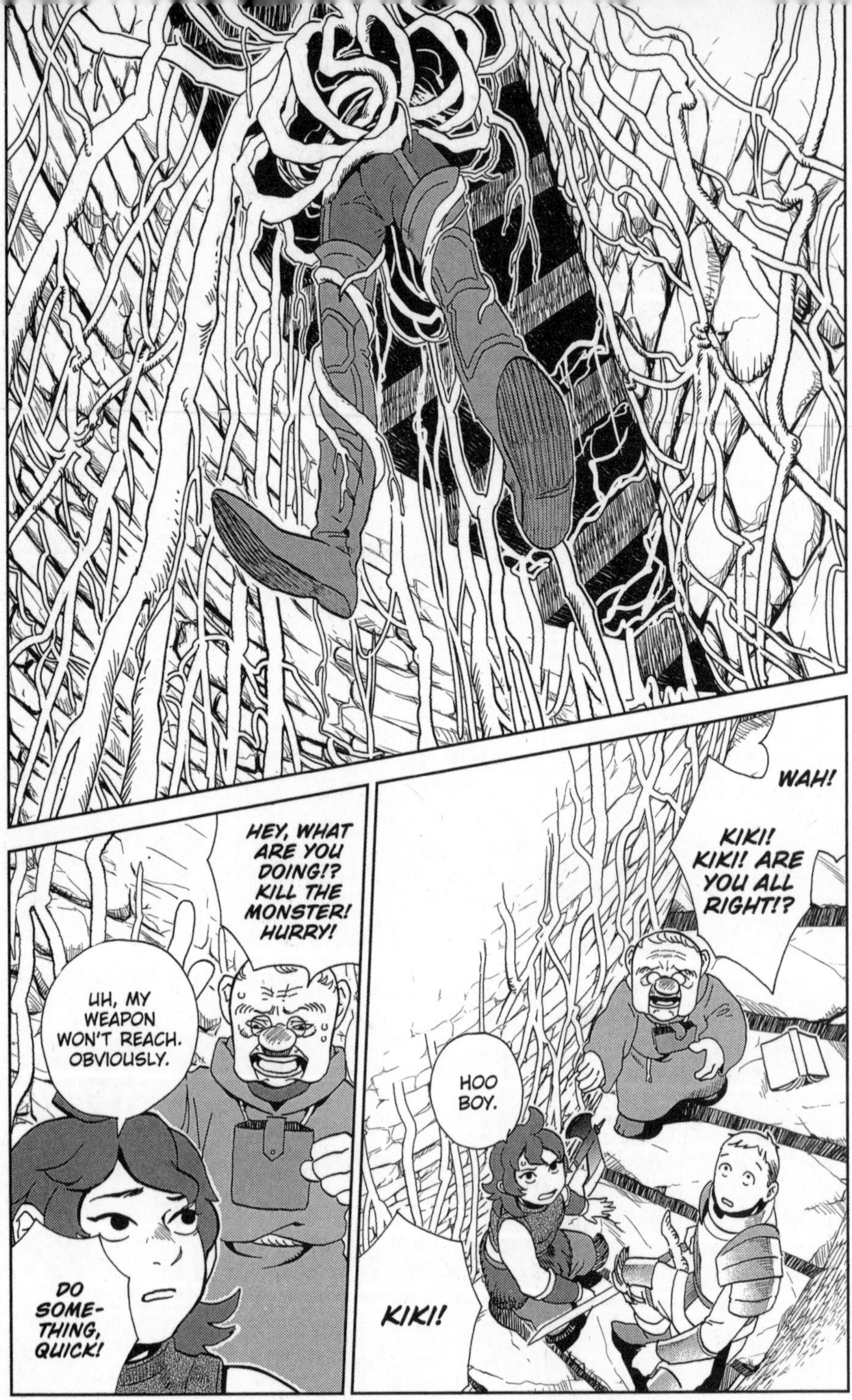
WAH!
KIKI! KIKI! ARE YOU ALL RIGHT!?
HOO BOY.
KIKI!
HEY, WHAT ARE YOU DOING!? KILL THE MONSTER! HURRY!
UH, MY WEAPON WON'T REACH. OBVIOUSLY.
DO SOME-THING, QUICK!

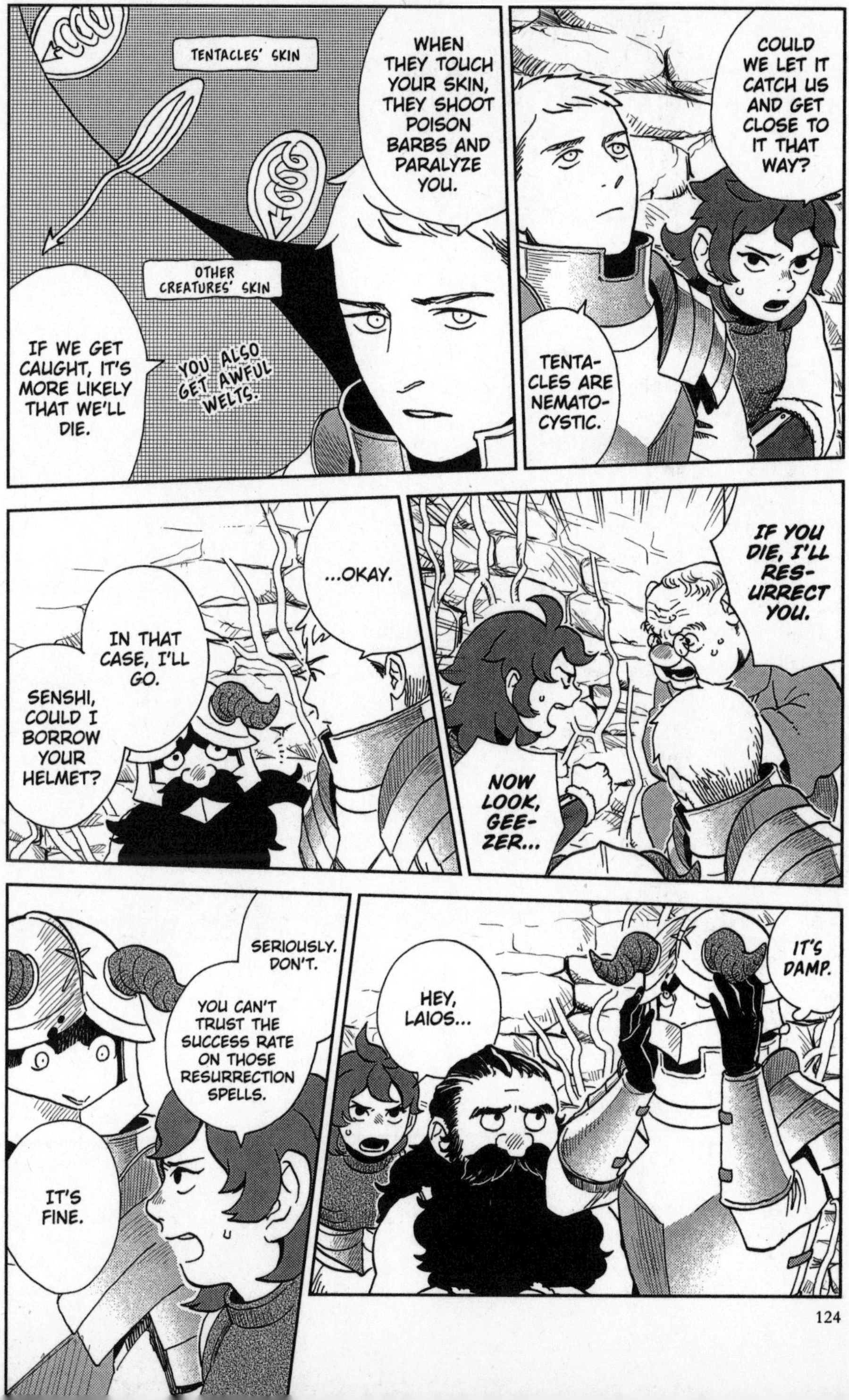
COULD WE LET IT CATCH US AND GET CLOSE TO IT THAT WAY?
TENTACLES ARE NEMATOCYSTIC.
WHEN THEY TOUCH YOUR SKIN, THEY SHOOT POISON BARBS AND PARALYZE YOU.
TENTACLES' SKIN
OTHER CREATURES' SKIN
YOU ALSO GET AWFUL WELTS.
IF WE GET CAUGHT, IT'S MORE LIKELY THAT WE'LL DIE.
IF YOU DIE, I'LL RESURRECT YOU.
NOW LOOK, GEEZER...
...OKAY.
IN THAT CASE, I'LL GO.
SENSHI, COULD I BORROW YOUR HELMET?
IT'S DAMP.
HEY, LAIOS...
SERIOUSLY. DON'T.
YOU CAN'T TRUST THE SUCCESS RATE ON THOSE RESURRECTION SPELLS.
IT'S FINE.

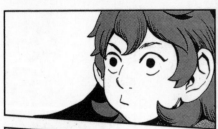

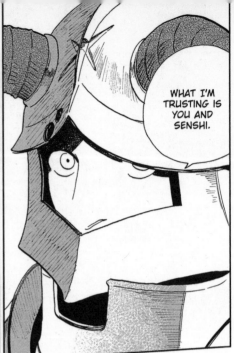

WHAT I'M TRUSTING IS YOU AND SENSHI.

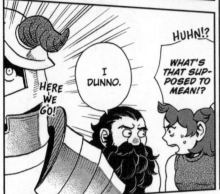

HERE WE GO!

I DUNNO.

HUHN!?

WHAT'S THAT SUP-POSED TO MEAN!?

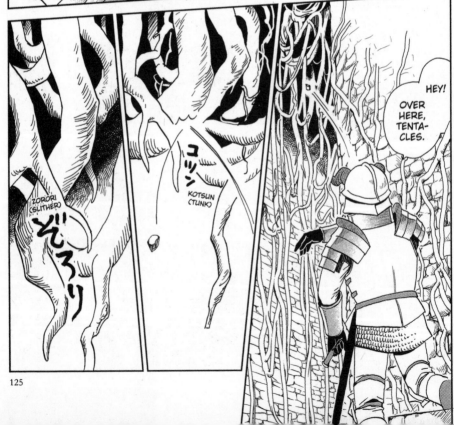

HEY! OVER HERE, TENTA-CLES.

ZORORI (SLITHER)

KOTSUN (TUNK)

125

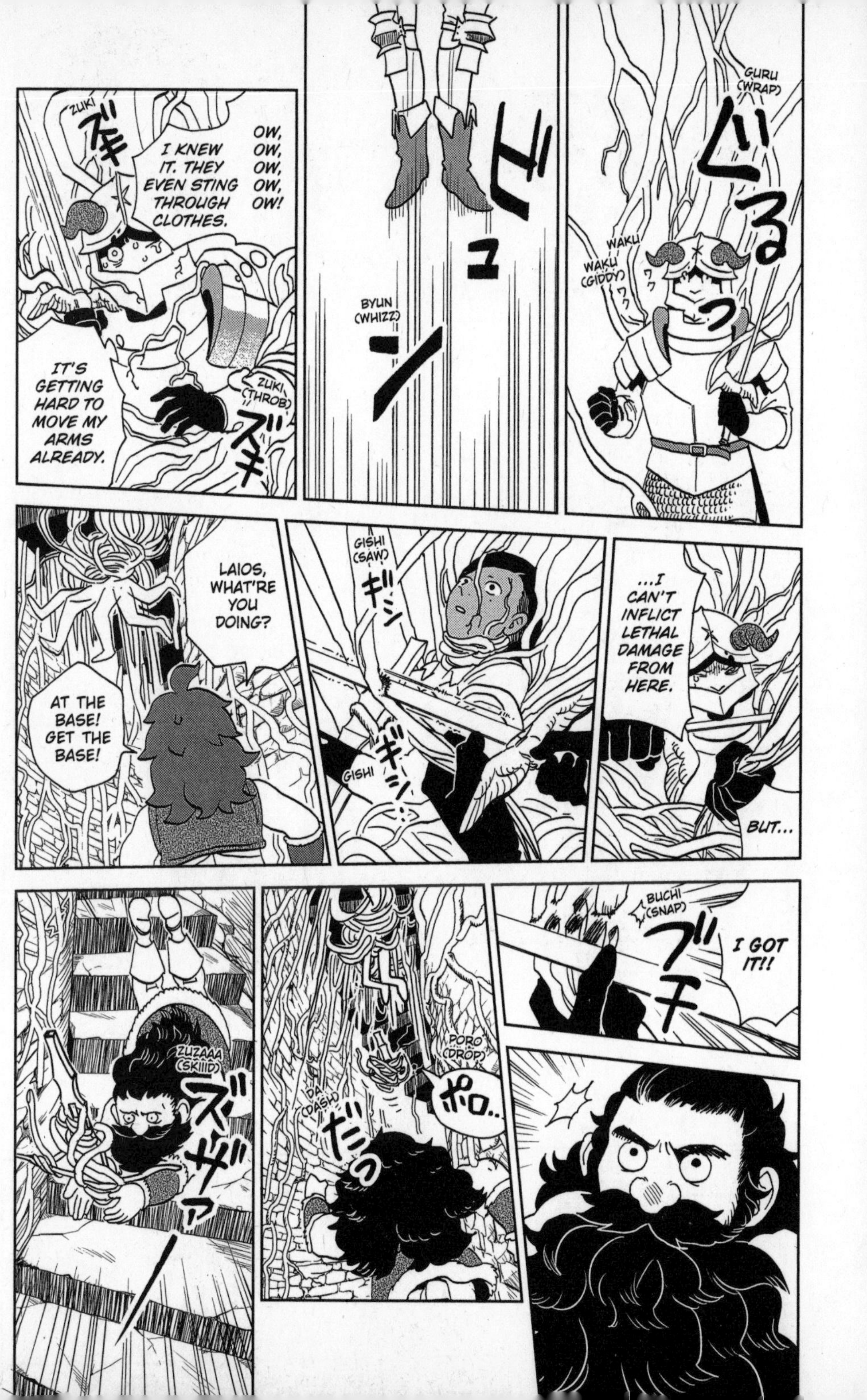

GURU (WRAP)
ぐるっ
WAKU WAKU (GIDDY)
ワクワク
BYUN (WHIZZ)
ビュン
ZUKI
ズキ
OW, OW, OW, OW, OW!
I KNEW IT. THEY EVEN STING THROUGH CLOTHES.
ZUKI (THROB)
ズキ
IT'S GETTING HARD TO MOVE MY ARMS ALREADY.
...I CAN'T INFLICT LETHAL DAMAGE FROM HERE.
BUT...
GISHI (SAW)
ギシ
GISHI
ギシ
LAIOS, WHAT'RE YOU DOING?
AT THE BASE! GET THE BASE!
BUCHI (SNAP)
ブチ
I GOT IT!!
PORO (DROP)
ポロ...
DA (DASH)
だっ
ZUZAAA (SKIIID)
ズザァ

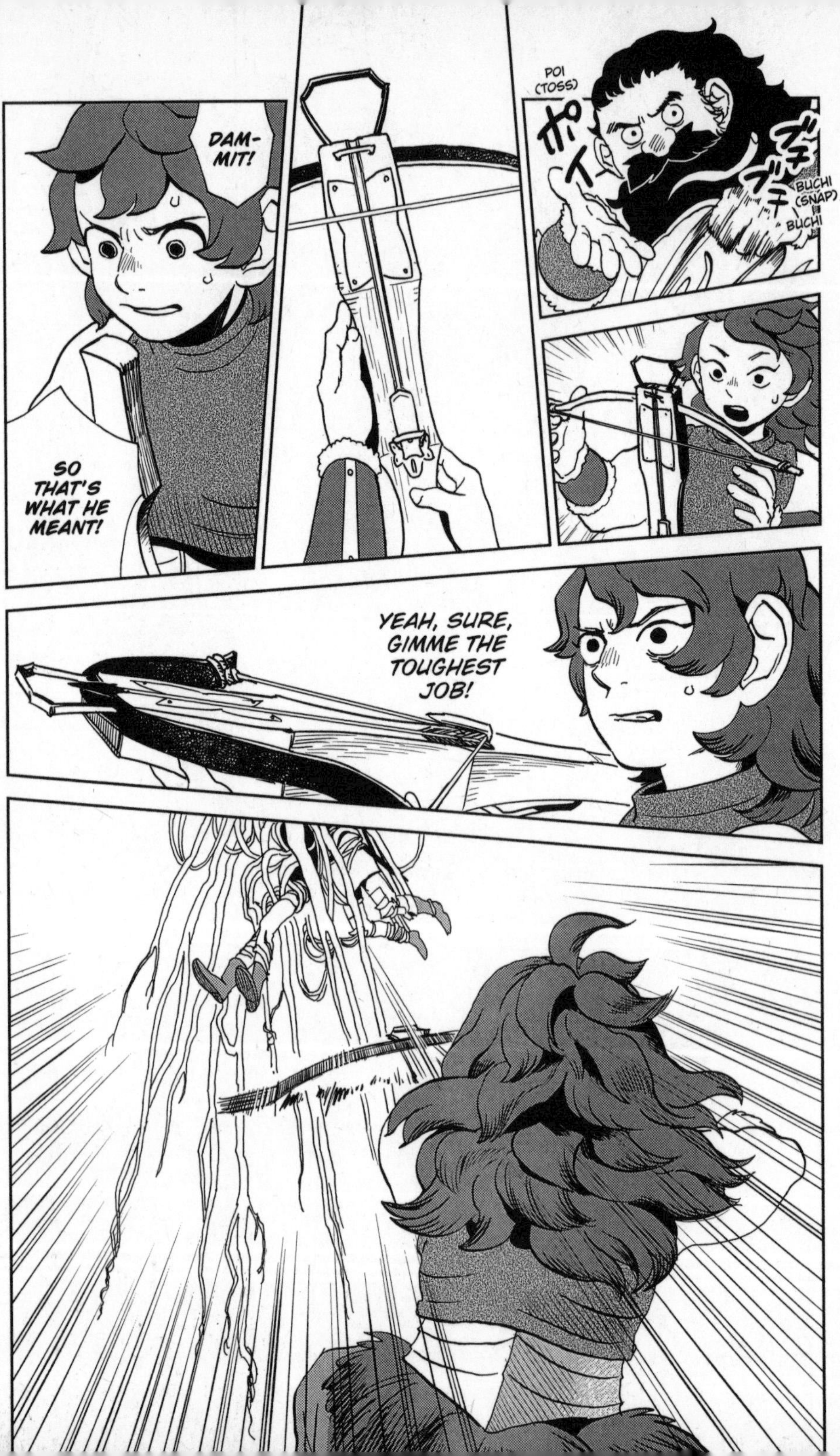
ポイ
POI (TOSS)
ブチブチ
BUCHI (SNAP) BUCHI
DAM-MIT!
SO THAT'S WHAT HE MEANT!
YEAH, SURE, GIMME THE TOUGHEST JOB!

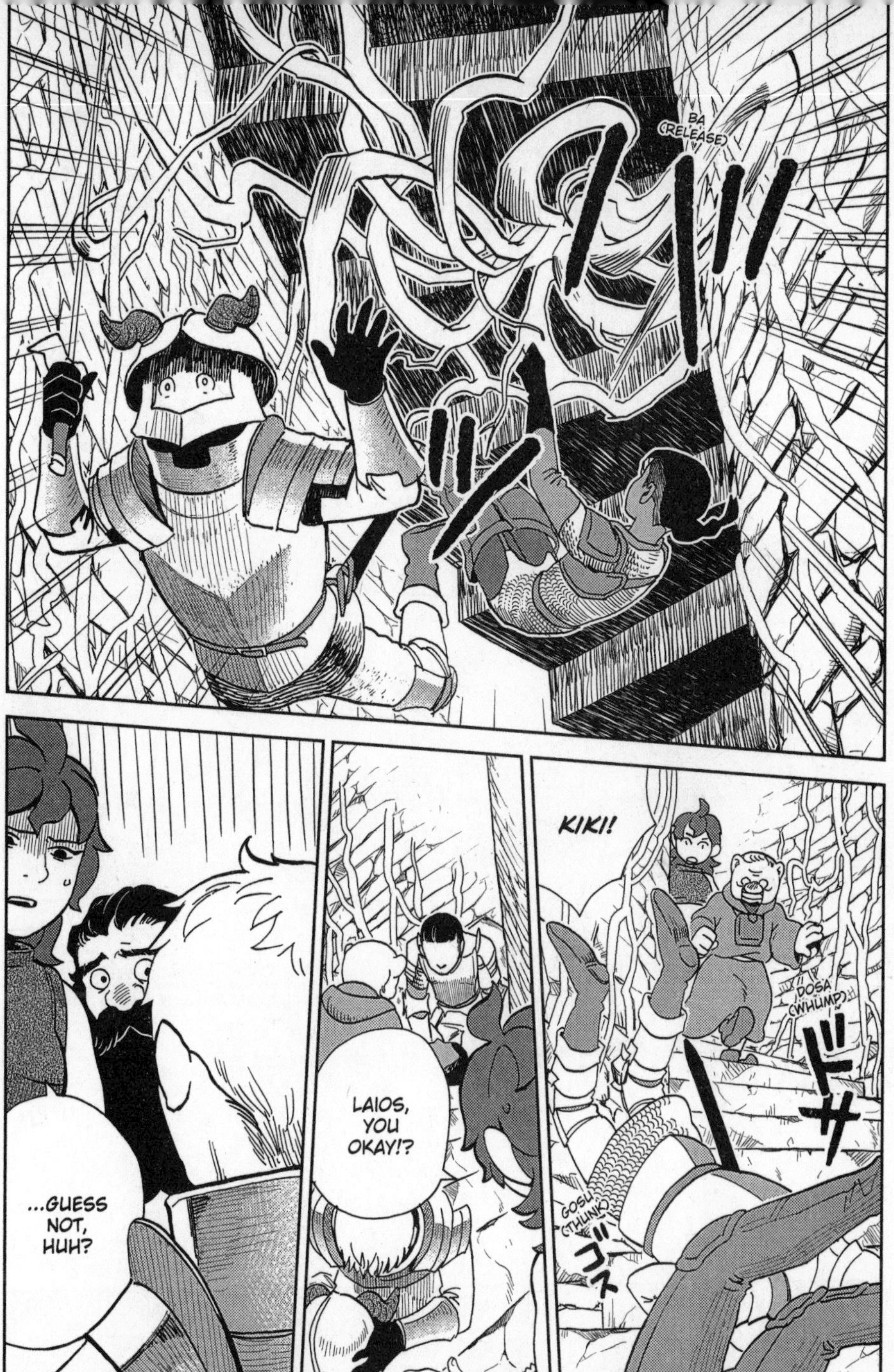
BA (RELEASE)
KIKI!
DOSA (WHUMP)
GOSU (THUNK)
LAIOS, YOU OKAY!?
...GUESS NOT, HUH?

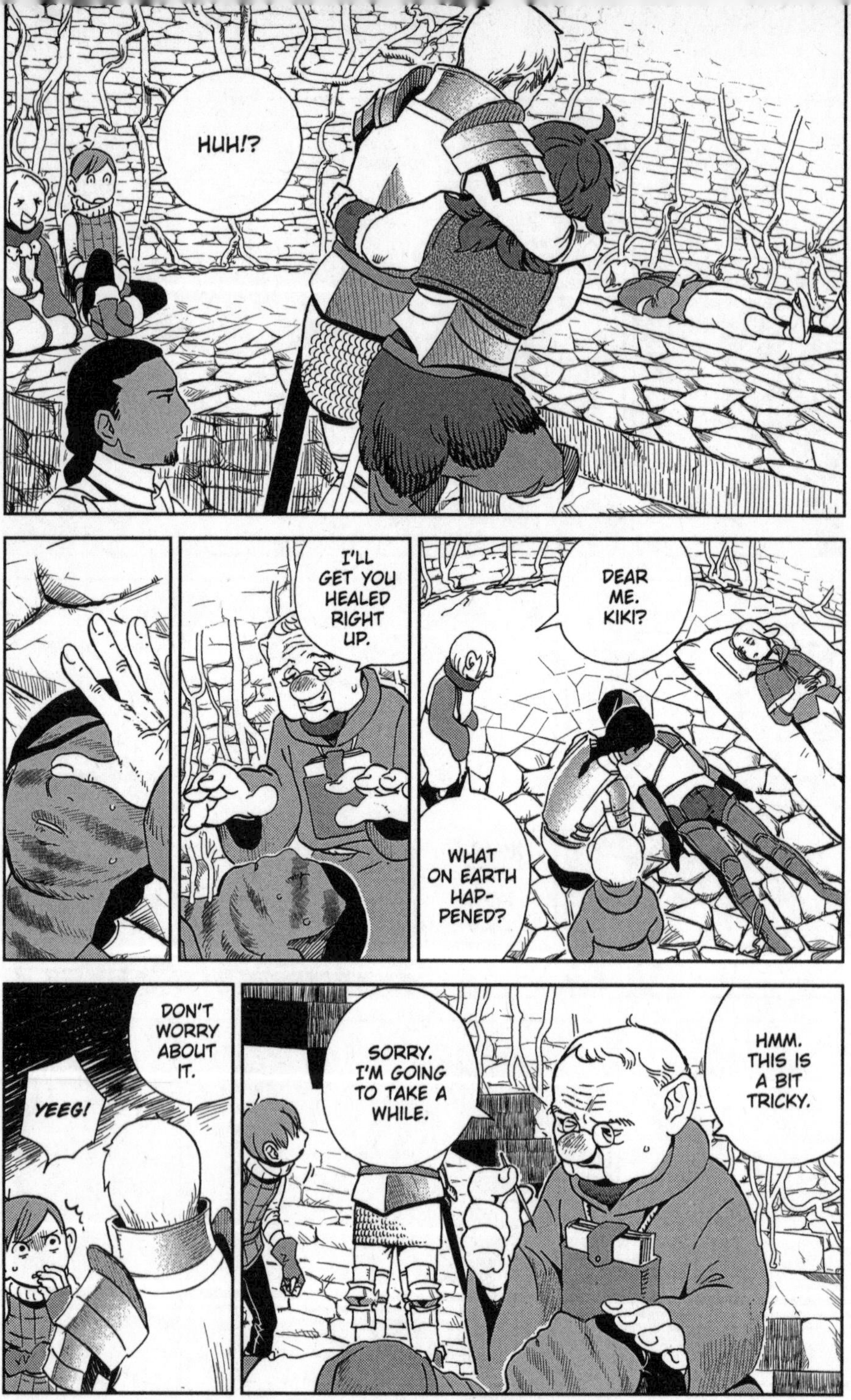
HUH!?
DEAR ME. KIKI?
WHAT ON EARTH HAP-PENED?
I'LL GET YOU HEALED RIGHT UP.
HMM. THIS IS A BIT TRICKY.
SORRY. I'M GOING TO TAKE A WHILE.
DON'T WORRY ABOUT IT.
YEEG!

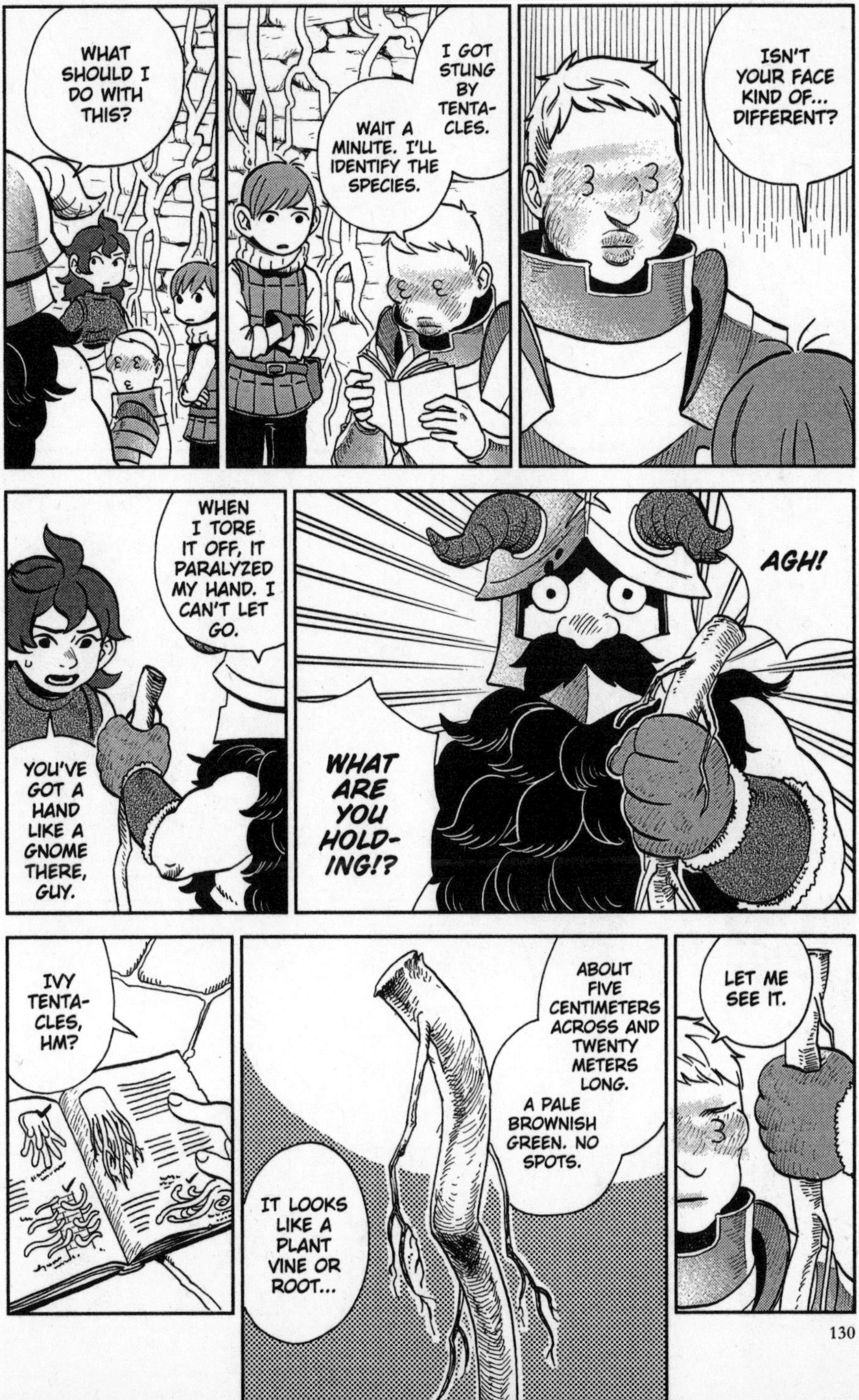
ISN'T YOUR FACE KIND OF... DIFFERENT?
I GOT STUNG BY TENTACLES.
WAIT A MINUTE. I'LL IDENTIFY THE SPECIES.
WHAT SHOULD I DO WITH THIS?
AGH!
WHAT ARE YOU HOLDING!?
WHEN I TORE IT OFF, IT PARALYZED MY HAND. I CAN'T LET GO.
YOU'VE GOT A HAND LIKE A GNOME THERE, GUY.
LET ME SEE IT.
ABOUT FIVE CENTIMETERS ACROSS AND TWENTY METERS LONG.
A PALE BROWNISH GREEN. NO SPOTS.
IT LOOKS LIKE A PLANT VINE OR ROOT...
IVY TENTACLES, HM?

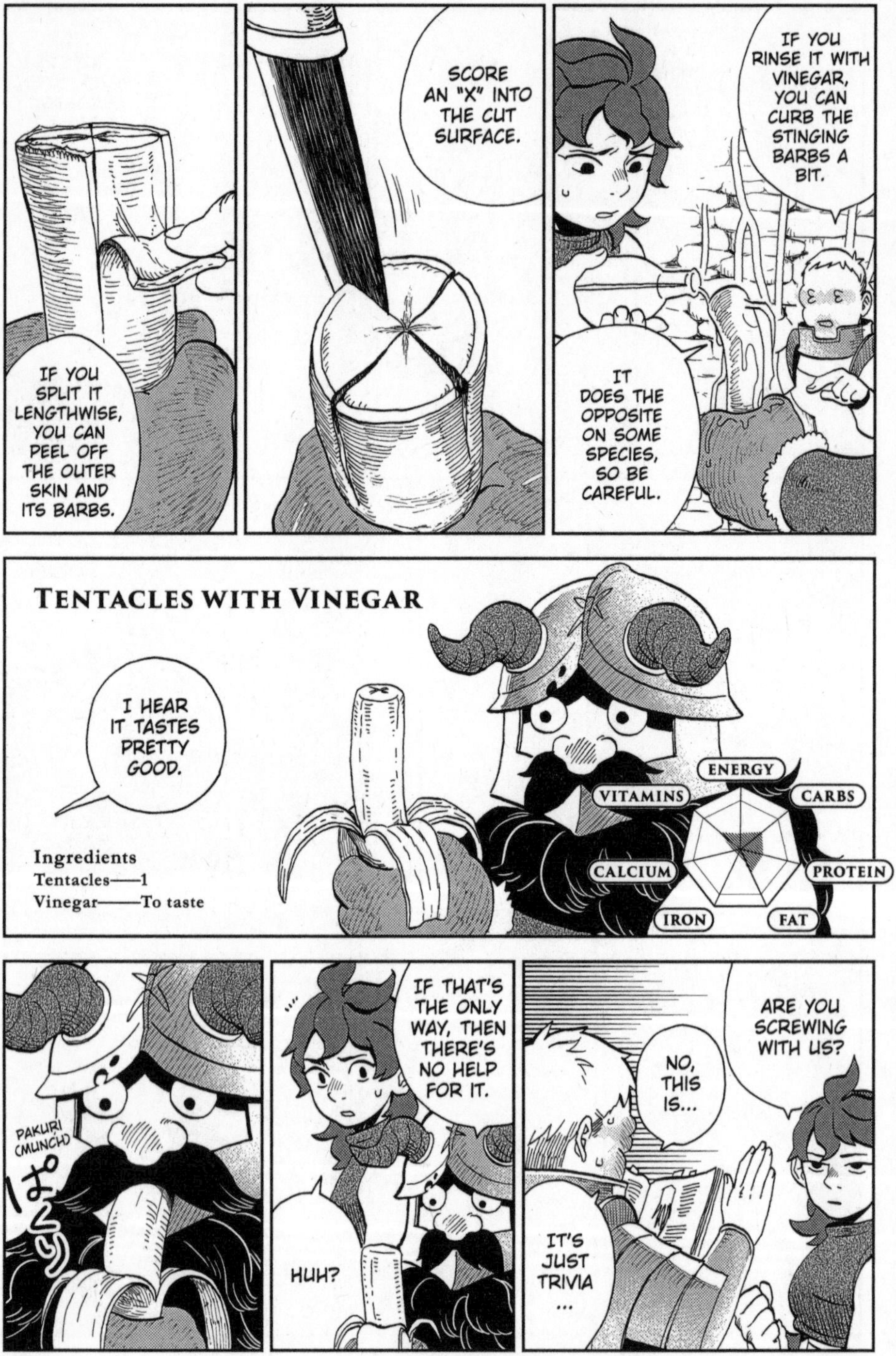
IF YOU RINSE IT WITH VINEGAR, YOU CAN CURB THE STINGING BARBS A BIT.
IT DOES THE OPPOSITE ON SOME SPECIES, SO BE CAREFUL.
SCORE AN "X" INTO THE CUT SURFACE.
IF YOU SPLIT IT LENGTHWISE, YOU CAN PEEL OFF THE OUTER SKIN AND ITS BARBS.
TENTACLES WITH VINEGAR
I HEAR IT TASTES PRETTY GOOD.
ENERGY
CARBS
PROTEIN
FAT
IRON
CALCIUM
VITAMINS
Ingredients
Tentacles——1
Vinegar——To taste
ARE YOU SCREWING WITH US?
NO, THIS IS...
IT'S JUST TRIVIA ...
IF THAT'S THE ONLY WAY, THEN THERE'S NO HELP FOR IT.
HUH?
PAKURI (MUNCH)
ぱくり

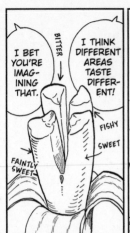

I SEE. NOT BAD.
COOKED PROPERLY, IT WILL BE BETTER.
LET ME HAVE SOME TOO!!
HM...
MOGU (CHEW)
もぐ
THIS IS...!
I THINK DIFFERENT AREAS TASTE DIFFER-ENT!
I BET YOU'RE IMAG-INING THAT.
BITTER
FISHY
SWEET
FAINTLY SWEET
NO, IT'S TRUE!
TRY SOME.
ALL I TASTE IS VINEGAR.
WANT TO TRY SOME, MARCILLE?
HUH? WHAT IS IT?
......
IT'S SOUR.
SLIMY TOO. WHAT...
WHAT IS THIS?

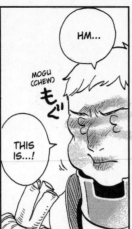

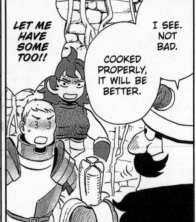

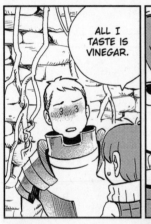

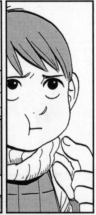

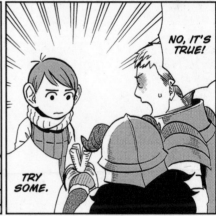

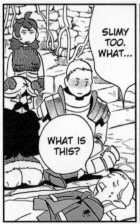

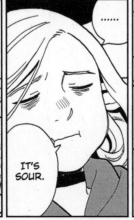

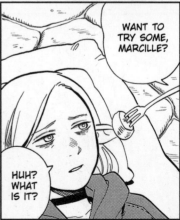

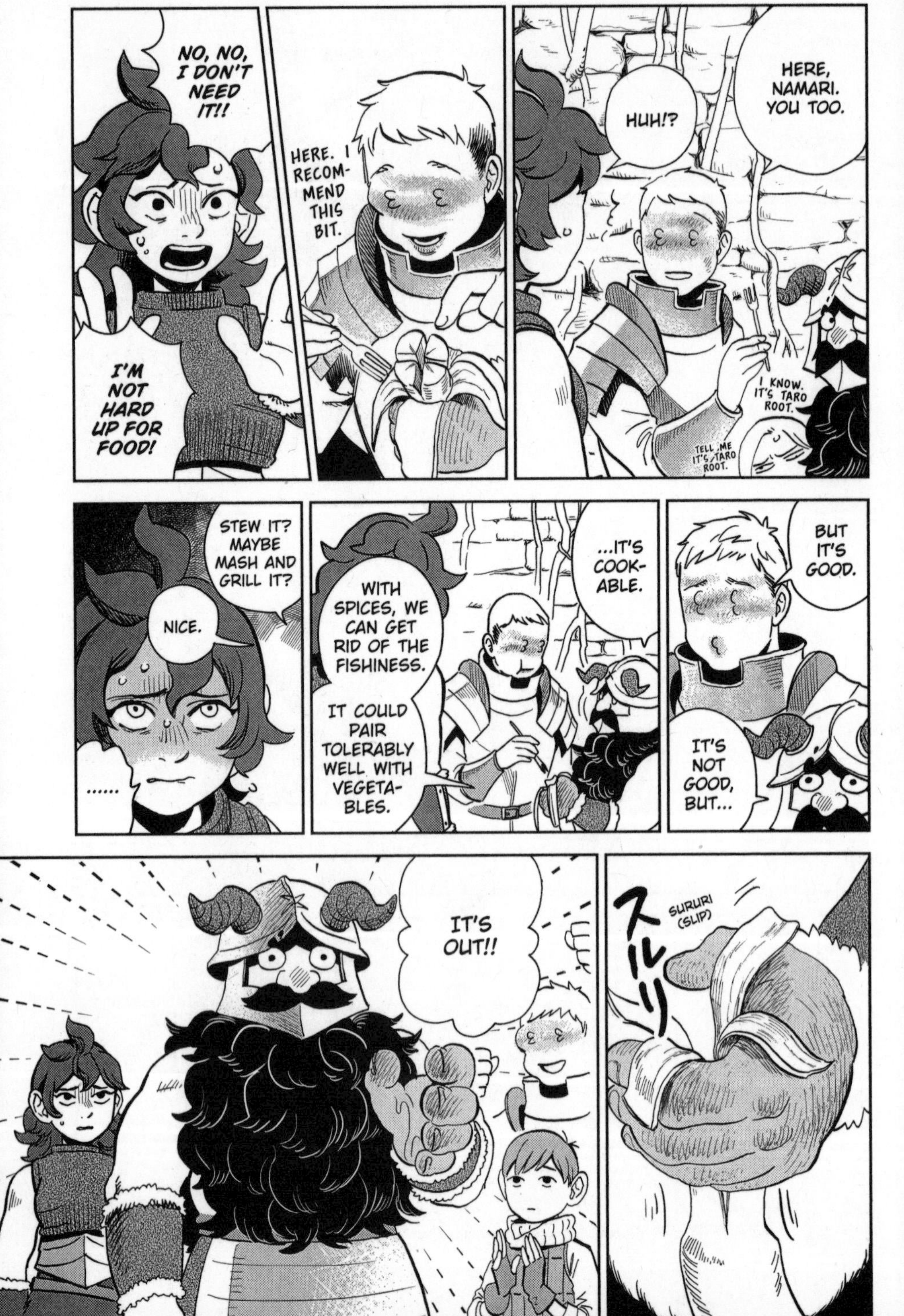
HERE, NAMARI. YOU TOO.
HUH!?
I KNOW. IT'S TARO ROOT.
TELL ME IT'S TARO ROOT.
HERE. I RECOMMEND THIS BIT.
NO, NO, I DON'T NEED IT!!
I'M NOT HARD UP FOR FOOD!
BUT IT'S GOOD.
IT'S NOT GOOD, BUT...
...IT'S COOKABLE.
WITH SPICES, WE CAN GET RID OF THE FISHINESS.
IT COULD PAIR TOLERABLY WELL WITH VEGETABLES.
STEW IT? MAYBE MASH AND GRILL IT?
NICE.
......
スルリ
SURURI (SLIP)
IT'S OUT!!

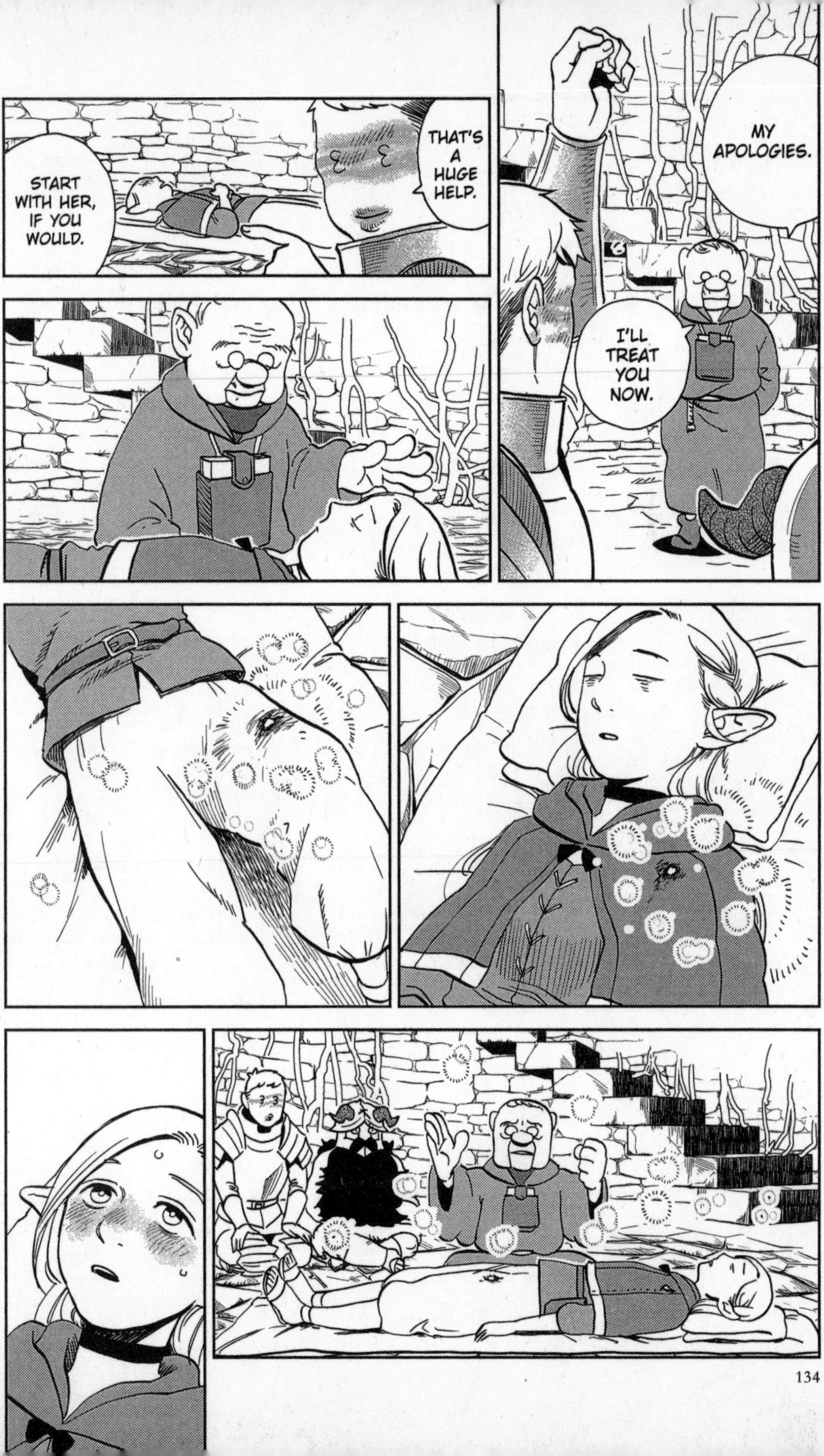

MY APOLOGIES.
I'LL TREAT YOU NOW.
THAT'S A HUGE HELP.
START WITH HER, IF YOU WOULD.

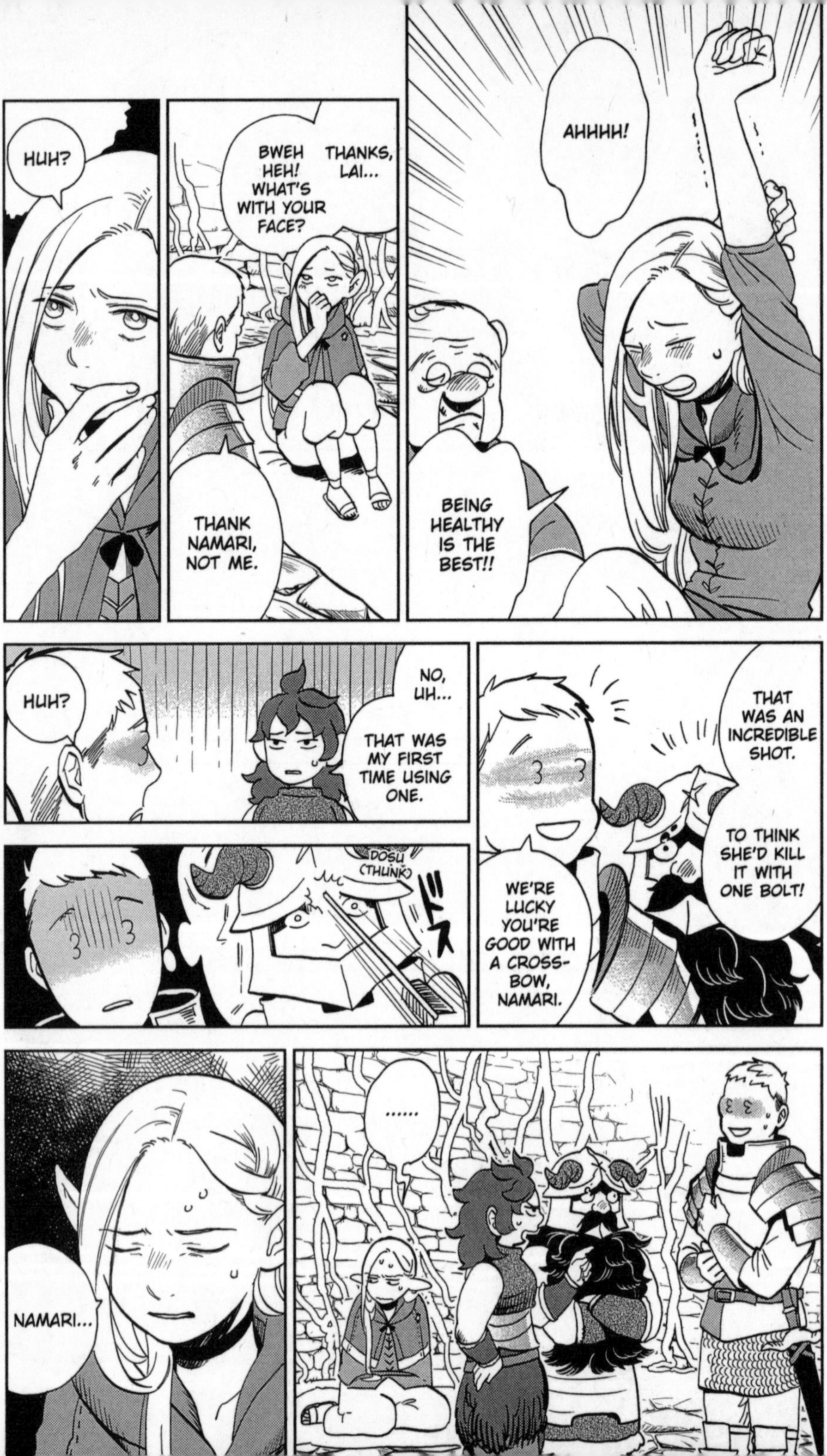
AHHHH!
BEING HEALTHY IS THE BEST!!
THANKS, LAI...
BWEH HEH! WHAT'S WITH YOUR FACE?
THANK NAMARI, NOT ME.
HUH?
THAT WAS AN INCREDIBLE SHOT.
TO THINK SHE'D KILL IT WITH ONE BOLT!
WE'RE LUCKY YOU'RE GOOD WITH A CROSS-BOW, NAMARI.
NO, UH...
THAT WAS MY FIRST TIME USING ONE.
HUH?
DOSU (THUNK)
ドス
......
NAMARI...

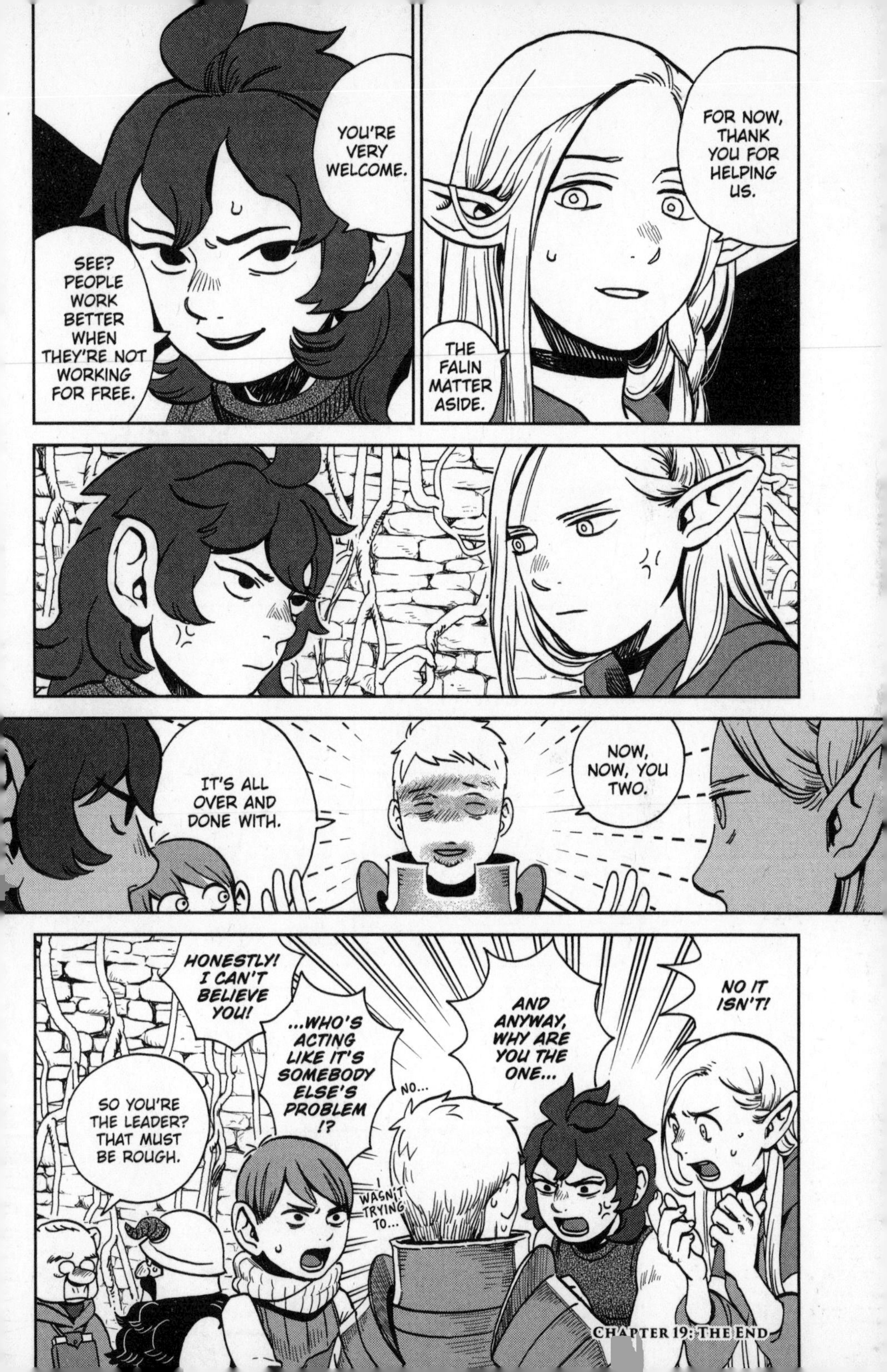
FOR NOW, THANK YOU FOR HELPING US.
THE FALIN MATTER ASIDE.
YOU'RE VERY WELCOME.
SEE? PEOPLE WORK BETTER WHEN THEY'RE NOT WORKING FOR FREE.
NOW, NOW, YOU TWO.
IT'S ALL OVER AND DONE WITH.
NO IT ISN'T!
AND ANYWAY, WHY ARE YOU THE ONE...
...WHO'S ACTING LIKE IT'S SOMEBODY ELSE'S PROBLEM!?
HONESTLY! I CAN'T BELIEVE YOU!
NO...
I WASN'T TRYING TO...
SO YOU'RE THE LEADER? THAT MUST BE ROUGH.
CHAPTER 19: THE END

20. Stew

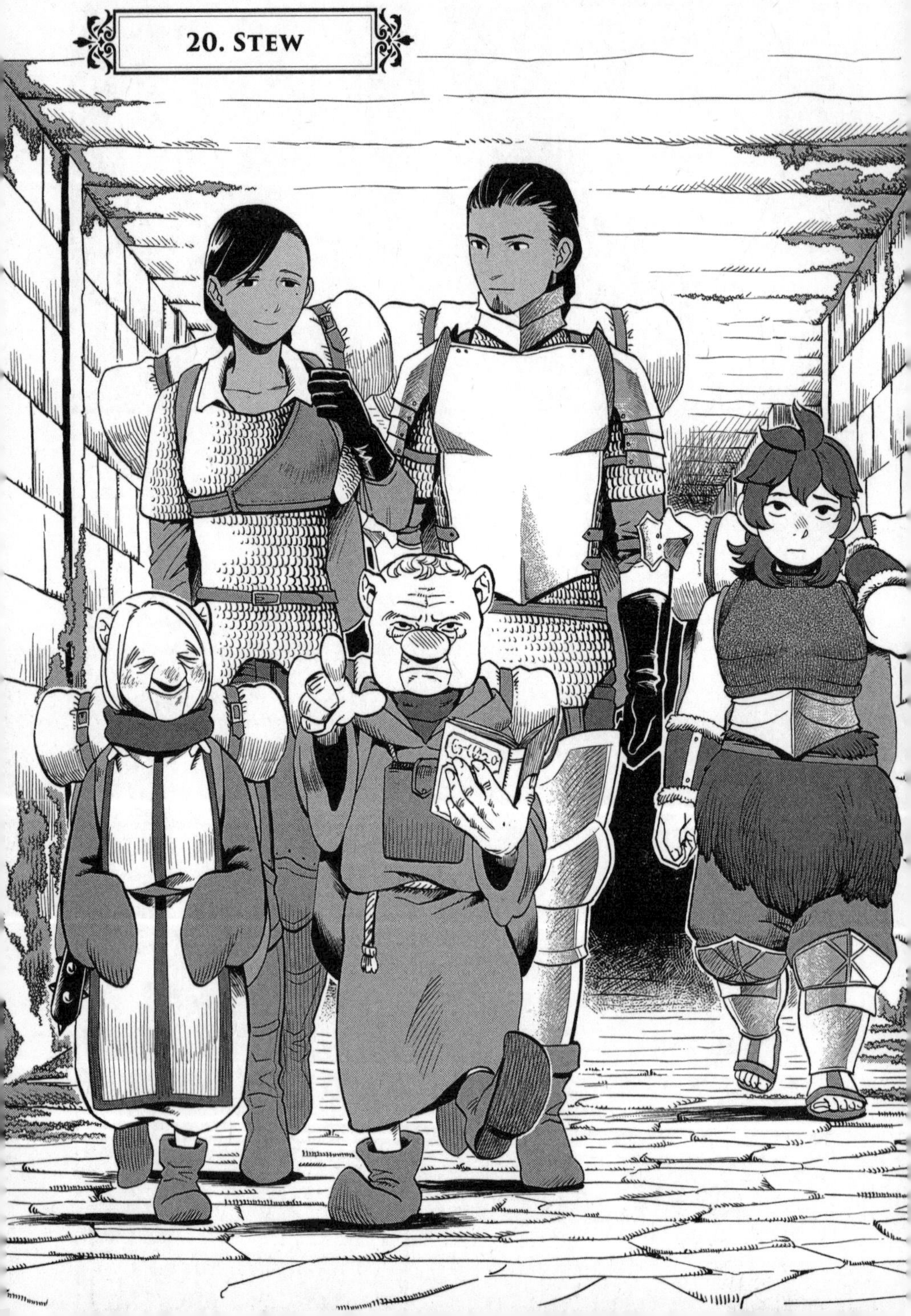

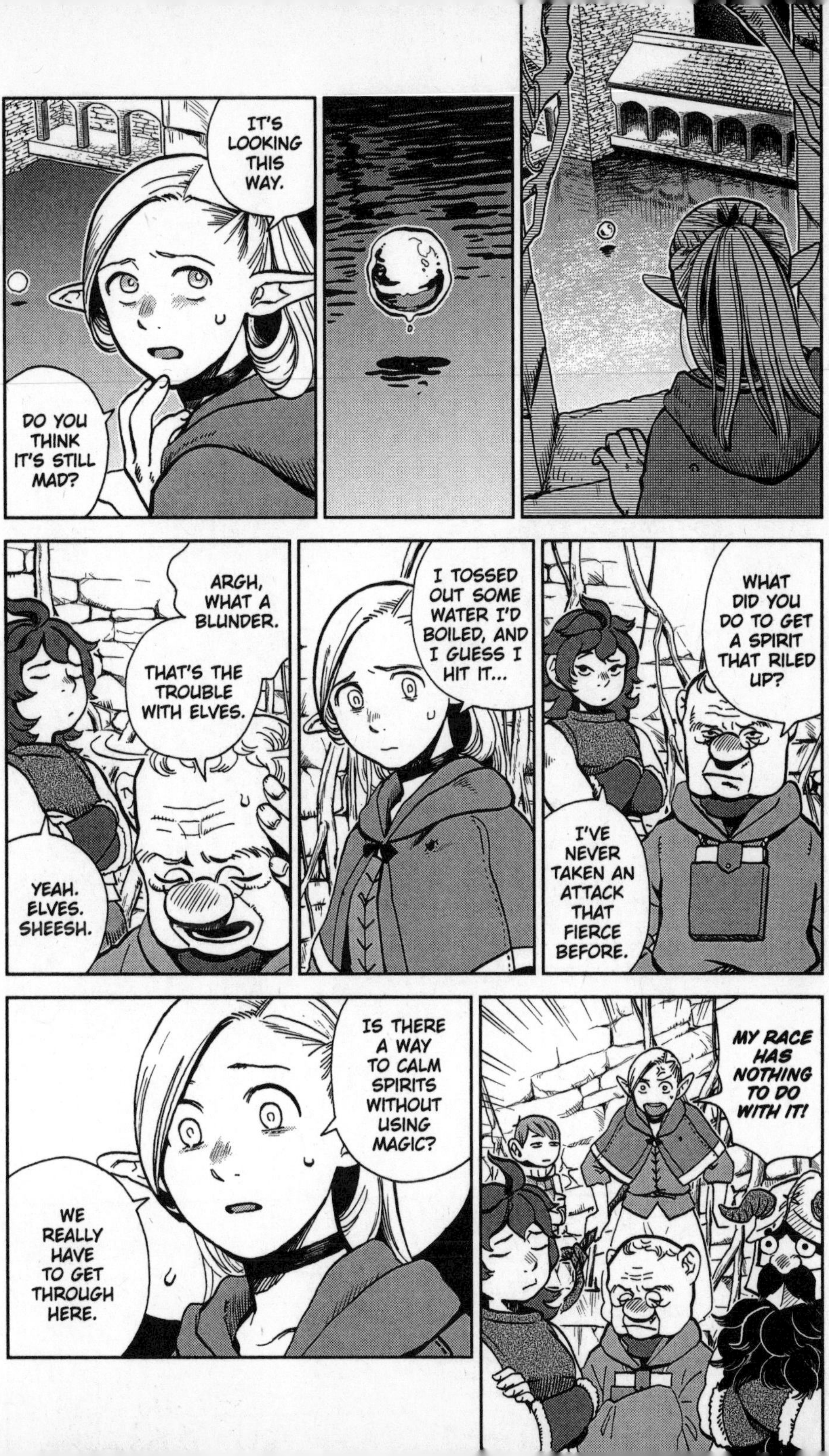
IT'S LOOKING THIS WAY.
DO YOU THINK IT'S STILL MAD?
WHAT DID YOU DO TO GET A SPIRIT THAT RILED UP?
I'VE NEVER TAKEN AN ATTACK THAT FIERCE BEFORE.
I TOSSED OUT SOME WATER I'D BOILED, AND I GUESS I HIT IT...
ARGH, WHAT A BLUNDER.
THAT'S THE TROUBLE WITH ELVES.
YEAH. ELVES. SHEESH.
MY RACE HAS NOTHING TO DO WITH IT!
IS THERE A WAY TO CALM SPIRITS WITHOUT USING MAGIC?
WE REALLY HAVE TO GET THROUGH HERE.

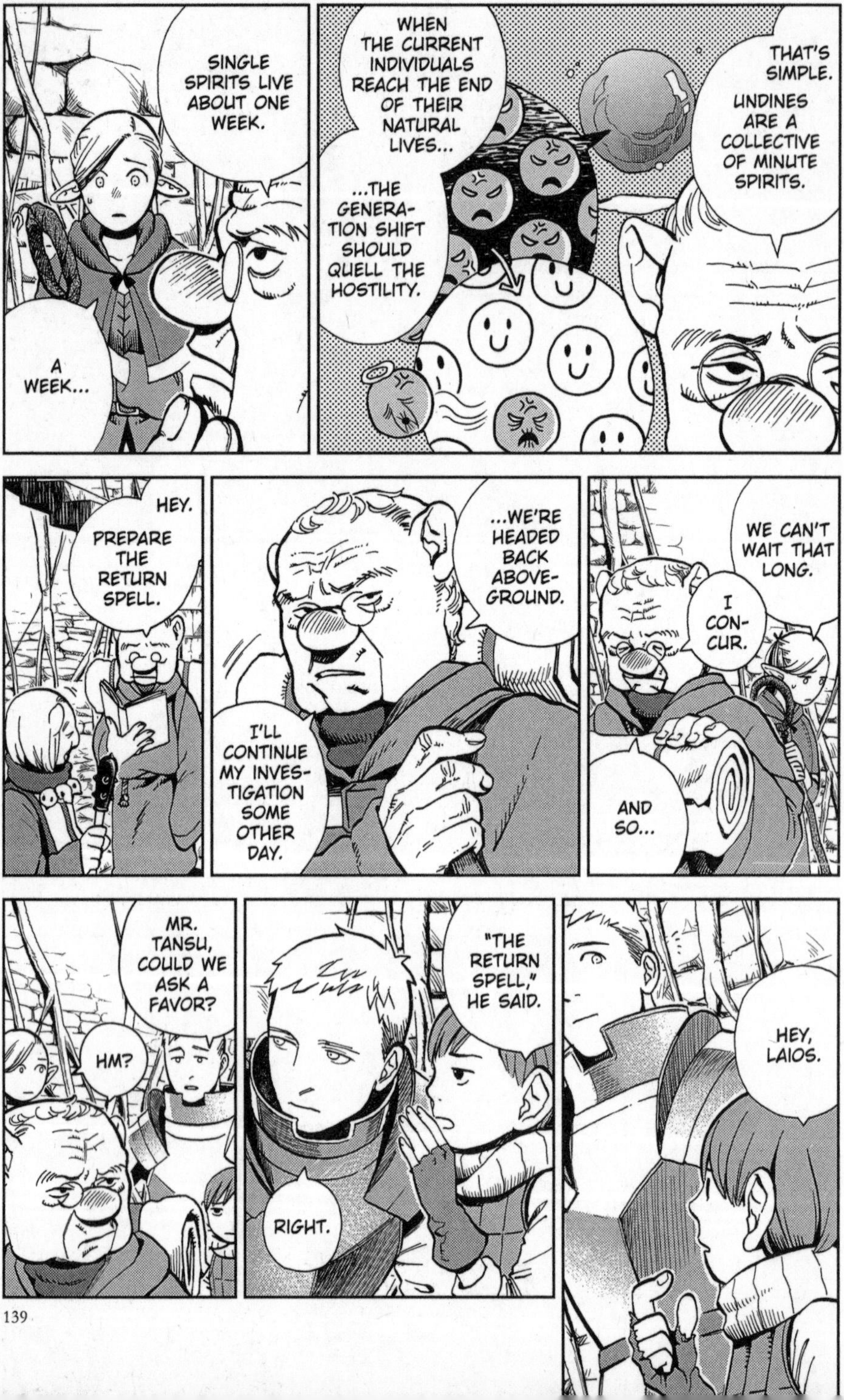
THAT'S SIMPLE.
UNDINES ARE A COLLECTIVE OF MINUTE SPIRITS.
WHEN THE CURRENT INDIVIDUALS REACH THE END OF THEIR NATURAL LIVES...
...THE GENERATION SHIFT SHOULD QUELL THE HOSTILITY.
SINGLE SPIRITS LIVE ABOUT ONE WEEK.
A WEEK...
WE CAN'T WAIT THAT LONG.
I CONCUR.
AND SO...
...WE'RE HEADED BACK ABOVEGROUND.
I'LL CONTINUE MY INVESTIGATION SOME OTHER DAY.
HEY.
PREPARE THE RETURN SPELL.
HEY, LAIOS.
"THE RETURN SPELL," HE SAID.
RIGHT.
MR. TANSU, COULD WE ASK A FAVOR?
HM?

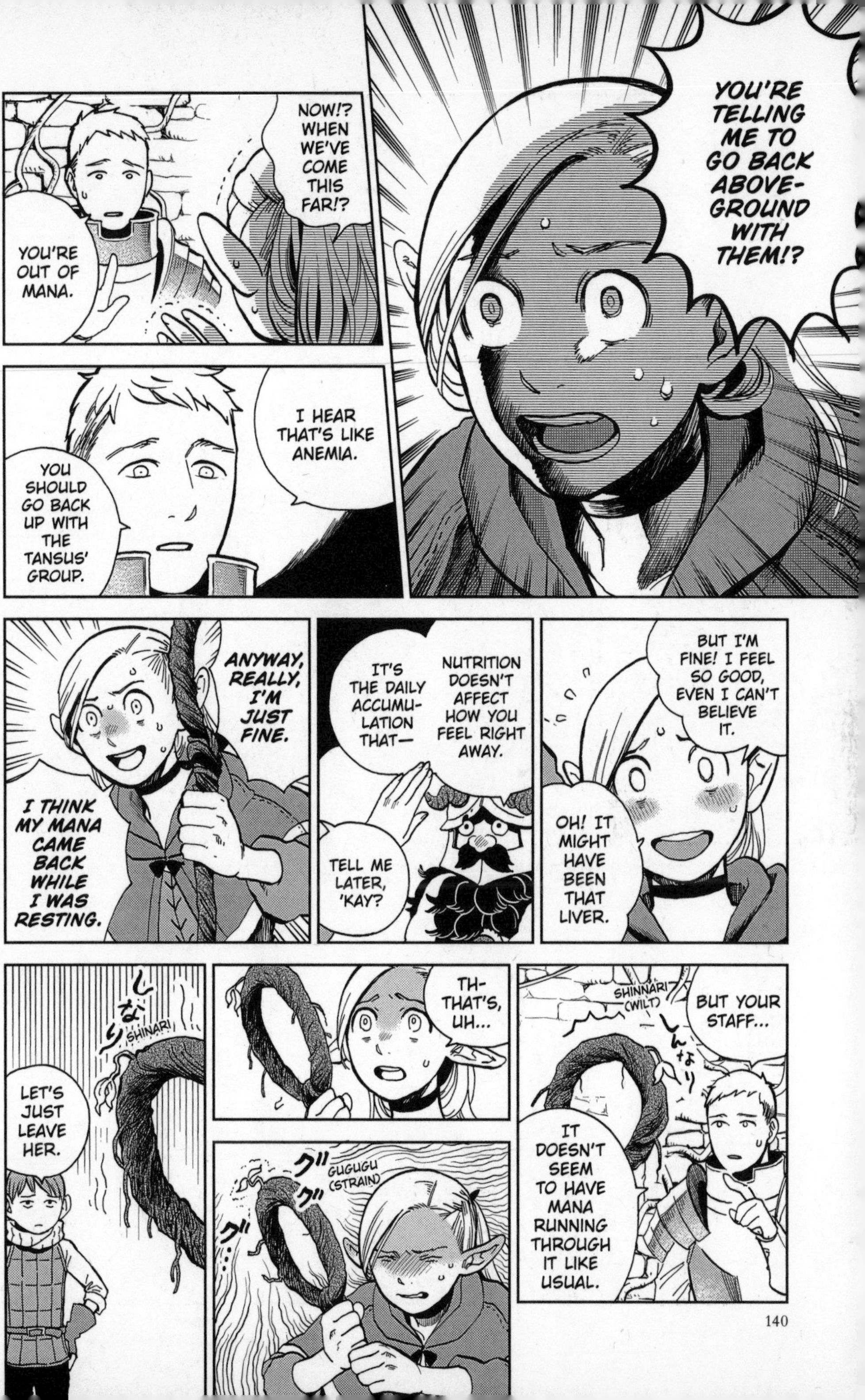
YOU'RE TELLING ME TO GO BACK ABOVE-GROUND WITH THEM!?
NOW!? WHEN WE'VE COME THIS FAR!?
YOU'RE OUT OF MANA.
I HEAR THAT'S LIKE ANEMIA.
YOU SHOULD GO BACK UP WITH THE TANSUS' GROUP.
BUT I'M FINE! I FEEL SO GOOD, EVEN I CAN'T BELIEVE IT.
OH! IT MIGHT HAVE BEEN THAT LIVER.
NUTRITION DOESN'T AFFECT HOW YOU FEEL RIGHT AWAY.
IT'S THE DAILY ACCUMULATION THAT—
TELL ME LATER, 'KAY?
ANYWAY, REALLY, I'M JUST FINE.
I THINK MY MANA CAME BACK WHILE I WAS RESTING.
BUT YOUR STAFF...
SHINNARI (WILT)
IT DOESN'T SEEM TO HAVE MANA RUNNING THROUGH IT LIKE USUAL.
TH-THAT'S, UH...
GUGUGU (STRAIN)
SHINARI
LET'S JUST LEAVE HER.

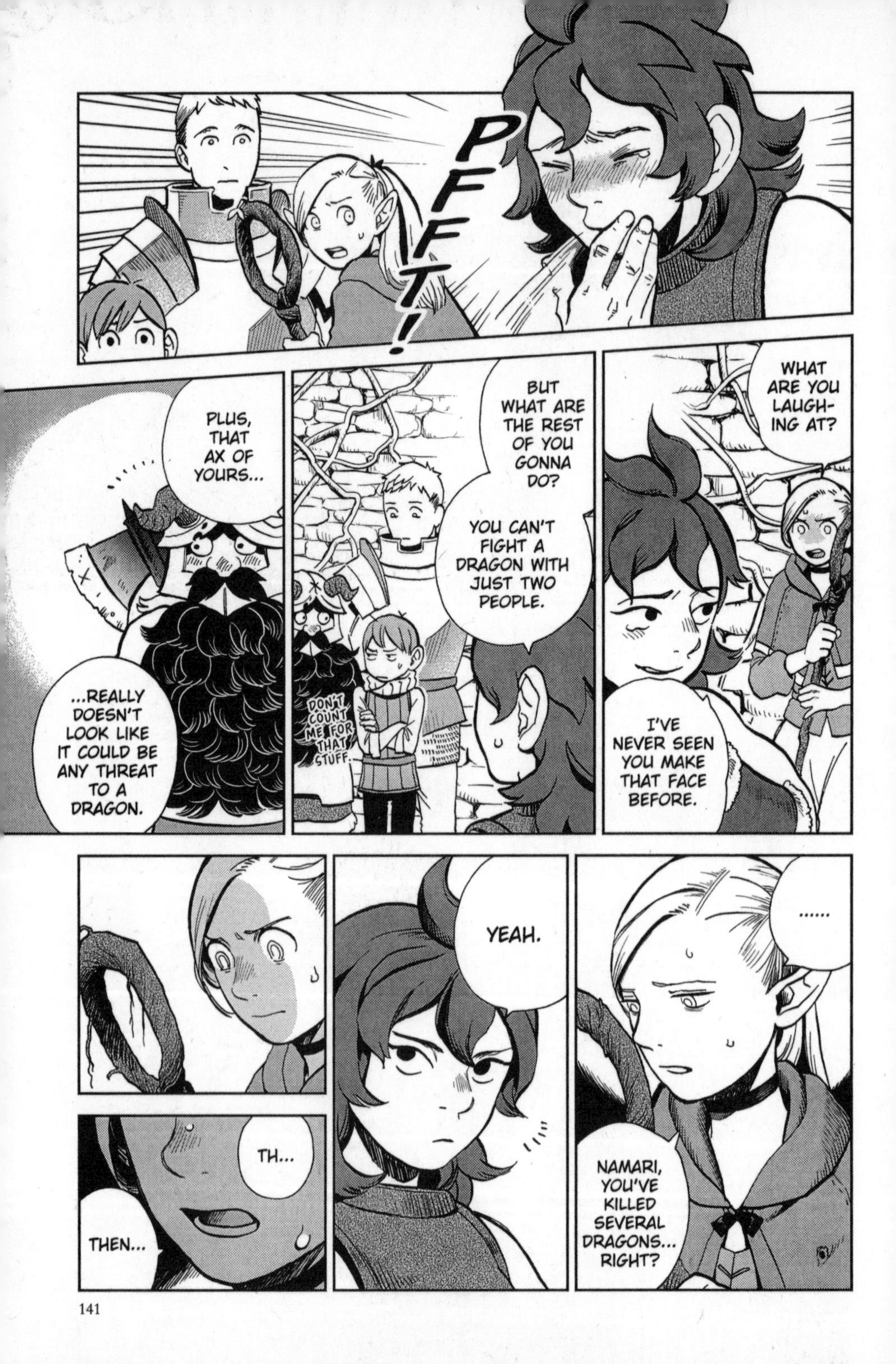
PFFFT!
WHAT ARE YOU LAUGHING AT?
I'VE NEVER SEEN YOU MAKE THAT FACE BEFORE.
BUT WHAT ARE THE REST OF YOU GONNA DO?
YOU CAN'T FIGHT A DRAGON WITH JUST TWO PEOPLE.
DON'T COUNT ME FOR THAT STUFF.
PLUS, THAT AX OF YOURS...
...REALLY DOESN'T LOOK LIKE IT COULD BE ANY THREAT TO A DRAGON.
......
NAMARI, YOU'VE KILLED SEVERAL DRAGONS... RIGHT?
YEAH.
TH...
THEN...

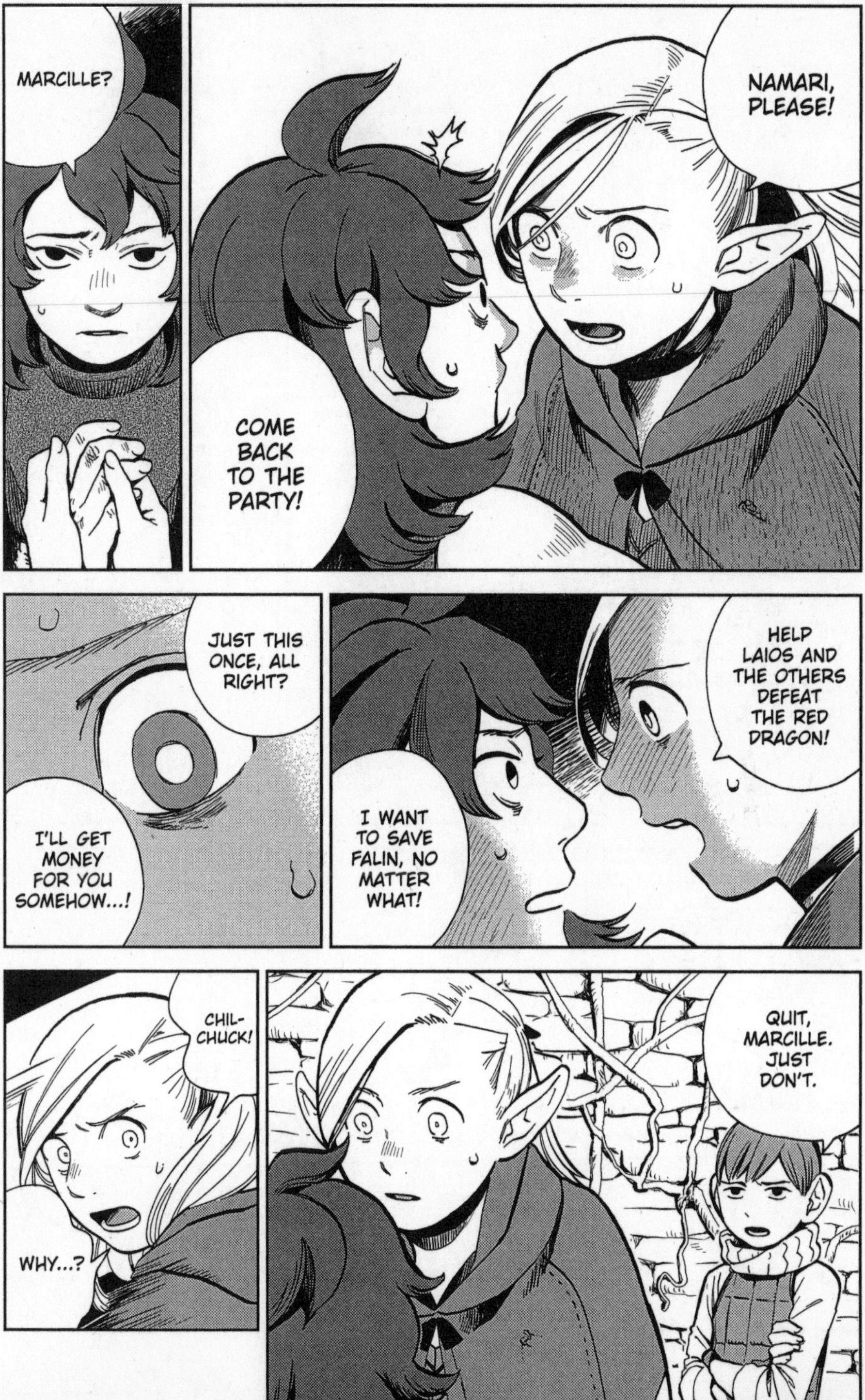
NAMARI, PLEASE!
COME BACK TO THE PARTY!
MARCILLE?
HELP LAIOS AND THE OTHERS DEFEAT THE RED DRAGON!
I WANT TO SAVE FALIN, NO MATTER WHAT!
JUST THIS ONCE, ALL RIGHT?
I'LL GET MONEY FOR YOU SOMEHOW...!
QUIT, MARCILLE. JUST DON'T.
CHIL-CHUCK!
WHY...?

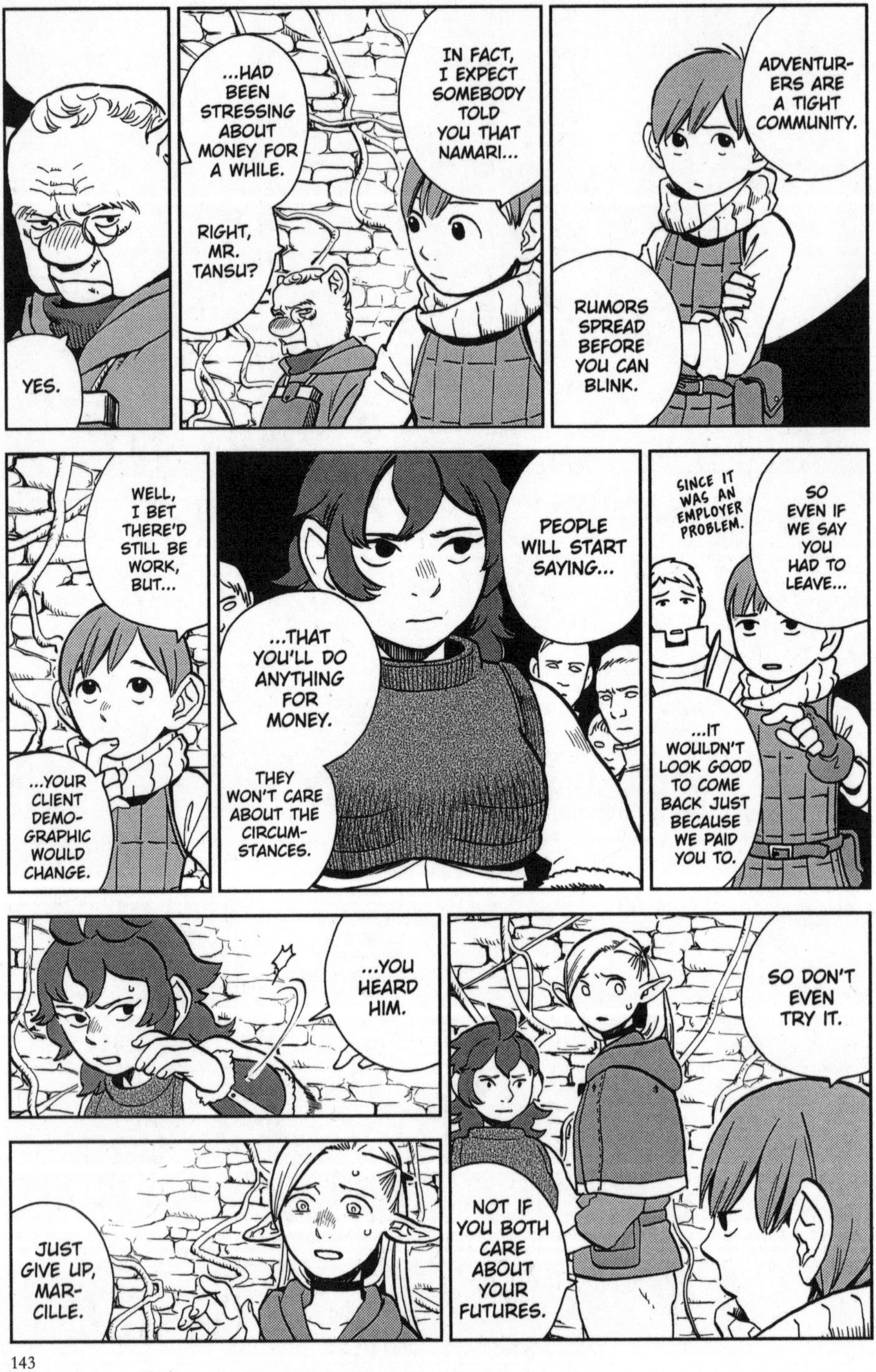
ADVENTURERS ARE A TIGHT COMMUNITY.
RUMORS SPREAD BEFORE YOU CAN BLINK.
IN FACT, I EXPECT SOMEBODY TOLD YOU THAT NAMARI...
...HAD BEEN STRESSING ABOUT MONEY FOR A WHILE.
RIGHT, MR. TANSU?
YES.
SO EVEN IF WE SAY YOU HAD TO LEAVE...
SINCE IT WAS AN EMPLOYER PROBLEM.
...IT WOULDN'T LOOK GOOD TO COME BACK JUST BECAUSE WE PAID YOU TO.
PEOPLE WILL START SAYING...
...THAT YOU'LL DO ANYTHING FOR MONEY.
THEY WON'T CARE ABOUT THE CIRCUMSTANCES.
WELL, I BET THERE'D STILL BE WORK, BUT...
...YOUR CLIENT DEMOGRAPHIC WOULD CHANGE.
SO DON'T EVEN TRY IT.
NOT IF YOU BOTH CARE ABOUT YOUR FUTURES.
...YOU HEARD HIM.
JUST GIVE UP, MARCILLE.

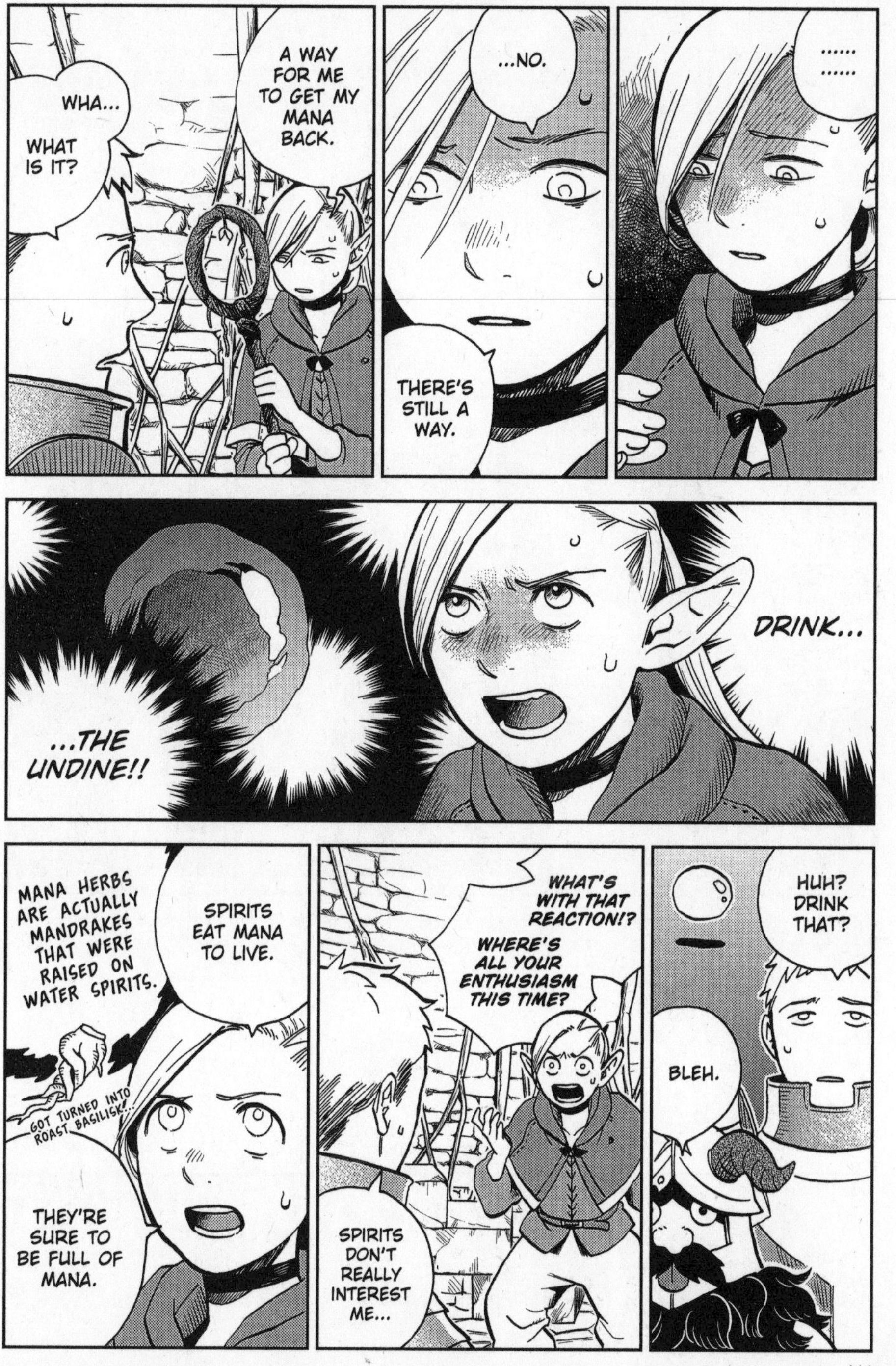

......
......
...NO.
THERE'S STILL A WAY.
A WAY FOR ME TO GET MY MANA BACK.
WHA...
WHAT IS IT?
DRINK...
...THE UNDINE!!
HUH? DRINK THAT?
BLEH.
WHAT'S WITH THAT REACTION!?
WHERE'S ALL YOUR ENTHUSIASM THIS TIME?
SPIRITS DON'T REALLY INTEREST ME...
SPIRITS EAT MANA TO LIVE.
MANA HERBS ARE ACTUALLY MANDRAKES THAT WERE RAISED ON WATER SPIRITS.
GOT TURNED INTO ROAST BASILISK...
THEY'RE SURE TO BE FULL OF MANA.

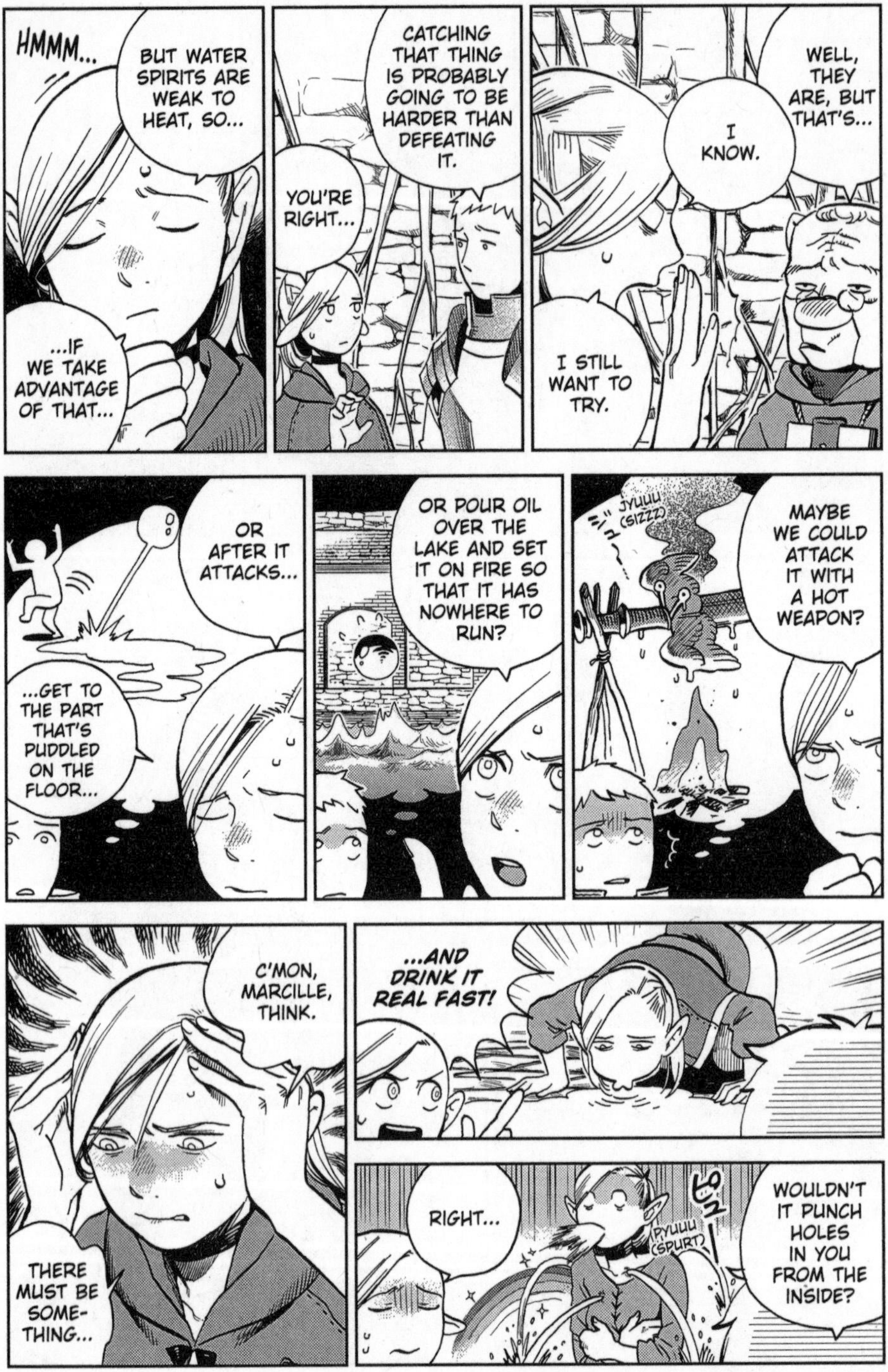
WELL, THEY ARE, BUT THAT'S...
I KNOW.
I STILL WANT TO TRY.
CATCHING THAT THING IS PROBABLY GOING TO BE HARDER THAN DEFEATING IT.
YOU'RE RIGHT...
HMMM...
BUT WATER SPIRITS ARE WEAK TO HEAT, SO...
...IF WE TAKE ADVANTAGE OF THAT...
JYUUU (SIZZZ)
MAYBE WE COULD ATTACK IT WITH A HOT WEAPON?
OR POUR OIL OVER THE LAKE AND SET IT ON FIRE SO THAT IT HAS NOWHERE TO RUN?
OR AFTER IT ATTACKS...
...GET TO THE PART THAT'S PUDDLED ON THE FLOOR...
...AND DRINK IT REAL FAST!
WOULDN'T IT PUNCH HOLES IN YOU FROM THE INSIDE?
PYUUU (SPURT)
RIGHT...
C'MON, MARCILLE, THINK.
THERE MUST BE SOME-THING...

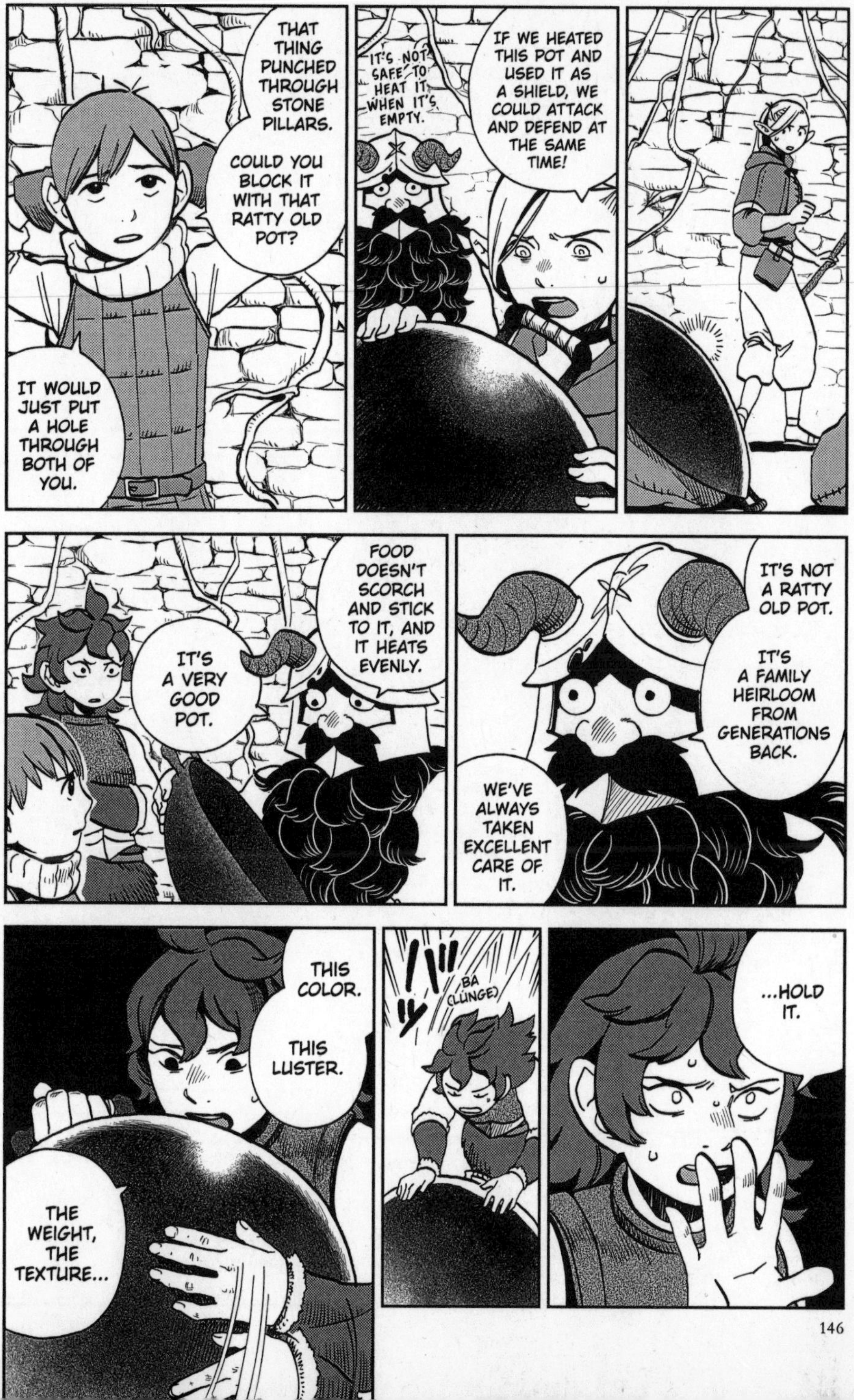
IF WE HEATED THIS POT AND USED IT AS A SHIELD, WE COULD ATTACK AND DEFEND AT THE SAME TIME!
IT'S NOT SAFE TO HEAT IT WHEN IT'S EMPTY.
THAT THING PUNCHED THROUGH STONE PILLARS.
COULD YOU BLOCK IT WITH THAT RATTY OLD POT?
IT WOULD JUST PUT A HOLE THROUGH BOTH OF YOU.
IT'S NOT A RATTY OLD POT.
IT'S A FAMILY HEIRLOOM FROM GENERATIONS BACK.
WE'VE ALWAYS TAKEN EXCELLENT CARE OF IT.
FOOD DOESN'T SCORCH AND STICK TO IT, AND IT HEATS EVENLY.
IT'S A VERY GOOD POT.
...HOLD IT.
BA (LUNGE)
THIS COLOR.
THIS LUSTER.
THE WEIGHT, THE TEXTURE...

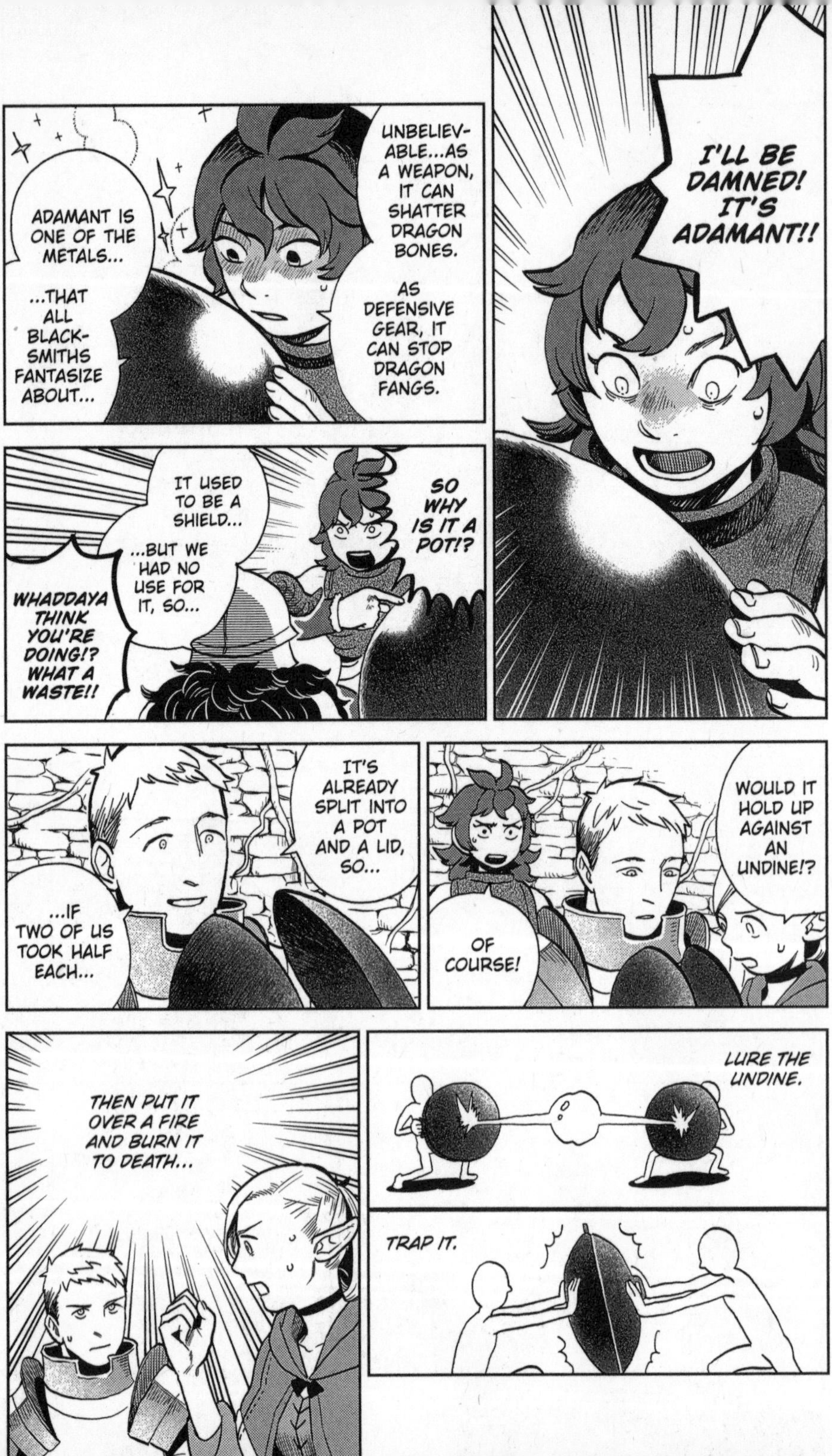
I'LL BE DAMNED! IT'S ADAMANT!!
UNBELIEVABLE...AS A WEAPON, IT CAN SHATTER DRAGON BONES.
AS DEFENSIVE GEAR, IT CAN STOP DRAGON FANGS.
ADAMANT IS ONE OF THE METALS...
...THAT ALL BLACKSMITHS FANTASIZE ABOUT...
SO WHY IS IT A POT!?
IT USED TO BE A SHIELD...
...BUT WE HAD NO USE FOR IT, SO...
WHADDAYA THINK YOU'RE DOING!? WHAT A WASTE!!
WOULD IT HOLD UP AGAINST AN UNDINE!?
OF COURSE!
IT'S ALREADY SPLIT INTO A POT AND A LID, SO...
...IF TWO OF US TOOK HALF EACH...
LURE THE UNDINE.
TRAP IT.
THEN PUT IT OVER A FIRE AND BURN IT TO DEATH...

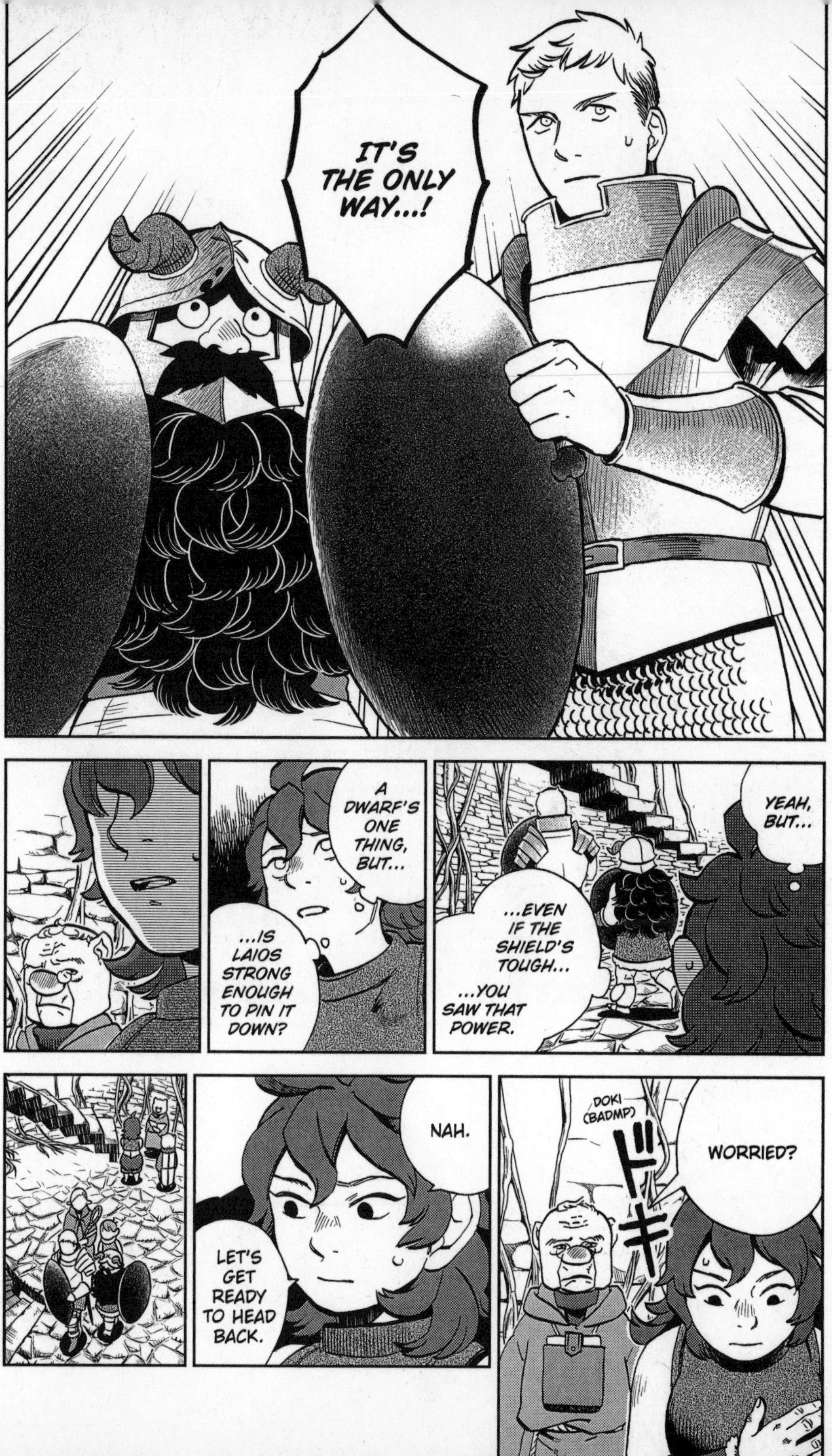
IT'S THE ONLY WAY...!
YEAH, BUT...
...EVEN IF THE SHIELD'S TOUGH...
...YOU SAW THAT POWER.
A DWARF'S ONE THING, BUT...
...IS LAIOS STRONG ENOUGH TO PIN IT DOWN?
WORRIED?
DOKI (BADMP)
ドキ
NAH.
LET'S GET READY TO HEAD BACK.

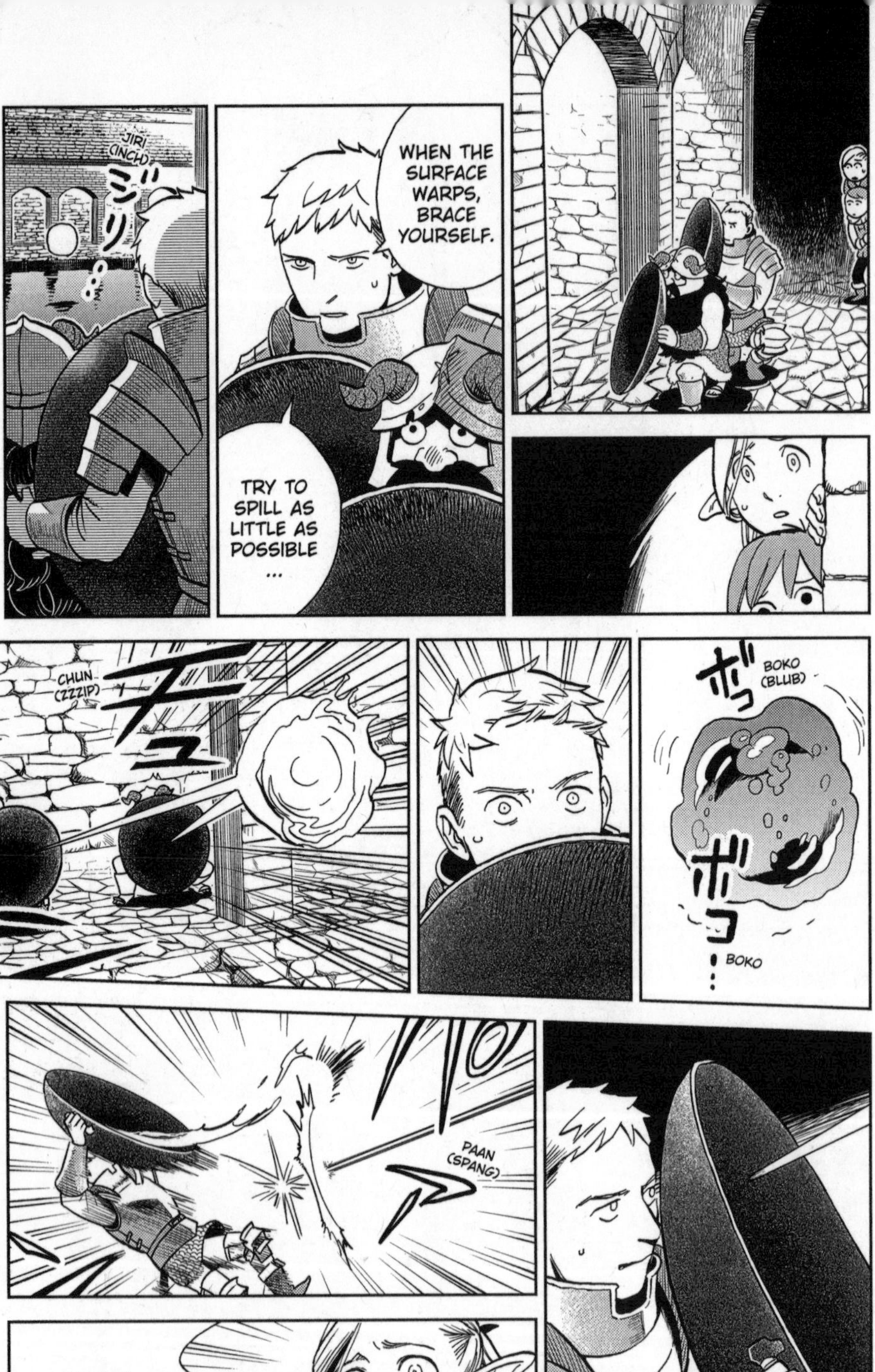
WHEN THE SURFACE WARPS, BRACE YOURSELF.
TRY TO SPILL AS LITTLE AS POSSIBLE ...
JIRI (INCH)
ジリ…
BOKO (BLUB)
ボッ
ボコ…
BOKO
CHUN (ZZZIP)
チュ
PAAN (SPANG)
パ
LAIOS!

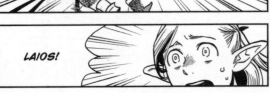

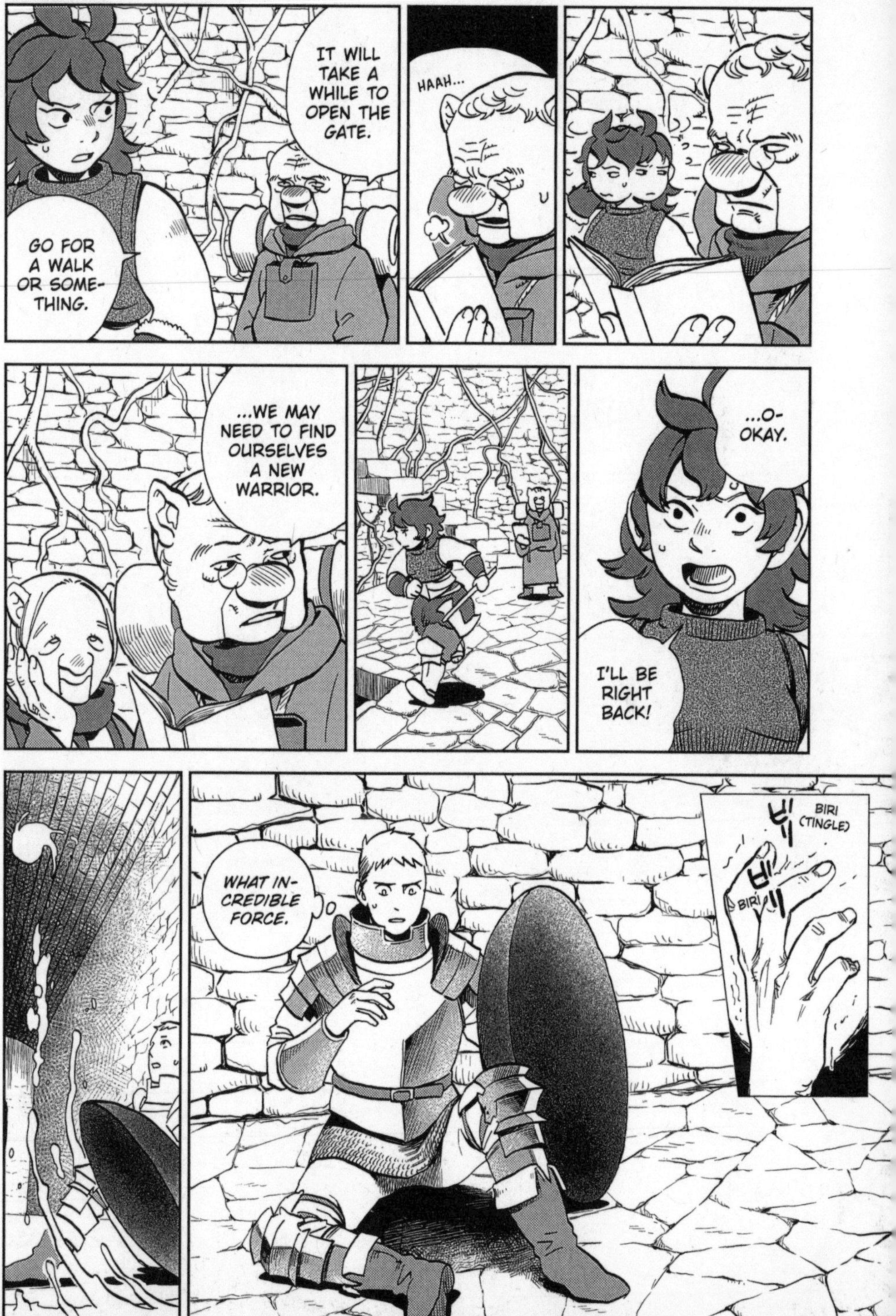
HAAH...
IT WILL TAKE A WHILE TO OPEN THE GATE.
GO FOR A WALK OR SOME-THING.
...O-OKAY.
I'LL BE RIGHT BACK!
...WE MAY NEED TO FIND OURSELVES A NEW WARRIOR.
BIRI (TINGLE)
BIRI
WHAT IN-CREDIBLE FORCE.

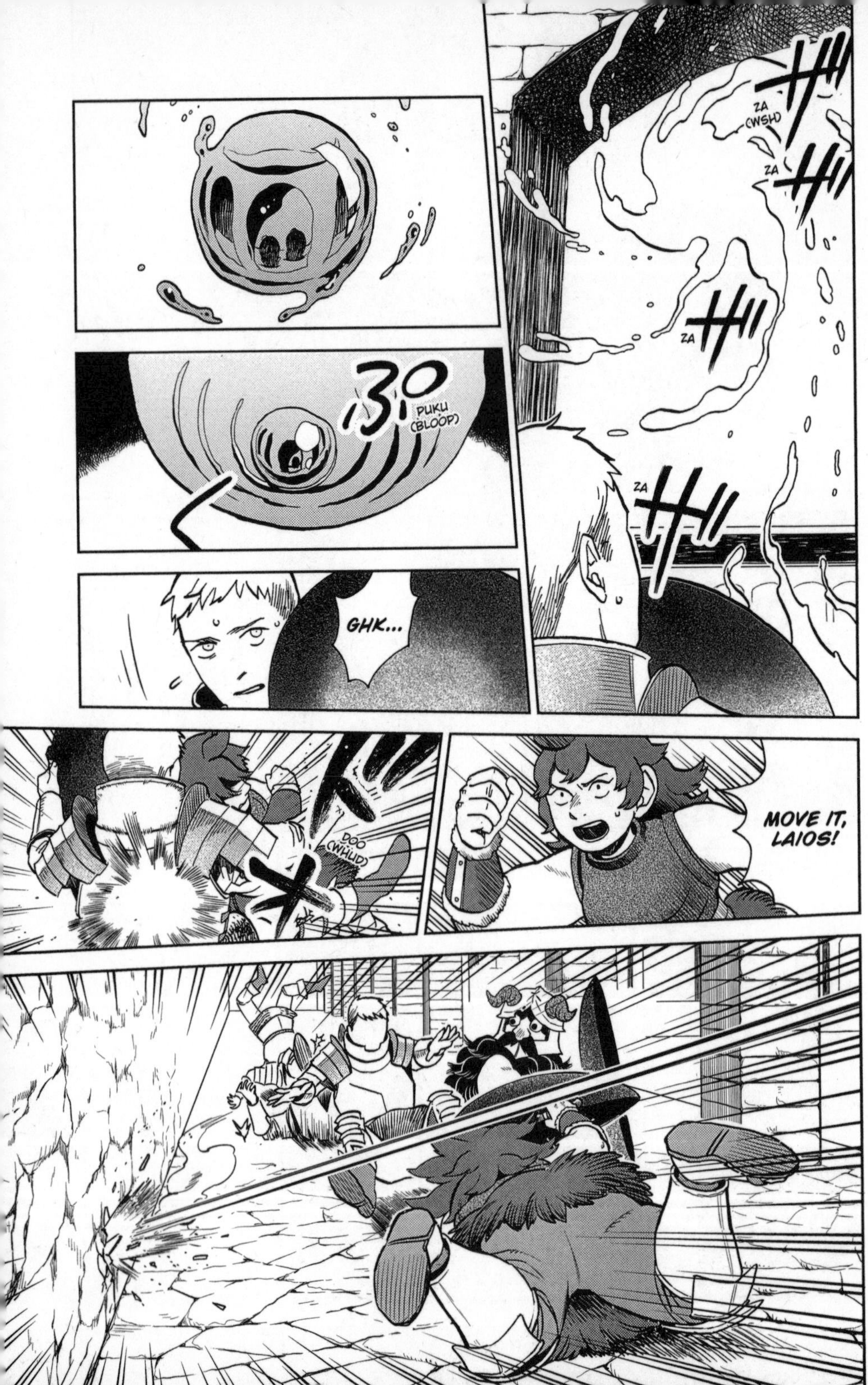
ZA (WSH)
ZA
ZA
ZA
PUKU (BLOOP)
GHK...
MOVE IT, LAIOS!
DOO (WHUD)

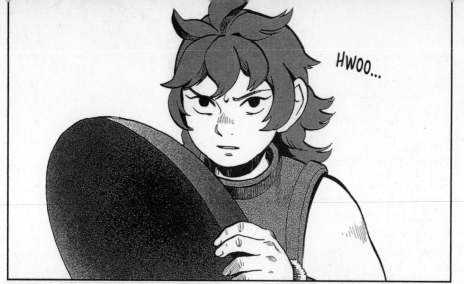

HWOO...

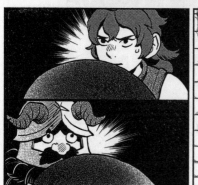

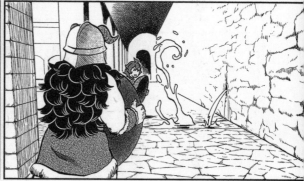

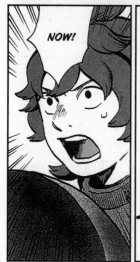

NOW!

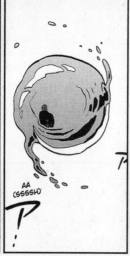

AA
(SSSSH)

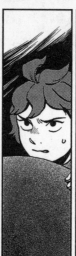

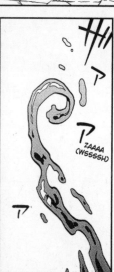

ZAAAA
(WSSSSH)

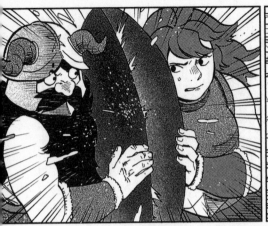

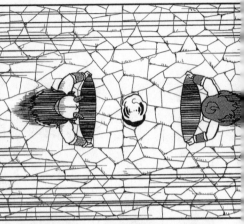

HOLD YOUR GROUND!!

GOOD... KEEP GOING...

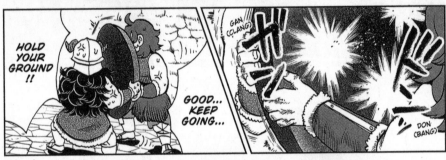

GAN (CLANG)

DON (BANG)

...ON THE FIRE!!

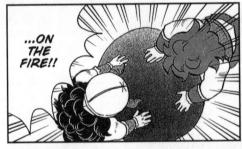

GET IT...

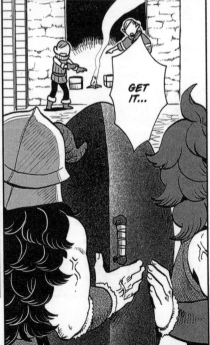

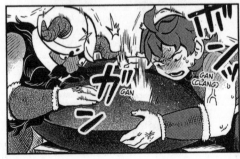

GAN (CLANG)

GAN

153

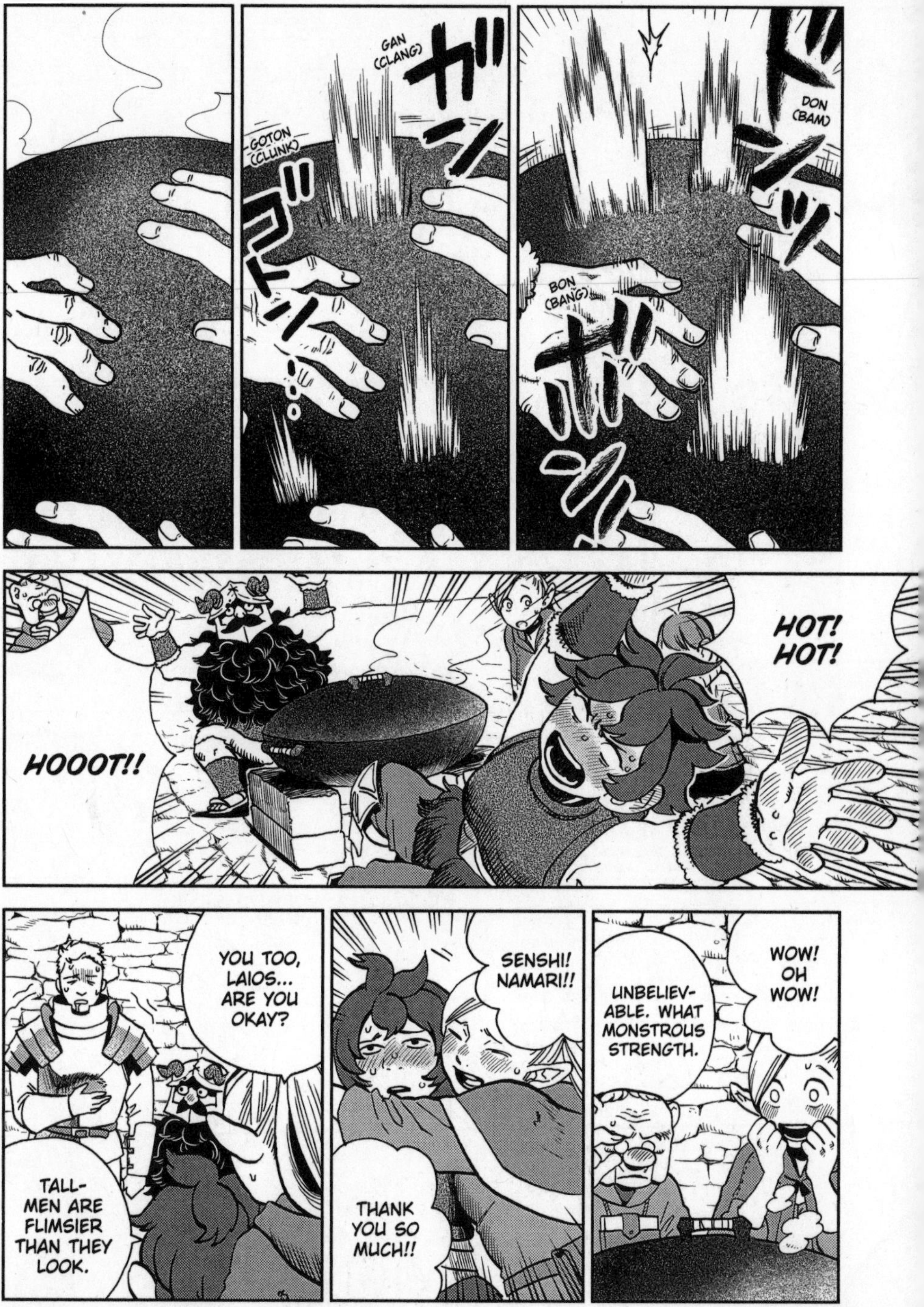
DON (BAM)
BON (BANG)
GAN (CLANG)
GOTON (CLUNK)
HOT! HOT!
HOOOT!!
WOW! OH WOW!
UNBELIEVABLE. WHAT MONSTROUS STRENGTH.
SENSHI! NAMARI!!
THANK YOU SO MUCH!!
YOU TOO, LAIOS... ARE YOU OKAY?
TALL-MEN ARE FLIMSIER THAN THEY LOOK.

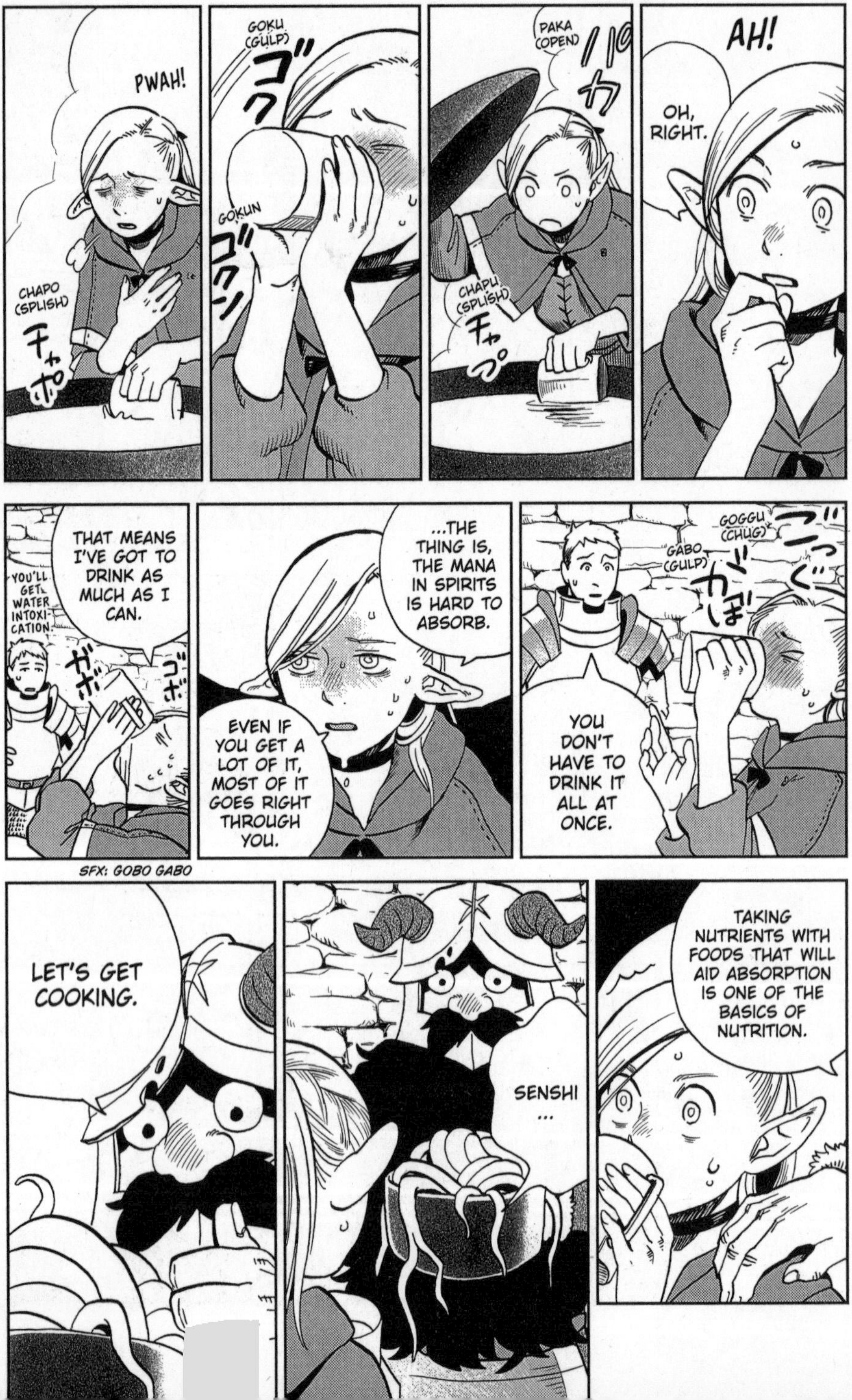
AH!
OH, RIGHT.
PAKA (OPEN)
パカ
CHAPU (SPLISH)
チャプ
GOKU (GULP)
ゴク
GOKUN
ゴクン
PWAH!
CHAPO (SPLISH)
チャポ
GOGGU (CHUG)
ごっく
GABO (GULP)
がぼ
YOU DON'T HAVE TO DRINK IT ALL AT ONCE.
...THE THING IS, THE MANA IN SPIRITS IS HARD TO ABSORB.
EVEN IF YOU GET A LOT OF IT, MOST OF IT GOES RIGHT THROUGH YOU.
THAT MEANS I'VE GOT TO DRINK AS MUCH AS I CAN.
YOU'LL GET WATER INTOXICATION.
ゴボ
ガボ
SFX: GOBO GABO
TAKING NUTRIENTS WITH FOODS THAT WILL AID ABSORPTION IS ONE OF THE BASICS OF NUTRITION.
SENSHI ...
LET'S GET COOKING.

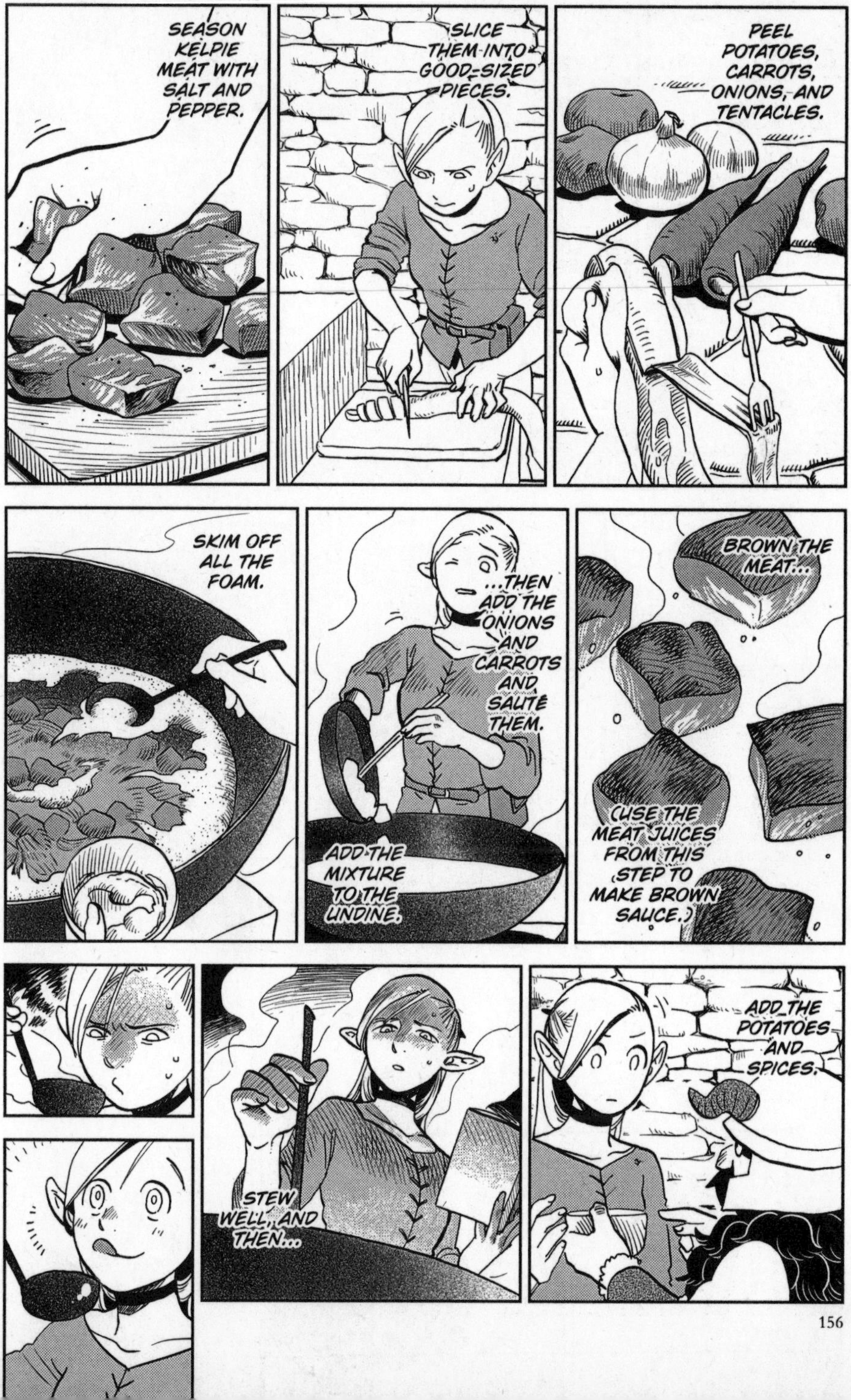
PEEL POTATOES, CARROTS, ONIONS, AND TENTACLES.
SLICE THEM INTO GOOD-SIZED PIECES.
SEASON KELPIE MEAT WITH SALT AND PEPPER.
BROWN THE MEAT...
(USE THE MEAT JUICES FROM THIS STEP TO MAKE BROWN SAUCE.)
...THEN ADD THE ONIONS AND CARROTS AND SAUTE THEM.
ADD THE MIXTURE TO THE UNDINE.
SKIM OFF ALL THE FOAM.
ADD THE POTATOES AND SPICES.
STEW WELL, AND THEN...

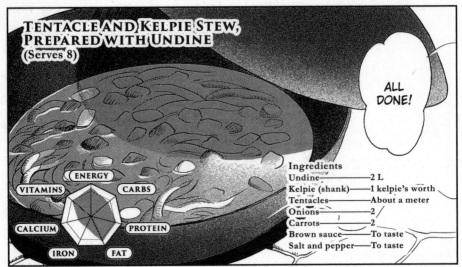

Tentacle and Kelpie Stew, Prepared with Undine
(Serves 8)

ALL DONE!

Ingredients

Undine	2 L
Kelpie (shank)	1 kelpie's worth
Tentacles	About a meter
Onions	2
Carrots	2
Brown sauce	To taste
Salt and pepper	To taste

ENERGY
VITAMINS · CARBS
CALCIUM · PROTEIN
IRON · FAT

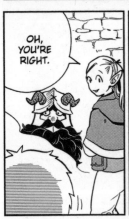

OH, YOU'RE RIGHT.

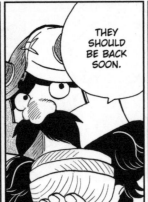

THEY SHOULD BE BACK SOON.

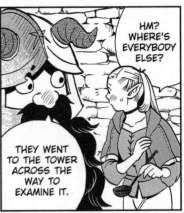

HM? WHERE'S EVERYBODY ELSE?

THEY WENT TO THE TOWER ACROSS THE WAY TO EXAMINE IT.

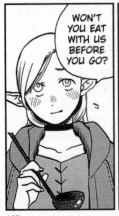

WON'T YOU EAT WITH US BEFORE YOU GO?

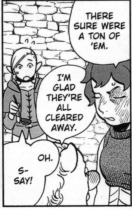

THERE SURE WERE A TON OF 'EM.

I'M GLAD THEY'RE ALL CLEARED AWAY.

OH. S-SAY!

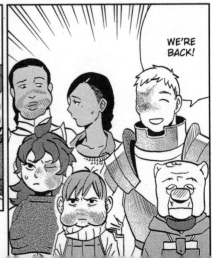

WE'RE BACK!

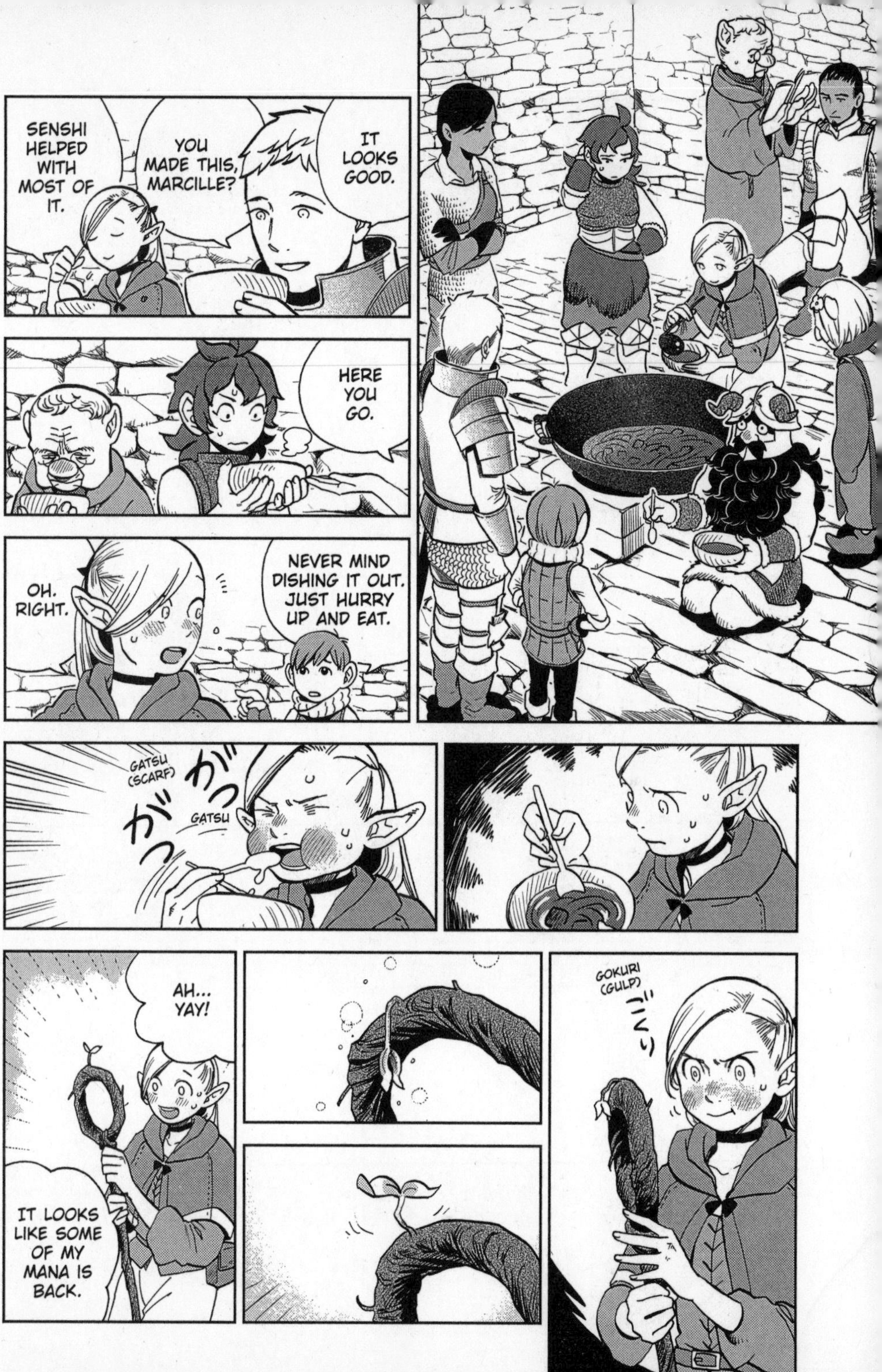
IT LOOKS GOOD.
YOU MADE THIS, MARCILLE?
SENSHI HELPED WITH MOST OF IT.
HERE YOU GO.
NEVER MIND DISHING IT OUT. JUST HURRY UP AND EAT.
OH. RIGHT.
がつ
GATSU (SCARF)
がつ
GATSU
ごくり
GOKURI (GULP)
AH... YAY!
IT LOOKS LIKE SOME OF MY MANA IS BACK.

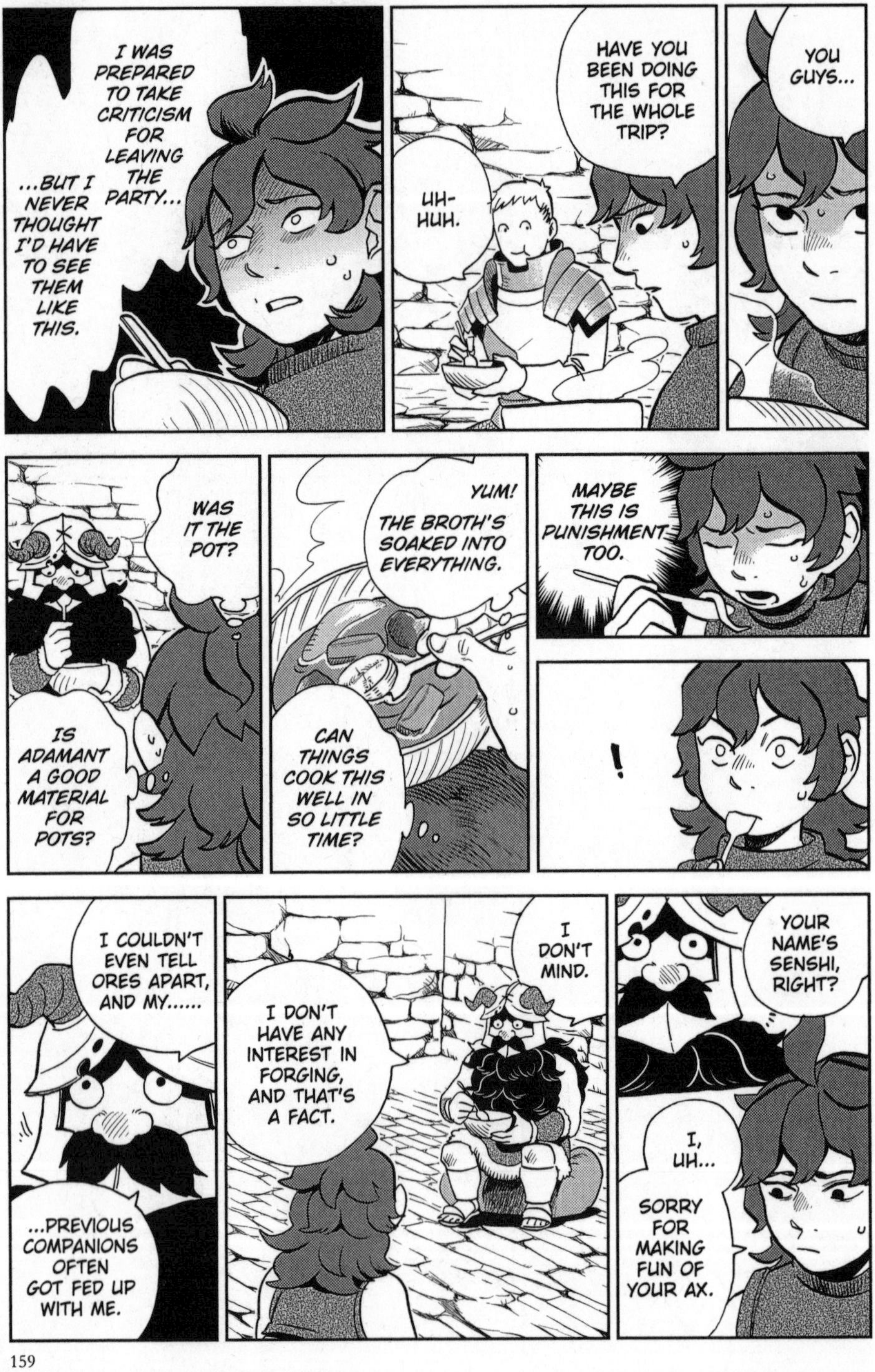
YOU GUYS...
HAVE YOU BEEN DOING THIS FOR THE WHOLE TRIP?
UH-HUH.
I WAS PREPARED TO TAKE CRITICISM FOR LEAVING THE PARTY...
...BUT I NEVER THOUGHT I'D HAVE TO SEE THEM LIKE THIS.
MAYBE THIS IS PUNISHMENT TOO.
!
YUM!
THE BROTH'S SOAKED INTO EVERYTHING.
CAN THINGS COOK THIS WELL IN SO LITTLE TIME?
WAS IT THE POT?
IS ADAMANT A GOOD MATERIAL FOR POTS?
YOUR NAME'S SENSHI, RIGHT?
I, UH...
SORRY FOR MAKING FUN OF YOUR AX.
I DON'T MIND.
I DON'T HAVE ANY INTEREST IN FORGING, AND THAT'S A FACT.
I COULDN'T EVEN TELL ORES APART, AND MY......
...PREVIOUS COMPANIONS OFTEN GOT FED UP WITH ME.

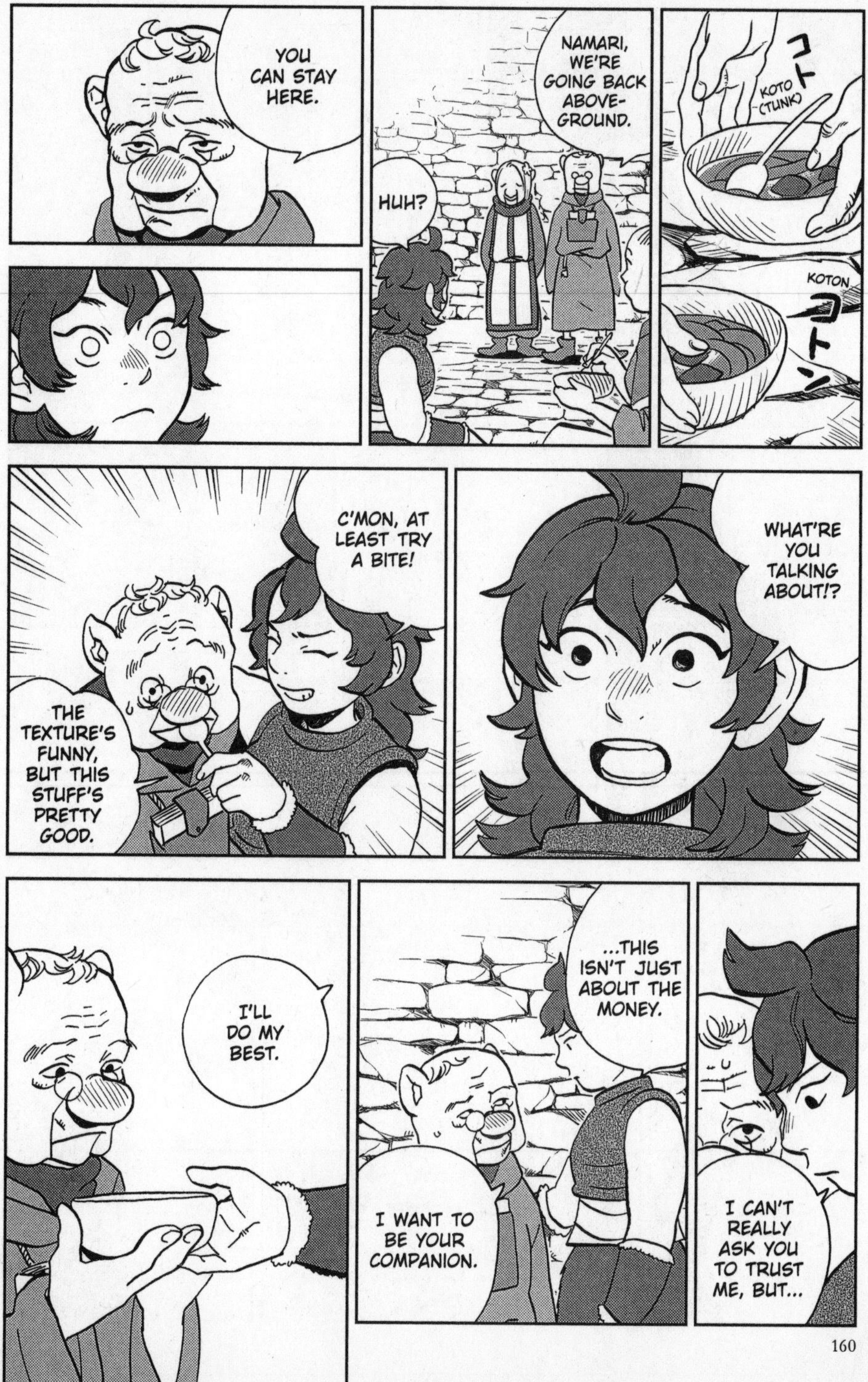
コト
KOTO (TUNK)
KOTON
コトン
NAMARI, WE'RE GOING BACK ABOVE-GROUND.
HUH?
YOU CAN STAY HERE.
WHAT'RE YOU TALKING ABOUT!?
C'MON, AT LEAST TRY A BITE!
THE TEXTURE'S FUNNY, BUT THIS STUFF'S PRETTY GOOD.
I CAN'T REALLY ASK YOU TO TRUST ME, BUT...
...THIS ISN'T JUST ABOUT THE MONEY.
I WANT TO BE YOUR COMPANION.
I'LL DO MY BEST.

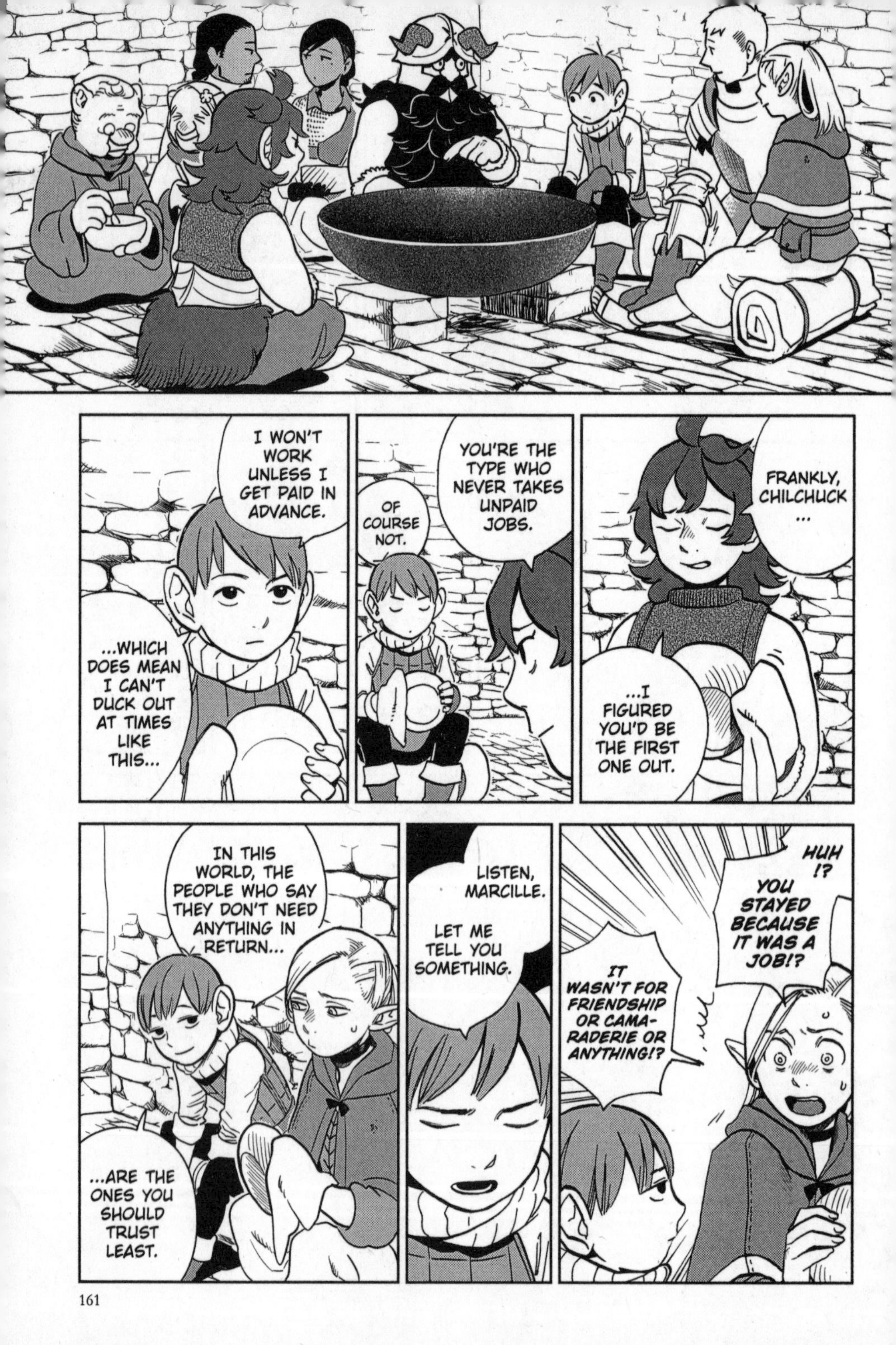
FRANKLY, CHILCHUCK...
...I FIGURED YOU'D BE THE FIRST ONE OUT.
YOU'RE THE TYPE WHO NEVER TAKES UNPAID JOBS.
OF COURSE NOT.
I WON'T WORK UNLESS I GET PAID IN ADVANCE.
...WHICH DOES MEAN I CAN'T DUCK OUT AT TIMES LIKE THIS...
HUH!?
YOU STAYED BECAUSE IT WAS A JOB!?
IT WASN'T FOR FRIENDSHIP OR CAMARADERIE OR ANYTHING!?
LISTEN, MARCILLE.
LET ME TELL YOU SOMETHING.
IN THIS WORLD, THE PEOPLE WHO SAY THEY DON'T NEED ANYTHING IN RETURN...
...ARE THE ONES YOU SHOULD TRUST LEAST.

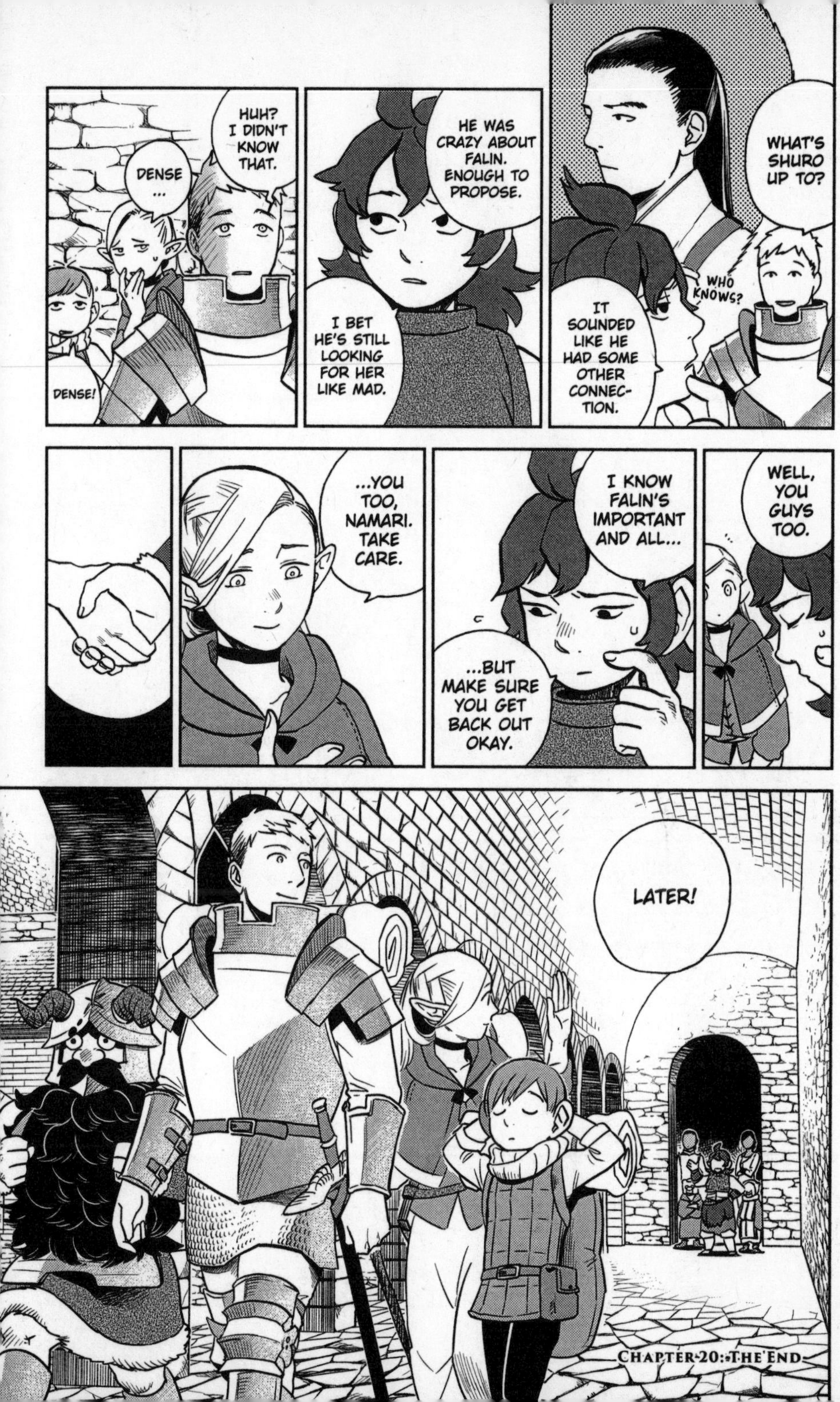
WHAT'S SHURO UP TO?
WHO KNOWS?
IT SOUNDED LIKE HE HAD SOME OTHER CONNECTION.
HE WAS CRAZY ABOUT FALIN. ENOUGH TO PROPOSE.
I BET HE'S STILL LOOKING FOR HER LIKE MAD.
HUH? I DIDN'T KNOW THAT.
DENSE...
DENSE!
WELL, YOU GUYS TOO.
I KNOW FALIN'S IMPORTANT AND ALL...
...BUT MAKE SURE YOU GET BACK OUT OKAY.
...YOU TOO, NAMARI. TAKE CARE.
LATER!
Chapter 20: The End

21. Giant Frogs

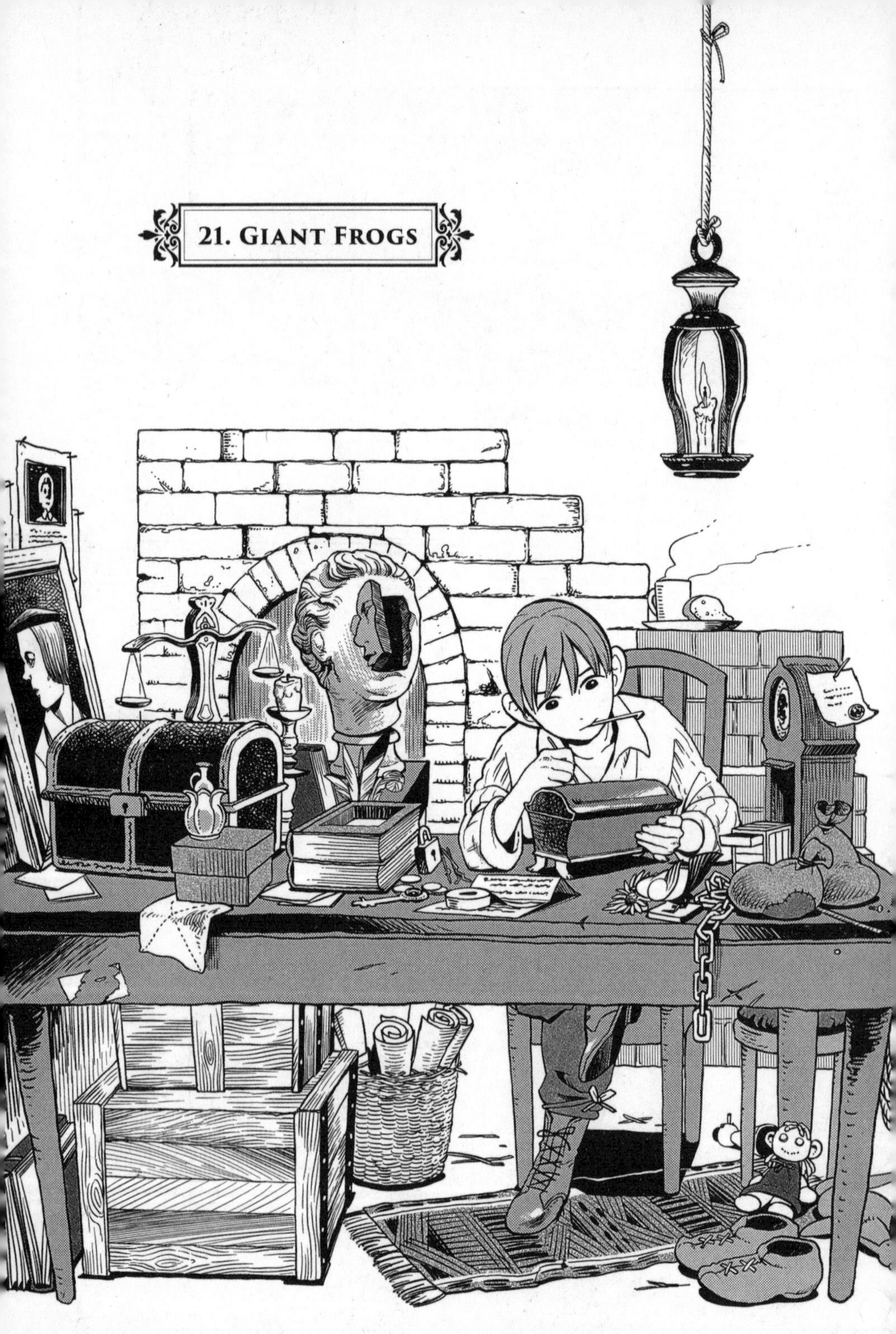

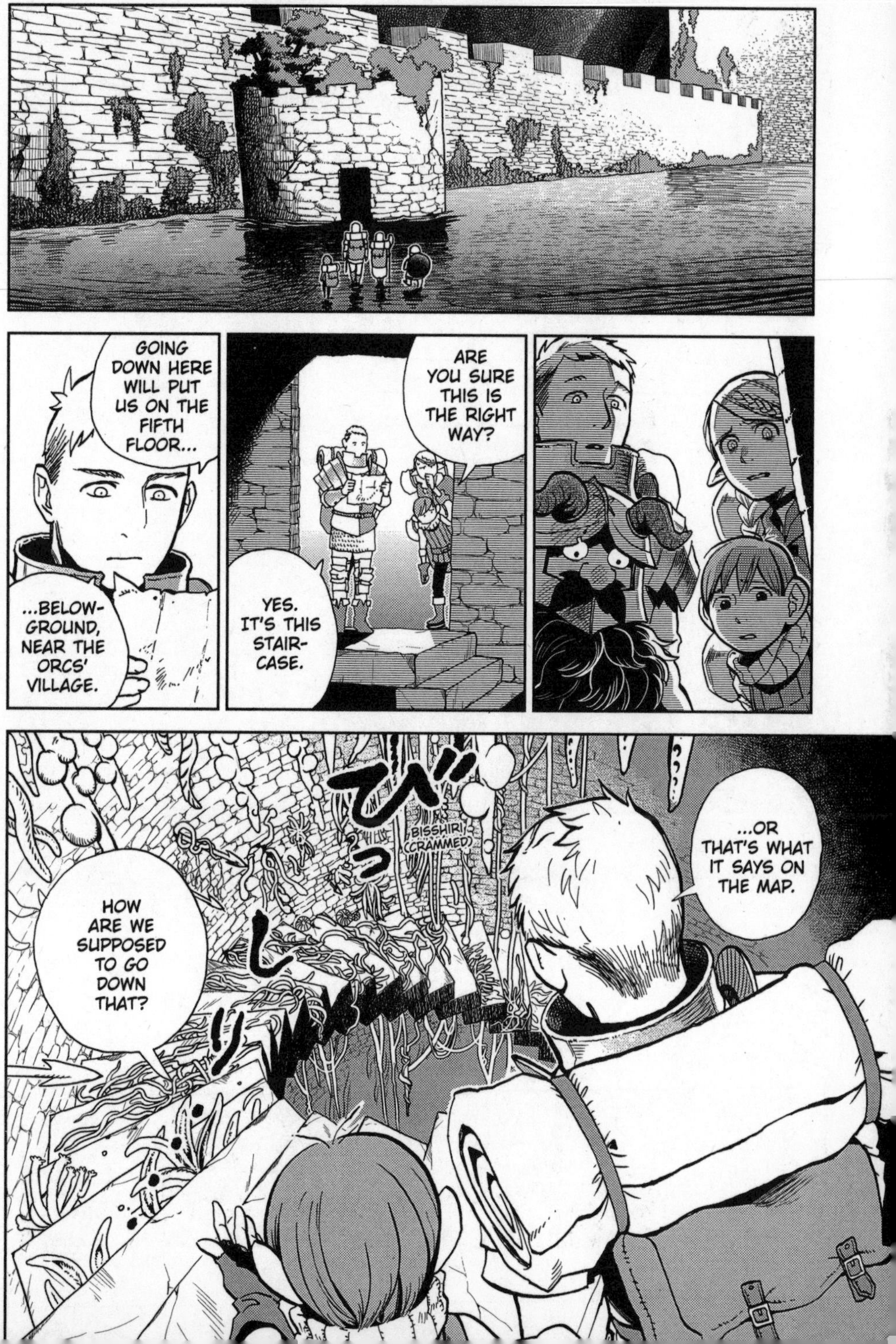

ARE YOU SURE THIS IS THE RIGHT WAY?
YES. IT'S THIS STAIR-CASE.
GOING DOWN HERE WILL PUT US ON THE FIFTH FLOOR...
...BELOW-GROUND, NEAR THE ORCS' VILLAGE.
...OR THAT'S WHAT IT SAYS ON THE MAP.
びっしり
BISSHIRI (CRAMMED)
HOW ARE WE SUPPOSED TO GO DOWN THAT?

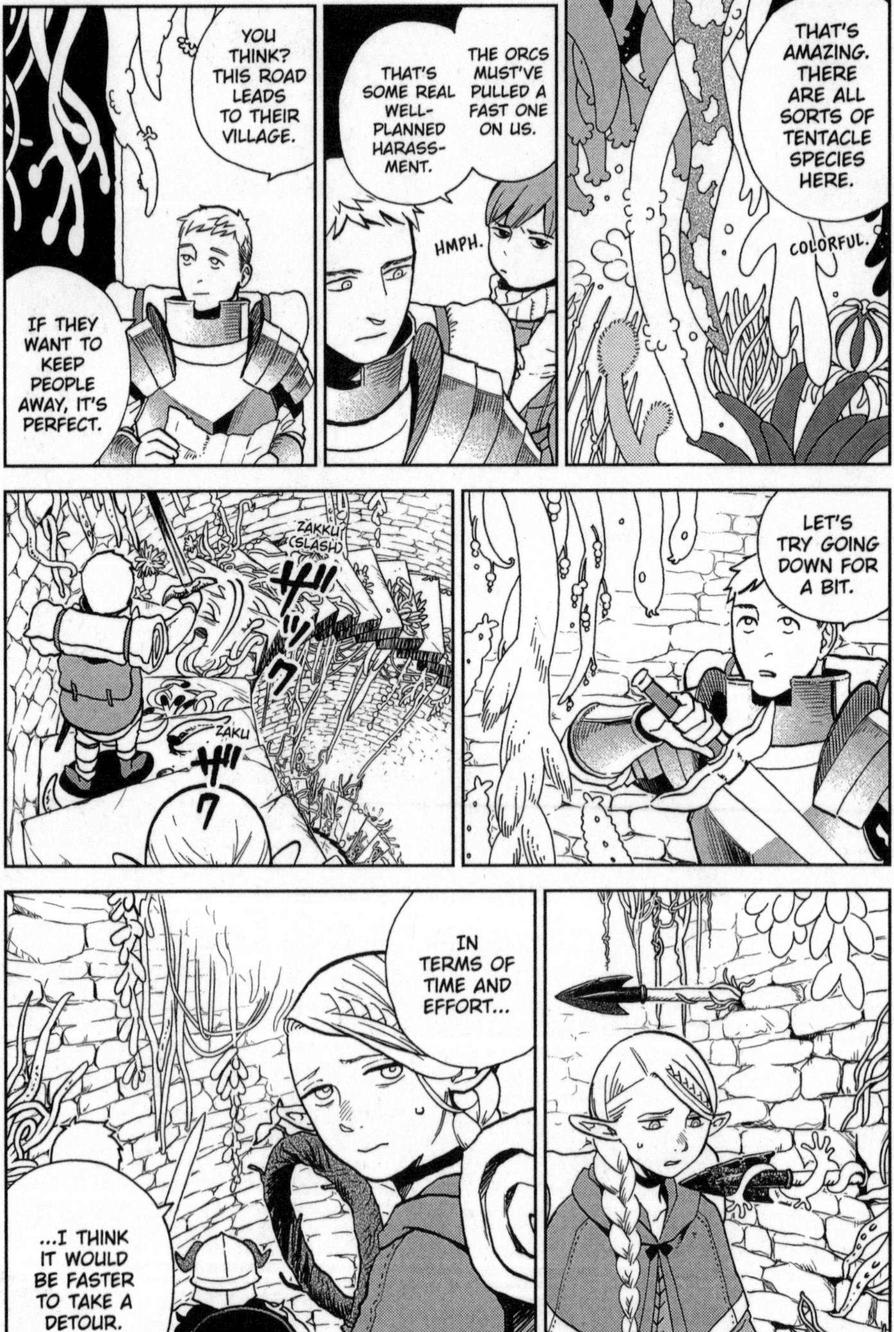
THAT'S AMAZING. THERE ARE ALL SORTS OF TENTACLE SPECIES HERE.
COLORFUL.
THE ORCS MUST'VE PULLED A FAST ONE ON US.
THAT'S SOME REAL WELL-PLANNED HARASSMENT.
HMPH.
YOU THINK? THIS ROAD LEADS TO THEIR VILLAGE.
IF THEY WANT TO KEEP PEOPLE AWAY, IT'S PERFECT.
LET'S TRY GOING DOWN FOR A BIT.
ZAKKU (SLASH)
ザック
ZAKU
ザク
IN TERMS OF TIME AND EFFORT...
...I THINK IT WOULD BE FASTER TO TAKE A DETOUR.

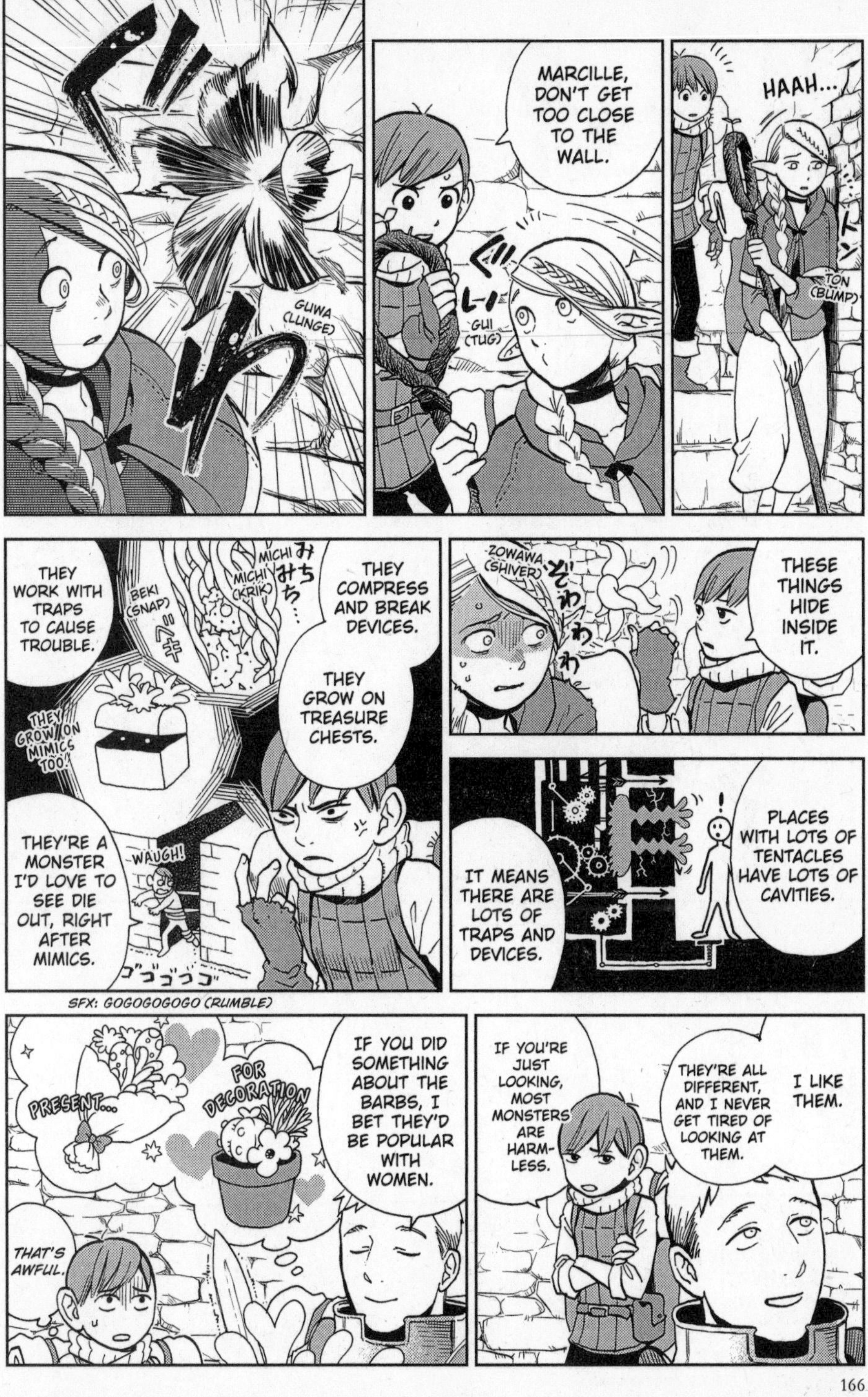
HAAH...
TON (BUMP)
MARCILLE, DON'T GET TOO CLOSE TO THE WALL.
GUI (TUG)
GUWA (LUNGE)
THESE THINGS HIDE INSIDE IT.
ZOWAWA (SHIVER)
PLACES WITH LOTS OF TENTACLES HAVE LOTS OF CAVITIES.
IT MEANS THERE ARE LOTS OF TRAPS AND DEVICES.
THEY COMPRESS AND BREAK DEVICES.
MICHI MICHI (KRIK)
THEY WORK WITH TRAPS TO CAUSE TROUBLE.
BEKI (SNAP)
THEY GROW ON TREASURE CHESTS.
THEY GROW ON MIMICS TOO!
THEY'RE A MONSTER I'D LOVE TO SEE DIE OUT, RIGHT AFTER MIMICS.
WAUGH!
SFX: GOGOGOGOGO (RUMBLE)
I LIKE THEM.
THEY'RE ALL DIFFERENT, AND I NEVER GET TIRED OF LOOKING AT THEM.
IF YOU'RE JUST LOOKING, MOST MONSTERS ARE HARMLESS.
IF YOU DID SOMETHING ABOUT THE BARBS, I BET THEY'D BE POPULAR WITH WOMEN.
FOR DECORATION
PRESENT...
THAT'S AWFUL.

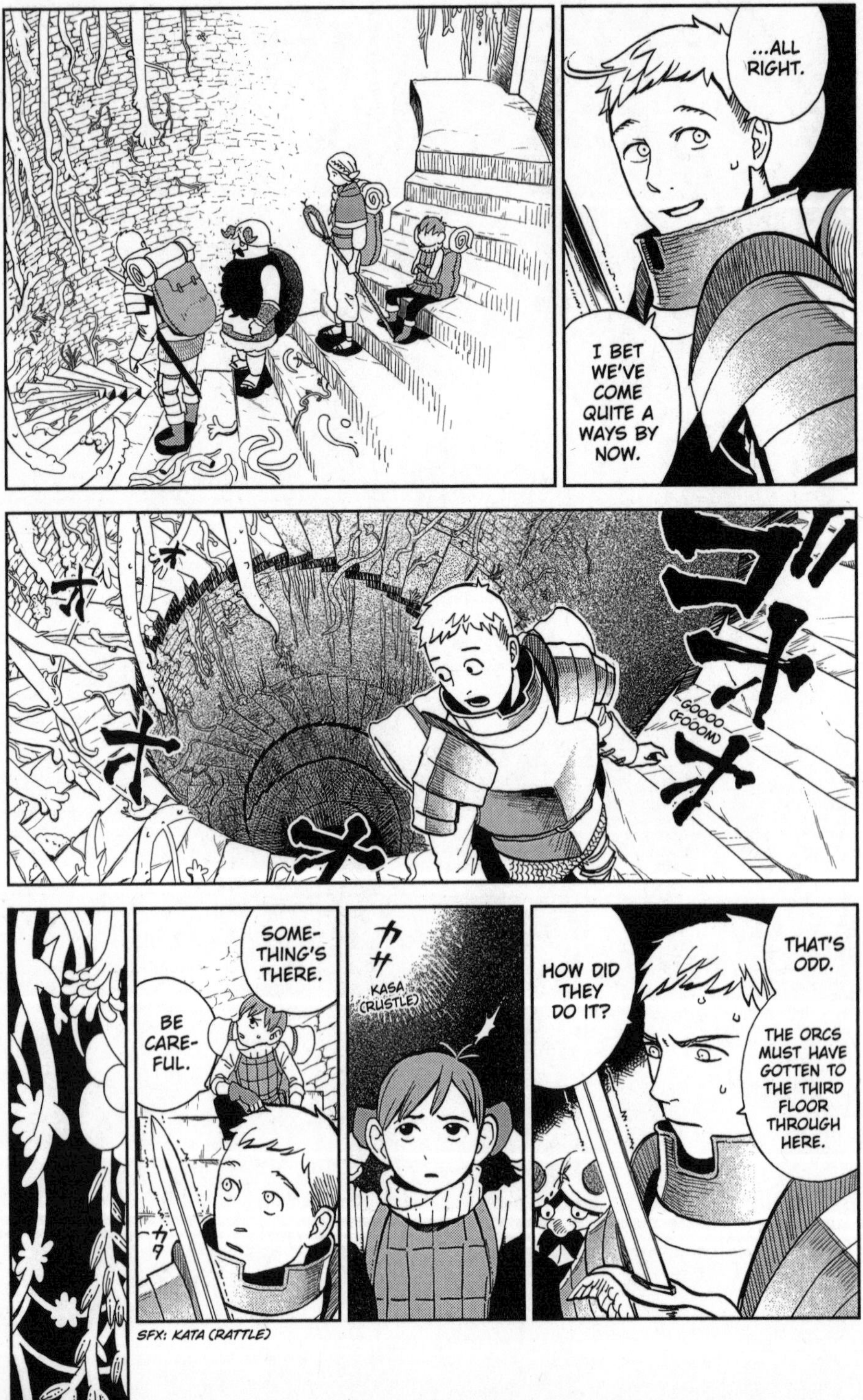
...ALL RIGHT.
I BET WE'VE COME QUITE A WAYS BY NOW.
GOOOO (FOOOM)
THAT'S ODD.
THE ORCS MUST HAVE GOTTEN TO THE THIRD FLOOR THROUGH HERE.
HOW DID THEY DO IT?
KASA (RUSTLE)
SOME-THING'S THERE.
BE CARE-FUL.
SFX: KATA (RATTLE)

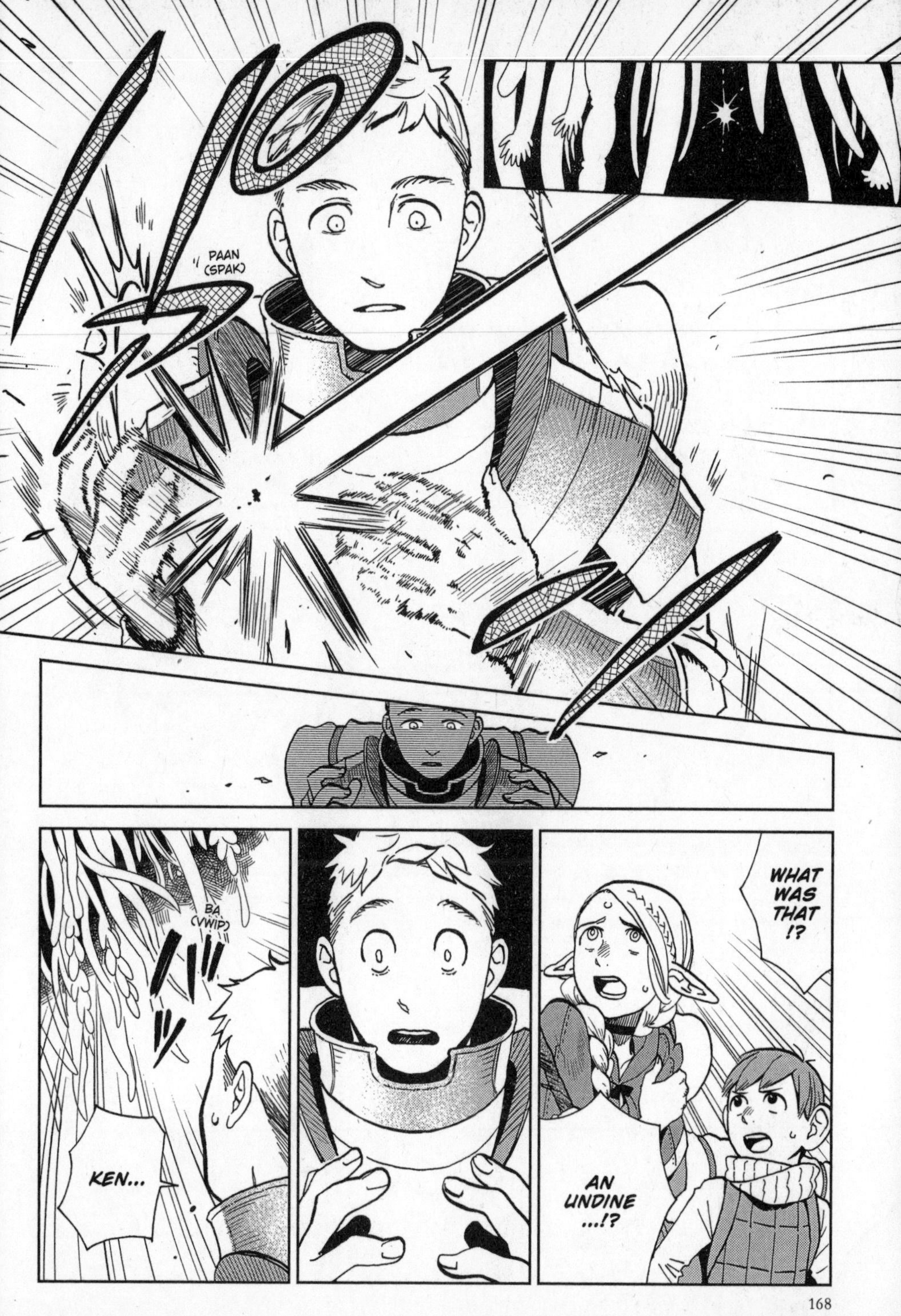
PAAN
(SPAK)
WHAT WAS THAT!?
AN UNDINE ...!?
BA
(VWIP)
KEN...

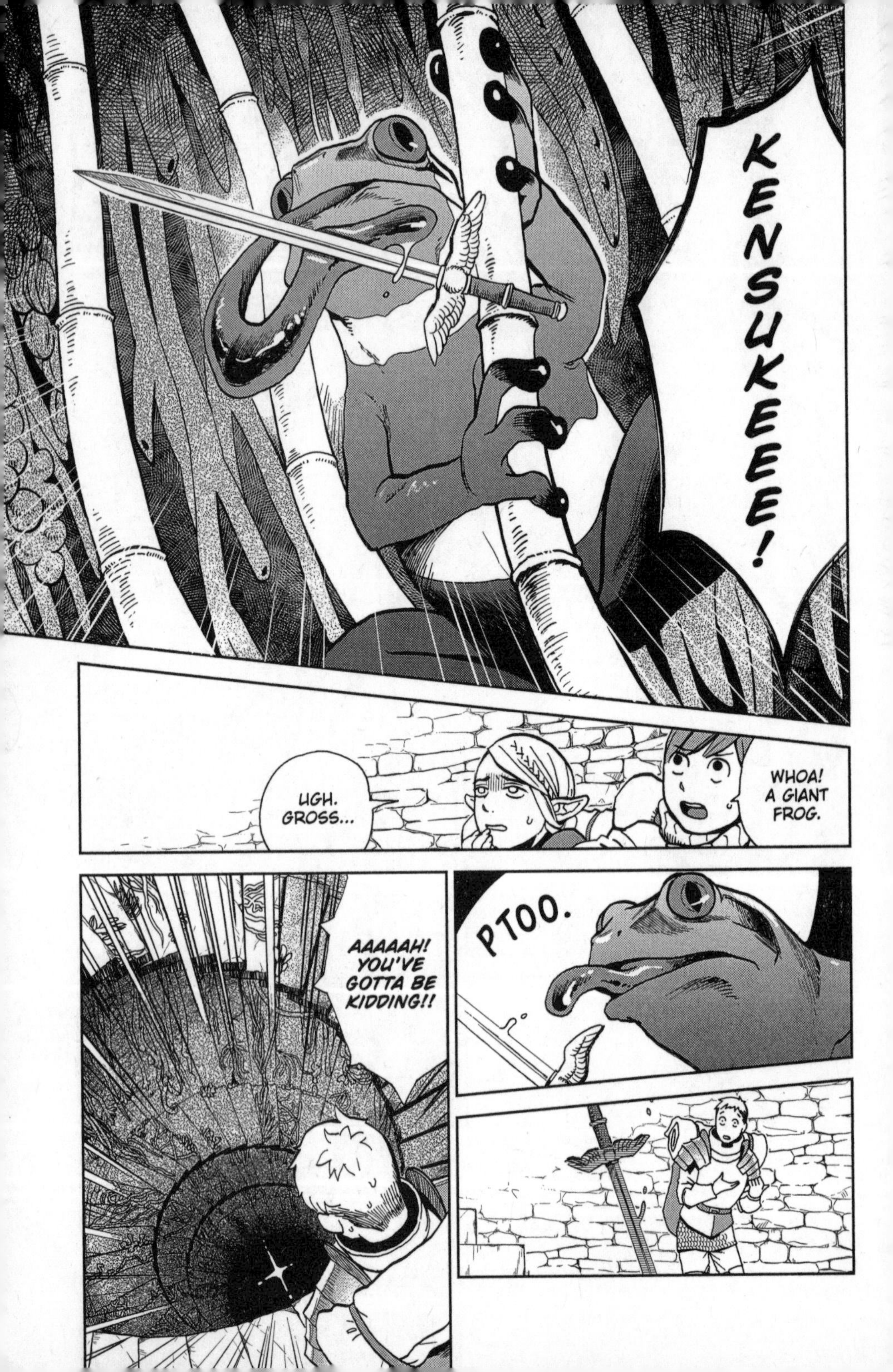
KENSUKEEEE!
WHOA! A GIANT FROG.
UGH. GROSS...
PTOO.
AAAAAH! YOU'VE GOTTA BE KIDDING!!

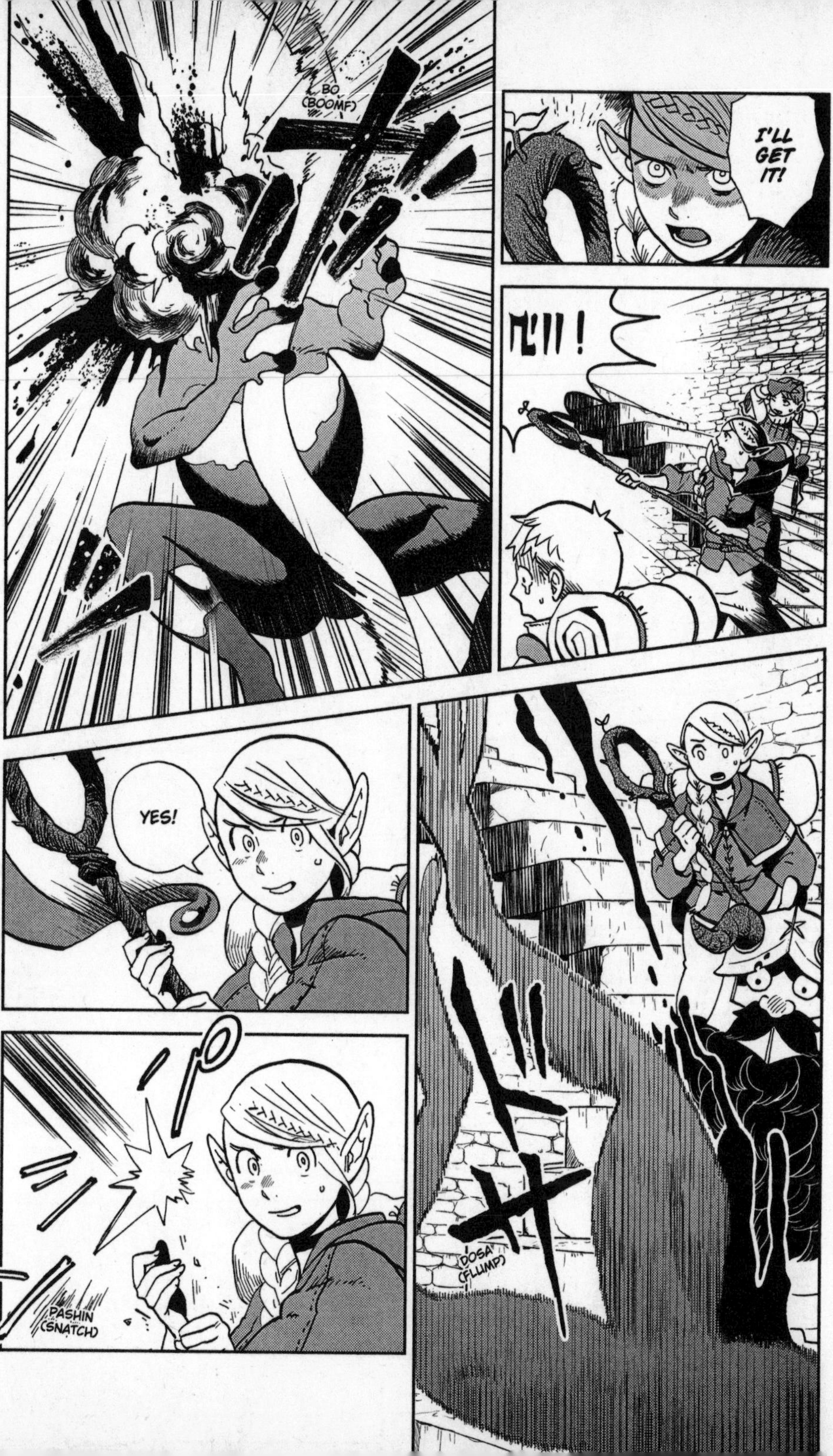
I'LL GET IT!
BO (BOOMF)
DOSA (FLUMP)
YES!
PASHIN (SNATCH)

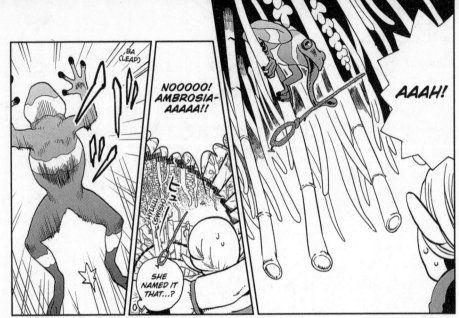

NOOOOO! AMBROSIA-AAAAA!!

BA (LEAP)

HYULU (SWISH)

SHE NAMED IT THAT...?

AAAH!

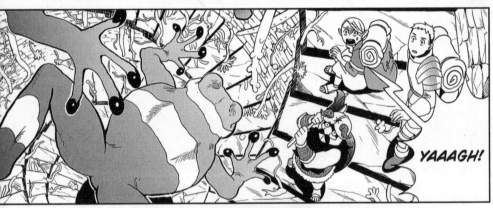

YAAAGH!

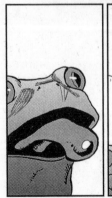

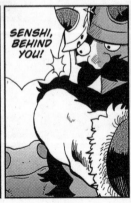

SENSHI, BEHIND YOU!

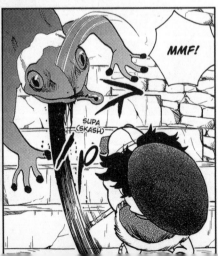

MMF!

SUPA (SKASH)

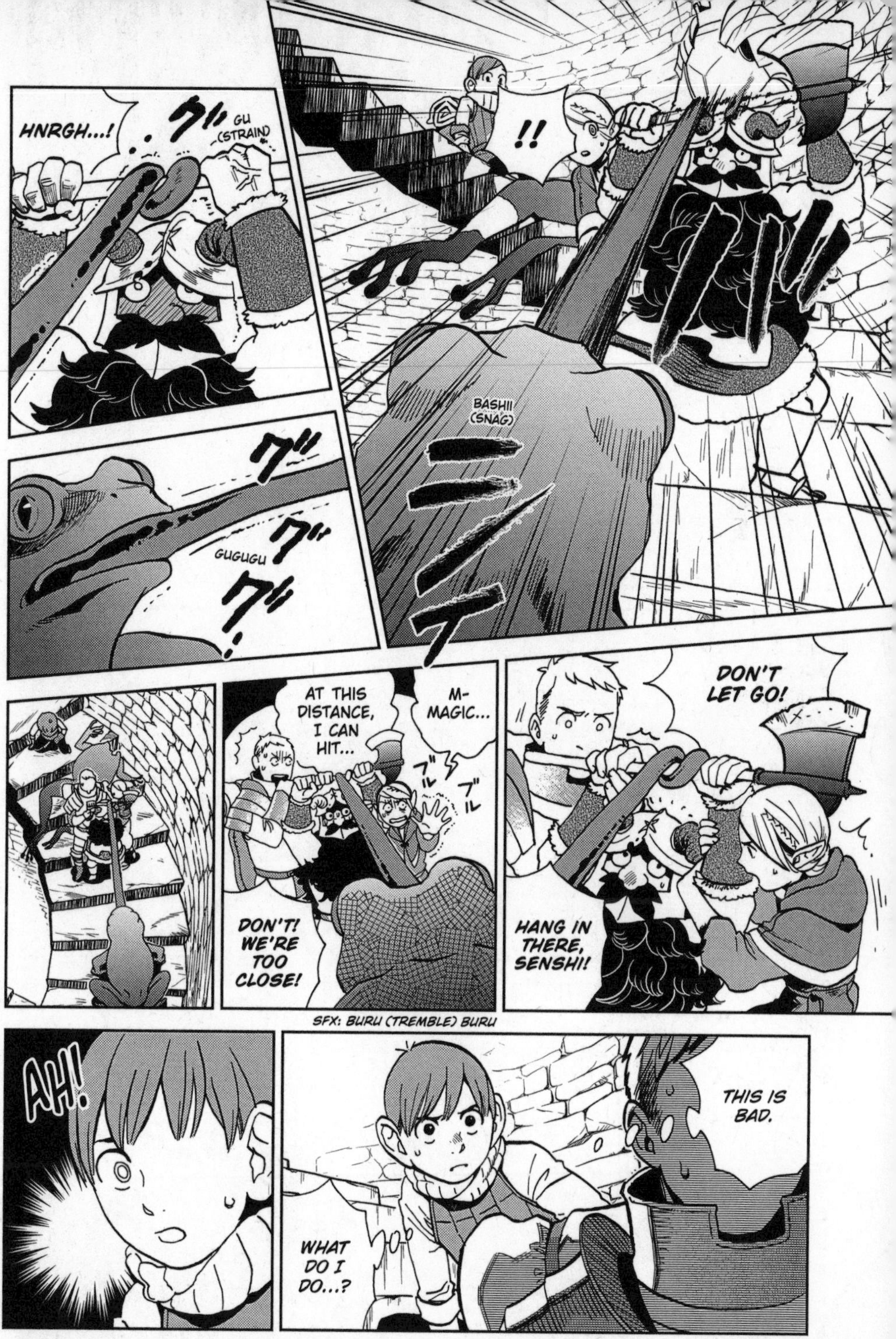
!!
BASHII (SNAG)
HNRGH...!
GU (STRAIN)
GUGUGU
DON'T LET GO!
HANG IN THERE, SENSHI!
M-MAGIC...
AT THIS DISTANCE, I CAN HIT...
DON'T! WE'RE TOO CLOSE!
SFX: BURU (TREMBLE) BURU
THIS IS BAD.
WHAT DO I DO...?
AH!

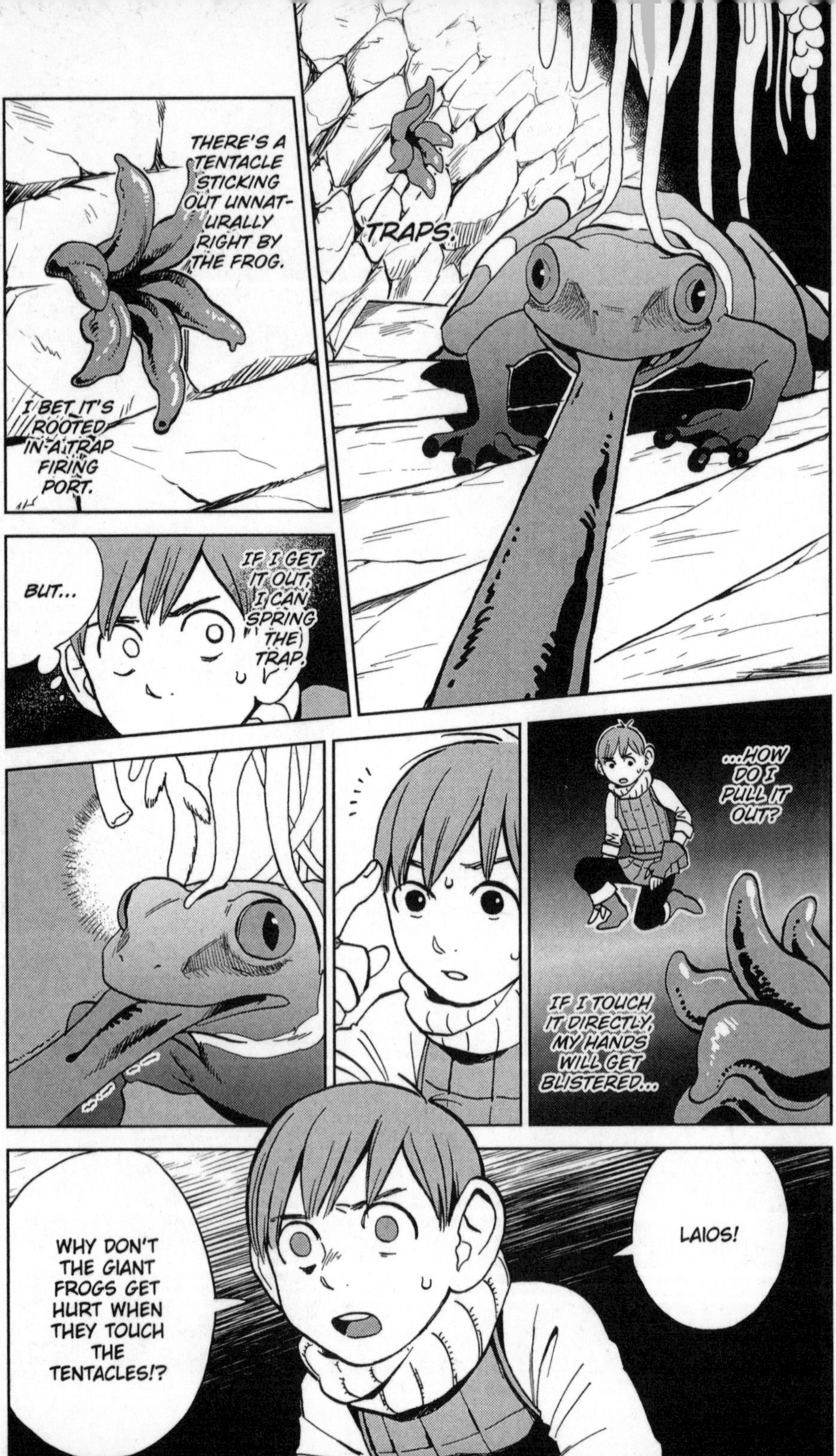
TRAPS.
THERE'S A TENTACLE STICKING OUT UNNATURALLY RIGHT BY THE FROG.
I BET IT'S ROOTED IN A TRAP FIRING PORT.
IF I GET IT OUT, I CAN SPRING THE TRAP.
BUT...
...HOW DO I PULL IT OUT?
IF I TOUCH IT DIRECTLY, MY HANDS WILL GET BLISTERED...
LAIOS!
WHY DON'T THE GIANT FROGS GET HURT WHEN THEY TOUCH THE TENTACLES!?

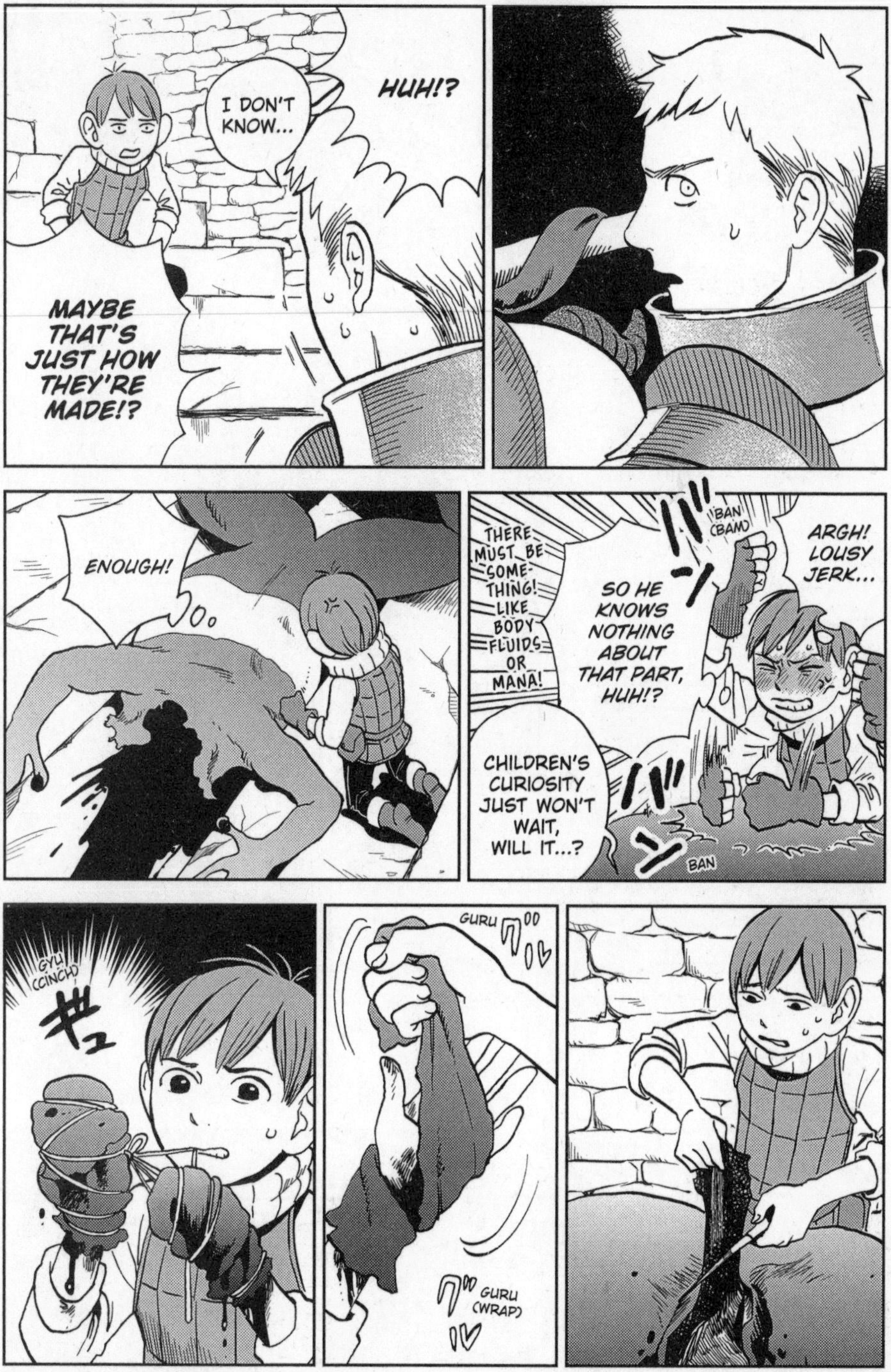
HUH!?
I DON'T KNOW...
MAYBE THAT'S JUST HOW THEY'RE MADE!?
ARGH! LOUSY JERK...
BAN (BAM)
SO HE KNOWS NOTHING ABOUT THAT PART, HUH!?
THERE MUST BE SOMETHING! LIKE BODY FLUIDS OR MANA!
CHILDREN'S CURIOSITY JUST WON'T WAIT, WILL IT...?
BAN
ENOUGH!
GURU
GURU (WRAP)
GYU (CINCH)

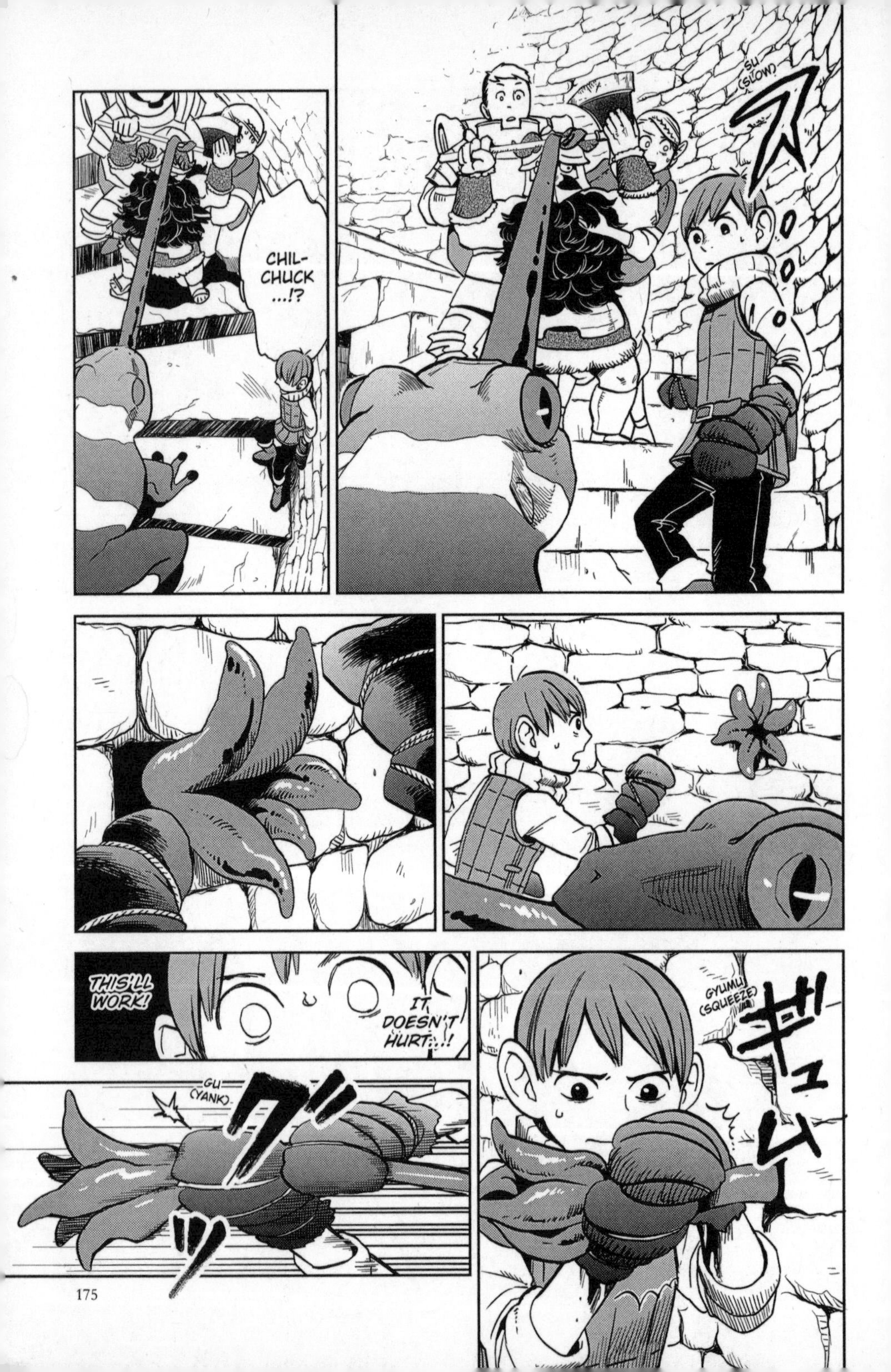
SU (SLOW)
ス
CHIL-CHUCK ...!?
GYUMU (SQUEEZE)
ギュム
IT DOESN'T HURT...!
THIS'LL WORK!
GU (YANK)
グッ

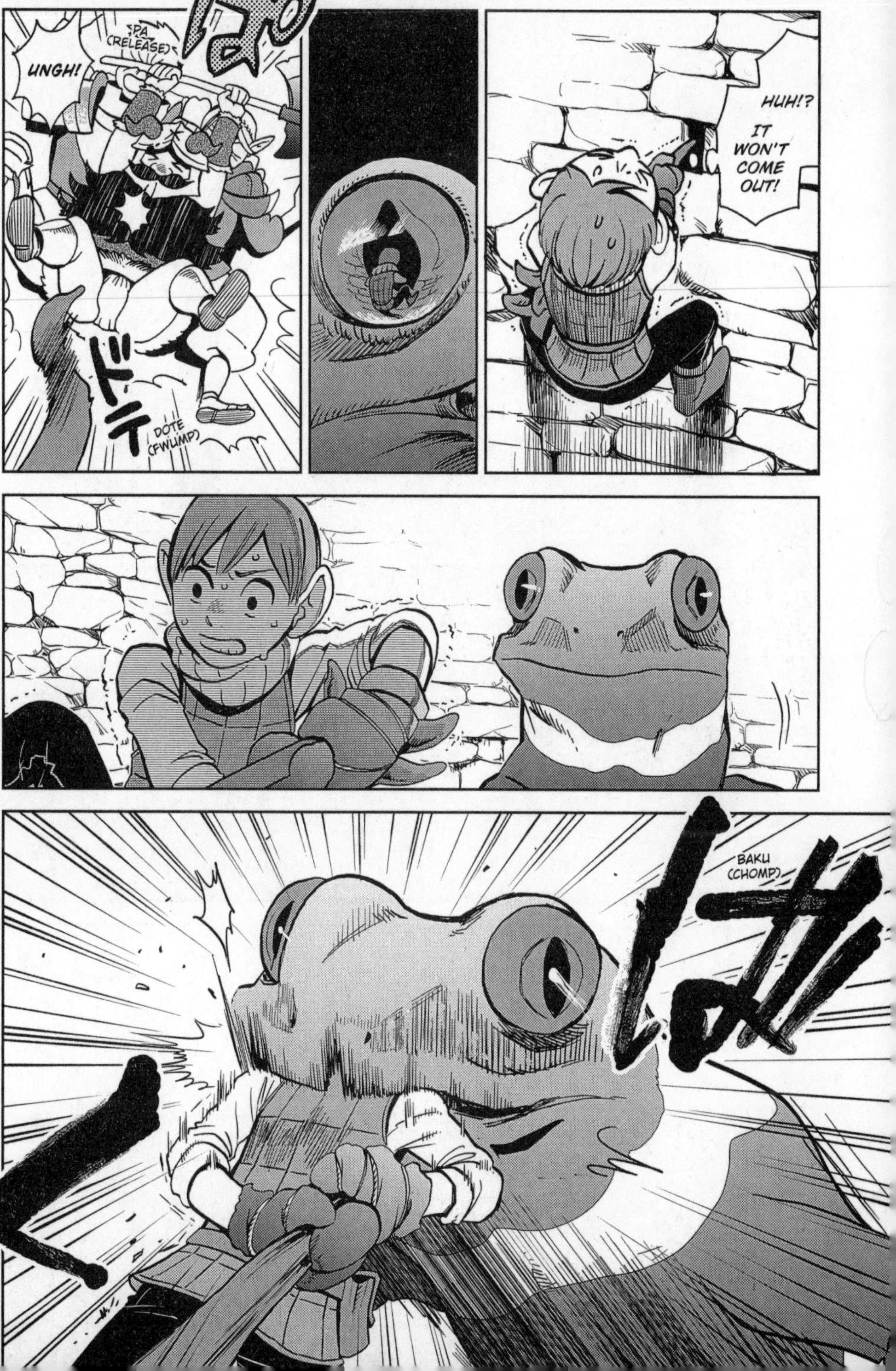

HUH!?
IT WON'T COME OUT!
PA (RELEASE)
UNGH!
ドテ
DOTE (FWUMP)
BAKU (CHOMP)

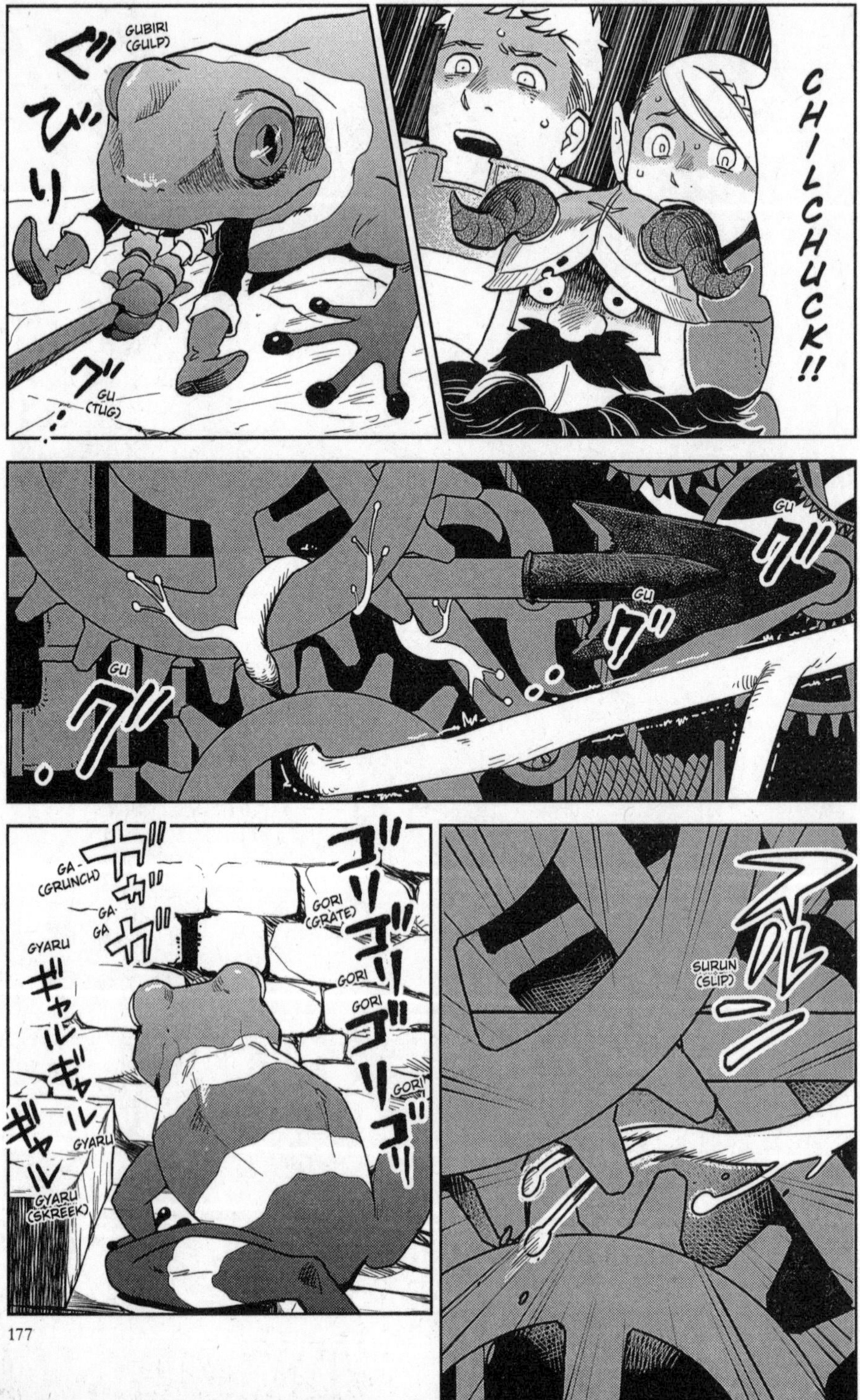
CHILCHUCK!!
ぐびり
GUBIRI (GULP)
グ
GU (TUG)
グ
GU
グ
GU
グ
GU
スルン
SURUN (SLIP)
ゴリゴリゴリゴリ
GORI (GRATE)
GORI
GORI
GORI
ガガガ
GA (CRUNCH)
GA
GA
ギャルギャルギャル
GYARU
GYARU
GYARU (SKREEK)

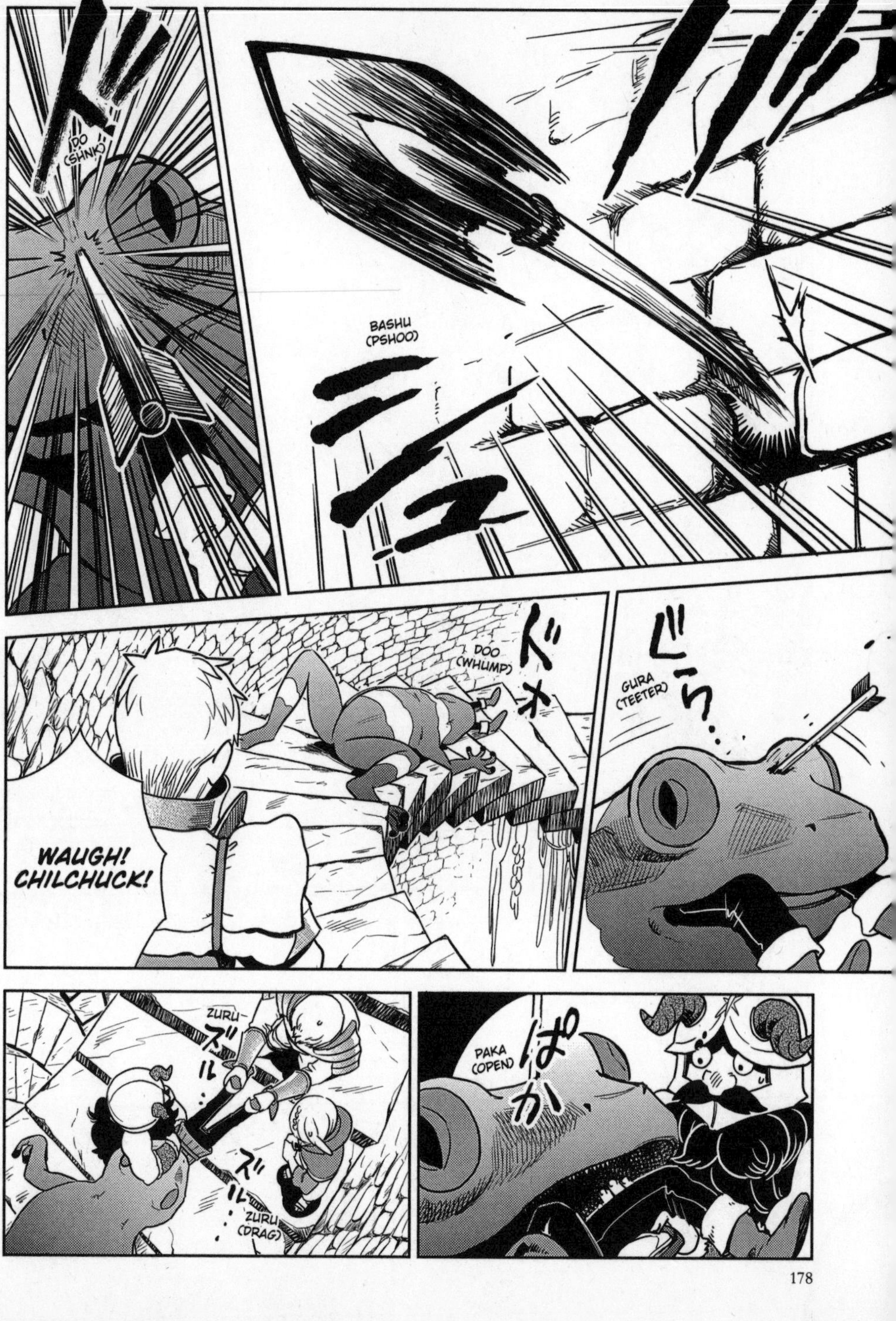
BASHU (PSHOO)
DO (SHINK)
GURA (TEETER)
DOO (WHUMP)
WAUGH! CHILCHUCK!
PAKA (OPEN)
ZURU
ZURU (DRAG)

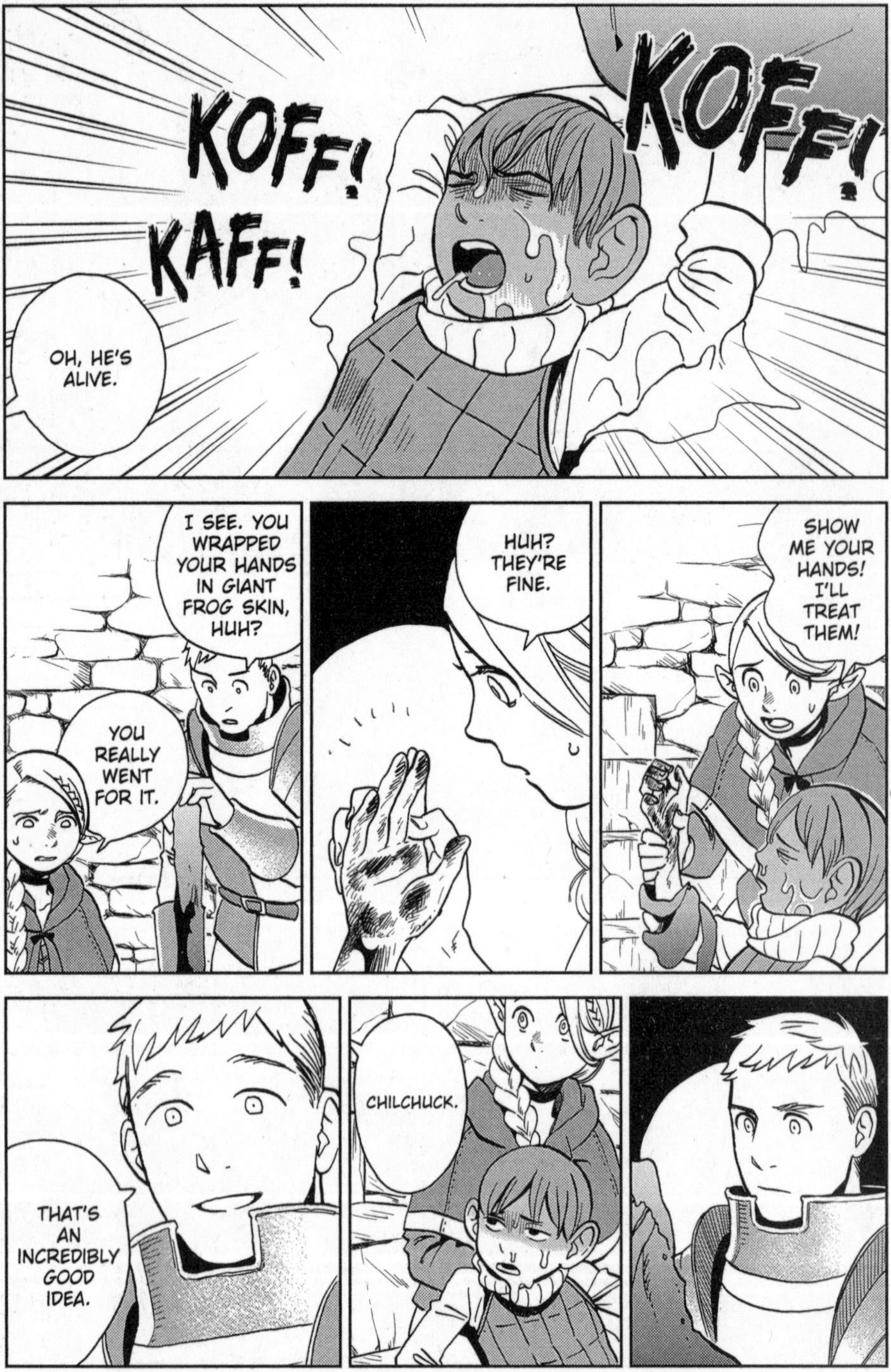
KOFF!
KOFF!
KAFF!
OH, HE'S ALIVE.
SHOW ME YOUR HANDS! I'LL TREAT THEM!
HUH? THEY'RE FINE.
I SEE. YOU WRAPPED YOUR HANDS IN GIANT FROG SKIN, HUH?
YOU REALLY WENT FOR IT.
CHILCHUCK.
THAT'S AN INCREDIBLY GOOD IDEA.

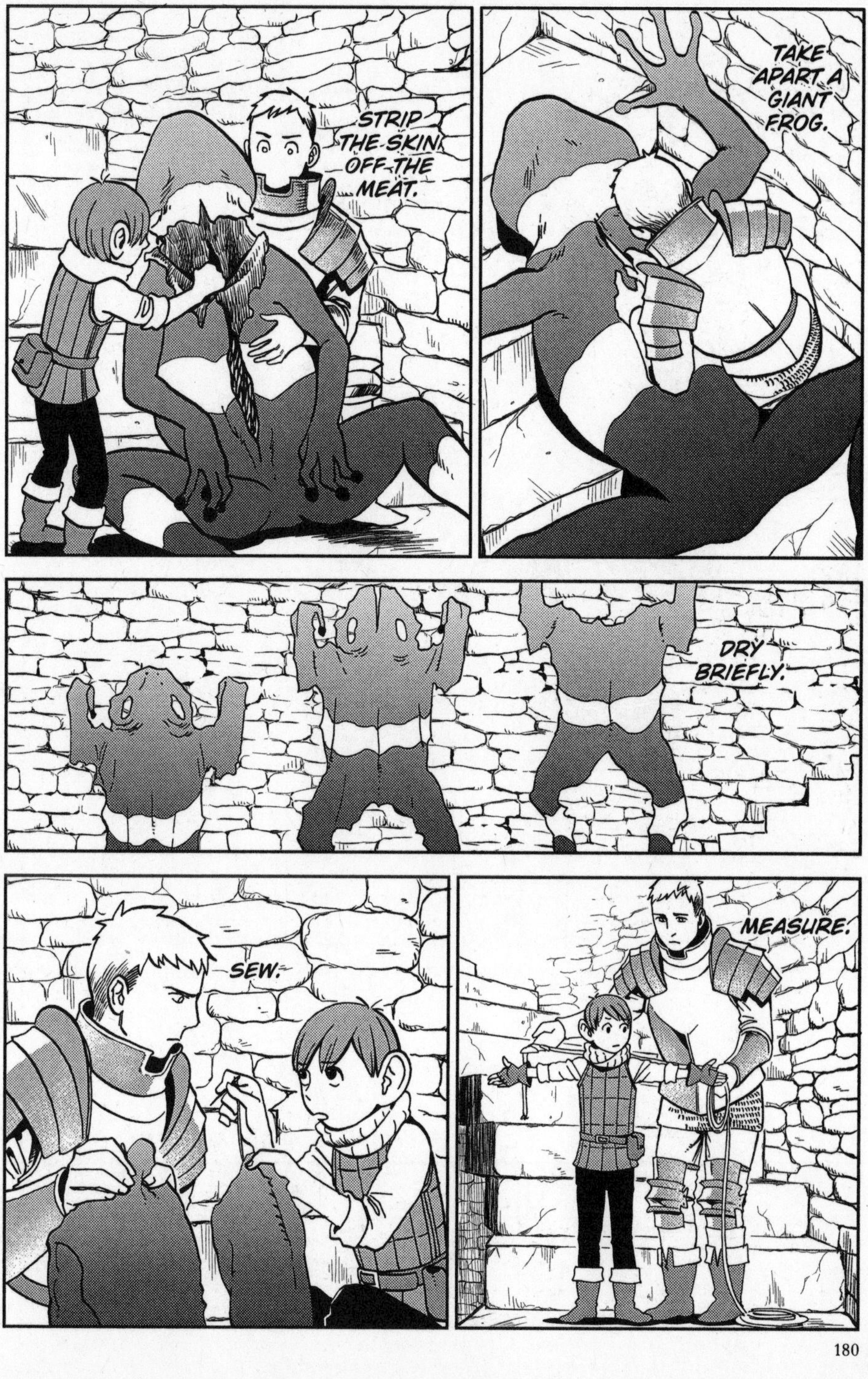
TAKE APART A GIANT FROG.
STRIP THE SKIN OFF THE MEAT.
DRY BRIEFLY.
MEASURE.
SEW.

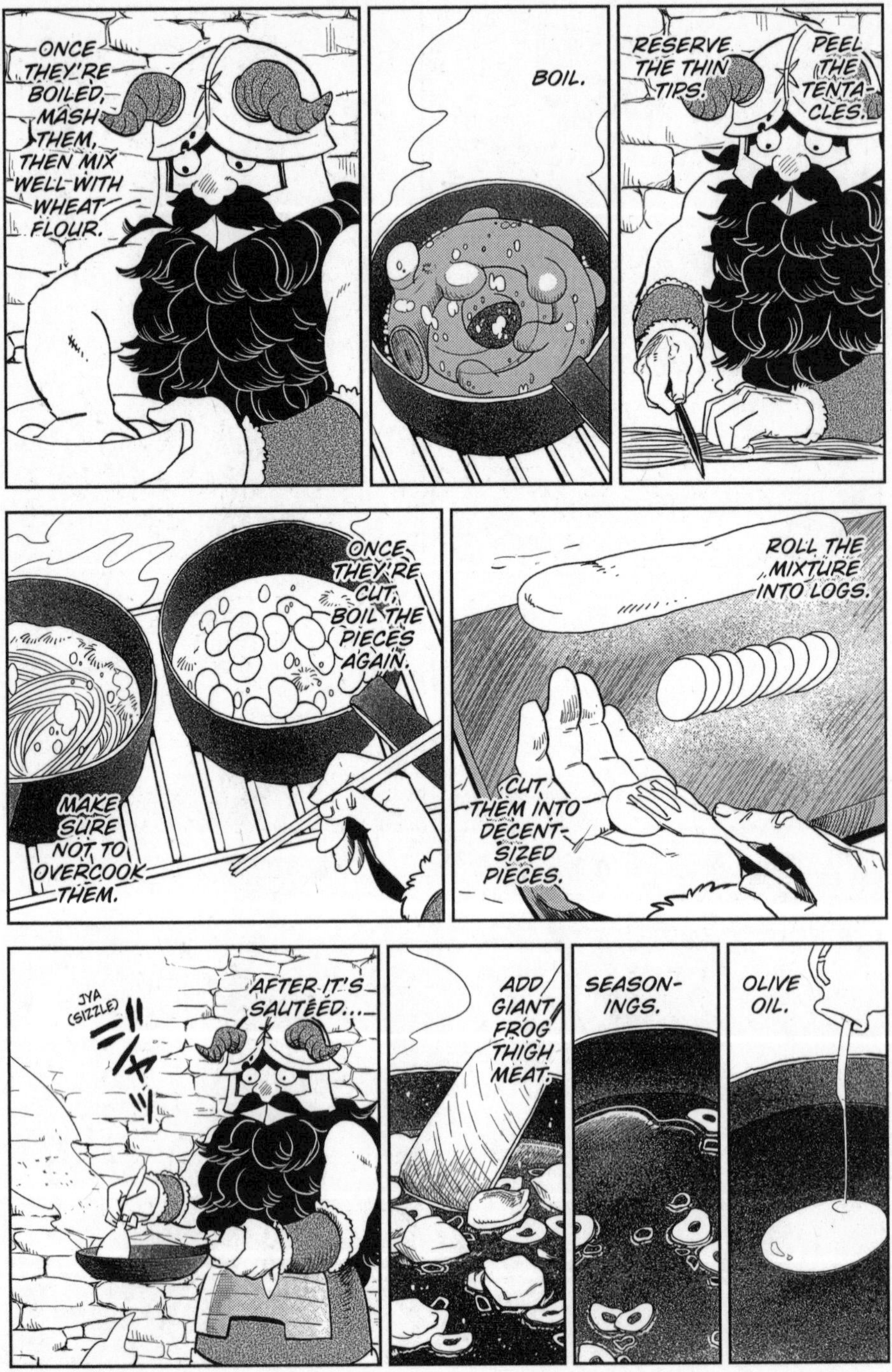

PEEL THE TENTACLES.
RESERVE THE THIN TIPS.
BOIL.
ONCE THEY'RE BOILED, MASH THEM, THEN MIX WELL WITH WHEAT FLOUR.
ROLL THE MIXTURE INTO LOGS.
CUT THEM INTO DECENT-SIZED PIECES.
ONCE THEY'RE CUT, BOIL THE PIECES AGAIN.
MAKE SURE NOT TO OVERCOOK THEM.
OLIVE OIL.
SEASONINGS.
ADD GIANT FROG THIGH MEAT.
AFTER IT'S SAUTÉED...
JYA (SIZZLE)
ジャッ

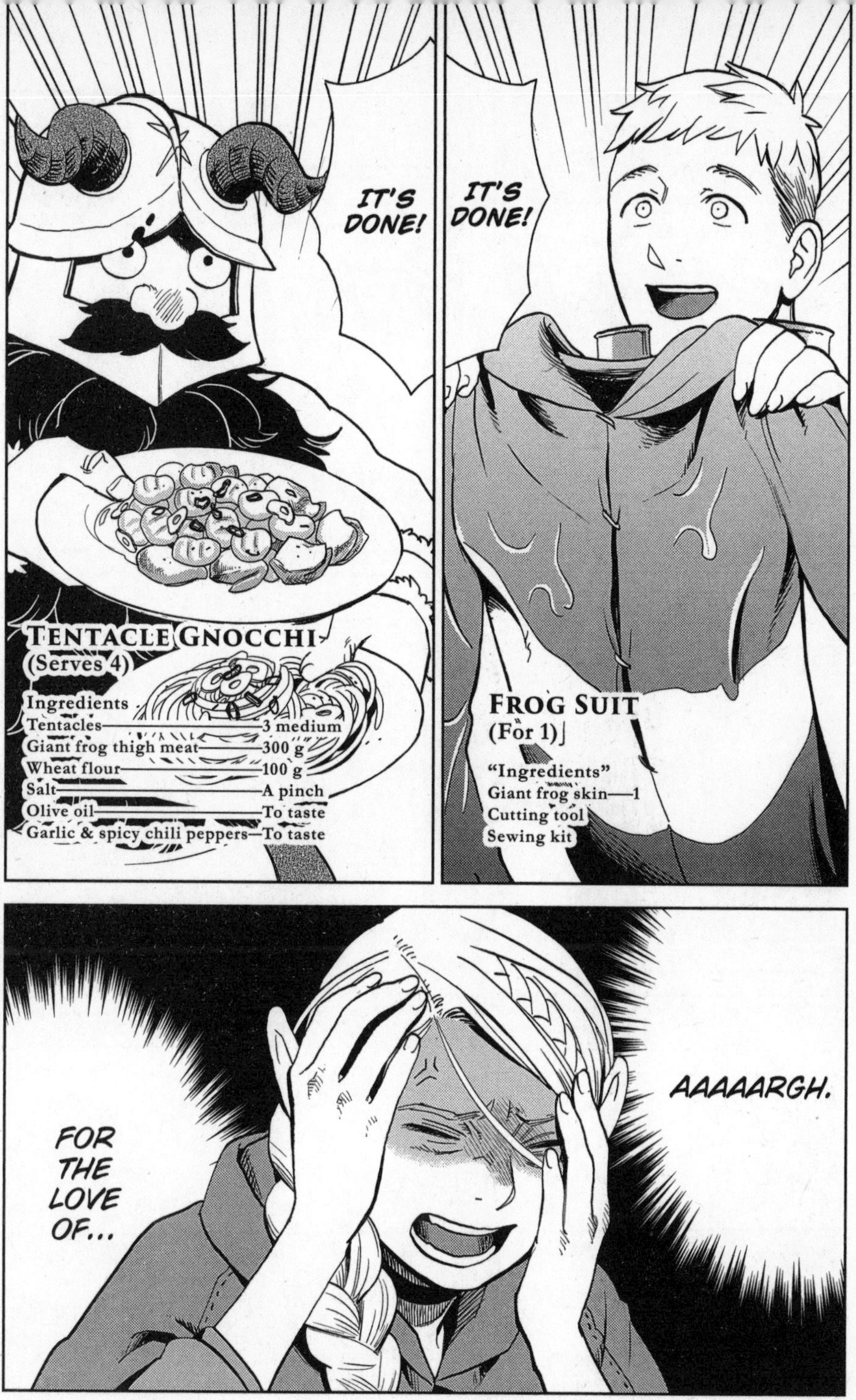
IT'S DONE!
FROG SUIT
(For 1)
"Ingredients"
Giant frog skin—1
Cutting tool
Sewing kit
IT'S DONE!
TENTACLE GNOCCHI
(Serves 4)
Ingredients
Tentacles—3 medium
Giant frog thigh meat—300 g
Wheat flour—100 g
Salt—A pinch
Olive oil—To taste
Garlic & spicy chili peppers—To taste
AAAAARGH.
FOR THE LOVE OF...

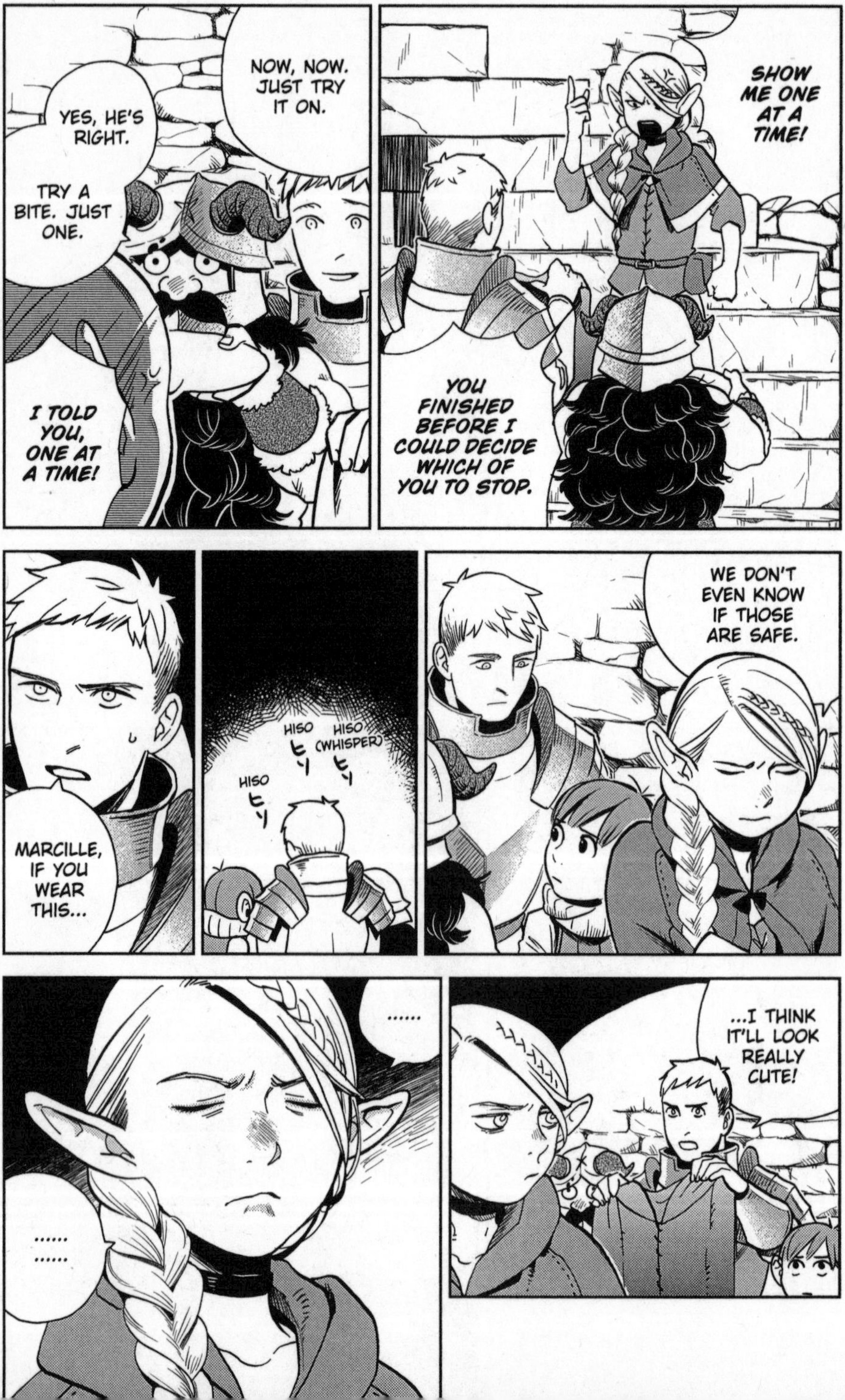
SHOW ME ONE AT A TIME!
YOU FINISHED BEFORE I COULD DECIDE WHICH OF YOU TO STOP.
NOW, NOW. JUST TRY IT ON.
YES, HE'S RIGHT.
TRY A BITE. JUST ONE.
I TOLD YOU, ONE AT A TIME!
WE DON'T EVEN KNOW IF THOSE ARE SAFE.
HISO ヒソ
HISO ヒソ (WHISPER)
HISO ヒソ
MARCILLE, IF YOU WEAR THIS...
...I THINK IT'LL LOOK REALLY CUTE!
......
......
......

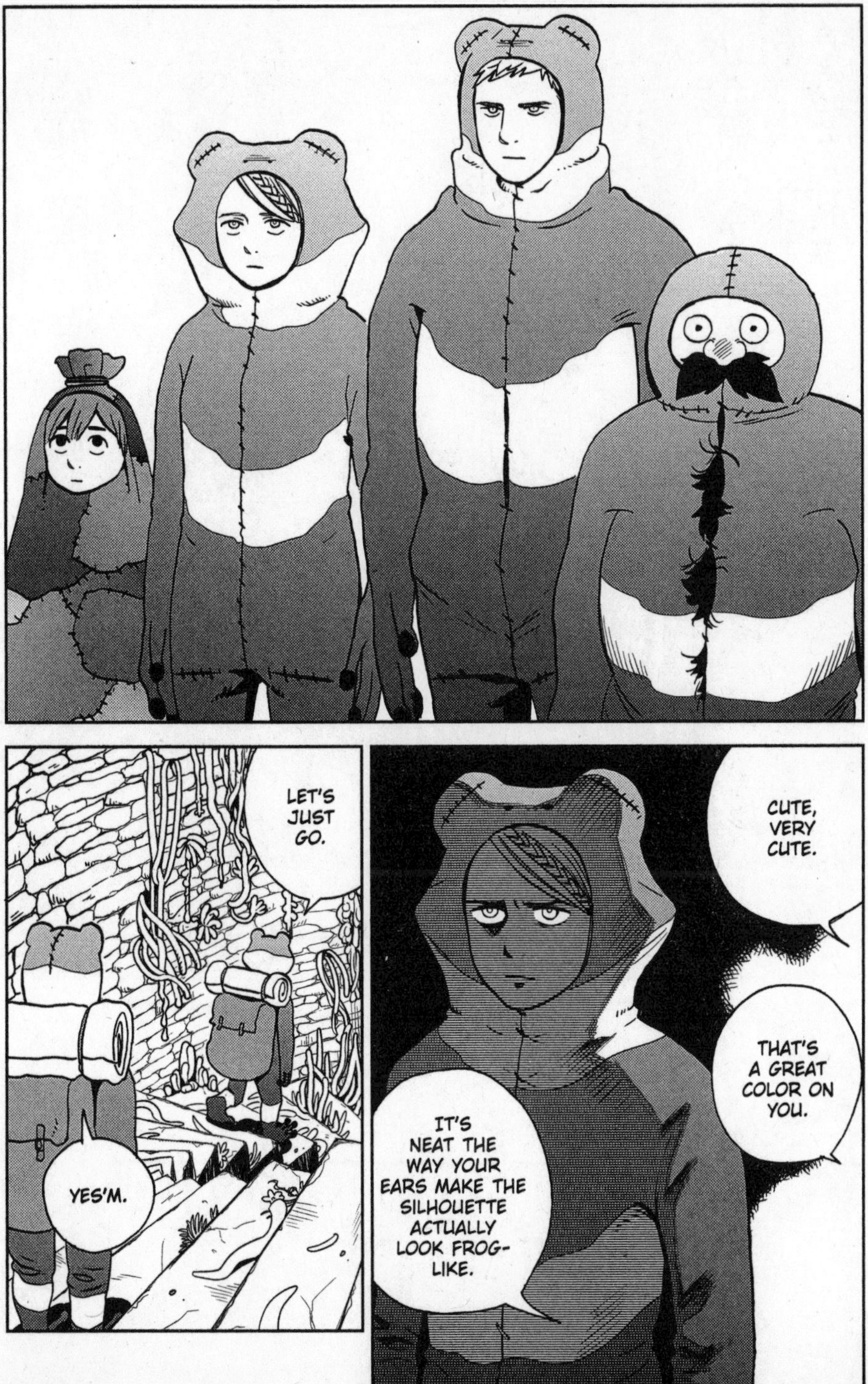
CUTE, VERY CUTE.
THAT'S A GREAT COLOR ON YOU.
IT'S NEAT THE WAY YOUR EARS MAKE THE SILHOUETTE ACTUALLY LOOK FROG-LIKE.
LET'S JUST GO.
YES'M.

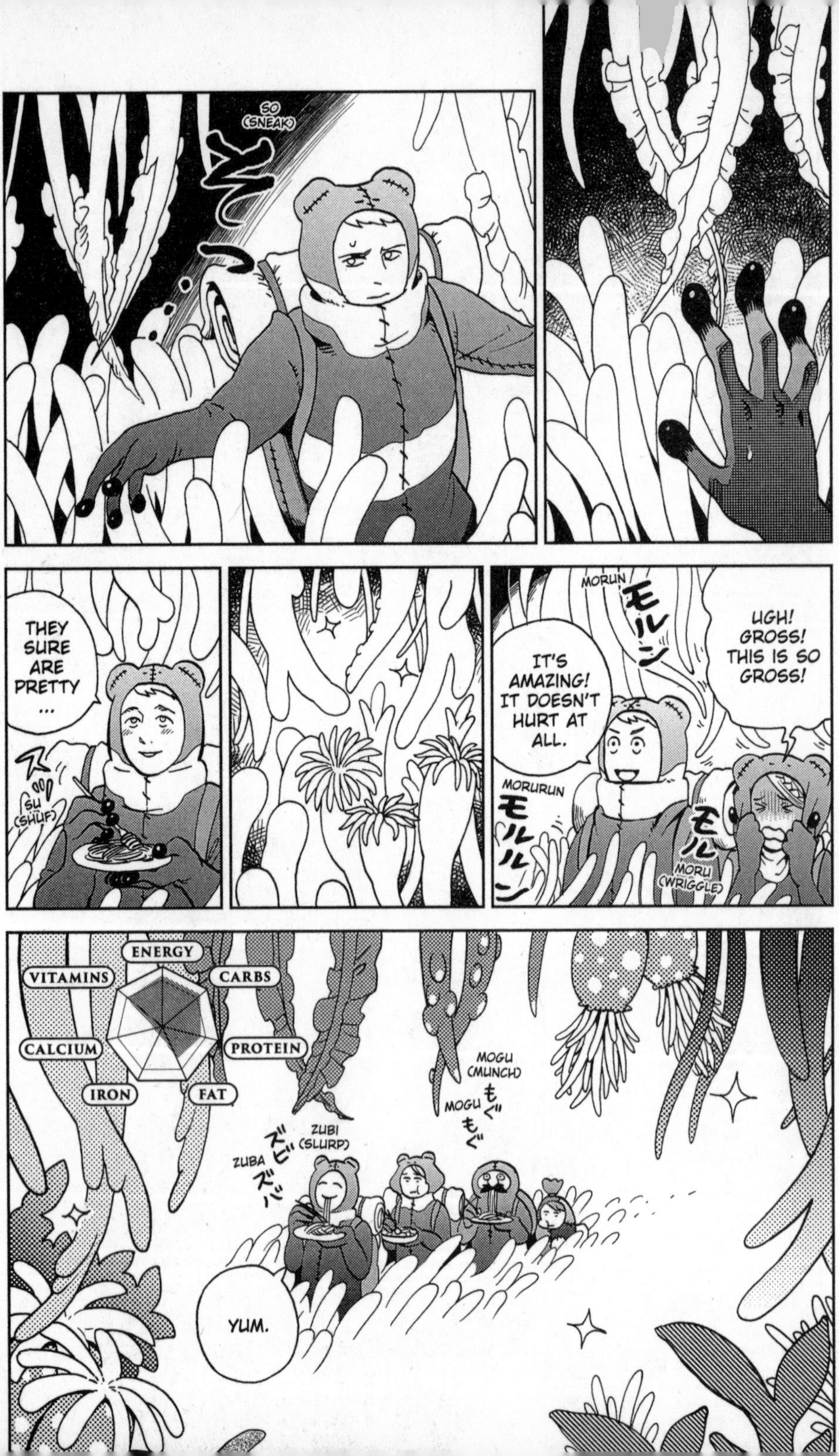
SO (SNEAK)
そっ
MORUN
モルン
UGH! GROSS! THIS IS SO GROSS!
IT'S AMAZING! IT DOESN'T HURT AT ALL.
MORURUN
モルルン
モル
MORU (WRIGGLE)
THEY SURE ARE PRETTY ...
ス
SU (SHUF)
ENERGY
CARBS
PROTEIN
FAT
IRON
CALCIUM
VITAMINS
MOGU (MUNCH)
もぐ
MOGU
もぐ
ZUBI (SLURP)
ズビ
ZUBA
ズバ
YUM.

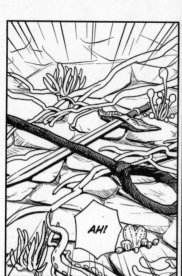

AH!

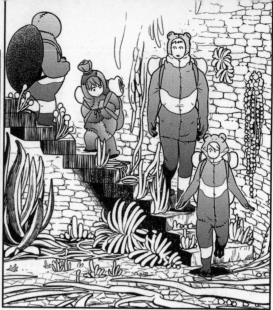

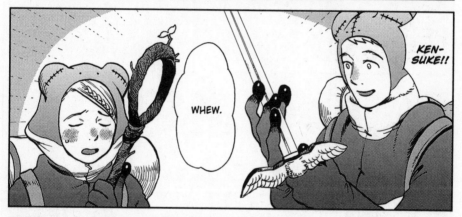

WHEW.

KEN-SUKE!!

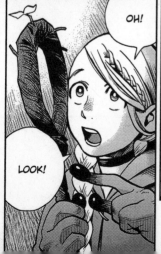

OH!

LOOK!

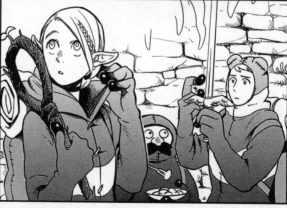

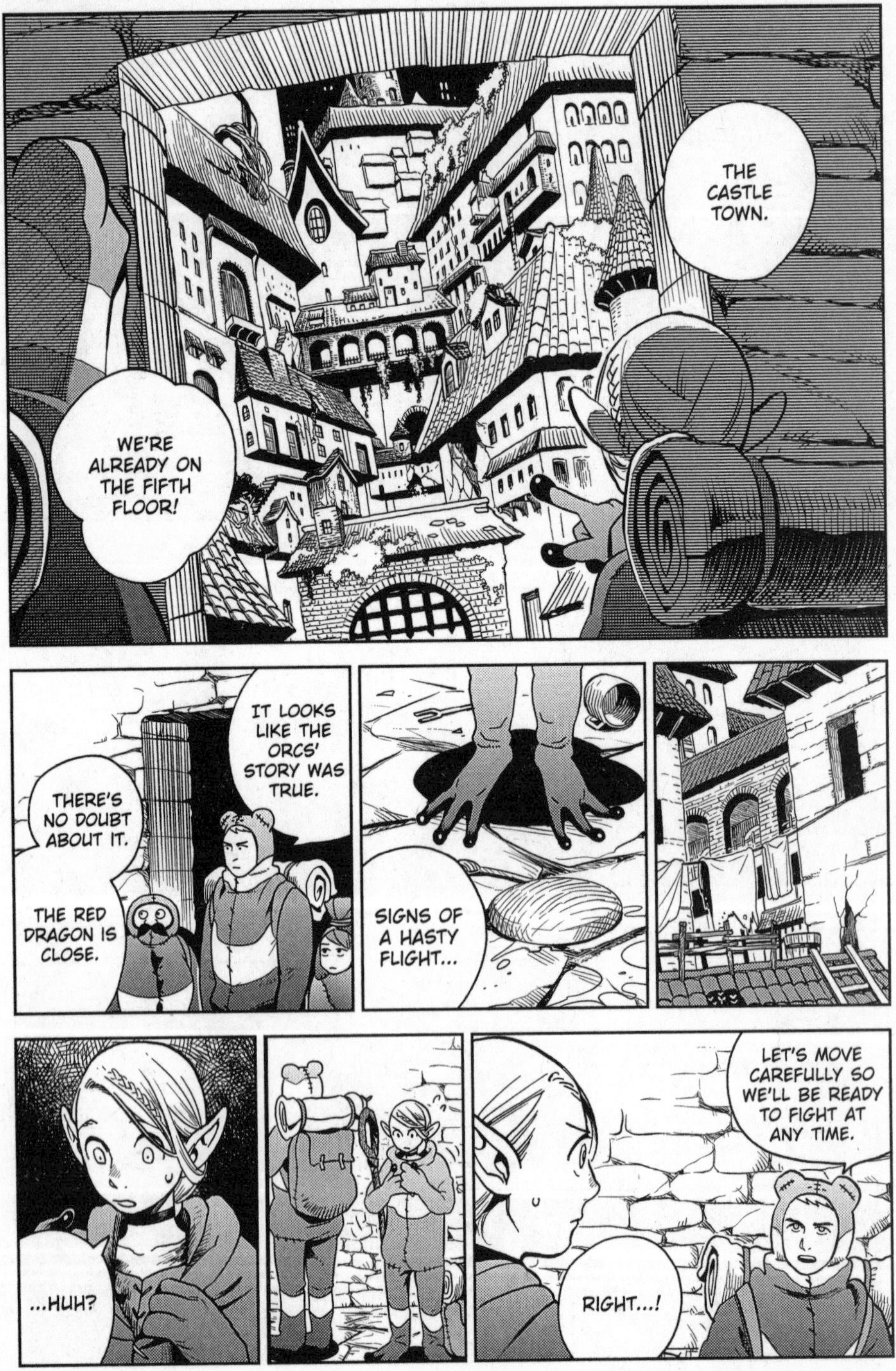
THE CASTLE TOWN.
WE'RE ALREADY ON THE FIFTH FLOOR!
SIGNS OF A HASTY FLIGHT...
IT LOOKS LIKE THE ORCS' STORY WAS TRUE.
THERE'S NO DOUBT ABOUT IT.
THE RED DRAGON IS CLOSE.
LET'S MOVE CAREFULLY SO WE'LL BE READY TO FIGHT AT ANY TIME.
RIGHT...!
...HUH?

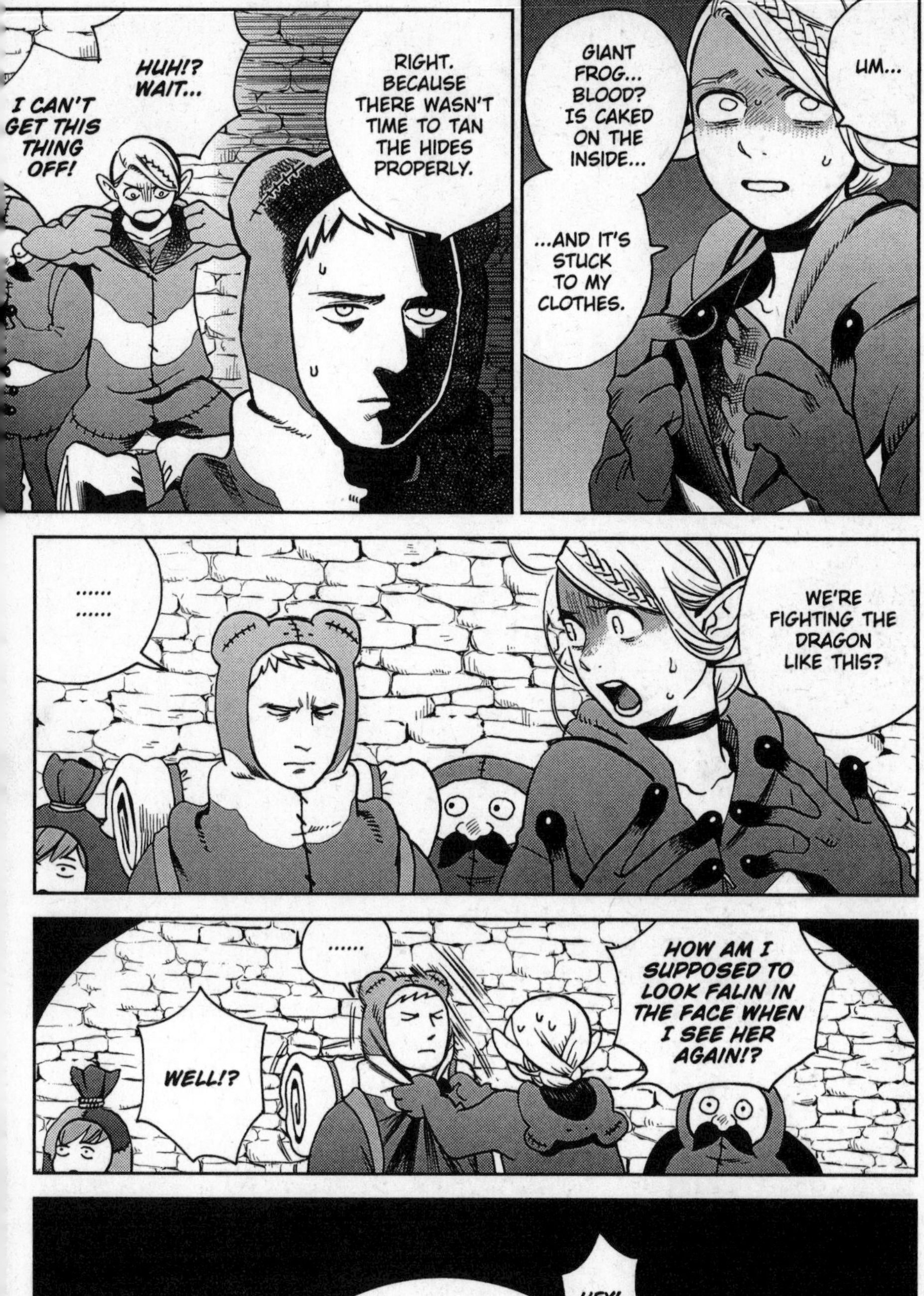
UM...
GIANT FROG... BLOOD? IS CAKED ON THE INSIDE...
...AND IT'S STUCK TO MY CLOTHES.
RIGHT. BECAUSE THERE WASN'T TIME TO TAN THE HIDES PROPERLY.
HUH!? WAIT...
I CAN'T GET THIS THING OFF!
WE'RE FIGHTING THE DRAGON LIKE THIS?
....
HOW AM I SUPPOSED TO LOOK FALIN IN THE FACE WHEN I SEE HER AGAIN!?
......
WELL!?
HEY!

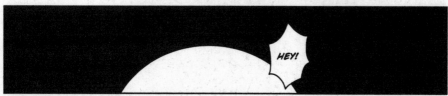

To be continued...

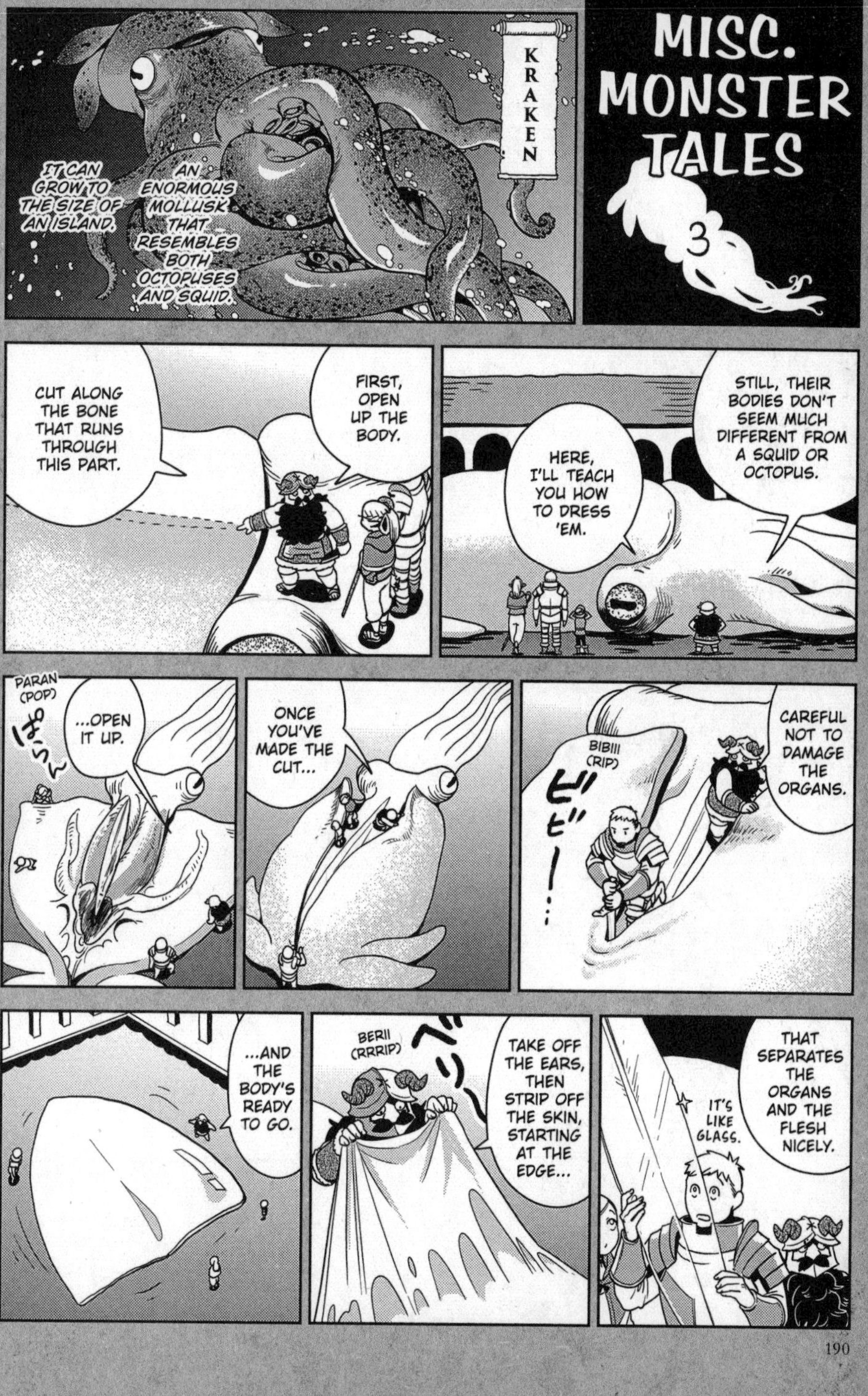
MISC. MONSTER TALES
3
KRAKEN
AN ENORMOUS MOLLUSK THAT RESEMBLES BOTH OCTOPUSES AND SQUID.
IT CAN GROW TO THE SIZE OF AN ISLAND.
STILL, THEIR BODIES DON'T SEEM MUCH DIFFERENT FROM A SQUID OR OCTOPUS.
HERE, I'LL TEACH YOU HOW TO DRESS 'EM.
FIRST, OPEN UP THE BODY.
CUT ALONG THE BONE THAT RUNS THROUGH THIS PART.
CAREFUL NOT TO DAMAGE THE ORGANS.
BIBIII (RIP)
ビビー…
ONCE YOU'VE MADE THE CUT...
...OPEN IT UP.
PARAN (POP)
ぱらん
THAT SEPARATES THE ORGANS AND THE FLESH NICELY.
IT'S LIKE GLASS.
TAKE OFF THE EARS, THEN STRIP OFF THE SKIN, STARTING AT THE EDGE...
BERII (RRRIP)
べりー
...AND THE BODY'S READY TO GO.

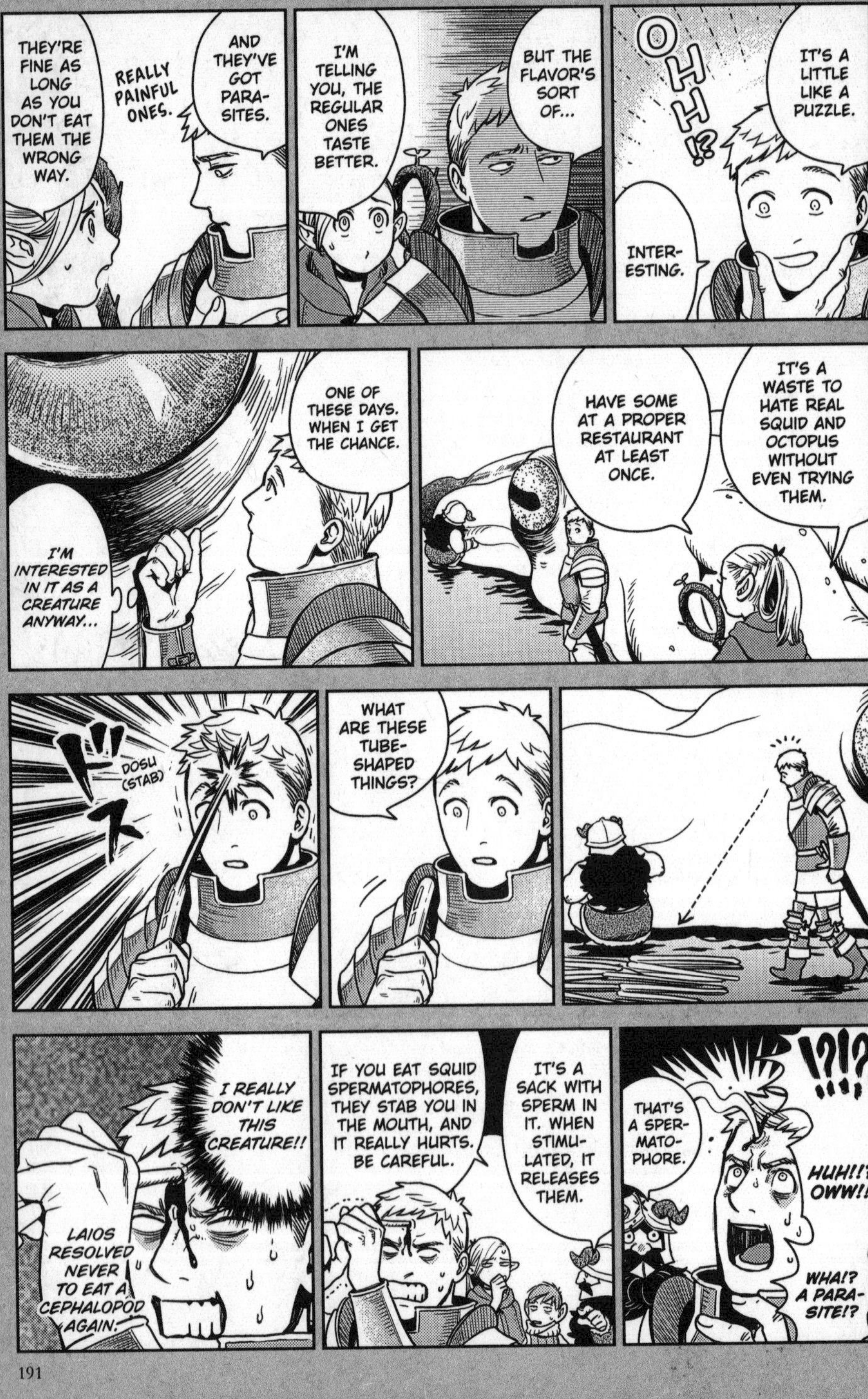
IT'S A LITTLE LIKE A PUZZLE.
OHH!?
INTERESTING.
BUT THE FLAVOR'S SORT OF...
I'M TELLING YOU, THE REGULAR ONES TASTE BETTER.
AND THEY'VE GOT PARASITES.
REALLY PAINFUL ONES.
THEY'RE FINE AS LONG AS YOU DON'T EAT THEM THE WRONG WAY.
IT'S A WASTE TO HATE REAL SQUID AND OCTOPUS WITHOUT EVEN TRYING THEM.
HAVE SOME AT A PROPER RESTAURANT AT LEAST ONCE.
ONE OF THESE DAYS. WHEN I GET THE CHANCE.
I'M INTERESTED IN IT AS A CREATURE ANYWAY...
WHAT ARE THESE TUBE-SHAPED THINGS?
DOSU (STAB)
!?!?
HUH!!? OWW!!
THAT'S A SPERMATOPHORE.
WHA!? A PARASITE!?
IT'S A SACK WITH SPERM IN IT. WHEN STIMULATED, IT RELEASES THEM.
IF YOU EAT SQUID SPERMATOPHORES, THEY STAB YOU IN THE MOUTH, AND IT REALLY HURTS. BE CAREFUL.
I REALLY DON'T LIKE THIS CREATURE!!
LAIOS RESOLVED NEVER TO EAT A CEPHALOPOD AGAIN.

3
DELICIOUS IN DUNGEON
RYOKO KUI

Translation: Taylor Engel   **Lettering: Abigail Blackman**

This book is a work of fiction. Names, characters, places, and incidents are the product of the author's imagination or are used fictitiously. Any resemblance to actual events, locales, or persons, living or dead, is coincidental.

DUNGEON MESHI Volume 3 © 2016 Ryoko Kui. All rights reserved. First published in Japan in 2016 by KADOKAWA CORPORATION ENTERBRAIN. English translation rights arranged with KADOKAWA CORPORATION ENTERBRAIN through Tuttle-Mori Agency, Inc., Tokyo.

English translation © 2017 by Yen Press, LLC

Yen Press, LLC supports the right to free expression and the value of copyright. The purpose of copyright is to encourage writers and artists to produce the creative works that enrich our culture.

The scanning, uploading, and distribution of this book without permission is a theft of the author's intellectual property. If you would like permission to use material from the book (other than for review purposes), please contact the publisher. Thank you for your support of the author's rights.

Yen Press
1290 Avenue of the Americas
New York, NY 10104

Visit us at yenpress.com
facebook.com/yenpress
twitter.com/yenpress
yenpress.tumblr.com
instagram.com/yenpress

First Yen Press Edition: November 2017

Yen Press is an imprint of Yen Press, LLC.
The Yen Press name and logo are trademarks of Yen Press, LLC.

The publisher is not responsible for websites (or their content) that are not owned by the publisher.

Library of Congress Control Number: 2017932141

ISBNs: 978-0-316-41279-7 (paperback)
        978-0-316-44634-1 (ebook)

10 9 8 7 6 5 4 3 2 1

BVG

Printed in the United States of America